MUNNAR TO MARINA
THE JOURNEY

W.I DAVARAM

INDIA · SINGAPORE · MALAYSIA

ISBN
Paperback 979-8-89498-351-6
Hardcase 979-8-89556-982-5

Contents

Acknowledgement

Before all else, I have to thank Covid-19 for getting me started on my book. If not for being under house arrest, I wouldn't be here thanking the following people:

A K Vishwanathan for providing me a steno to record my memoirs of the past, activities of the present, and dreams for the future, and also for pushing me to write.

My wife Prema for the rhyme at the head of each chapter; our idea of having a rhyme at the start of the book developed into one for every chapter.

Prema, once again, and my daughter Anita for editing the book and giving me valuable suggestions throughout.

My grandson Amitesh for the front and back cover pictures and for all his suggestions and ideas.

Charles Nehemiah for the wonderful job he did with the cover page.

P. Ganesh, Chief Reporter, Police Shorthand Bureau, who dedicated all his free time to recording my narratives.

DGP Dr. Jayant K Murali, a brilliant writer with many books to his credit, for the foreword for the book.

K. Thukkiandi, an outstanding police officer who started his career under me during the Naxalite operation, for suggesting and taking charge of the Tamil version of my book; not only translating it from English but getting it published as well.

Preena Sam for patiently handling all the computer work related to the book.

Notion Press for publishing the English version and Student Xerox for the Tamil.

It would be remiss of me not to thank my family, friends, the sports fraternity, and the police force for all their support and encouragement.

Note from the Author

My memoir titled "Munnar to Marina" traces a small-town boy's journey from the tea estates of Munnar to the office of the Director General of Police on Chennai's Marina.

The front cover picture has a meaningful tale to tell. Barring the managers' bungalows, our house, like most other estate houses, could be reached only via footpaths through tea bushes or by crossing trenches dug to keep elephants out of residential areas.

On my father's promotion as Labour Welfare Officer covering all the estates in Kerala as well as those in the Anamalais in Tamil Nadu, he was provided with a motorbike to facilitate his estate visits.

Having a bike was very well; but how was he going to take it to a house surrounded by mounds covered with tea bushes and no means of approach? The problem was sorted out when we had a pathway, 20ft long and 5ft wide, cut through the mound closest to the house.

It is a picture of this pathway, with a photograph of me in uniform striding out into the world, that has taken pride of place on the front cover of my book.

Foreword

A memoir offers the same joy and excitement as an engaging story. Memoirs are immersive, like living another person's real story and the closest we can get to walking a mile in another's shoes. The first time I read a memoir, it immediately became apparent why they are so popular. Reading someone's life through their own eyes, in their own words, is a powerful experience and an incredible window into another person's life. There is nothing quite like immersing yourself in someone else's real-life story and taking away lessons for your own life. The more memoirs I read, the more lessons I learn, especially about the spirit that drove them to extraordinary achievements, the altitude of their thoughts and the depth of their wisdom.

And if the memoir happens to be that of a legend such as Walter sir.

Then, it will undoubtedly be a blockbuster that will breathtakingly lift and transport the reader, holding him spellbound in a cop universe where the protagonist superhero Walter in the face of danger, battles charlatans, terrorists, gangsters and anti-socials through feats of ingenuity, courage and strength to emerge victorious. That's what Walter-sirs present memoirs did to me and more. The readers who read this book will never be disappointed but will get spellbound by the magic that the author weaves with his real-life action and super deeds. The book opens with the author's childhood days, which were carefree in the beautiful salubrious hills of Munnar, where much time got spent wandering like a deer in the open fields, enjoying the natural beauty of the jade green hills. His long walks to the school and encounters with wild animals on his way to school do a fascinating reading. Further, as you read, you will discover that the author, even in his younger years, showed tremendous courage and maturity as superintendent of Police and made an indelible mark wherever he served. The present memoir is replete with lessons for young police officers to learn and emulate from the various challenging situations that the author deftly dealt with as they arose. For instance, the racy narration of how a developing law and order situation at the Cordite factory at Aruvankadu Coonoor was dealt with by the author is a case in point.

As Superintendent of Police of the combined Tanjore District, the tremendous manner with which the author handled the conflict between agricultural workers, mostly Dalits and the landlords in 1968 speaks volumes of the competence and maturity of the officer. It was a revelation that this conflict was responsible for enacting the Minimum Wages Act post-Keezhvenmani carnage. I found the author's days as the Deputy Inspector General of Vellore Range even more compelling and exciting.

As I read on, I was awestruck by how the author singlehandedly staved off the Naxalites from striking their roots in Tamil Nadu. But for the author, Tamil Nadu would have become a haven for Naxalites as it had happened to our neighbouring state of Andhra Pradesh which had to battle them for several years before they could breathe easy. The story of the killing of three top Naxalites blew my mind away, and it's no wonder that the author rightly got bestowed with the gallantry medal for this heroic act. The daredevilry of the author was phenomenal, and there are several incidents and stories in the book where this aspect becomes obvious. He always led the team from the front, so when Madam Jayalalitha's government decided to hunt down the sandalwood smuggler Veerappan in the 6,000 sq. km jungle, the honourable CM could not think of anyone else but the author himself. This foreword has the propensity to go on endlessly as the author has packed the memoir with several thrilling, magnificent deeds, making this book engaging and unputdownable. Specifically, one of the many things that stand out is the sterling leadership of the author as the Chief of the Joint Special Task Force of Tamil Nadu and Karnataka that crushed the Veerappan's gang and brought down their strength from "150 to five", Also the brilliant handling of the situation inside the Tamil Nadu Legislative assembly when Mrs Janaki Ramachandran was the Chief Minister of Tamil Nadu. The story of the arrest of the LTTE Chief Prabhakaran by the author in 1985 at Adyar Chennai was another delightful revelation to me.

Compressing the author's enormous firearm shooting prowess and his contribution to athletics into a para is challenging. Although I am attempting to do that here, keeping in mind the requirement of adherence to the word limit. The author was such a fantastic shot that he was unbeatable at the National Shooting championships. As the President of the Tamil Nadu Athletics Association, the author's contributions to the development of athletics were nothing less than marvellous. I was amazed to read the story of how his suggestion for enhancement of reward money met with an even higher grant of ₹ five lakhs for a gold medal, ₹ 3 lakh for Silver and ₹ 2.5 lakhs for a bronze medal by the then Honourable CM. Finally, memoirs have become a popular form of storytelling. These personal narratives allow readers to enter another person's world, especially when that person is famous. This memoir helped me relive the author's days and times and experience the author's beautiful world in my mind. Memoirs show us the truth about a person's life, as they remember it and want to tell it. Walter-sir is truly inspiring for all of us, mainly me. I have been so fortunate to have had an opportunity to work under a legend like him.

Albert Einstein speaking of Gandhi said - Generations to come will scarcely believe that such a one as this ever in flesh and blood walked upon this earth. The same holds for Tamil Nadu police when it comes to Walter, sir. Generations to come to Tamil Nadu Police will love, admire and derive inspiration for their lives from him.

I consider myself lucky to write the foreword for the author who is, by all means, a legend and for whom I have the most profound admiration. I have no words to express how honoured I feel to have been conferred this privilege of writing a foreword for my real-life hero. To me, it is the ultimate honour, and I cherished it immensely throughout the way.

Dr. Jayanth K Murali

DGP (retd)

A Tribute to Walter Davaram

by N. Balachandran, IPS

Balachandran was in a class of his own'
As 'Bobby Nair' he was better known;
Straight and unwavering was the path he trod,
Said, all were same in the eyes of God.
To humble folk, celebs et-al,
Rules were rules, for one and all.

N. Balachandran

"When the history of Tamil Nadu Police is written, one name that bridges many decades and stands out for outstanding service is Walter Davaram."

After he passed the UPSC examination, he joined the Central Police College, later named the National Police Academy, at Mount Abu in Rajasthan. He was joined by many other young men who went on to become leaders of the force. But his fellow trainees always maintained that try as they could (and did), they could not match him either in outdoor activities or in academics.

Winning the President's Baton and the PM's Revolver for standing first in the order of merit, his name peppers almost every Roll of Honour in the Academy. It was wistfully recalled by one batchmate that others like him got one or two prizes which Walter did not contest.

It was time to bid goodbye to the alma mater. Drill and sports instructors Menon and J.B. Joseph, Chief Drill Instructor Spadigam, and Vice Principal in charge of outdoor training Davenport admitted that they were not likely to get another who could equal Walter.

Workers at the Cordite Factory, Aravankadu, had struck work in his first district, The Nilgiris. It is the fundamental right of every union member to lay off the tools, with or without reason. While talks were going on with the labour officers, the workers—obviously egged on by the union—decided to block the movement of the finished product. For a country that had witnessed a war a few years earlier, ammunition was vitally required at the borders. This did not cut much ice with the rebellious strikers who disregarded all appeals. Walter was called in. Young but confident, he asked the workers to lift the blockade. "If you don't, I'll have no option but to disperse you with force." It was a warning delivered in the firm voice which many later generations of agitators came to recognise only too well.

There were some local reserve police, but Walter was not too sure of their marksmanship. In any case, he adopted a stand that was his trademark: "If anybody shoots, it'll be me," he warned his men. Facing the crowd, he said, "I have six rounds in my service revolver. Six of you will get shot. Would you want that?"

A momentary madness made them surge, and Walter had no option but to empty six rounds on the front rank. As they fell, one by one, the crowd became very quiet. Better sense prevailed. Turning around, they fled as fast as their skinny legs would take them. Restraining the men from chasing, he was about to show another facet of his character.

"If the unruly mischief-makers have withdrawn, we need not lose control and expend our anger on the people—some of whom may be innocent bystanders," he told his restive and impatient constables. Not wanting to earn the ire of the new SP, the men sullenly stood by till he reminded them of their duty towards the fallen.

This was an eventful start to an illustrious career, punctuated by firings elsewhere but always in a planned and telling manner. "Our job is not to shoot our people," he'd say, "but if they take the law into their hands and damage public property, they'll have to face the consequences." For a soft-spoken gentleman, every firing where people died was a wrenching experience, but he never retreated.

Later years saw him entrusted with the containment of Communists in Thanjavur District and Anti-Naxalite work in the old Vellore area. Unwilling to submit to dialogue, the violence generated had to have only one response: fight fire with fire. Human Rights were not a buzzword then, and both the Government and the people were confident that Walter would not use force unless he had no other choice.

It is easy to say that Walter was trigger-happy, but the truth was that he got enough satisfaction hitting the bull's-eye on the shooting range.

A regular entrant as a competitor in local and national tournaments, he brought back many trophies for the state.

Veerappan—a nondescript sandalwood smuggler—entered the public domain no less dramatically than Robin Hood, a character he was said to imitate. For some reason, he became an enemy of the state. Orders went forth to apprehend and bring him to justice. Easier said than done. It took more than a decade, millions, many lives, and some close misses before he was cornered.

If Walter set the ball rolling, he was not there to kick it in. His deputy for many years, Vijay Kumar, got to score the goal. But haven't we heard of assists? Nobody scores all by himself. A series of passes, tricking the opposition and freeing the scorer to boot the ball in: all these team moves contributed.

The crafty bandit tried to lure Walter into a trap by suggesting negotiations. "I don't dance with the Devil," he said. A few gullible younger officers from the Forest and Police forces were brutally killed when, like the spider to the fly, the invitation to enter her parlour was accepted.

Walter is unmistakable—walking, sitting, talking, or taking a meeting. His handlebar moustache has been a constant. It did not shrink or grow with age, circumstance, or adversity. As mentioned earlier, he has kept himself very trim. Some years ago, he used to ride out on the beach. But the demands of office pinned him to Chief Office.

As a hill person, he has not been very complimentary of the sticky, moist weather of Madras. Perhaps he was in his element climbing the Sathyamangalam Hills. What has slowed him down these days are the side effects of a horrendous road accident some years ago. A fighter to the core, he came back and served many more years.

When he marched down the road with the marriage procession, which also included the Chief Minister, critics were quick to point out that it was not appropriate for the sitting ADGP to escort the baraat party. But would you rather that he sit in his vehicle while all the VIPs are walking? And how could he extend security cover in an open area if not by being present himself?

Walter has had his share of critics, both within the department and outside. They were uneasy with his clean hands. His ready and immediate disposal of contentious issues was legendary. Punishment Rolls were non-existent, and officers were encouraged to be bold—but correct. He would lend his shoulder to any officer who was being victimised.

At a station visit, he'd peruse the records and question the officer in charge. There was no PA or stenographer, and he did not take any notes either. With a remarkable memory for dates and events, Walter would send a brief but precise Visit Note.

Walter had a facile and good pen, a style of recording his remarks that was uniquely his own. While most of his contemporary colleagues struggled with spoken and written expression, Walter was in his element, either with an impromptu speech or a morale-boosting message to the Force. This was not expected of a so-called field officer, a man of action.

Walter always took everyone along. Not for him were these restrictive barriers and administrative boundaries, which were alright in good times but very fragile in testing times. Thus, when the Holy Father visited Madras and held a High Mass on the sands of Marina, he consulted Mr. John Lobo, the Papal Adviser on security matters, and got ready a 'Pope-mobile' at very short notice.

It would take a stout volume to list all of Mr. Davaram's achievements. Suffice it to say that when he retired from active service, he left behind a rich legacy. With his departure, many felt that an era was coming to a close. As a leader, he led not by prescription but by example. The state would not see another officer with his qualities of head and heart.

Sd/- N. Balachandran, IPS ®

Prologue

Friends said, "Write"! The entire force said, "Write"!

But the "push" I needed was nowhere in sight.

But when locked down by COVID with its wide, wicked grin,

I knew then, 'twas time, my book to begin.

Growing up in the High Ranges

When I was just a little lad,
Tea-gardens around me made me glad;
Slopes in myriad shades of green,
Such beauteous sight, elsewhere not seen;
Those hills and dales were a joy to see,
With nature's beauty enfolding me.

Bison Valley, Mattupatti, Yellapatti, Pallivasal, Gundumalai, Lockhart, Nallathanni, Sivanmalai, Parvathi, Letchimi, Kannimalai, Chokkanadu, Aathikadu, Grahamsland, Periyakanal, Chinnakanal, Periyavarai, Chenduvarai are exotic names of tea estates in the High Ranges; of mountain peaks, clear-water brooks, and evergreen glades and Sholas; names given in their respective tongues by the Muduvans, the original tribal inhabitants of the High Ranges, and by the pioneering planters, British, Tamil, and Malayalee. The very mention of these places lifts my spirit and gives me a sense of superiority over those who have not been blessed with such a priceless heritage. Today, seven decades have gone by since I left the High Ranges for the harsh climes of the plains, but my heart still yearns for the breathtaking grandeur of the Western Ghats, the immaculately manicured tea gardens, the endless stretches of grasslands, the silvery waterfalls, the enchanting valleys carpeted with lilies and wild roses, the swift-flowing, clear mountain streams, the impenetrable rainforests, and above all, the grassy peaks towering above 7500 feet. I still hear the trumpeting of elephants as they splash about at the waterhole, the distant growl of the tiger, the howl of the jackal, the agitated jabbering of the langur, the melody of jungle birds, and the crackling of giant bamboo swaying in the wind.

The steamy heat of Chennai on the Coromandel Coast deepens my longing for the winter frost that gave the tea gardens a picture-postcard look, the never-failing monsoon that brought the heavens down in great sheets of water, the cotton-wool mist gently blanketing the hills, woods, and valleys and disappearing through the mountain passes as silently as it had sailed in; and the welcome rays of the summer sun that soothed and never scorched.

I see in my mind's eye the beautifully manicured tea gardens; I breathe the bouquet of tea leaves plucked with delicate care by the women workers and carried to road junctions to be transported by head-loads, ropeway, mules, or tractors to factories to be processed; I delight in the all-pervading fragrance of freshly processed tea wafting from the factories.

In my early college days in Madras, I would attribute my longing for the High Ranges to the unfamiliar heat and dust of the plains, the mosquitoes and flies, the strange taste of the water, the polluted air, and the natural human tendency to romanticise one's childhood. But my subsequent acquaintance with almost all other mountain ranges and hill plantations of India, as well as those of neighbouring countries, has convinced me that my infatuation with James Finlay and Company, later renamed The Kannan Devan Hills Tea Limited, with Munnar as its headquarters, is no childhood illusion. Munnar town is situated at the confluence of three rivers, the Nallathani, Kundalai, and Muthirapuzha; hence the name 'Munnar,' which in Tamil means three rivers. These rivers feed the Chitrapuram Power House, which accounts for much of Kerala's power requirements.

One of my earliest recollections of those days gone by is of the perilous and eventful road journey from the plains to Munnar from Udumalpet, a distance of 85 km over the thickly wooded and panoramic Amaravathy and Chinnar Hills, or from Alwaye, the nearest railhead on the Cochin-Madras railway line 120 km away; or the 5000-foot trudge from Kurangani on the torrid plains of Bodinayakanur up to the imposing cliffs of Top Station. Top Station was the highest point of the ropeway that carried tea from the hills to the Lower Station near Theni. Thereafter, the tea would be taken to Kodai Road railway station and transported by train to Trichy for the tea auctions there. The ropeway was meant to carry only tea, definitely not people, lest, in the rather unlikely event of a mishap, they plunge to their death 4000 to 6000 feet below. Yet, it was the dream of every child to take a ride on that ropeway. Before the ropeway came into being, a railway called 'Kundaley Valley Light Railway,' commissioned in the year 1908, transported the tea. But those railway lines were washed away in the floods of 1924. Walking up and down hilly terrain was the only way one could get around from one estate to another or from the estates to Munnar town.

As children, we would be fascinated by the stories of tea workers, men and women from the plains of Tirunelveli, Ramanathapuram, and Madurai, who were recruited by middlemen called 'kankanis' with the promise of a salary of four annas (a quarter of a rupee) per day. To people who had never seen or handled money and who were used to carrying out all transactions by barter (work in exchange for rice, coconuts, fruits, milk, etc.), the prospects were very attractive.

At the end of the day, each worker had to pay the 'kankani' a quarter of an anna out of his or her salary of four annas. Naturally, the 'kankanis' soon became well-off enough to be able to send some of their children to colleges on the plains of Kerala or Tamil Nadu. Then, there were the field officers whose duty was to oversee the pruning and weeding by the men and the plucking of the "two leaves and a bud" by the women labourers. The office staff took care of the administrative details, and the factory staff supervised the processing of tea leaves into 'broken orange pekoe' (BOP) and 'tea dust.' The supervisory staff were school-educated men from both sides of the linguistic border—Travancore and Cochin on one side and the Madras Presidency on the other.

The sudden disappearance of vast stretches of the road caused by massive landslides, the breakdown of overloaded and rickety buses, and the intransigent bull elephant in the middle of the road bringing traffic to a standstill were rather essential and not incidental to every trip to and from the hills. Munnar was really no 'easy to access' destination. I remember students of the American College, Madurai, leaving their estates by 3 o'clock in the morning, walking to Top Station, and down to Kurangani on the plains from where they took the first bus to Madurai to be in class by 10 o'clock, covering a 5000-foot descent down the hill followed by a bus ride of 150 km. Whichever route was taken to reach Munnar from the plains of Kerala or Tamil Nadu, it transported the traveller to another world, to another age.

The social life on the Estates was also very different from that on the plains or even that of towns in The Nilgiris. In the High Ranges, the British were still the masters. The newly won Independence was yet to be felt up in the hills. The High Range Club was still out of bounds for Indians. Rugby, Golf, Hunting, Fishing, and horse racing were still the exclusive preserve of the British. Yet there was no animosity or bitterness. The Indian staff showed their fierce loyalty to their respective 'Dorais' (English Managers) at the weekly horse races, steeplechase, and tent pegging, and the 'Dorais' and 'Doraisanies' were at the homes of their Indian staff to share with them in their joys and sorrows. Everyone was conscious of the fact that it was the combined effort of the Highlanders from Scotland and the impoverished Tamilians from the plains of Tirunelveli, Ramnad, and Madurai that converted the inhospitable jungles into magnificent and highly profitable tea gardens.

I remember the friendly cricket and football matches between the High Range Club and the Kannan Devan (Indian) Club played on Saturdays. Sunday, being the Sabbath, was considered a day of rest; as such, all social activities would be scheduled for Saturday. I remember the annual rugby tournament hosted by the all-white High Range Club when teams from the Anamalais, The Nilgiris, Coorg, Bangalore, Bombay, Madras, Ceylon, and the Armenian Club team from Calcutta and even a team from Singapore vied for the trophy. I also remember Munnar's best player, J.C. Gouldsbury, driving around in his little car that tilted to one side because of his weight. By and by, the game of rugby died a natural death, and the Indian managers were not quite up to taking part in the somewhat rough game.

Kannandevan club

More than all these events, it was the Inter-Estate "Finlay Cup Football Tournament" that brought together, as one, all three classes of the estate community: the British managers, the Tamil and Malayalee supervisory staff, and the predominantly Tamil labourers. "James Finlay and Company" found its noblest expression on the football field, where teams comprising all three categories battled it out for the glory of their respective estates. This tournament, which started way back in 1941, was the oldest in the State of Travancore. Almost every estate took part in the tournament, watched by the workers of the competing estates. They would walk all the way to Munnar from their estates in lively anticipation, unmindful of the distance of 15 or 20 km. The end of the match, whatever might have been the result, always warranted a visit to the local arrack shop before the long trudge back to their estates. The teams of Munnar, Sivanmalai, and Pallivasal estates and that of the Munnar Workshop had won the trophy the most number of times. It was this football background that produced players who found places in the College teams of Kerala and Madras. We often met each other at inter-collegiate or inter-University matches. Also, boys who had passed out of Munnar High School proved their class in long-distance running. They owed their innate strength and stamina to their long walks to school, playfields, markets, and places of worship.

Other features that set Munnar apart from the plains were the vast 18-hole golf course and the racecourse, the two separated by the Munnar River gurgling its way down to join the Mullai Periyar River on the plains below. Sadly, the racecourse no longer exists as it has been converted into an Athletic Coaching Centre by the Sports Development Authority of Kerala. I say "sadly" because, in those days, the racecourse was very much a part of our lives. On Saturdays and holidays, we looked forward to being there to watch the Gymkhana Horse Races. These races had been the preserve of the British until A.S. Rangasamy, one of the first two Indian Assistant Managers, became part of this sport, and, much to the chagrin of the British, outclassed them. He was also a good hunter. I remember having gone to his bungalow to take a look at the tiger which he, seated on a 'Machan' (platform built on a tree), had shot down, using a goat tied to the tree as bait. He was also a champion tennis player. Perhaps the British authorities did not take kindly to his versatility, which outsmarted them, or perhaps he did not quite measure up to their managerial job expectations; his probation was terminated.

The other Indian, N.S. Dhar, rose to the highest position of Chairman of the Kannan Devan Planters Association. His daughter Letika, allotted to the Tamil Nadu cadre in the IPS, became the first woman officer to hold the post of Commissioner of Police, Chennai, and later, that of DGP, Tamil Nadu.

The connection between Munnar and Bodinayakanur on the plains goes back more than a century. It was to a family of Chettiars from Bodi that supplied rice and other essential commodities to the estates in Munnar that the short-term manager A.S. Rangasamy belonged. The family grew in wealth, and one of them, Alaganan Chettiyar, even married a British lady, an unthinkable happening in those days.

For those who, like me, were born and brought up in Munnar, the Kannan Devan Hills Tea Estate Limited was everything. Except for the post office and the occasional visit of a solitary policeman from the distant Devikulam Police Station located in the Taluk headquarters, there was nothing to remind one of the existence of a government. Buildings, roads, bridges, hospitals, schools, the market, the township—all belonged to the Company.

I cherish the memory of the one-room, one-teacher elementary school in Kadalar Estate, where I was born and where I started my formal school education. The children of class I sat in the first row, class II in the second, and so on up to the fourth. After singing the glory of the King-Emperor and the Maharaja of Travancore, we children would be sent out to study under the trees. The teacher would then call us in, one class at a time, for lessons.

The Kadalar School

Outside my first school in Kadalar, I remember my 10-mile walk to and from the High School in Munnar, the only High School in the entire hills. The three-storeyed school had once been a tea factory that had lost all its machinery to the major flood of 1924. Many children, boys and girls, had to walk greater distances than I did to reach the school. But distance was never considered an inconvenience because, apart from the invigorating climate, there were distractions aplenty along the way: barking deer playing hide and seek around tea bushes; wild boar and porcupines scurrying across one's path; exquisite butterflies fluttering over wildflowers; and jackals making off with domestic fowl. One could see herds of bison grazing on the distant slopes, forming a kaleidoscopic picture of black dots against a green background, constantly changing patterns as the herd moved on. I especially remember my daily encounter with an otter sunning itself on the banks of the river, which, after waiting for me to get to within 10 feet of it, would dive gracefully into the icy water and disappear.

The Munnar High School had an excellent team of teachers, all of whom, suited and booted, taught in both Tamil and Malayalam. The headmaster was Thomas John, a strict disciplinarian but a kind-hearted person. Hindi was introduced as a compulsory subject when I was in standard 9; this, in later years, gave me an advantage over the student community of Tamil Nadu. As a Boy Scout, I enjoyed monthly outings around the hills. I remember Scout Master C.V. Mathew taking us on an excursion to Madras and giving us our first experience of a train ride and the cold delight of ice cream at the Erode railway station. My most memorable excursion, however, was the climb to Eravikulam Ibex (mountain goat) Sanctuary and Anaimudi Peak, from where we could see all of the Anaimalai Hills up to Pollachi on the Madras side and all of Devikulam and Peermedu taluks on the Kerala side.

On my father's promotion to Labour Welfare Officer, he was allotted a bungalow on the Letchmi estate. As he had to travel extensively between the Anamalais and Munnar, and the walk to school and back, especially for my younger siblings, proved a little too much, my father took a house in Palya Munnar, nearer the school. The house was on a hill surrounded by tea, with no motorable path to it. It was forbidden to uproot tea bushes, and it took a lot of going back and forth before permission was granted to cut a 20-foot-long and 5-foot-wide pathway through the tea bushes for his bike to go through.

The house at Letchmi Estate

The house in Palaya Munnar

The pathway that led to the house.

There was only one cinema theatre in the entire district, the Pankajam Theatre. It was a tin shed opposite the Munnar High School. It had three classes of seating; the lowest was tharai (floor), costing three annas. The second enclosure had benches and cost 6 annas per person, while the highest class, again a set of benches, cost 8 annas (16 annas made a rupee). Tamil movies would be screened every night without disturbing the work on the estates. Thursdays and Saturdays were for English movies, usually a war or a cowboy movie on Thursday and a serious one on Saturday. The 3-anna ticket remained the same for the English movie; the 6-anna ticket became eight annas, and the 8-anna ticket became Rs. 2. The two-rupee enclosure was used only by the British even long after independence, and Indians, even if they could afford the two-rupee ticket, refrained from going into that upper-class enclosure.

Most of all, I remember and cherish the bonhomie and geniality of Munnar's mixed society. Everyone was known to everyone else, and needless to say, everyone also knew what everyone else was doing! Everyone spoke both Malayalam and Tamil. Every motor vehicle, a rarity in those days and of which there were just a few in Munnar, was recognised by the sound of its horn. Everyone was 'Uncle,' 'Auntie,' 'Chechie,' or 'Thambi.' One was never alone on the road. There were estate workers, the men armed with pruning knives and women with wicker baskets strapped onto their foreheads, under the watchful eyes of their Indian supervisors; cowherds taking the estate cattle to the grasslands, often returning home minus a cow or 2, which had ended up as food for tigers or leopards. The British Manager or Assistant Manager rode by on horseback, overseeing the multiple activities of the estates. They would all stop to exchange greetings or to enquire about the health, job, or family of the staff and workers. Even the drivers of the buses to Kottayam and Udumalpet would wave out to those whom they passed on the road.

The strife-free and almost crime-free society was unique in more ways than one. Cent per cent employment, free education, free medical care, and the homogeneity of the Company's employees rendered locks and keys redundant. Every family had its own vegetable garden, fruit trees, and milch cows. Petty commercialisation was yet to enter the hill economy. Politics was unknown.

It was a mutually beneficial society which saw no difference between the Malayalee and Tamilian, Caste Hindu and Harijan, Christian, Hindu, and Muslim. Everybody celebrated the Hindu festivals of Aadi, Onam, Vishu, and Deepavali, the Christian festivals of Christmas and Easter, and the Muslim festivals of Ramzan and Bakrid. It is to this society that I owe my personal development and my present position. It is the fond memory of this fabled land that sustains me when all else fails. It is the heart-warming influence of Munnar, along with her mountains, rivers, tea estates, and warm-hearted people, that has governed my life down the years.

Today's Idukki district, which has been carved out of the old Kottayam district, is the largest district in Kerala, with 97% of its area being forest or plantation. Its borders extend up to the Chinnaar and Amaravathi Rivers in the Coimbatore district in the north, Bodi and Gudalur (lower camp - Kumuli) of Theni district in the east, Pattanamthitta district in the South, and Kottayam and Trichur districts in the west. The headquarters of the district is Painavu, located near the 555-metre-high Idukki Dam, the third-largest arch dam in the world. Important places in the district other than Munnar are Thodupuzha, Devikulam, Udumbanchola, Pallivasal, and the new settlement of Maraiyur outside the tea-growing area close to the Tamil Nadu border. It is this mountain district in Kerala that grows most of the tea for export and also produces about one-third of the state's electricity requirements at the Chitrapuram Power Station. Incidentally, Chitrapuram was named after Maharaja Chitirai Tirunal, the last King of Travancore. This district boasts the largest number of dams, the main ones being the Gundalay, Mattupatti, Munnar, Mullaiperiyar, and

Idukki dams. The only police station and the Magistrate's court were in the headquarters of the Taluk, Devikulam, 15 km out of Munnar. There was one well-equipped hospital in Munnar under a senior British doctor. Each estate had its own clinic under a Licensed Medical Practitioner (LMP).

At that time, children of the company employees who finished school chose to follow in their parents' footsteps, taking up jobs on the estates. The situation has now changed, and many of them take up jobs not only in Tamil Nadu and Kerala but all over India and abroad.

I am the first IPS officer from Munnar, and 13 years later, Letika Saran became the second one. There have been others, too, and I cannot adequately describe the elation I feel every time I meet someone in khaki who tells me, 'I am from Munnar,' or one who is married to a 'Munnarite.' It is possible there are more Munnarites I have yet to meet. I hope that someday, those of us police officers with our roots in Munnar get together to renew our connection with our beloved hills.

Letika Saran née Dhar

Just like a bird of passage that longs for its woodland home, I longed for the place of my birth—the cloud-kissed mountains, the clear-water streams, and the tea gardens that stretched out as far as the eye could see. The incomparable High Ranges! These truly are the memories of my youth.

Fast Forward to 2022:

It is the 12th of November 2022. I was once again on the Ghat Road from Udumalpet to Munnar, my heart filled with eager anticipation. I was on my way to attend a get-together of the alumni of my school, the Munnar Government High School.

This trip was a dream come true for Prema, daughter Anita, and grandson Amitesh, who so badly wanted to see the place where I was born and the various houses I had lived in until destiny brought me to where I am today.

It seemed to me, as we drove through the Anamalai and Chinnar Wildlife Sanctuaries, that nothing much had changed since my last trip up that road. But Maraiyur was not the sleepy village I had left behind; it was abuzz with eateries catering to the hordes of tourists going to or returning from Munnar. We found that if we missed our tea at Maraiyur, there were other possibilities all along the way.

The next rude shock came when we entered Munnar Town. Anita manoeuvred the car down those familiar but now overly crowded roads and drove into the compound of a multi-storeyed building, our hotel, Isaacs Residency. I looked for my tin-shed Pankajam Theatre to find in its place the multi-storeyed 'silver Tips' Hotel. At least the yesteryear cinema posters outside and inside spoke of the place's heritage. There was even a projector at the entrance to remind me of the days gone by.

I longed for the one-horse town I'd left behind nearly 6 decades ago. I could not find it. I was dismayed, but at least the estates were still the same. The houses I had lived in were there too. But to see them unkempt, with their compounds overgrown with weeds instead of pretty gardens and orchards, was heartbreaking. Didn't the present occupants care? My disappointment was somewhat allayed when I visited my schools in Kadalar and Chokanad and the house in Nayamakad, which had been so much a part of my growing years, and found that not much had changed.

The school reunion brought together more than 700 past students. I was the oldest, having passed out in the year 1954, and quite understandably, there was no one there who had been in school with me. I looked at the cheery gathering around me; some of them might not have even been born at the time I was there. But then school reunions are joyous occasions and bring back memories of those bygone carefree days. However, I did miss my three-storeyed tea factory-turned-school building, which has been replaced by a single-storeyed one.

We were in Munnar for 4 days, visiting various estates and viewpoints and doing "touristy" things, the most important ones being the Eravikulam Ibex Sanctuary and a trip to Idukki Dam, the third-highest arch dam in the world, for after all, we were in "today's Munnar."

This walk down memory lane was made more meaningful thanks to Letika Saran, who connected us with Mohan Verghese and Pereira and took us to all the places that were so much a part of my childhood and youth.

With Mohan Varghese

With Joseph Pereira

As I left Munnar at the end of our visit, it was with a tinge of sadness the Munnar I was leaving behind was not the Munnar I had left behind those decades ago.

> How I long for my home where wild animals roam
> And the people are happy all day;
> That good life in which one is never alone
> As one travels along on life's way.

My Second Choice

With all in the army, grand-dad, uncle, dad,
The army to me, was much more than a fad.
But as days went by, I began to see,
life in the army eluding me.
Though I wanted the army, no matter what rank
For what I'm today, my second choice I thank.

What is or was my first choice? It had always been the army that held my fascination because of my family background. My maternal grandfather was a Subedar Major in the Karnataka Regiment in the First World War, later renamed the Madras Regiment. He was recalled when the Second World War broke out. My father, my maternal uncle, and many of the British managers who were on the estates in Munnar also enlisted in the army and served on the Burma front against the Japanese. Although they never talked much about their tenure in the army or the war, their uniforms, medals, ceremonial swords, and photographs left a lasting impression on my young mind.

My Maternal Grandfather, Subedar Major Isaac,
After Whom I've Been Named

When my father left for the war front, my mother, with my older
sister and me, moved to Trivandrum, where I still remember watching
with fascination as the Maharaja made his daily procession to the
Padmanabhaswamy Temple, surrounded by his bodyguards and led by
the royal band. To me, at that time, it was a delightful pageant. Back in
Munnar after the war, my sister and I resumed our studies, first in the

one-room estate school and later in the government high school, where we completed our SSLC, as did my other siblings. My only brother joined the Air Force; my older sister became an academic and ran a primary school in a village in Salem district. The oldest of my younger sisters did a secretarial course, worked for several years in the USA, and returned to India after her retirement. The next one is a paediatric surgeon, and the one younger than her is a housewife. The youngest was a University athlete. She retired from Bishop Appasamy College, Coimbatore, where she worked as an administrator.

Another event that further fuelled my interest in the army was the Poppy Day ceremony at the "Victory Pillar" in Munnar on the 11th of November every year, which I would attend with my father. The buglers would sound the Last Post at the 11th second of the 11th minute of the 11th hour of the 11th day of the 11th month of the year. After a two-minute silence, the buglers would sound the Reveille. This ceremony was in memory of those who had sacrificed their lives in World War I and later also for those who died in World War II. It was called 'Poppy Day' because the battle-scarred fields of Flanders in France, where World War I ended, were soon covered with poppy plants in bloom. The closing lines of John McCrae's poem 'In Flanders Fields' say it all:

> 'If ye break faith with us, who die,
> We shall not sleep, though poppies grow
> In Flanders fields'

The Victory Pillar at Munnar

As soon as I could read and understand English, I would get colourful, illustrated magazines and books on World War II from the High Range Club and go through them from cover to cover, with my parents helping me with words I could not understand. The result of all this was that the army became a permanent fixation in my mind; I wanted nothing more than to be a part of the Indian Army.

After school, I chose to go to Madras Christian College, which at that time was one of the few colleges that offered the NCC. Meanwhile,

I had also written the entrance exam for the National Defence Academy (NDA). I received the result just as I was writing my Intermediate final examination. I had completed Part I and Part-III, with only Part II (language) left, when I was called for the final selection by the Services Selection Board, Bangalore. I could easily have asked for a change of date for my interview, citing my pending language paper. But I was so sure of getting into the army because of my NCC training and proficiency in sports that I decided to forgo the exam. My father took me to Bangalore after giving me a lesson on the use of cutlery at the high-end Spencer's Restaurant on the first floor of Madras Central Station. In those days, Spencer's had a similar restaurant in Coimbatore junction as well, where a meal at Christmas time included delicious plum pudding with an equally delicious brandy sauce.

Unfortunately, I did not get selected. That meant I had to take the pending Part-II exam in September and wait until the following academic year to continue my studies. Instead of wasting that year, I took a one-year certificate course at the YMCA College of Physical Education. The YMCA College was founded in 1920 by the American Harry Crowe Buck. It happened to be the only one of its kind in South Asia. This gave me the rare experience of meeting students not only from all over India but also from Ceylon and Malaysia. The only discordant note in this harmonious setup was the enmity between the Sinhalese and Sri Lankan Tamil students; they would not even talk to each other.

Back in MCC for my B.A. and with my mind still focused on the army, I passed the C-Certificate of the NCC and reached the highest rank of Under Officer. Four of us from our college unit of the NCC were called for an army interview in Bangalore. Only one of us got selected and retired as a Major General after a glorious career. Philip Jacob, my fellow Under Officer, went on to study medicine and later migrated to the USA. Sergeant Ramakrishnan, the fourth candidate, who, unlike the rest of us, passed his B.A. on his first attempt, became a Sub-Inspector of Police. This became the subject of a joke for us all. The only person who had got his degree on his very first attempt ended up as an SI, while those of us who failed fared much better in life! But it is to his credit that Ramakrishnan, who passed out as the best cadet in his batch of SIs and who was No.1 in seniority, had a glorious career. He is one of the few SIs who retired as an IPS officer following his commendable service, which included saving the body of Rajiv Gandhi from the shocked and emotionally charged crowd in Sriperumbudur, taking it safely to the general hospital in Chennai for post-mortem, and later, to the airport. For this commendable effort, he was awarded a Gallantry medal.

I cleared my B.A. in September and applied to MCC for my M.A. But as the college seemed to have had enough of me, I had to go to Annamalai University for my post-graduation. There, I represented the University in two Inter-University Athletic Meets, one in Lucknow and the other in Bangalore. I also represented the University in football and hockey.

It was at Annamalai University that my scholarly professor, Sathyanatha Aiyar, an authority on history who had authored several books, told me that I had sufficient proficiency in English to try for the IAS. But the IAS did not appeal to me. The IPS, on the other hand, seemed to be a good alternative to the army. I lived up to the expectations of my professor by getting a first class in M.A. History and also the first rank.

My classmate Santhana Krishnan and I took the UPSC exam; he took the IAS, and I took the IPS. Shortly after the examination, in October 1962, the Chinese War broke out. That rekindled my longing for life in the army. Without a second thought, I left for the North East Frontier Agency (NEFA) with the hope of getting into the army on the strength of my NCC training and its C-Certificate. The journey took 5 days, including a steamer crossing across the river Brahmaputra, as the construction of a bridge across it was yet to be completed. By the time I reached Dimapur, the war was over. But I decided to stay on and apply for the Emergency Commission instead of returning home. I took the opportunity to visit a few places in the North East Frontier Agency, Nagaland, and Manipur. While on my way to Imphal from Dimapur, my bus made a tea stop at Maram on the Nagaland-Manipur border. There, to my surprise, I heard the sound of a language alien to where I was but familiar to me. I turned towards the source of the conversation to find two men in police uniform talking in Tamil! I learnt from them that they belonged to the Malabar Special Police II Battalion with headquarters in Imphal. The Battalion was there to provide protection from the Naga insurgents to convoys travelling between Kohima and Imphal.

Another pleasant surprise awaited me in Imphal. I walked out of my hotel and into my classmate and fellow NCC Under-Officer from Madras Christian College, Lokendra Singh, a brilliant Manipuri who had also been Captain of the Madras University and Christian College football teams. He suggested that instead of going back to Munnar to wait for the IPS results, I could work as a member of the teaching staff at the Government College Imphal, where he was working. When I told him that I did not even have my MA certificate with me, he said that, on his word, the Principal would accept my application. I was appointed the same day. This was indeed a happy break for me. I shall always be thankful to Lokendra Singh for the opportunity to meet and teach students who are totally different from those in the rest of India. My mind goes back to an incident that caused me great embarrassment. At the request of my Naga and Mizo students, I once attended a Church service. When everyone rose for the final prayer, I was shocked to hear one of the students making an announcement: 'Professor Walter will now lead us in prayer.' The congregation bowed their heads and closed their eyes. It was with much discomfiture that I had to inform them that I did not know how to pray and, as such, was not in a position to lead them in prayer. It is not that I do not pray. I do, but within myself.

My sojourn in Imphal gave me the opportunity to trek to my heart's content. One of my treks took me through the thickly wooded 'no-man's-land.' I had somehow missed the Indo-Burmese border check-post and reached the Burmese border town of Tamu. There, I met the owner of an eatery, a Tamilian who was originally from Dindigul and who, when the British Army surrendered Burma to the Japanese, chose to stay back in Burma, unlike most of the other Indians who returned to India. He was one of the few Indians who felt no threat from the Japanese. Later, he became a citizen of Burma, now known as Myanmar. When trekking in Manipur, the locals would stare at me and refer to me amicably as Mayang (stranger). In Nagaland, however, it was different. The Nagas overwhelmed me with their hospitality and insisted I join them at meal times. I could not refuse whatever they offered: a locally brewed liquor and a rice meal with meat, the source of which I dared not ask. All I can say is I was aware of kennels with dogs reared specially for occasions like Christmas, New Year, and weddings. Dog meat was a delicacy for the Nagas, or at least for my hosts, the tribe of Angamis.

Two months into my stint at the college, I was called for the IPS interview in Madras. I wrote to the UPSC requesting a change of centre from distant Madras to relatively closer Calcutta. I took the flight to Calcutta, attended the interview, and returned by flight. That trip cost me my entire salary of Rs.250/-. But it was worth it, considering the fact that it would have taken me 5 days just to reach Calcutta from Imphal by road and rail. At that time, the airfare to and from Imphal and Agartala, the capital of Tripura, and Calcutta had been subsidised by the Government because of the remoteness of the North Eastern States.

The IPS result was announced 2 months later, and I had finished second in the overall ranking behind R.K. Raghavan of Tamil Nadu. It was then that the head of the Indian Military Academy in Dehradun advised me to take up the IPS, as the Emergency Commission that I had applied for was not a permanent one. Thus, my olive-green dream turned to khaki.

I joined the course at the Indian Administrative Academy in Mussoorie after a delay of almost a month, as I needed time to say goodbye to my friends, fellow teachers and students in Imphal, the officers and men of MSP-II, and friends in Nagaland and Burma who had enlivened and enriched my weekends. I then went home to Munnar, from where I went to Trivandrum for the mandatory medical test before joining the Academy.

I had given Nagaland, which at that time was still fighting for independence, as my first choice of cadre, not for the dog meat but for the exciting life which I thought the state would offer me. However, while in Mount Abu, I was informed that there was no cadre for Nagaland as it was only a union Territory and not a state. Once again, I had to make a second choice. I chose Madras State in preference to my home state, Kerala.

Now, when I compare my service in the Police department with what it might have been in the army, I have no regrets. I feel happy that my life has been action-packed all through, dealing with agitators, Naxalites, Separatists, Religious fundamentalists, and jungle bandits. Had I been in the army, I might not ever have even seen action, depending on the deployment of my Regiment in the 1971 war. As such, I am grateful that my second choice has been fruitful, giving me opportunities to trek, explore, and visit places of historical and religious importance.

But then, I must admit that I continue to have a lot of respect for India's Armed Forces, which are second to none in the world. I still treasure the greeting card dated 6th March 1964 sent to me by Subedar Major Ganju Lama VC (Victoria Cross) of the Gurkha Rifles when he was a member of the President's Body Guards. It was in reply to my letter congratulating him on his prestigious award, although when I wrote to him, 20 years had gone by after the extraordinary heroism displayed in Burma in 1943 as a member of the Fifth Gurkha Rifles.

Incidentally, the Indian Army's maximum number of Victoria Crosses has been won by the Gurkhas, "the bravest of the brave." Following the progress of my career with its high-risk operations, there are also those who ask me whether I am always fearless. To them, I repeat the famous quote of Field Marshall Manekshaw, 'If anybody says he is not afraid, he is either a liar or a Gurkha!' But me? I'm neither.

At this juncture, I must appreciate my cousin Ivor Devavaram from Munnar for his glorious career in the Madras Regiment, from which he retired as a Major General. He is the highest-ranked army officer in Munnar as well as in Kanyakumari district, where he eventually settled down. Following in his footsteps, his son is also in the army and is now a Colonel in the same Regiment.

I would also like to introduce my readers to a rather unlikely military family. Narasimhan was the District Forest Officer, Thanjavur, when I was the SP there. Both his sons, Mahendran and Vijayaraghavan, grew up to become army officers. His only daughter, Lakshmi, is the wife of Lt. Gen. Pattabiram, who is now retired and settled in Coonoor. Moving down the line, Vijayaraghavan's son is also an army officer. An army family from a non-martial race!

I see myself as the odd man out because all the menfolk in my family, starting with my grandfather, then my father and uncle, and finally my only brother, served in the armed forces. My brother-in-law, Prema's only sibling, was a fighter pilot in the Indian Air Force, and I, who really longed to be there, did not make it. Today, as I look back on my years of service, I have no regrets at all. It was my second choice that took over my action-filled life and gave me my greatest satisfaction and sense of fulfilment.

In Principio

The training in Mussoorie just happened to be
A chance, the mighty Himalaya to see.
But the course in Mount Abu was focussed enough
To convert us all into policemen tough.
The best cadet I turned out to be,
In the batch of nineteen sixty-three.
I served in the force for years thirty and four;
Years of fulfilment they were, and much more.
Of the events of those years, I'd now like to write
Future generations must know, 'tis right that is might.

Those who had cleared the UPSC examination were required to undergo the first phase of their training at the Lal Bahadur Shastri National Academy of Administration in Mussoorie. By the time I reached the academy, the others were already 3 weeks into the course. I got there and found there was no accommodation in the main block. Another latecomer, IAS-Trainee S.L. Verma from Rajasthan, and I were accommodated in a portion of the quarters allotted to an office staff member, 300 metres downhill below the main academy building. The climb to the Academy took almost 20 minutes, and we had to do it at least thrice a day. To my delight, I saw that the accommodation was close to the riding arena. As such, I enjoyed not only the climb up to the academy but also the opportunity to ride twice in the morning and twice in the evening instead of just once every other day.

At that time, the course in Mussoorie for the IPS candidates was only an introductory course of 6 months. We had no exams and no marks to worry about. As such, I would skip classes, which were meant mainly for the IAS, and attend only the guest lectures. I spent the rest of my time trekking in the hills, often crossing the river Yamuna, which flowed 10 km away from the academy. It was not long before I was joined by my batchmate, A.V. Liddle of the Madhya Pradesh cadre. Together, we planned longer treks. We trekked to Rishikesh, Haridwar, Chakrata, and even to distant Shimla, crossing the river Yamuna twice. On our return to Mussoorie from Shimla, we took a shortcut which, at 132 km, was hardly 'short' and took us a day and a half to cover. Liddle had more stamina than I and would offer to carry my haversack whenever I got too tired. The Director of the Academy took kindly to our leisure activities and even made us regale the trainees with accounts of our treks. At the end of 6 months, we left for Mount Abu.

The Indian Police (IP), founded on 15th September 1948, was the precursor of the Indian Police Service (IPS) when its first batch of officers was trained at the Central Police Training College, Mount Abu, the only hill station on the Aravallis in Rajasthan. The course was exacting for most of the trainees who, over the years, had lost touch with sports and other physical activities. They would all be so drained that they had to use their Sundays to reinforce themselves for the demanding week ahead. As for me, I would go riding with the Mounted Branch, scaling the nearest mountains, or walking up to Dilwara, the Jain Temples, or to the sunset point further away. I was later joined by another brilliant trekker, Warwade, who was one of the 10 DSPs from Madhya Pradesh sent for training with us. Both of us would go down to Abu Road Railway Station by bus and jog back to Mount Abu, a distance of about 30 km, all of it uphill.

I was delighted to be in Rajasthan, with its legendary forts, historical monuments, unforgettable battles, and, above all, the legend of Rana Pratap Singh of Chittoor. Although I managed to visit only a few of those places over weekends and during the 10-day break in June, I had no time to visit all of them; this I did with Prema 10 years later when we were there for the Senior Officers' Course.

The trainees found the IPS training schedule demanding, even gruelling, but the training staff, drawn mostly from the legendary Malabar Special Police of the Madras Presidency and headed by Chief Drill Instructor DSP Spadigam, resolutely turned a blind eye to this aspect and remained unmoved, stern, and exacting. The strenuous training wore out most of the trainees, leaving them with no energy for studies. I, on the other hand, could easily cope with it all. Riding was also taught by expert riding instructors led by a Rajput Inspector. I enjoyed cross-country riding with them on Sundays.

It is customary for the best cadet of the course to lead the Passing-Out Parade every year. Owing to my four-year training in the NCC, which had honed my expertise in drill, shooting, weapon training, and sports, as well as my experience in having commanded the Republic Day Parade in Delhi, I won all the outdoor trophies except the one for riding, in which I had to face a better rider in Damodar Singh of the Manipur Rifles, who, along with another officer, had been sent to Mount Abu for training with us. In sports, the only competition I had was from N.K. Singh, a DSP trainee from Madhya Pradesh. Surprisingly, I won the Mehta Cup for studies as well.

The Chief Guest for the passing-out parade was Sukhadia, Chief Minister of Rajasthan. I led the parade on horseback and received the President's baton and the Prime Minister's revolver from him. He made a few enquiries in Hindi, and I replied that they were also in Hindi. Thirteen years were to pass when, as DC, L&O, Chennai City, I commanded the Police Medal Parade in Chennai. Sukhadia, who had by then become the Governor of Tamil Nadu, was the Chief Guest. I was pleasantly surprised that he recognised me. Could it have been the Rajput moustache? He even asked about my hometown in Rajasthan! My answer took him by surprise, but that did not affect his regard for me.

Mohan Lal Sukhadia

I find that the syllabus for the IPS trainees has now undergone major changes. Fifty marks have been allotted for an examination conducted in Mussoorie; only 600 marks have been allotted for outdoor activities and a whopping 1200 marks for studies in addition to 400 marks for the Director's assessment. The activities include physical training, drill, shooting, unarmed combat, yoga, fieldcraft and tactics, map reading, and ambulance drills. Yoga? Am I glad I belonged to the batch of 1963?

Over the last 72 years, about 7000 IPS officers have been trained in the academy, besides DSPs from some of the Indian States and neighbouring countries like Nepal and Bhutan. In 1975, the Institute was shifted to the centrally located Hyderabad by the then Director, IGP S.M. Diaz of Tamil Nadu. I have been to Hyderabad a few times to conduct riding and drill tests.

Here, I must mention an anomaly in recalling trainees who failed to ride for a re-test. As ASPs or even SPs, they would have had no chance of improving their riding skills because Mounted Branches are maintained only at the State Headquarters. I had to wait for more than 10 years after leaving Mount Abu to ride again. Bearing that in mind, I would pass all those who were there for the re-test. It is time for the present system of conducting practical tests in outdoor activities to be revamped.

There was a time when the highest number of trainees in the All-India Services came from Tamil Nadu. In my batch of 75 cadets, as many as 16 were from Tamil Nadu. Other than Haryana, Punjab, and Uttar Pradesh, all the other Indian States had officers from Tamil Nadu. All three officers allotted to Andhra Pradesh were from Tamil Nadu because there was no one from the home state. Officers are allotted to various states on a ratio of outsiders and insiders. In Tamil Nadu, R.K. Raghavan was the insider; E. Hariharane from Pondicherry and I from Kerala were the outsiders. But all three of us happened to be Tamilians.

Sadly, representation from Tamil Nadu has been on the decline. In the 2016 batch, only eight out of 150 were from Tamil Nadu; in 2017, only nine out of 121; in 2018, only five out of 144. Of the 5, only one candidate, Kiran Shruthi, was allotted to the Tamil Nadu cadre. She won the best cadet award and ten other trophies, setting a record that is hard to beat.

Every year, the best officer-trainee is awarded the President's Baton and the Prime Minister's revolver. The following officers from the Tamil Nadu cadre have won this prestigious award:

1. C.V. Narasimhan (1948)

2. M.K. Narayan (1955)

3. W.I. Davaram (1963)

4. K.V.S. Moorthy (1976)

5. K. Ramanujam (1978)

6. Dr. Senthil Velan (2004)

7. D.V. Kiran Shruthi (2020)

As part of our training, we were taken in batches to various states so that we would have an idea of basic police duties and acts and regulations peculiar to them. I was sent with a few others, first to Mumbai and then to Pune. We were also sent for army training in field areas. I was lucky to have been sent to a well-known Indo-Pakistan war front of the 1965 war, the Hajipur Pass at an altitude of 8652 feet. The military engagement from 26th to 28th August 1965 resulted in India capturing the entire Pass. India's taking over the Pass was a major strategic victory as it plugged the ingress routes of infiltrators from Pakistan. Brig. Bakshi and Major Dayal were awarded the Maha Vir Chakra (MVC), and the first para-regiment was awarded the battle honour 'Hajipur.'

This trip also took us to Srinagar, where each one of us was presented with a carton of apples. I sent mine to my parents in Munnar; I booked the parcel by train from Delhi to Alwaye and informed them by telegram. My brother went down to Alwaye railway station, picked it up, and carried it back to Munnar, 110 km away. Those were days when apples were a rarity in South India and totally unknown in Munnar. In fact, the only 'apple' we were acquainted with was the one that adorned the first page of an English Primer, which read 'A for Apple!' Needless to say, my carton of apples was a rare treasure that was shared with neighbours and friends.

Vellore – My Home Away from Home

My first stint in Vellore saw me just a trainee;
By my second stint there, I'd become an SP;
But stint number three was as long as could be,
By which time, I'd become a DIG
And once I was free of the naxal syndrome,
I could look upon Vellore as my second home.

Vellore to the Tamil Nadu Police is what Wellington in The Nilgiris is to the Madras Regimental Centre, and Dehradun in Uttarakhand is to the Indian Military Academy. But the heritage of the last two post-independence centres is not as ancient as that of Vellore's 125-year-old police heritage.

The Police Training College in Vellore was established in 1896, and those selected as Inspectors underwent a three-month course there; for ASPs, however, it was 6 months. Both categories were recruited in England. There was also a training centre for constables in Vellore. Three more Recruit Schools were opened in Vijayanagaram, Coimbatore, and Ananthapur in 1908. But Vellore continued to be the centre for the training of various categories, from constables to the ASPs of the IP (Indian Police). It was only later that Indian DSPs were recruited and trained there.

Vellore was seen as the most suitable location to house a Police Training Establishment, as the Fort had ample accommodation for trainees in the Hyder and Tippu Mahals; there was also ample open area for parade grounds, playfields, and other facilities. In fact, the entire fort area, with the exception of the Jalakandeswarar Temple, St. John's Church, and a mosque, was available for outdoor police training. Besides, other than in the Church, there was no worship in either the mosque or the Temple. Now that the police training facility has been shifted to the Tamil Nadu Police Academy in Oonamachery and the Police Training College at Ashok Nagar in Chennai, the Fort has once again regained its past glory.

This Fort is one that ought to be maintained like other historical heritages elsewhere in the country, like the forts in Agra, Ginjee, Udaipur, Jaipur, Jodhpur, Jaisalmer, Sinhagard, Pratapgard, and Jhansi, to name a few. The 16th-century Vellore Fort is protected by a massive rampart and a wide moat, which, at one-time, harboured crocodiles to prevent enemies from entering it. Access to the Fort was over a drawbridge that could be lowered or raised as required.

This bridge still exists but as a fixed structure. The Fort is now under the care of the Archaeological Department. The entire area at that time was available for the training of police officers and men. As such, it was the obvious choice for a Police Training Centre for the entire force, from IPS officers down to SIs and PCs. Devasagayam and Sanjeevi Pillai were the first Indian IP officers to be trained there, and E.L. Stracey was the last. India's independence marked the induction into the IPS of officers K.R. Shenoy and S.M. Diaz from the disbanded British Indian Armed Forces.

The training of IPS officers allotted to the Madras Presidency, Group-1 officers of the state (Dy. SPs), SIs, and constables continued in Vellore. The Madras Presidency, however, underwent many changes in the fifties. The State of Andhra Pradesh was formed in 1958. Five taluks of Travancore district and the Sengottai Taluk of Quilon district were transferred to the Madras Presidency, later renamed Tamil Nadu. But nothing changed for Vellore, which continued to be the training centre for the reconstituted Tamil Nadu. When our batch of 3 IPS officers arrived at the college in Vellore, two state Dy. SPs and two Assistant Commandants selected by the TNPSC were already under training there. With them were two senior Dy. SPs of the Armed Reserve and four Deputy Commandants of the Tamil Nadu Armed Police on their one-time conversion to Dy. SPs of the local police. Little did I think then that Vellore would become my second home, with me returning to spend one year as SP, North Arcot, and returning yet again for a record number of five-and-a-half years as DIG, Vellore Range. No wonder then that I was the obvious choice to deal with the Sri Lankan militants who had risen in rebellion in the Vellore Fort and again later, to recapture the militants who had escaped from the Fort by tunnelling their way out.

Now, let me take you back to my training days. An annex had to be built for the three of us as the Officers' Mess was already overcrowded. We cycled to the Fort thrice a day for drills, classes, and sports. While all other trainees went home over holidays and even weekends, I would stay back because, for me, my home, Munnar, was more than 700 kms away. But I did not waste those breaks. I would cycle to Chittoor, Chandragiri Fort, Horsely Hills, and Madanapalli, all located in neighbouring Andhra Pradesh. I also visited Ambur Fort, Ratnagiri Temple, the Sholingur Lakshmi Narasimha Swamy Temple, Amirthi Zoo, Vallimalai Murugan Temple, Pallikonda Perumal Temple, and other heritage sites.

Would anyone believe that I learnt to cycle only after I went to Madras Christian College? For that matter, forget cycling itself; I had not even seen a cycle in Munnar, probably because of the rugged, hilly terrain; cycling was not a practical mode of transport.

The anti-Hindi agitation put an end to all my trekking and cycling activities. K.V. Subramaniam, SP, North Arcot district, would take us to places where the anti-Hindi agitators had caused heavy damage to public property. Vellore Town itself was well-protected by a determined

DSP, Dhanraj, who stood in the middle of the road, valiantly facing the agitators. While under training in Vellore, we also had the pleasure of meeting E.L. Stracey, DIG, Coimbatore, while he was on a tour of his Range, which extended from Travancore and Cochin state in the South to the newly formed Andhra Pradesh in the North. It was his usual practice to meet trainees over breakfast or lunch and to informally chat with them about the do's and don'ts of good policing. It was on one such occasion that he told us about Vellakoil Police Station in Coimbatore district, which had been attacked by anti-Hindi agitators. HC Mariappan, who happened to be the only policeman in the police station, locked the door from the inside. But the agitators climbed onto the roof and tried to enter the building. The HC shot one of them dead and injured 4 others, thus saving himself and the police station. DIG Stracey gave him an on-the-spot promotion to the rank of SI. It is unfortunate that the government that came to power soon after demoted him to his old rank. The upright and proud SI could not accept the humiliation and put in his resignation.

E.L STRACEY, I.P.

K.V. Subramaniam, my first SP.

As an example of how not to be, Stracey also told us about an incident in Namakkal where anti-Hindi agitators were on the rampage. The ASP did not stir out of his residence and guarded himself with the armed strength he was supposed to use to deal with the agitators. The ASP had to be pulled out of his residence to face the situation.

I am sure it would interest readers to know that it was in the Vellore Fort that the first Sepoy Mutiny against the British took place on 10th July 1806. This was the first time that the Indian soldiers had risen in rebellion against the British and was the forerunner of the epoch-making 'Sepoy Mutiny' that broke out in Meerut 51 years later in 1857, spreading all over North India. Protesting against a piece of cowhide used on their new caps and perhaps at the instigation of the sons of Tippu Sultan, who were being held prisoners in the Fort, the sepoys rose in revolt and massacred more than 200 British soldiers belonging to the 69th South Lincolnshire Regiment. A few survivors rushed to the main gate and held down the drawbridge across the moat, foiling repeated attempts by the sepoys to raise it and prevent British reinforcements from entering the Fort.

In the morning, the news of the Mutiny reached Arcot, five kms away. Col. Gillespie immediately collected the few soldiers who were available and rushed to Vellore. He crushed the Mutiny in a matter of 6 hours from the time he received the news in Arcot. Altogether, 350 mutineers were killed, six of their leaders were blown up by cannons, five were shot dead by a firing squad, and eight were hanged. Col. Gillespie did not have speedy transport, wireless equipment, telephones, or any other means of quick communication. When he received the news of the mutiny, he did not wait for any reinforcements or instructions. He did not waver on the point of jurisdiction as staff of our police stations often do. It was his commitment to his king and country that motivated him. Eventually, he was killed while leading an attack on the Gurkhas at Fort Nalapani near Dehradun in the Anglo-Nepal War of 1814.

The graveyard of the Church of South India outside the fort stands testimony to that part of British history covering Vellore. It holds the largest number of graves of British officers and men who had been killed in the Sepoy Mutiny on 10th July 1806. Among them is the grave of Lt. Col. John Fancourt of the 34th Regiment. In this cemetery can also be found the grave of Lushington, Governor of Madras. The oldest tomb here is that of Major Brenton, who had been killed in Wandiwash (the present Vandavasi) in the war against the French in 1760.

Recently, retired ADGP M. Balachandran reminded me of an incident that took place when I was the Superintendent of Police, North Arcot district, and he was the DSP, Gudiyatham. People of a hill tract informed us of the presence of a sloth bear in their area, which was posing a threat to the inhabitants and livestock. Both of us went on reconnaissance to pinpoint the bear's area of operation. The very next day, we came across the animal's spoor and followed it to a cave in which it had taken shelter. All our efforts to bring it out of the cave did not succeed. So, I decided to crawl into the cave, torch in one hand and rifle in the other. Balachandran was to stand guard outside with a rifle. He still remembers my instructions to him that day: 'When you hear a gunshot, if I come out of the cave, well and good, but if the bear comes out, you shoot it.'

M. Balachandra

Thankfully, I was able to kill the animal in one shot. Later, when I was DIG Armed Police, the grateful public of that area brought me a bear cub they had found abandoned in the forest. We named him Tyson. Before he was handed over to the II Battalion in Avadi, he spent most of his time in my office, sleeping at my feet. He became the mascot of the battalion and even led their parades as Subedar Tyson. Realising that it was not proper for us to keep a wild animal in captivity, however well it was being looked after, we presented him to the Guindy Children's Park, where he brought great joy to the visitors, especially children.

It was during my tenure as SP, North Arcot (1976-1977) that a new Range was formed with Krishnagiri as its capital. The old Coimbatore Range was bifurcated with the Coimbatore, The Nilgiris, and Erode districts forming the Coimbatore Range and the North Arcot, Dharmapuri, and Salem districts forming the Vellore Range. S. Palanivel, the first DIG, got the headquarters shifted from Krishnagiri to Vellore but was so magnanimous that he refused to dislodge the SP from his quarters, as some others used to do when taking charge of newly created posts. He moved into the Officers' Mess until he was transferred in 1976. There were as many as 4 DIGs over the next 4 years until the Naxalite menace came to a head, and in 1980, I was back in Vellore, this time as DIG. I was there for a record tenure of five-and-a-half years.

With Vellore practically infused in my blood, how can I not but write about the seven wonders of Vellore? Of the 7, I choose to mention only 5, as the other 2 show the men and women of Vellore in a not-too-complimentary light.

i. Fort without a King (after the takeover by the East India Company)

ii. Temple without a God (after the removal of the idol of Lord Jalakandeswarar from the Temple)

iii. River without Water (River Palar, which carries sub-soil water but is always dry on the surface)

iv. Hills with no trees (referring to the bald rocky mounds around the town)

v. Police with no powers (referring to the trainees of the Police Training College, who outnumbered the regular police force)

Brushing aside these negative aspects, Vellore is home to one of the best medical college-cum-hospitals in the country, the Christian Medical College and Hospital, best known as CMC. This institution, started by Dr. Ida Scudder in 1900, boasts several medical advancements, including the first open-heart surgery by Dr. Stanley John.

During my tenure as DIG, the idol of Lord Jalakandeswarar was brought back to the Temple from nearby Satuvachari, where it had been housed by the Department of Archaeology. The people of Vellore are ever grateful to Collector Gangappa, who, on 16th March 1981, got the idol installed in its rightful place, countering pointless opposition from the Archaeological Department. I still remember the 'Pratishtapana' (Pradishtie) of the 1,000-year-old idol. Yet another heritage monument within the fort is the Muthu-Mandapam, a memorial built around the tomb of Sri Vikramaraja Singa (1798-1815), the last ruler of Sri Lanka.

Another incident that made me an inseparable part of Vellore took place on 14th January 1991. The LTTE militants confined in the Vellore Fort rioted and held the police at bay by bolting the only gate from the inside. I was then IGP, Armed Police. I was asked by the DGP to rush to Vellore and take charge of the situation. I reached Vellore at midnight and planned the strategy to capture the Mahal from the militants. I knew the layout of the Fort well, as I used to walk the ramparts during my tenures as SP, North Arcot, and DIG, Vellore Range. I picked out a few spots on the rampart from where the main gate of the Mahal could be watched and posted armed policemen there with instructions to shoot any militants if they approached it. At dawn, we kept the rioters away from the gate by firing a few shots over their heads, and then, releasing the bolt through the grill, we quickly opened the gate and entered the Mahal, arrested all the militants, sent the injured ones to the hospital, and brought the curtain down on that incident.

It was in Vellore that Prema and I forged friendships with IPS trainees Sahi, Sawani, Deepak Samal, P.R. Thapa, N. Balachandran (Bobby Nair), and T. Radhakrishnan. Also, it was in Vellore that, for the first time, civilians came into our lives: philanthropist Mohanlal; Dr. Mohini, now in Barbados, and her sister and brother-in-law, Dr. Mrs. and Dr. C.D. Jacob; Dr. Devaprasad Jeyasekharan, his wife Dr. Renu, Dr. Sabu Jeyasekharan and his wife Beena, and the doctor couple Thomas and Molly Banu. Incidentally, Molly was from Munnar, 2 years my senior in school. And then, there was Mrs Abraham (fondly referred to by everyone as 'Katpadi Kochamma' or 'Katpadi Aunty'), who, we were pleasantly surprised to find, was the mother of Prema's college mate Kitchu Mathew Abraham. Sadly, Molly Banu, Mrs. Abraham, and Kitchu have passed on, but we are still in touch with the others.

While on the subject of ASPs under training, I recall the jollity brought about by a message one of them received from the Control Room. "By order of the DIG, a murder has been committed. The ASP is directed to proceed to the scene of the crime." This was the closest I ever got to providing, shall I say, real-life study material! Prema and I thought it hilarious.

Apart from my service in the State headquarters for 12 years in various capacities as DC L&O, Commissioner of Police, DIG, and again as IG Armed Police, ADGP, and DGP Law-and-Order, and DGP Training, and my postings in Thanjavur, Nagapattinam, Trichy, and Madurai, it is my tenure in Vellore, first as ASP under training, then as SP North Arcot District for a year followed by five-and-a-half years as DIG Vellore Range, years remembered by everyone for the total eradication of Naxalism, and finally, dealing with the LTTE militants confined in the Fort on two occasions that have made me so much a part of Vellore. This is what draws me to Tirupattur of North Arcot district (presently

Tirupattur district) on 6th August, year after year, over the past 42 years, to observe 'Martyrs Day' in memory of the Inspector and two constables who had been killed by the Naxalites on 6th August 1980. Vellore is, indeed, my home away from home.

My Practical Training in Madurai

I trained as a constable, head-constable too;
S.I. and Inspector to learn what they do;
The Revenue Department was a bit of a bore,
Still, how it worked, I was supposed to know.
The Forest Department? I loved there to be,
Those coffee estates were just my cup of tea.

After my three-month training in PTC Vellore, I was sent to Madurai for 8 months of practical training, which included working as a constable, head constable, SI, and Inspector. I was also, for a few days, attached to the Revenue Department to learn the workings of the lower revenue staff like the Village Munsif, Karnam, and others, as well as that of the tahsildar and RDO. But the part of my training I enjoyed most was training with the Forest Department when I was taken to a few reserve forests and a few coffee estates in Megamalai above Chinnamannur. The owner of one of those coffee estates, A.D. Jayam Pandian, became a close friend of our family, sharing with us his joys and sorrows till his death 2 years ago.

As destiny dictated, his older brother Jawahar Pandian, an exporter and founder of the first college in Nagapattinam, was our neighbour when I settled down in a rented house after I formed and took charge of the new Thanjavur East district, later named Nagapattinam. Again, when I was seriously injured in a car accident, it was to Jawahar Hospital in Madurai, and Jawahar's son Dr. Sarathy, stabilised me for my flight to Madras. We are still in touch with the survivors of the two families, although the first generation of Pandians is no longer alive.

My means of transport in Madurai was, just as it had been in Vellore, a bicycle. During one of my cycle trips, I visited the lesser-known dargah of Khan Sahib Md. Yousuf Khan, the East India Company's most famous Indian General. Born Maruthanayagam Pillai, he became a Muslim and joined the British Army as a soldier. He rose to the rank of General and led the Company's Indian troops to several victories over the rebel Palayakarars (or Polygars) of Madurai and Tirunelveli before leaving the British to command an army of his own. Finally, his old masters succeeded in capturing him from Madurai Fort after a long siege. Yousuf Khan was hanged at the site of the present Jhansi Park in Madurai on 14.10.1764. His name still lives on in several villages in and around Madurai—Kansapuram, Kansamettu, etc. But his final resting place in Sammattipuram remains inconsequential even to the residents of Madurai. Whenever I had time, I would visit important Temples like the Madurai Meenakshi Amman, Alagar Koil, Pazhamudir Sholai, and Thiruparakundram, both Murugan Temples of 'Aaru Padai Veedu,' and Thirumogur Perumal Temple, all of them within my cycling range.

At that time, there was a government regulation which required every IAS/IPS officer to have a car of their own within 6 months of joining the service. To buy myself a vehicle, the government gave me an advance of Rs. 4,800/-, which was to be recovered in instalments from my salary of Rs. 400/-. With that meagre amount, I could only buy an apology of a car. I would drive it around Madurai, only to abandon it whenever and wherever it broke down, and walk back to my room. I could do that without a care, as I was sure no one would want that jalopy. It was left to the Madurai traffic police to bring it back to the Madurai Cosmopolitan Club where I was staying.

After my training in Madurai, I took the old heap to Tuticorin, where I enjoyed the luxury of a vehicle attached to the sub-division. So, there she lay, neglected and in anticipation of a trip, which came when I was promoted and posted as SP of the Nilgiris. She got me as far as Coimbatore, after which she had to be towed to Mettupalayam and up the ghats to Ooty. The Nilgiri police had thoughtfully sent me a vehicle to reach Ooty. I must credit Prema with some guts. She drove the 'old thing' a few times to Coonoor, spent some time with her parents, and returned to Ooty with no problem at all. Eventually, we replaced the rickety car with an Ambassador, also second-hand but roadworthy. This car saw us through several trips to Coonoor from Tanjore and Nagapattinam. I must mention here that those were the days when there were more bullock carts on the roads than cars. This meant more lost horseshoes and consequently, more punctures en route. Since we never took a driver along with us, Prema and I took turns at the wheel, managing to replace the punctured tyre with the stepney, getting the puncture vulcanised, so we would be ready for the next puncture! Well, those were the days.

Readers of this chapter will find it hard to believe that I had not, in my entire service, met any minister or political leader, past or present, other than the three Chief Ministers—M. Karunanidhi, MGR, and Jayalalithaa. This was because Tuticorin and The Nilgiris, my first two postings, had no ministers but came directly under the Chief Minister, M. Bakthavatchalam. I had met M. K. Stalin of the DMK, D. Jayakumar and Veeramani of the AIADMK but before they became Ministers. After that, except during the spells of President's rule, I worked directly under Chief Minister M. Karunanidhi for 13 years, MGR for 10 years, and Jayalalithaa for five. During my training in Madurai, I had met Kakkan but had never talked to him. He was then Home Minister of the Madras Presidency and would come by train to Madurai once a fortnight to visit his native village, Thumbipatti, near Melur. I would accompany the SP of Madurai district, Achuthan Nair, and ASP Sripal, and sometimes DIG S. M. Diaz to the station to receive him. Kakkan would alight with a two-rupee note in his almost see-through shirt pocket. This he gave to the porter who carried his suitcase to his car. He never allowed any police officer or party member to carry his bags. Such was his simplicity, so different from the present-day practice of even senior police officers carrying the bags of ministers and junior police officers carrying those of their seniors.

I had heard that Kamaraj, too, was of the same calibre and owned nothing of his own. But to me, Kakkan's sacrifice was greater than that of Kamaraj because Kamaraj had no family to make demands on him as Kakkan did. However, Kakkan's children and grandchildren have, on their own merit, come up in life. S. Rajeswari, a granddaughter of his, is now a DIG of Police in Tamil Nadu. Another granddaughter, Meenakshi Vijayakumar, is one of the first two women to be recruited as Divisional Fire Officers. She is presently the Deputy Director of Fire and Rescue Services. Unfortunately, Kakkan's son, Kasi Viswanathan, who joined the police department as DSP, died young. His daughter is married to an IPS officer, IGP P. Harisekaran of the Karnataka cadre. Such was the calibre of freedom fighters turned politicians. My heart longs for leaders like Kamaraj, Kakkan, Karuppiah Moopanar, Periyar, C. N. Annadurai.

It was in Madurai that, by chance, I met my Christian College classmate Md. Kasim, who had become a professor at the Madras Presidency College. Less than a year after that, he was selected as DSP in the Group-1 service and rose to the level of IGP. We worked together on several occasions, including two Mahamahams in Kumbakonam in the years 1980 and 1992. More than our college and police careers, it is an incident in college that we both so clearly remember. My friends and I had got Kasim unanimously elected as Chairman of the College Union. In return, he had promised to take us to Buhari, a well-known restaurant, but kept dodging. Meanwhile, Lakshmanasamy Mudaliar, Vice Chancellor of Madras University, had accepted the position of Chief Guest at the inauguration of the college union. Kasim, as the newly elected Chairman, had to welcome the Chief Guest, but he needed a coat to 'dress up' for the occasion. It was my coat that came to his rescue. As soon as Kasim took up position on the stage, the words 'Osi Coat,' meaning 'free coat,' wafted across the auditorium in a crescendo until the entire two thousand strong audience started chanting 'Osi coat' 'Osi coat.' Later, when the Principal, Dr. Macphail, asked Kasim what the chanting was about, he explained to him that he had borrowed the coat from Walter Davaram and that his friends wanted to make sure everybody knew that. Incidentally, for me, too, it was an 'Osi coat.' It happened to be my father's. The result of all that chanting was that Kasim lost no time in taking us to Buhari for the promised treat.

Kasim wore my coat again when he went to see his bride-to-be, the pretty daughter of a rich business magnate, S. E. Varisai Md. Rowther. Even now, Kasim talks about this because he believes that my coat brought him luck. After his retirement, he has held important posts such as a member of the Academic Council of the University of Madras, a Member of the National Committee of the Finance Ministry, a Member of the Moulana Azad Education Foundation, and also a non-executive Indian Director of the board of ELNET Limited. He continues to write books on different subjects, both in English and Tamil, which have been well received by the learner. But at the end of it all, do I see any change in him? Not at all. He is the same 'Osi coat' person of our college days.

My Near-Foul Start

In the beginning, in my very first post,
I saw the blue sea with its vast sandy coast.
What stretched out before me, just filled me with awe
A beckoning ocean, t'was all that I saw
My job, like that ocean, had its calms and its storms
With challenges aplenty, in so many forms;
But then, every experience was a lesson for me
All of them readying me for my future to be.

After my eight-month practical training in Madurai, I was posted as ASP Tuticorin Sub-Division, a difficult and demanding charge because of the communal and caste-based rivalries, high crime rate, proximity to Sri Lanka with its associated problems of fishing rights, clashes at sea, illicit trade, and illegal immigration.

I reached Tuticorin on the 31st of December 1965 and took charge of the sub-division on the 1st of January 1966. Accompanied by Inspector Nambiar of the Town Police Station and a Sub-Inspector of Police, I went around the town to familiarise myself with my charge. After covering the town, the Inspector took me to Tuticorin Port. The new harbour was, at that time, under construction. At the port, I saw a passenger ferry about to leave for Colombo. The Captain invited me on board to take the trip to Colombo, spend the night on the ferry, and get back the next day. The Inspector, aware of the rules that governed visits to other countries, advised me not to go. But the vast blue sheet of water that stretched out before me into the horizon beckoned. I thought the offer was too good to miss. I made the trip, during which the Captain briefed me about the prevalence of illicit trade between the two countries and also of illegal immigration from Tamil Nadu to Ceylon through kallathonis (boats used by smugglers). I spent the night on the ferry berthed in Colombo and returned to Tuticorin the following day. The Inspector warned me that I had made an unauthorised trip on the very first day of my service and that it could result in the termination of my probation. As such, he advised me not to mention it in what was to be my very first weekly report.

I chose to be open about the trip rather than hide it and put myself into a 'what-if-they-found-out' bed of thorns. The return of my weekly report was anxiously awaited by the Inspector as well as the staff in my camp office. The SP and the Collector had made no comments on it. But DIG Madurai Range S. M. Diaz had made the following remarks:

"Very good! Prepare a detailed report on illicit trade and illegal immigration between the two countries and steps to be taken to prevent them."

The senior officers, especially those who had been recruited from the army and the Navy after the Second World War, officers like S. M. Diaz and K. R. Shenoy and I. P. officers like E. L. Stracey, were magnanimous and broad-minded, so I was spared the ordeal of having my probation extended or, worse, terminated on the very first day of my service. Diaz was later honoured by the Government of India with his appointment as Director of the Central Police Training College (CPTC), Mount Abu. It was he who had the college shifted from Mount Abu to the centrally located Hyderabad, naming it "Sardar Vallabhbhai Patel National Police Academy." It was he who invited me to Hyderabad to conduct the riding test for one of the batches of IPS probationers. Sadly, he passed away in Chennai in the year 2000. One of our best senior officers had passed into eternity.

When I took over the Tuticorin Sub-Division as Assistant Superintendent of Police, my first independent charge, I was dismayed to see the acute casteism that prevailed at every level of administration. Even before a new officer took charge of his post, his subordinates would have found out details of his caste, and through them, the general public also would have this needless information. If only such diligent application of investigative skills could have been used to solve many undetected cases! It was this factor of casteism, more dominant in the Southern districts than in the rest of the state, that led to the practice of posting officers from states other than Tamil Nadu to these districts. Such a trend was not prevalent in the Western, Central, and Northern districts where I worked subsequently, where any enquiry about the caste of the incoming Police Officer would always draw a blank from the subordinate staff as well as from members of the public. The ancestry of the officers did not concern them as long as they handled the demands of their post diligently.

My Kerala and tea estate origin, Christian first name, and Hindu-sounding surname frustrated the efforts of self-appointed investigators and led them to very wrong conclusions. Soon, they gave up their futile efforts and started taking me for what I was and for my professional worth. But, during my early days in the sub-division, I would see, to my dismay, policemen, especially those belonging to the Armed Reserve, getting together in caste-based groups during their lunch breaks as well as during their periods of rest. However, on the other hand, it must be said to their credit that at the call of duty, they set aside their caste considerations and worked together to maintain law-and-order, thereby upholding the prestige of the department.

The first major caste clash that I had to deal with took place in the village of Katcheri Dalavoipuram, close to the historic Panchalamkurichi Fort, which had, towards the end of the 18th century, defied the armed might of the British East India Company. The Poligar of the Palayam and the master of the Fort was "Veera Pandia Kattabomman," belonging to the warrior class of Kambalathu Naickars. He was ultimately hanged by the British in Kayathar, and his Fort was razed to the ground. The graves of the British officers who were killed in that siege can still be found near Ottapidaram Police Station. The most characteristic feature of this historic conflict was the Naick's ability to unite the conflicting castes into one unified army, jointly led by his own brother Oomaithurai, along with a Tamil-speaking Marava, Vellaya Thevar, and Sundaralingam, a Palla. It is, therefore, ironic that casteism was so rampant in his domain in the 19th and 20th centuries and remains so even now.

On an extremely warm afternoon, 5 months after I had taken charge of the sub-division, I was returning to my headquarters from Ettayapuram, which, interestingly, happens to be the birthplace of the patriotic poet Subramanya Bharathi. I had gone there to investigate a case of murder. When I was about 12 km out of Tuticorin, I noticed a column of heavy smoke rising skyward from the Kacheri-Dalavoipuram village. Knowing that the village had a long history of Nadar-Pallar animosity, I directed the driver to go towards the source of the smoke. On reaching the village, I found the Dalit half of the village ablaze and villagers trying to salvage whatever they could from their burning houses. I directed my driver to rush to Tuticorin, alert the Fire Service, and return to the village with as many Police personnel as possible. Those were the days before the introduction of the Police Wireless Network and the handy V.H.F. handsets; what's more, there was not a single telephone in the village.

I entered the village alone and joined the Pallas in dousing the fire with what little water was available in the almost dry well. I also learnt from them that, following an altercation, the Nadars had opened fire with country-made guns and killed 2 Dalits. They had then dragged the bodies to their side of the village after setting fire to the Dalit huts. The fire had, by then, spread to the Nadar side as well, threatening to burn down the whole village. I made my way to the Nadar side of the village to be told that it was the Dalits who had started the arson. Pointing my revolver towards the two groups, I managed to keep them apart until the Police and Fire Service arrived. The search for the bodies of the two

Dalits seemed futile until three Nadar widows admitted that they had helped their menfolk burn the bodies and that, on seeing my police vehicle approaching the village, they had hurriedly buried the half-burnt bodies in the cow-dung pit.

We dug out the bodies and sent them to Tuticorin for post-mortem. We also recovered the guns used in the killing. It took the fire service the rest of the day and all night to put out the fire. All the Nadar accused were arrested over the next few days and arraigned in the court for arson and murder. My eye-witness account of the whole sequence went a long way in getting a deterrent verdict: a life term for three accused and varying terms of imprisonment for six others. The Sessions Judge commended me for my timely intervention and for my valuable and clinching evidence.

Most of the cases of murder, arson, and rioting in the district were against a backdrop of caste. I received information about one such incident on the morning of Republic Day 1967, when I was in Tirunelveli, commanding the Republic Day Parade. Soon after the Parade, I left for Vilathikulam Village, where the murder had taken place, 95 km away, close to the border of Ramanathapuram district. When I got there, I found no evidence and absolutely no motive for the murder of a Marava youngster. However, the village's crime history, preserved in Part IV of the Police Station records, gave me a vital clue. It was in the form of another murder that had taken place in the village 22 years earlier, in 1945. The victim in that case was a Kambalathu Naiker, and the accused was a Marava. Interrogation of that murdered man's widow revealed an interesting tale of revenge. At the time of her husband's murder, she had been pregnant and, soon after, gave birth to a boy. As the posthumous son grew, she kept telling him of his father's murder. The murder accused had, meanwhile, died in prison. But that did not matter to either the mother or the son. What mattered was that the family honour had to be upheld. They decided to kill the innocent son of the murderer. This, the boy did, avenging the murder of the father he had never known. The widow was proud of her son for having avenged the murder of her husband. I shuddered to think of the next round of revenge killings when the boy, sentenced to life imprisonment, came out of prison after serving his term. Such was the code of conduct handed down from generation to generation by the erstwhile martial communities.

Even other communities of Tirunelveli district were not far behind in resorting to such brutal killings. Inter-gang rivalries and political enmity often led to such murders. The murder of Thalamuthu, an upcoming DMK leader in Tuticorin, and the tit-for-tat killing of a Communist leader the very next day; the massacre of five members of the family of a leading medical practitioner, Dr. Maragathavel, by two burglars; the ghastly end of notorious rowdies Andy Konar and Komba Konar. All these were still fresh in the minds of the citizens of Tuticorin, the murder capital of Tamil Nadu, where every caste and community had its share of rowdies and professional killers.

The General Election of 1967 changed the entire profile of Madras State. The Congress Party, which had won independence for the country and which had been in power since then, never thought it would be defeated. The Communist Party was of no consequence. As such, it was the Congress versus the DMK in that election.

As the DMK had won only 50 seats in the 1962 election, the Congress was confident of victory in 1967. The campaign in Tuticorin town was going on smoothly until, all of a sudden, it took an ugly turn. Both Congress and the DMK were involved in a door-to-door campaign on the same street, creating some tension. The Inspector and the party were confronted by a Congress leader known to everyone as 'Captain Natarajan,' who insisted that the entire road should be set aside for the Congress Party till the party's volunteers had completed their canvassing. The Police under the Inspector were helpless in stopping him as he happened to be a leader belonging to the ruling party; besides, he was armed with a revolver. On receiving a message in my camp office, which was just a short distance away, I rushed across to find a man in white Congress attire brandishing a revolver and threatening not only the public but the police as well. I went up to him and directed him to hand over the revolver. He was defiant. I gave him a powerful football kick, which not only threw him to the ground but also sent his revolver flying. That was the signal for the other police officers and men who, till then, had been holding back helplessly to act with renewed vigour. They clobbered him, tied him up, and took him to the police station. It was then that I learnt that he was no Army or Naval Captain; he had been just the Captain of the Police Armed Reserve (AR) football team before he resigned to enter politics!

Over the next few days, there was a lot of conjecture concerning my future once the election results were declared. If the Congress won, what would become of me, who had kicked their 'Captain?' But it was the DMK that won the election, and the so-called Captain remained behind bars. I continued in the sub-division for the next 3 months until I was promoted and posted as SP of the Nilgiris. How ironic that the high and mighty rule of a football Captain should end with a football kick! I was grateful to my father for having taught me the toe-kick, a handy manoeuvre in football. Incidentally, Congress never returned to power in Madras State, which was later renamed Tamil Nadu.

Baptism by Fire

T'was a cold winter morn,
And a white, frosty dawn,
When my new charge I viewed,
By its grandeur subdued.
How like Munnar my childhood home,
With hills and dales for me to roam!

When my father retired and left Munnar for good, I felt despondency. It seemed to me that a delectable slice of my childhood and growing years had faded away into the past; life in my beloved Munnar was never to be had again. But then, a cheer came in the form of my posting to Ooty as SP of the Nilgiris, a district similar to the High Ranges, the place of my birth and growing years that have been closest to my heart.

In The Nilgiris, there were tea estates, hydroelectric projects, and wildlife sanctuaries. If my High Ranges had, in the 8,842-foot Anaimudi, the highest peak South of the Himalayas, The Nilgiris had, in the 8,642-foot Doddabetta, the second highest one. While the High Ranges were home to the Mudhuvan tribe, The Nilgiris were home to the tribes of Todas, Kurumbas, and Irulas; the Badagas, too, were there. But they were not indigenous, having come in from the old Mysore state over 500 years earlier to make The Nilgiris their home. The similarities ended there, but still, there was enough in The Nilgiris to keep a hardcore Munnarian happy. While life in the High Ranges was mainly estate-oriented, life in The Nilgiris was more urbanised. There were tea estates aplenty, but the towns of Ooty, Coonoor, and Kotagiri also catered to a large non-estate population of businessmen, merchants, and traders who had, several generations earlier, set up their concerns within the gated market-places as well as outside of them. Coonoor, I saw, was also home to the renowned Pasteur Institute of India, housed in a beautiful building sporting golden domes and manufacturing anti-rabies vaccine as well as the DPT, the vaccine against diphtheria, pertussis (whooping cough), and tetanus.

The Nilgiris also included the Gudalur plateau at a lower altitude of about 3,500 feet, totally different from the rest of the district. It originally belonged to the Rajas of Nilambur and Nelliyalam and had been divided into the Cherengode, Nambalacode, and Munnabawadu Amsams. After the area and the entire Malabar region were recaptured from Tippu Sultan by the British in the year 1792, it was made a part of the Malabar district with its headquarters in Calicut. On 3.3.1877, Wyanad was bifurcated, and its eastern half, referred to as British Wyanad, was attached to The Nilgiris, providing the British with direct access to the Mysore Kingdom.

Three years later, the system of policing that had been prevalent in the Madras Presidency was extended to the Gudalur Plateau, which was then given the status of a 'circle' with an Inspector of Police who worked directly under the SP. This was how it was even when I took charge of the district. The Gudalur Circle was referred to as the main Range, and I, as SP, had to investigate grave crimes and inspect the police stations in that circle. The only other gazetted police officer in the district was the DSP, stationed in Ooty, with jurisdiction over Ooty Town, Ooty Taluk, Coonoor, and Kotagiri Circles.

When I left Munnar, most of the estate managers were Scots, but in The Nilgiris, the estates were owned and managed by Indians, most of the British managers having returned to England. Let me take you back in time to the year 1820. It was the year in which John Sullivan, the Collector of Coimbatore, brought to the world's attention the beautiful

Nilgiri Hills, which were to become the main attraction and the go-to haven for the British who made it their summer retreat and also for those who chose to stay back in India after retirement to enjoy their last days in the place they had grown to love. The Tiger Hill Cemetery in Coonoor stands solemn and tranquil, testimony to this chapter in Indian history. At that time, The Nilgiris were under administrative charge, not as Collectors but as Commissioners. The first Commissioner was James Williamson Breeks, and Ooty's Breeks Memorial School stands to this day, a fitting tribute to his contribution to these hills.

The Nilgiris was given the status of a district in the year 1882, with Richard Wellesley Barlow as its first Collector. Do go to Coonoor and take a walk down Barlow's Road, which, even today, is an important part of every 'Coonoorian's' life. On the police side, however, all of The Nilgiris, at that time, had only one DSP who reported to the SP who was based in Coimbatore. It was only in 1906 that it was given the status of a separate police district, with Bernays as the 1st SP and I the 44th.

I took charge of the district on a cold winter morning in January 1968. As the district had no official quarters, I had to rent a private house for my residence-cum-camp-office, just as my predecessors had done all those long years ago. But I was in luck. I became the first SP of the district to enjoy the luxury of official quarters: the beautiful colonial bungalow that had been the residence of the Governor's Military Secretary, a post which had been abolished. The vacant bungalow had been earmarked by my predecessor, Rajasekaran Nair. With Perumalsamy, who was in Ooty as the ADC to Governor Ujjal Singh, following up, the bungalow became the official quarters of the SP of the Nilgiris, and I, its first occupant. There it stood in the upper reaches of the Botanical Gardens in serene splendour, so beautiful with its ivy-clad façade, the haven into which, 2 months later, I led Prema, my bride.

1.3.1968 was found to be the 'good day' to move into my new quarters. My mother, sister and I were preparing to move in when I received a call from Aravankadu informing me that a crowd of workers from the

Cordite Factory had blocked the Coonoor-Ooty road. Incidentally, this factory had been opened in 1904, and the police station was just across the road from it in 1906.

DSP P.L. Viswanathan and I left for Aravankadu at once after directing one section of Armed Reserve personnel to rush there. When we reached the area, we found a crowd of workers blocking the road completely, requiring us to get off the jeep and jostle our way through the mob to reach the police station. I managed to calm the clamorous crowd just enough to be able to find out the reason for their unlawful behaviour, which had totally paralysed the movement of traffic between Coonoor and Ooty. They told me that the Sub-Inspector of Aravankadu Police Station had taken two factory workers who had been fighting on the road to the police station for further enquiry. The crowd not only refused to disperse but also questioned the right of the State Police to arrest Central Government employees, the Cordite factory being part of the Ordnance setup of the Government of India. I insisted they clear the road for traffic before I questioned the Sub-Inspector of Police to see if he had indeed acted beyond his brief. The arrival, at that juncture, of the AR section of eight constables made the crowd more aggressive; they insisted on the immediate release of their arrested colleagues that I refused to do.

As the impasse continued, I took stock of the situation. There were 15 of us: the Inspector of Coonoor Circle, the SI and three constables of the Aravankadu PS, eight men of the AR, the DSP, and I, all of us outside the small station building, which stood beside the main road. It was impossible for us to disperse the crowd by force as it had swelled to about 800, with the off-duty staff also joining the agitators.

The situation changed drastically at 4:30 pm when the siren announcing the end of the day shift sounded. Within minutes, more than 2,000 workers, already aware of the confrontation, poured out of the factory gate right across the road from the police station and joined their colleagues who were already there in front of the station, obstructing traffic on the road and shouting slogans. They then surrounded the station building and started attacking us with stones, sticks, and iron rods, injuring all of us. My peak cap was crushed by a stone hurled at me, leaving a bleeding injury on my head. Our first warning to the crowd that we would have to open fire fell on deaf ears. They seemed emboldened by the DMK government's pre-election assurance that the police would never open fire on workers and students. At that point, my attention was drawn to my jeep parked on the road in front of the station. One of the mob had opened the bonnet and was about to strike a match to set the engine on fire. Fearing an explosion and a catastrophic fire, I shot him down; he dropped dead onto the engine, and the jeep's bonnet crashed onto his body. Meanwhile, a constable opened fire on the mob trying to enter the station from behind the building. I had to fire 3 more rounds before the crowd realised that the firing was no warning and that I meant business. Panic set in, and the workers ran helter-skelter, many of them crashing through the barbed wire fence that separated the factory from the highway. As soon as I saw signs of dispersal, I held my fire.

News of the firing had, by then, reached the Madras Regimental Centre, the Defence Services Staff College, and the Military Hospital in nearby Wellington. The injured were swiftly shifted to the hospital, barely 2 km away. The prompt treatment saved the lives of many of the injured, who were mostly those who had crashed through the barbed wire fencing in a frantic effort to escape into the factory campus.

DIG K.R. Shenoy rushed to Aravankadu from his headquarters in Coimbatore, 80 km away, and conferred with the District Collector, the General Manager of the Aravankadu Cordite Factory, and the Commandant of the Madras Regimental Centre to bring about the early return of normalcy to the area. He visited the Military Hospital, reassured the injured, and offered blood from Police personnel for transfusion to the severely injured. He also arranged to have me and other injured Policemen taken to the Government Hospital in Ooty for treatment. Each of the 15 Police personnel on duty in Aravankadu that day had received injuries of varying degrees, but they dutifully held on to their posts until, with the arrival of further reinforcements from Coimbatore, normalcy was restored. By the time I had visited the injured and had my own injuries attended to by Dr Ravindran in the Ooty Government Hospital, my mother and sister had moved into my new residence.

The very next day, the Government ordered a judicial inquiry into the firing and appointed Justice Ganesan as the Inquiry Officer. When the IGP took the news of the first Police firing since the DMK came to power to Chief Minister C.N. Annadurai, he broke down. Such was his compassion for the people. At the same time, not once did he question the Police action. Such was his administrative wisdom.

Within a week, Justice S. Ganesan started his enquiry from the tahsildar's Office in Coonoor. The DIG remained in Coonoor until the Justice completed the judicial inquiry, personally attending to every aspect, from summoning experts to assist the Commission to brief the witnesses. He also resolved the misunderstanding between the police and the staff of the Cordite factory; he left the district only after the Judge had completed his inquiry. I make special mention of the DIG's total involvement because The Nilgiris was the smallest of the five districts—Coimbatore, Salem, Dharmapuri, North Arcot, and The Nilgiris—in his charge. His jurisdiction extended from the state's border with Kerala and Karnataka in the South and West to its border with Andhra Pradesh in the North. Still, he chose to remain in the place of action to uphold the morale of the District Police, especially that of the young and 'inexperienced' Superintendent of Police. Since then, I have faced several inquiries, both judicial and magisterial, but never have I received such encouragement and support from officers immediately senior to me in the hierarchy.

Justice S. Ganesan, who conducted the judicial inquiry, not only justified the Police firing, which had resulted in the death of four rioters and bullet injuries to six others, but also praised me. I quote here the relevant portions of the Inquiry Report:

i. *"I have come to the conclusion that the Superintendent of Police acted with great moderation and ordered firing only after giving the necessary prior warning, and as the Officer in charge of the Police Station (as per the Cr. P.C, the senior-most officer in the Police Station assumes the powers of the Station House Officer), his action was perfectly justified in resorting to shooting for dispersing the unlawful assembly of workers. In ordering the firing in self-defence and out of necessity, he had not exceeded the right of self-defence in any manner."*

ii. *"The SP endeavoured his level best to appease and conciliate the workers to the maximum extent possible, consistent with reason and dignity. It is extremely unfortunate that the workers, goaded by their leaders, indulged in violence, resulting in injuries to policemen and officers, and had driven the SP, out of necessity and self-defence, to order firing, resulting in the loss of four lives and injuries to a large number of workers."*

iii. *"In the present situation, the policemen, few in number, though armed, were forced to face great odds. Pitted against a menacing, boisterous crowd of more than 2,000 workers armed with stones, brickbats, mortar, and tile pieces, they did their job well. The courage and discipline displayed by them in the discharge of their onerous duty to the state and society, at great risk to their lives, calls for compliments, not censure."*

iv. *"The Superintendent of Police is a young officer of 29 years, and he deserves praise for the tact and firmness with which he tackled the delicate situation at the outset and for the courage and devotion to duty in handling the violent and unruly mob at grave personal risk."*

My 'baptism' by fire within 3 months of my first district charge was to stand me in good stead throughout my service and guide me in all my subsequent actions. I must mention here that this happened to be the first and the last police firing in the otherwise peaceful and tourist-oriented Nilgiri district, the serene, tranquil Blue Mountains.

From the Hills to the Plains

My stint in the hills was varied and more,
With VIPs, tourists and film-shoots galore.
But then, all good things must come to an end,
So off to the plains they did me send.
Tanjore was not quite where I wished to be,
But they said, kisans and landlords needed me.

The police firing at Aravankadu was, at most, an aberration because The Nilgiris happened to be the most peaceful district in Tamil Nadu. It wasn't that there were no law-and-order situations in the one year and 8 months that I spent there. There were a few, like the Badaga-non-Badaga confrontation that followed a clash between the students of the Government Arts College, who vandalised a cinema theatre in Ooty, and the residents of the Ooty market, most of them from the districts on the plains, who went in support of the staff of the theatre, resulting in injury to a few students, some of whom happened to be Badagas. This led to the Badagas from the villages lying within a radius of about 15 to 20 kilometres around Ooty, marching into town seeking revenge. The situation appeared grim, especially because communal or sectarian violence was unheard of in the district. Eventually, the large Badaga congregation that had blocked the main Bazaar Road dispersed peacefully when I assured them of appropriate action against those who had assaulted the students.

Another situation that threatened to become serious and create an inter-state confrontation was an incident at the check-post in Choladi on the Tamil Nadu-Kerala border. The staff manning the Tamil Nadu check-post had had an altercation with a few cyclists smuggling ration rice from the Gudalur Taluk of Tamil Nadu into Kerala. An exaggerated version of the incident by the cyclists, upon reaching the first major village in Kerala, resulted in a protest march to the check-post by a large number of Malayalees. I managed to reach the check-post, 95 kilometres away from my headquarters in Ooty, just in time to confront the marchers on the other side of the bridge that marked the boundary between the two States. By then, the policemen who were at the check-post to provide protection to the check-post staff had positioned themselves, their rifles aimed at the protesters, warning them that anybody crossing the state border would be shot down. With more people joining the protesters and swelling their numbers, the smallest incident or even the use of an abusive term might have snowballed into a serious border incident, causing acute embarrassment to both State governments.

The protesters demanded the immediate removal of the check-post that was marring the relationship between the people living on either side of the border. They raised slogans against the check-post staff and against the Tamil Nadu Police and refused to listen to me. Suddenly, it dawned on some of them that I was addressing them in Malayalam! The leaders then told the protesters that I was one of them and that they should listen to me. After that, it was all bonhomie, and I was taken to the hospital in Kerala, where the three cyclists had been admitted for injuries alleged to have been sustained at the check-post. I also visited the local police station there before returning to Gudalur and then back to Ooty.

Here, I must explain why the Superintendent of Police had to rush to a checkpoint 95 kilometres away to deal with a situation that normally would have been attended to by the sub-divisional officer concerned. The Nilgiri District at that time had only one Deputy Superintendent of Police. He was stationed at Ooty and had jurisdiction over the higher hill areas of Ooty, Coonoor, and Kotagiri, each of which was looked after by an Inspector of Police. The Deputy Superintendent of Police had no jurisdiction over Gudalur Taluk, which lay at a much lower altitude of about 3,500 feet and which had been a part of the Malabar district until the year 1877 when it was annexed to The Nilgiri District.

Gudalur Taluk, also known as British Wyanad, had only five Police Stations. They came under an Inspector of Police with his headquarters in Gudalur Town. In an administrative arrangement peculiar to the district, the Superintendent of Police had direct control over Gudalur Circle, which was referred to as the SP's Main Range. As such, it was the SP's duty to conduct the annual Police Station inspections and also to take up the investigation of grave crimes, just as it was the duty of the Deputy Superintendents of Police elsewhere in the state. Thankfully, the direct intervention of the SP was rarely needed in this Taluk, as it was made up largely of tea plantations, reserve forests, and the Mudumalai Wildlife Sanctuary.

It was only in the seventies, when Government-run tea estates were opened up for the large-scale settlement of Tamil repatriates from Sri Lanka, that new Police Stations, Circles, and Sub-divisions were created. The Taluk now has two Sub-divisions, Gudalur and Devala, whereas earlier, there had been none.

Film shooting was a regular feature in Ooty, but in no way did it disturb the routine of the local population as it does on the plains. My meeting with a popular and well-known film star took place on the very day I took charge of the district. I reached Ooty on 3rd January 1968 from Tuticorin, where I spent 2 years as Assistant Superintendent of Police. After taking charge of the Nilgiri district, I retired to the official guest house for government officers, the 'Gate House,' which was named after its location at the entrance to the Government Botanical Gardens. I was to stay there until I could rent suitable accommodation for myself.

Around midnight, I was woken by the watchman, who told me that a Hindi actor, Raj Kapoor, wanted to see me urgently. I found the actor outside, shivering in the cold, with the mercury having dropped to zero that night. He had travelled to Ooty with the crew of R.K. Productions to shoot a few scenes for his movie 'Mera Naam Joker' at Lovedale's Lawrence School and Railway Station. Some students of the Government Arts College, with the anti-Hindi agitation still fresh on their minds, had prevented the shooting at the Lovedale station, saying they would allow neither Hindi films to be shot nor screened in Madras State. I assured him of Police protection when they resumed shooting the following day.

When we reached Lovedale railway station the next morning, the film crew and the artistes were there on the platform with their paraphernalia. The students were also, certainly, not the serious ones who must have been in their classes. I gave them a stern warning not to interfere with the shooting and drew a line over which they were not to cross. The shooting commenced with the students raising derisive slogans. But soon, sensing our strength and determination, they melted away. The shooting went on peacefully over the next 3 days. Before leaving Ooty, the actor-producer called me on the phone to thank me for the police protection. So, it was with shock and a sense of betrayal that I read his statement to the press back in Bombay, saying that in Madras State, and especially in Ooty, his crew had been prevented from shooting the scenes. There was no mention of the help given by the police; neither was there any explanation for the appearance of the lengthy scene in the movie featuring the Lovedale railway platform, showing the boys, including the hero, boarding the train on their way home at the end of the school term. But then, one does not expect gratitude from people of his ilk. We, on our part, were happy with a job well done and with the students having been made to understand their limits.

The second film shoot during my tenure in Ooty was more memorable because it was then that I met two future Chief Ministers of Tamil Nadu. Unlike other film shoots in Ooty, the ones featuring MGR drew large crowds of enthusiastic fans, requiring regulation. This time, adding to their excitement, was the presence of the sensation of the time, J. Jayalalithaa. She was to be the heroine of the movie. MGR's position as "Chairman, state Small Savings," equated to that of a Cabinet Minister, was eligible for a courtesy call by the Collector and the Superintendent of Police. When Deputy Superintendent of Police P.L. Viswanathan and I 'called on' him at the Mysore Palace Guest House, he overwhelmed us with his charm and courtesy. There was no question of us leaving without breakfast with him, his fellow actors, the film shoot crew, and every single policeman drafted for bandobust at the shoot. It was then that I understood the eagerness of policemen to be part of the bandobust for MGR and not for that of any others.

I was new to the department and not known to him. That did not prevent him from receiving me cordially and introducing me to his co-star J. Jayalalithaa, who was the embodiment of courtesy, grace, and politeness, indicating her superior upbringing and convent-school background. That day, in 1968, little did I think that I would be serving both of them, MGR for ten long years and J. Jayalalithaa for 5. MGR made me Commissioner of Police of Chennai City. I held that post for 3 years until the AIADMK government was dismissed following the power struggle in the party between the factions of Jayalalithaa and Janaki after MGR's death on 24.12.1987. Jayalalithaa made me the ADGP (L&O) and later, the DGP when she became the Chief Minister.

My third meeting with a film celebrity also took place at a film shoot. The celebrity was Shivaji Ganesan, and the film shoot was going on in the Botanical Gardens. My camp office, a part of the SP's residence, was in the upper reaches of the same garden.

I was in my camp office when I received a call from Police Sergeant (the present-day Sub-Inspector of the Armed Police) Padmanabhan. He had been regulating the students of the Government Arts College who had come to the Botanical Gardens to watch the film shoot. While trying to keep them at a respectable distance from the scene of action, his baton had inadvertently touched one of the students. In protest, the students gheraoed the film crew and actors, forcing them to stop the shoot.

I rushed down from my camp office to where the shoot was taking place. Once I had taken stock of the situation, I told the students to stay a reasonable distance away to enable the crew to carry on with their shoot. But they demanded the suspension of the Sergeant, who they said had caned one of them. I had no time to waste on reasoning with them as time was running out for the crew to complete their day's shoot. I lined up the men, brought them to the 'Ready' with their lathis, and delivered my ultimatum to the students that if they did not disperse before I counted 10, they would be lathi-charged. Their confidence that the police would not attack the 'privileged' students started evaporating when I began counting. By the time I reached 8, they realised that I meant business and took to their heels. I then walked up to Shivaji Ganesan, told him to go ahead with the shoot, and returned to my camp office.

It was 3 years later when I was SP of Thanjavur district, that I met Shivaji Ganesan again. He had come down to Thanjavur Town to act in a play, "Vietnam Veedu," and I was introduced to him by D. Narayanaswamy, one of the Commandants of the Malabar Special Police, who had been selected for the post of DSP and posted to Thanjavur Town. Shivaji Ganesan then told him that I needed no introduction and that he had already introduced me in his film "Thanga Padakkam." He added that he had modelled his role in the movie as a Police Officer on what he had observed of me in Ooty. He also invited me to watch the movie, which I did soon after, in Kumbakonam. Possessing a brilliant conceptual mind, remarkable memory, and an extraordinary ability to imitate anybody, the great thespian had modelled his walk, manner of speaking, demeanour, and even his visage, marked by a prominent moustache, after me—all that after watching me for less than 10 minutes in Ooty!

My penchant for seeking out and unearthing secret arrack distillation points in the Sholas once led me into trouble. As I was getting ready to go into the jungle with the team, I got news of Chief Minister C.N. Annadurai's unexpected death, an event that I knew would cause widespread disturbance all over the state. But The Nilgiris was different, with its population of only Todas and other Tribals, Badagas, Kannadigas, Tamils, and Malayalees. As such, I did not expect any trouble and went on the raid. On my return to headquarters that night, a radio message from DIG K.R. Shenoy awaited me, admonishing me for not having remained in the district headquarters on such a day. I acknowledged my mistake and apologised. The DIG, in his magnanimity, closed the matter.

Only the next day, after reading in the papers of the mass hysteria that Annadurai's death had caused all over the state, did I realise how wrong I was not to have remained at my headquarters that day. I read with consternation of the unprecedented rush of mourners from the districts to Chennai, of the death of a large number of people in overcrowded trains and even atop them, of mourners crowding onto a false ceiling of Rajaji Hall to get a better view of their leader's body placed on a catafalque just below, causing the structure to collapse and injuring many of them; of the need to relocate the body onto the steps leading up to the hall; of the police having had to use lathis, fire tear-gas shells, and even open fire to control the mob.

Had even a fraction of the turmoil that rocked the state hit The Nilgiris, I would have lost my job, and deservedly so. Never again in my service did I take lightly any incident involving the death of a popular leader. That day, I learnt the lesson, 'Better be prepared for a holocaust than expect an eventless day.'

I consider myself fortunate to have been posted to the Hill district. The Nilgiris was not too different from the High Ranges of Kerala, where I was born and brought up, where my father worked for the British-owned Kannan Devan Tea Estates Limited. Naturally, I was very much at home in my new surroundings. Visits to the tribal hamlets hidden deep in the forests and prohibition raids covering forbidding hill slopes and impenetrable jungles kept me physically fit and active. It seemed so easy to combine work with pleasure. Beyond working hours, there was time enough to indulge in my passion for trekking, exploring, riding, and hunting.

At that time, the licensing system for selective hunting was in practice. With a licence issued by "The Nilgiri Wildlife Association," one could, in one season, shoot one bison, one sambhar, ten spotted deer, and any number of wild boar. However, there were rules to be strictly followed—no shooting from vehicles or with the help of headlights or torches, and no shooting of females or young ones of any species; only old males, past the age of reproduction, could be killed. Additionally, the minimum horn measurement of the animals had to be strictly observed—no less than 24" for a spotted deer, 32" for a sambhar, and 36" for a bison. Animals that satisfied these requirements were naturally old males. I had followed all the rules very strictly but later gave up hunting animals. Due to the widespread misuse of licences and poaching, the concessions were withdrawn, and a total ban on shooting wild animals and exotic birds was imposed by the government. Looking back, I regret participating in the 'Royal Sport' brought to the hills by the British. I wish I had trained my rifle only on targets at the shooting range instead of on wildlife.

I must also mention a village in The Nilgiri district, Thengumarada, situated 130 km away from the Solur Mattam Police Station to which it was attached. This is probably the only village in the world so distant and remote from its police station. The road journey from the station at Solur Mattam to the village requires four changes of bus, at Kotagiri, Mettupalayam, Sathyamangalam, and Bhavani Sagar; in an emergency, however, the villagers could reach the station in 3 hours, walking up the jungle path!

The rivers Bhavani and Moyar, which drain The Nilgiri Hills, almost encircle the district before converging at the Bhavani Sagar Dam. Situated on the right bank of the River Moyar, 1500 metres below Solur

Mattam, this village can be considered a geographical accident and an ethnic necessity.

In the year 1946, a band of enterprising Badagas from Kil Kotagiri, where the Solur Mattam police station is located, expressed their desire to reclaim the narrow strip of forest land between the Eastern slopes of the Hills and the River Moyar for paddy cultivation. Collector H.H. Carlstone and Sub-Collector J.P.L. Gwynn took the initiative and paved the way for the formation of the 'Thengumarhada Co-operative Farmers Society Limited.' The society came into being on 5.8.1948, with the Collector as the President. 5 hundred acres of land were cleared and given to the society, which in turn distributed it to its 141 members.

These founder members and their families were the initial settlers of this village, which, along with the tribal hamlets of Kallampalayam and Hallimoyar, today forms a part of Kotagiri Taluk. The villagers, led by the founder of the Society, Kalla Maistry, did not wait for the district administration to provide their basic needs. They built a school, a dispensary, and a godown and laid a road through the elephant-infested forest to Bhavani Sagar, 32 km away. Today, the school, with classes up to standard 8, and the dispensary have been taken over by the respective government departments. The cost of maintaining the road is being shared by the Forest Department.

My first visit to the village was on 3.2.1968 when I trekked down from Kodanadu viewpoint, almost 6000 feet above MSL. Time stood still in this picturesque village, with the lofty Nilgiri Mountains on one side and the swift-flowing Moyar River on the other. It is still cut off from the rest of the world by the river, which can be crossed only on coracles (parisals).

My next visit to the village was on 1.9.1993 while pursuing the Veerappan gang. In my first visiting notes, I had expressed the hope of seeing a bridge across the River Moyar and also the revival of the Moyar Valley road that connects Bhavani Sagar on the northern end of the Valley to Masanagudi on the South eastern end. Fifty-two years had passed since my first visit and 28 years since my second, but nothing had changed. There is still no bridge, and people continue to cross the river on coracles. Attempts to attach the village to the neighbouring Erode district have also failed because the residents, all Badagas, prefer to be part of the district of their nativity.

During my tenure as Superintendent of Police, Nilgiris, I married Prema, who belonged to a well-respected family of third-generation settlers in Coonoor, thus extending my hill heritage further from the High Ranges in Kerala to The Nilgiris in Tamil Nadu. The difference between life in the High Ranges and that in The Nilgiris was striking. They moved in the same circles as the British planters, something that did not happen in Munnar. Throughout most of his tennis career at Upasi Sports, my father-in-law played alongside British planters.

My father-in-law on the left

Prema and my mother-in-law at Upasi

The wedding took place in Coonoor at the All Saints' Church, beautiful with its stained-glass windows and red-cushioned pews. Built in 1854, it stood in serene splendour, surrounded by weeping willows. Arrangements for our wedding reception in Ooty 2 days later were supervised by DIG K.R. Shenai. It was attended by Governor Ujjal Singh and all the prominent citizens of The Nilgiris. We also welcomed into our lives our daughter Anita, who was born in Coonoor a year later.

The Governor Ujjal Singh at our wedding reception

A few days after our wedding, we were going through my photo album when Prema exclaimed, "I know her!" She was looking at my batchmate R.K. Raghavan's wedding photo. She explained that Raghavan's wife Shanthi, a student of Queen Mary's College, used to attend a weekly inter-collegiate class at Madras Christian College, where Prema was a student. Over lunch, Shanthi would leave her own classmates to join Prema and her friend Helen, who later became an officer of the Indian

Foreign Service. I must also mention that the very first 'police wife' Prema met was Sowdha, wife of Perumalsamy, who, at the time of our wedding, was in Ooty as Aide-de-Camp to the Governor. They met a few days after the wedding and have been friends ever since.

With Sowdha and Perumalsamy

Prema and Shanthi Raghavan

Apart from incidents like the ones mentioned earlier in the chapter, the job of the Superintendent of Police of The Nilgiris was light and enjoyable, except, of course, during the summer and autumn months when Ooty, rightly called the 'Queen of Hill Stations,' drew a large number of tourists and VIPs from all over India.

Sadly, my time in the mountain paradise was running out. Inspector General of Police, Tamil Nadu, R.M. Mahadevan, I.P., who had come to Ooty in May 1969 for the customary South Zone IG's meeting, told me that in September that year, I would be taking charge of Thanjavur District from the Superintendent of Police, S. Subarayan, who would take over the post of Superintendent, Special Branch, Madras, which would be falling vacant on the retirement of the incumbent.

The IGP must, of course, have first discussed the cycle of transfers with the CM, Karunanidhi, who was from Thanjavur district, the district I was being posted to. Thanjavur was, at that time, a district plagued by never-ending kisan unrest and a highly politicised atmosphere, and I had been chosen to be the SP of that district, the largest and most populous one in the state. I was, naturally, elated, but I must admit, The Nilgiris did tug at my heartstrings.

Those days, nobody ever thought of questioning or changing any orders once they were issued or even while they were being contemplated. Neither did officers cultivate friendships with the political leaders of the districts in which they were posted. The SP's reach stopped with his DIG and that of the DIG with the IGP. Needless to say, the system worked well, with the head of the department assuming full administrative responsibility. That meant responsibility rested on the senior-most officer at every level, be it Range, District, sub-division, Circle or Police Station, each one discharging his decentralised responsibility sincerely.

I close this chapter with my eternal gratitude to K.R. Shenoy for his personal interest in my life and career. His reassuring presence throughout the judicial inquiry into the Aravankadu firing, his supervision of my wedding reception in Ooty, his presence in Kumbakonam as IGP Tamil Nadu throughout the Mahamaham in the year 1980, and finally, his concern for my safety during the River Adyar flood operation in the year 1987 will always be in my mind.

K.R. Shenoy

Green Fields of Thanjavur

The rice fields of Tanjore so lush and green
Stretched out before me like I'd never seen;
Munnar's greens told a different tale,
Up and down, they went, o'er hill and dale
Here, flat acres of rice fields were all I could see;
Wherever I looked, green fields greeted me.

The undivided Thanjavur district was the most populous district in Tamil Nadu, extending from the river Kollidam (Coleroon) in the North to Kodikarai (Point Calimere) in the South, a stretch of nearly 240 km. The district, with more than 1,650,000 acres under paddy cultivation, has rightly been called the "Granary of the South." To someone like me who had never seen a paddy field, let alone acres of it, being posted to Thanjavur district with its ever-increasing socio-economic problems, especially after the Kilvenmani tragedy, was a big challenge. Moving from the smallest district in the state, with only 23 police stations to the largest one with 81 police stations, was daunting. Even more daunting was the fact that the posting made me directly answerable to the Chief Minister M. Karunanidhi, who came from that district.

The social pattern in the district was determined to a large extent by the nature of the ties that bound the various communities to the soil. In the Western parts of the district, where holdings were small, the landowners themselves attended to the cultivation, thereby establishing direct and inalienable rights over the soil. In East Thanjavur, however, extensive holdings running into thousands of acres in some cases led to absentee landlordism and the existence of a large working class, drawn mostly from the landless Dalits. The landlords and their agents took full advantage of the helplessness and lack of awareness of the agricultural labourers and treated them no better than slaves. In fact, their living conditions were not unlike those of the cotton plantation slaves of America before the Civil War. They lived in perpetual poverty and abject misery, huddled in insanitary hovels, and were paid just enough to sustain themselves. Any sign of disobedience or recalcitrance was put down ruthlessly.

It was at this juncture that the nascent Communist Party of India, which could not make much headway among the industrial proletariat, succeeded in formulating a method of interpreting and adapting Marxist doctrines in light of the conditions obtaining in rural areas. This shift in their strategy was accomplished by drawing the peasantry and the landless agricultural labourers into a struggle for basic rights like better living conditions and higher wages.

Nothing could have been more propitious for the success of their endeavour than the dismal conditions in which the agricultural labourers of East Thanjavur found themselves. The task of spreading Communism in East Thanjavur had been entrusted to veteran leader Manali C. Kandaswamy. He was ably assisted by a band of dedicated repatriates from Malaya who had been initiated into Marxism by Ducroux, a Frenchman. By the late forties, the entire kisan population had flocked to the Red-banner. The fight for their emancipation had begun.

Although the Communist Party of India had put forth a series of demands like land-ceiling, transfer of land-ownership to the tillers, and better living and working conditions for the kisans, the basic and immediate demand was for higher and uniform wages. The Communist agitation reached its peak between the years 1948 and 1952. This period was marked by several cases of organised attacks on the landlords, trespass into their lands, and the forcible harvesting of their crops.

Several Communist leaders went underground to direct the terrorist movement; six of them were killed in encounters with the Police. After the agitation had run its course, the Communists had nothing much to show on their credit side, apart from the achievement of a minor increase in wages and partial recognition of tenancy rights. On the other hand, the kisans, who for the first time had become a unified force, proved themselves formidable. Several of their party candidates were successful in the assembly elections, even though they were in jail or underground during the entire period of election campaigning as well as on the day of the elections.

All was quiet on the kisan front in the 16 years that followed. During that period, several ad hoc agreements regarding wages were made at the village, Taluk, and district levels between the representatives of the kisans and the landlords, keeping in mind the rising cost of living. However, no effort was made to evolve a uniform system of wages for the district as a whole. The balance of mutual indispensability ensured peaceful co-existence, however unreal and ephemeral it might have been.

Meanwhile, the Communist Party itself underwent a major change, and the great schism that split the party into two set both groups in a frantic race to consolidate their position among the kisans. The kisans' allegiance was largely determined by the local leadership; as a result, the division of spoils found Mayavaram, Sirkazhi, Mannargudi, and Thiruthuraipoondi taluks going to the Communist Party of India (CPI) and Nagapattinam, Nannilam, and Thiruvarur to the Marxist Communist Party (CPM).

The split had an important bearing on kisan activities. Both groups, CPI and CPM, in their bid to prove their sincerity to the kisans' cause, launched large-scale agitations for further wage increases. Their usual method of agitation, refusing to work in the fields until higher wages were promised, was countered by the landlords employing outside labour. To facilitate this move, the landlords formed the Paddy Producers Association, which, besides representing the landlords in arbitrations and conciliatory meetings, served as an agency to muster and transport outside labour.

But in this manoeuvre and counter, the kisans stole a march over the landlords, as the so-called 'outside labourers' from neighbouring taluks and villages were also members of the Communist Party and would not betray the greater cause of the kisans. The landlords then resorted to large-scale import of non-communist and non-Harijan labourers from neighbouring districts. This step gave a definite communal colour to the hitherto purely kisan-landlord dispute.

It was against this background of mutual mistrust and hostility that the Keelvenmani tragedy came to pass. While the Communist Party of India showed a willingness to resolve the dispute at the conciliatory table, the Marxist Communist Party tried to force the issue by resorting to direct action. By doing so, they turned the clock back by 16 years, and the violence of 1948-1952 was repeated, only on a much larger scale. Police parties sent to prevent lawlessness were attacked. One such incident on 5th October 1967 in Poonthalankudi Village led to police firing in which one kisan lost his life. On 29th October 1968, in Puducheri Village, a police party was attacked with spears and knives, resulting in serious injuries to three policemen.

Tension mounted with the commencement in November 1968 of the harvest of the short-term Kuruvai crop. Meanwhile, the tripartite conference convened by the Collector at a meeting in Mannargudi had stipulated the payment of one-and-a-half litres of paddy in addition to the prevailing wages of 6 litres of paddy for every 54 litres harvested.

Keelvenmani Village, 10 miles away from Nagapattinam, had always been a Communist stronghold. In 1948, a police party had to resort to firing to save itself from a violent kisan mob. But by 1968, the Paddy Producers Association had consolidated its position in the village, with P. Gopalakrishna Naidu, a landlord of the neighbouring village of Irinjur, as its President.

On 24th December 1968, the Marxist kisans refused to harvest the crops of three landlords in Killukudi Village, 3 miles away from

Keelvenmani, because they had been offered only four and a half litres of paddy as wages. The landlords approached Gopalakrishna Naidu to get outside labour. Gopalakrishna Naidu directed Pakkiriswamy Pillai, a member of the Paddy Producers Association, to take 25 workers from Irinjur and complete the harvest in the fields boycotted by the local labourers. The harvest was completed on 25th December.

Meanwhile, the Harijan kisans who had thus been deprived of their livelihood met in Thevur Village under Gopal, a prominent Marxist leader, to decide upon their course of action against the Caste Hindu labourers who had jeopardised their cause by working for lower wages. In keeping with the decision taken at this meeting, they, armed with sticks, sickles, and spears, attacked the workers who were on their way home after the day's harvest. Pakkiriswami Pillai, who tripped and fell, was carried away to Harijan Street in Kilvenmani village by Gopal and three others. The others scattered in different directions, leaving behind six injured men who then made their way to nearby hospitals.

It was another hour before a few of the loyal workers reached Irinjur Village to inform Gopalakrishnan Naidu about the assault and the kidnapping of Pakkiriswamy Pillai. Gopalakrishnan Naidu, instead of reporting the incident to Keevalur Police Station, which was just seven kilometres away, decided to take the law into his own hands. He hurriedly gathered a retaliatory party to raid Kilvenmani Village and rescue Pakkiriswami Pillai.

The raiders, numbering about 50, descended on Kilvenmani at 10:30 pm with shotguns, machetes, and burning torches. Upon coming across the Harijans, Gopalakrishna Naidu, his nephew Balakrishna Naidu, and another landlord, Govindaraju Naidu, opened fire, injuring several of the villagers. The Harijans, who had not bargained for a confrontation with firearms, fled the village. A few old men, women, and children who could not keep up with the fleeing villagers hid themselves in the hut farthest out on the street, hoping to escape the notice of the raiders. The Harijans, while running out of the village, locked the hut from the outside, hoping the attackers would think it was unoccupied.

Meanwhile, the raiders, who were already in a highly agitated state of mind, came upon the mutilated body of Pakkiriswami Pillai on Harijan Street. Seized by savage fury, they set fire to all the thatched huts of the Harijans. Having exacted their revenge, they left the doomed village in a blaze of burning huts.

What met the eyes of the police when they arrived on the scene by midnight was a totally deserted village. Twenty-five huts had been burnt down completely, and Pakkiriswami Pillai's corpse had been left leaning against a coconut palm as if surveying the carnage through his lifeless eyes. The Inspector, who had gone to the village with vague information about a clash, had no way of knowing anything about what had happened in the past few hours. He posted pickets in the village, sent express reports to all concerned, and commenced the inquest over the body of Pakkiriswami Pillai. When dawn broke on the 26th, he saw one of the huts still smouldering and ordered a closer examination.

Those who beheld the horror that revealed itself were not likely to forget it in their lifetime. One by one, the charred remains of 42 people were brought out. All the bodies were found in one of the two mud-walled rooms measuring 9' x 7.' It had to be seen to be believed that so many people could have taken shelter in so small a room. Altogether, 2 old men, 18 women, and 22 children had perished in the inferno.

Slowly, the Harijans returned to their village to nurse their injuries and mourn their dead. Fourteen of them had received gunshot injuries, and nine others, injuries caused by sickles and sticks. One of them had lost his entire family, 11 in all, to the arson.

The state CID investigated both cases. Hundreds of witnesses were examined, and on 26th March 1969, charge sheets were laid against Gopal and 21 other Harijans for kidnapping, assault, and murder and against

Gopalakrishna Naidu and 22 others for arson, attempted murder, and murder. The trial itself roused unprecedented interest among the public. Altogether, one hundred and 31 witnesses were examined, and on 30th November 1970, C.M. Kuppannan, Sessions court Judge, pronounced judgement on both cases in a court hall packed to the gills.

The Marxist leader Gopal was sentenced to life imprisonment and his associate to 5 years' R.I. for the murder of Pakkiriswami Pillai. Three others were sentenced to 2 years' rigorous imprisonment each and three to one year's rigorous imprisonment. The remaining 14 were acquitted in the arson case, as the intention to commit the murder of the 42 people was held to have been 'not proved.' Gopalakrishna Naidu and eight others were sentenced to 10 years of rigorous imprisonment for unlawful assembly, attempted murder, and arson.

The most significant outcome of the tragedy was the Government's appointment of a Commission of Inquiry to investigate the cause of the agrarian unrest in East Thanjavur. The "Tamil Nadu Agricultural Labourer Fair Wages Ordinance, 1969" was promulgated based on the Ganapathia Pillai Commission's recommendations. It stipulated, among other things, uniform wages for the entire district at the rate of Rs. 3/- per day for men and Rs. 2/- for women for work related to cultivation and 6 litres of paddy for every 54 litres harvested. These rates, incidentally, were what the kisans had all along been fighting for.

I took charge of the district during the transition period between the announcement of the minimum wages by the Commission and its actual implementation. The landlords continued to pay the old wages, and that, in-kind (paddy), not cash. They also continued to employ the more pliable and obedient workers from the neighbouring districts. From the day I took charge, I was fully engaged in providing protection to the migrant labourers and in ensuring a peaceful Kuruvai harvest. I hardly returned to headquarters and was continuously on the move, keeping a watchful eye on the several 'trouble spots' in the vast district.

I still remember the newly posted Deputy Superintendents of Police, Saravana Perumal, M. Balachandran, and K. Subbiah, following me from village to village to report that they had joined duty in their respective Sub-divisions. They entered into the fray straightaway, staying in the villages at night and supervising field operations during the day. In my continuous absence from the District Police Office, the Additional Superintendent of Police, Srinivasa Ramanan, in a post that had been created especially for the heavy charges of Thanjavur, North Arcot, Coimbatore, and Ramnad districts, took care of routine administration.

The land-grab agitation by the Communist Party of India in the year 1970 gave further impetus to the Land Reforms Movement. It was aimed at recovering vast tracts of Temple land that were being enjoyed by just a few landlords like Thiyagaraja Mudaliyar of Vadapathimangalam, Sambasiva Iyer of Kunniyur, Srinivasa Iyengar of Perugavazhndan, Krishnasamy Vandaiyar of Poondi, and Appavu Thevar of Ukkadai.

The agitation was of an unprecedented scale. In the space of 3 days, more than 20 thousand agitators, including 3 MLAs, were arrested and remanded to custody. The entire operation, right from picking up the agitators from points of forcible entry into the landlords' fields until they were lodged in the Central Prison at Trichy after arduous road journeys through the troubled countryside, went off without a single incident. The Chief Minister Karunanidhi complimented the District Police on its achievement. The panic-stricken landlords heaved a sigh of relief and cooperated with the Government in surrendering benami lands. The CPI leadership also earned universal praise for conducting such a massive agitation without a single instance of violence. The highly motivated, welfare-oriented, and people-friendly District Collector T.V. Antony, I.A.S., sped up the process of redistributing the surrendered lands. He had been brought to Thanjavur district specifically to solve the kisan problem that had plagued the district for decades.

The Marxist-led kisans, however, were not as peaceful in their agitations and protests. Force had to be used on several occasions to protect the landlords as well as the migrant labourers. The young DSPs and I had to lead police parties personally to clear roadblocks and to liberate the gheraoed landlords, revenue officials, and even medical staff. Luckily, the police were spared the need to open fire.

After the successful conduct of three Kuruvai and an equal number of Samba cultivations and harvests, I was asked to give effect to the pending proposal of creating a separate Police district in East Thanjavur to deal more effectively with the kisan problem and to reduce the workload of the Superintendent of Police of Thanjavur district. This plan had been mooted after the Kilvenmani tragedy. As per the proposal, the district administration was to remain undivided under a single Collector. The Police district was to be bifurcated with Nagapattinam as the headquarters of the Superintendent of Police, Thanjavur East district, covering the Marxist-dominated areas of Sirkazhi, Mayavaram, Nannilam, Tiruvarur, Tiruthuraipoondi, Vedaranyam, and Nagapattinam. As was the healthy practice at that time, the first Superintendent of Police of the new district had already been named before the actual partitioning work had begun. He was my second in command, the Additional Superintendent of Police Srinivasa Ramanan. This made my job easy. I told him to attend to the bifurcation work, including that of the Armed Reserve, Headquarters Units, District Police Office staff, vehicles, wireless sets, arms, and ammunition. He completed the work well before 1st November 1971, the date set for the creation of the new Police district, and prepared to move to his new headquarters in Nagapattinam along with the staff, movable properties, and the vehicles that he had allotted to the new district.

But the day before the new district was to be inaugurated, the Chief Minister told the Inspector General of Police that he wanted me to take charge of the district because of my familiarity with the area and the people, and also because of my experience in dealing with the kisan problem. Accordingly, I moved out to Nagapattinam and set up the District Police Office and other Units in dilapidated rented buildings which, 4 years later, were either damaged or washed away in a cyclone, making way for the construction of a new set of buildings including quarters for the Superintendent of Police and the men of the Armed Reserve. It was only later that this Police District was upgraded to a Revenue District with its own Collector.

Prema and I moved into the building rented out for my residence. It had been built in the twenties in 40 days by a Muslim dignitary to host the visiting Governor of Madras. It faced the sea and had just two halls, one on the ground floor and the other upstairs. We had the halls partitioned with hard-board panels to give us two bedrooms upstairs with one common bathroom outside in a corner of the verandah, which ran around three sides of the hall; the large hall downstairs was partitioned to give us a drawing room and dining room. A small room on the side served as my camp office. Behind the main block was an open quadrangle and a small kitchen.

The large, low-set windows of our bedroom were like picture windows. The joy of being able to effortlessly watch the beautiful sun and moon rises through them more than made up for the inconvenience of not having a proper bungalow. These windows also gave us an unbroken view of the beach with the Nagapattinam-Nagore stretch of the railway line running across it and the seemingly endless Bay of Bengal beyond. Anita, our two-year-old daughter, loved to watch the trains from these windows, especially the last one of the day as it chugged across with all its lights aglow. On her first evening there, as she watched the train go past, she remarked in Tamil, much to our amusement, "Onga train, light ellam potittu styla poguday" (Your train is going along stylishly with all its lights on). Incidentally, thanks to a Hindi-speaking neighbour in Coonoor, she often used the three-language formula – "I, joola, mela going" (I am on the swing). The passenger trains on this route went with such precision that the locals lived by them, and so did we. If, by chance, the early morning train was late, so were the milkman and the maid!

Even my return home from my office was scheduled by the train as there was a level crossing between.

It was in Nagapattinam that Anita, whose world had been only the hills and valleys of The Nilgiris, had her first thrilling and delightful experience of the vast ocean and endless stretches of the sands on which she played, toy bucket and spade in hand. We did, however, have to watch out for the prickly tumbleweed, known locally as "Ravana's Meesai" or "Ravana's Moustache," driven by the breeze rolling around merrily all over the beach. But this did not, in any way, detract from the joy of having a beach for our backyard.

Nagapattinam was a port with a natural harbour which could not accommodate steamers. But it was a port of call for several cargo ships and two passenger ones. These had to be berthed out at sea, and the passengers and cargo ferried to and fro on launches. From our veranda, we watched ships coming in, recalling how our geography teachers proved the earth was round. The view at night was fairy-tale-like when the ships docked and put on their lights. On stormy nights, the ships would go further out to sea lest the strong winds dash them against the shore. What we saw then was literally a 'dance of lights.'

The two passenger ships, 'S.S. Rajula' and 'S.S. State of Madras,' sailing between Madras and the Malaysian Peninsula with an overnight stop at Nagapattinam, offered affordable transport for Indian labour working in Malaysia and Singapore and students from there, studying in Madras. Those were the days when flights were few and unaffordable. Even students from Sri Lanka (Ceylon in those days) travelled by train from their hometowns to Thalaimannar and took the ferry across the Palk Strait to Dhanushkodi, from where they took the "Dhanushkodi Boat Mail," a daily overnight express train service between Dhanushkodi and the Egmore terminus in Chennai. When the college term ended, the process was reversed.

The cargo ships that called at Nagapattinam belonged mostly to foreign companies, and the captains would invite us on board for informal parties. Getting to the ship was an adventure in itself. We had to reach it by launch. Once the launch reached the ship, it was up to us, on a launch bobbing any which way on the restless waves, to navigate the ship's gangway, which seemed to have a mind of its own, and the outstretched hand of a helpful member of the crew. Prema and I made it every time and enjoyed every visit. Many of those ships belonged to Japanese companies. Spending time with the friendly Japanese captains and crew got us interested in the Japanese language, and 'Linguaphone' found its way into our lives.

I continued to be busy with the maintenance of agricultural peace and also with the almost semi-monthly visits by Chief Minister Karunanidhi to Tiruvarur, the town where he had started his political career and perfected his skills as an astute politician, able organiser, administrator, writer, and orator.

I recall how, on one of his visits, he decided to go to Poompuhar, the ancient Chola capital. Poompuhar is also where the river Kaveri meets the Bay of Bengal. While there, he said he would like to go up to the point where the river actually met the sea. As the area was not accessible by car, he walked up to my jeep and got into it. I took the wheel and drove as far as the jeep would go. He got out of the jeep and walked down the small stretch of sand to the sea. I walked with him, and then we both returned to the jeep. When we got back to it, I was taken aback to see the driver's seat occupied; wasn't I amused that the new 'driver' was none other than my DIG who had hastily arrived on the scene?

Once the district had settled down to a peaceful routine, Prema and I had the time to enjoy our posting in Nagapattinam. Point Calimere, in my jurisdiction, was a wildlife and bird sanctuary with blackbuck and migratory flamingos. It was a cape, so one could enjoy sunrises as well as sunsets when the sky was clear. Muthupet, with its mangroves, was another fascinating part of my jurisdiction. Thiruthuraipoondi, another bird sanctuary with its salt pans, was also within my limits. What's more, I became an authority on Temple festivals, including Kumbabishekams, because of the plethora of Temples with their year-round festivals that this land of the Cholas boasted of.

The never-ending cycle of cultivation and harvest kept me in Thanjavur for more than 4 years, 2 years in the composite district and two in the newly formed Thanjavur East district. This prolonged stay in Thanjavur district deprived me of any chance of a deputation. I was not interested in the Intelligence Bureau, which I ought to have gone to in accordance with the earmarking system prevalent at that time, requiring the No.1 in each batch to be deputed to the Intelligence Bureau. On the other hand, I was keen on joining the newly created Indo-Tibetan Border Police (ITBP) because of its area of operation, where I would once again be in the mountains—not the 4,500- to 8,842-foot-high mountains of the Western Ghats where I was born and brought up, but in the world's highest mountain range, the mighty Himalayas, through which ran the boundary between India and Chinese-occupied Tibet. I had made full use of the weekends and holidays during my training at the National Academy in Mussoorie to trek up the hills of the Garhwal, the Kumaon, the Shivaliks, and to the picturesque and holy spots of Haridwar, Rishikesh, Devprayag, Karnaprayag, Rudraprayag, Kalsi, and Chakrata. A stint with the ITBP would, I thought, fulfil my longing to see for myself the higher reaches of the Himalayas, including the sacred and more alluring destinations of Gangotri, Yamunotri, Kedarnath, and Badrinath, collectively known as the Char-Dham, as well as the Valley of Flowers. But every time my deputation papers were put up to the Chief Minister, he would tell the IGP to renew the request after the never-ending 'nadavai' (cultivation) and 'aruvadai' (harvest). Naturally, the ITBP could not be expected to wait indefinitely, and my batchmate, E. Hariharane, was deputed instead. My other batchmate, R.K. Raghavan, went to the Intelligence Bureau. Another chance for a Central deputation came with my posting to the Madras Unit of the Research and Analysis Wing in place of B.P. Rangasamy, who was proceeding to Guwahati on promotion. Once again, the harvest intervened. In any case, a desk-bound mufti-job was not quite my cup of tea.

Finally, I made use of the convention that required IPS Officers to undergo the Senior Officers' Course before they completed 10 years of service. This convention was observed more in its breach than in its application, as not many officers wanted to be away on this six-month course. When my request was taken up to the Chief Minister by the Inspector General of Police, he agreed to let me go on the condition that I rejoin the same post after completing the course at the Central Police Training College, Mount Abu. I joined the course in April 1973, only to find, to my dismay, that the six-month course I had been looking forward to had been reduced to 3 months. But then, at least, I could go.

While in Mount Abu, our trips by local buses to Jodhpur, Udaipur, Pokaran, and Jaisalmer gave us the heart-warming experience of rural Rajasthani hospitality and their concern for the 'strangers' in their land. Our co-passengers ensured that our water pot (an essential part, in those days, of a traveller's paraphernalia) was never empty, and every time our bus stalled on a patch of desert sand, it was with much difficulty that I could persuade the locals to allow me to push the bus with them. It was in Rajasthan that Prema and I had our first camel ride, experiencing something akin to an earthquake when our mounts 'unfolded' their long legs to stand and, once again, when, at the end of the ride, it was time to dismount. I must admit, we enjoyed being 'pampered civilians.'

After the course in Mount Abu, Prema and I spent 3 days in Goa, thanks to the hospitality of my batchmate and IGP of Goa, Mukund Kumar Kaushal. We took it easy and planned to return home at leisure when we got an urgent message from R.K. Raghavan, my batchmate and Chief of the IB in Chennai, telling me that I had been selected by the Government of India to undergo a 3-month course at the "United Nations Asia and Far-East Institute" in Fuchu, Japan. But my nomination papers had to reach Delhi within 3 days. We rushed back to Chennai, and Raghavan arranged to send the nomination papers to Delhi through a special messenger, and my trip to Japan was secured. The course in Japan was a dream come true for Prema and me. When we learnt to speak Japanese, inspired by our visits to the Japanese ships that called in at Nagapattinam Port, we never dreamt we would get a chance to visit the country. By the time we left for Japan, we had become proficient enough in the language to manage on our own. The two courses gave me a welcome and enjoyable break from routine police work. The two enjoyable stints, one in Mount Abu and the other in Japan left us truly rejuvenated.

Rice Up and Away

Up, up they went, high o'er the hills,
With rice to Kerala from TN's rice mills;
The toil was demanding, but the profits were high;
So, to stop this traffic seemed impossible, well-nigh;
They smuggled the rice, just any which way;
But we ended it all and called it a day.

Rice had never been a part of my diet, but I could not escape the "Rice Factor" despite having been away from the state for almost a year, partly in Mt. Abu and partly in Japan. On my return to Tamil Nadu, I found myself posted to the Food Cell CID, a post newly created to prevent the hoarding and smuggling of rice. Mannai Narayanasamy, who had been the District DMK Secretary during my four-year tenure in Thanjavur district, had become a Minister in my absence from the state and had been allotted the sensitive Food portfolio. Hoarding and, more seriously, smuggling of rice from Tamil Nadu to Sri Lanka and Kerala, over sea and mountain, by road, rail, and waterways, had become a serious problem. At the Minister's insistence, I was posted to the newly created post of SP Food Cell with headquarters in Madurai. My area of operation covered all the districts that had a common border with Kerala, as well as the long-established illegal sea routes to Sri Lanka. I looked back on my Thanjavur days and began to feel like Christian in John Bunyan's 'Pilgrim's Progress,' he weighed down with a sack of his sins on his back, and me, with a sack of rice!

Smuggling of rice from Tamil Nadu was only to be expected, for in Tamil Nadu, ration rice sold through the PDS (Public Distribution System) was being sold at Rs.2 per kg. Across the border, often only a street away, as in the villages of Kerala bordering Kanyakumari district, it fetched Rs.8 to Rs.10 per kg. In Sri Lanka, the profit was even higher. The vast Cauvery Delta of the Madras Presidency and Nanjil Nadu of the erstwhile Travancore state, which in 1956 became part of Tamil Nadu, were the rice bowls of the state. Most of the other districts also had sizeable areas of rice cultivation, thanks to the optimal utilisation of every available water source. The excellent irrigation system that dated back two thousand years with the construction of the Grand Anaicut on the River Cauvery by Chola King Karikalan had been further improved upon by the British engineers who dammed all the major rivers like the Periyar, Cauvery, Krishna, and Godavari in the erstwhile Madras Presidency, and supplemented them with an elaborate canal system. On their part, the progressive Maharajas of Travancore tapped every water source available in Nanjil Nadu by constructing dams in Pechiparai and Perunchani, thereby diverting the mountain streams for rice cultivation. What little was left was harnessed after independence by the Congress Government of the Madras Presidency. As a result, not a drop of water was wasted, and the state was in a comfortable position with regard to rice production. But then, 2 years of drought brought in the system of rationing, which in turn, became a source of forbidden joy to smugglers and hoarders. A profit of Rs.6 to Rs.8 per kg was too tempting a lure, not only for the traditional inter-state and inter-district smugglers but also for the common villagers who were earning no more than 3 or 4 rupees a day. Overnight, the entire population in the border areas had turned to rice smuggling.

Enforcing regulatory laws on the production and sale of liquor, gambling, smuggling of forest produce, river sand, and the like makes the Government and the enforcing agencies unpopular. Besides, enforcement results in the emergence of criminal gangs and mafia-like organisations. The USA gave the world early lessons on these phenomena when it introduced prohibition in the twenties. Although it was suspended as unworkable, the damage had been done. The origin of most of the present-day gangs can be traced back to the lawless twenties, characterised by gang warfare, revenge killings, extensive corruption, and the virtual emergence of parallel governments underground.

A similar situation arose in Tamil Nadu. The introduction of Prohibition in Salem district by Premier Rajaji in 1937 turned a large number of villagers from law-abiding citizens into distillers, sellers, and transporters of illicit arrack. As prisons started filling up with prohibition offenders, the stigma attached to law-breaking and incarceration lost its sting. It is not surprising, then, that Salem, along with North Arcot—the second district where prohibition was introduced—still leads in illicit distillation and allied offences. People who became wealthy because of their success in this clandestine business even gained a degree of respectability later. Under these circumstances, rice smugglers were never bracketed with perpetrators of conventional crimes like murder, assault, rape, dacoity, robbery, and theft. The word 'rice-smuggling' even lost its true meaning when the villagers indulged in it en masse.

A considerable part of the first 10 years of my service had been spent in the Tuticorin Sub-Division and in the districts of The Nilgiris and Thanjavur, where I used to personally lead parties on prohibition raids, partly for the thrill of exploring the hills, jungles, and the major areas of illicit distillation, but more importantly, for the opportunity it gave me to accompany the rank and file, thereby fostering a sense of camaraderie and team spirit with them. After each raid, I focused more on the distillers, transporters, and sellers of the prohibited concoction and went easy on those who bought and drank it. Those who added spurious chemicals and other questionable ingredients to the arrack or rectified spirit to enhance the intoxication level came in for more drastic attention and were detained under the preventive sections of the Prohibition Act.

Smuggling of paddy and rice, on the other hand, was a different proposition. The villagers who took to large-scale smuggling did not think they were doing anything wrong or against the law. Besides, the high-profit rate was irresistible. A head-load of 15 kilograms of rice taken from the villages in the foothills of Bodinayakanur, Thevaram, Uthamapalayam, Gudalur, and Cumbum in Madurai district and delivered at Kumuli, Thekkadi, Santhamparai, and Udumbancholai in the Kottayam district of Kerala state, would fetch a profit of more than 100 rupees. The more enterprising smugglers engaged gangs of coolies to carry heavier loads across the borders, thus making greater profits. Using donkeys and ponies to carry rice bags was, no doubt, much more profitable because each animal could carry between 50 and 60 kg of rice. There were also attempts by lorries to smuggle rice across the border check posts. These, however, could be easily checked if provided. Of course, the check post staff were duty-conscious and honest.

The Cumbum Valley became the main theatre of our operations. I was back in the old familiar hills, climbing the steep slopes, slithering down them into the valleys, crossing jungle streams, and encountering wild animals like porcupines, bears, wild boars, bison, and even an occasional panther. My very first raid in the hills overlooking Kombai, Hanumanthanpatti, Pudupatti, and Uthamapalayam is still fresh in my memory. Inspector Fazulludin, who had a thorough knowledge of the smugglers' routes and their tactics, took me with a party of ten policemen on a circuitous route to the hills, eluding the look-outs posted by the smugglers at several points to watch out for and report the movement of police parties. After 3 hours of climbing, we reached a vantage point overlooking the entire valley below. We set up an ambush and waited.

The drama began to unfold shortly after midnight. Processions started from several villages on the plains. The advance scout and every fifteenth or sixteenth man in the line following carried a lighted cycle tyre or blazing torch to light the way. We could count at least 15 columns, each one between one hundred and two hundred strong. Slowly, the lines snaked their way towards the foot of the hills. Three or four of them converged to form a single line for the upward climb. When the climb started, there were six columns, 4 headed our way and two going up another path, about 3 or 4 kilometres beyond.

It took another hour and a half for the head of one of the combined columns to reach our ambush point. As soon as we confronted them with whistles and torch lights, panic set in. As going downhill with the head loads was well-nigh impossible, the smugglers dropped their loads and scrambled to the safety of the bushes on either side of the footpath. We could get hold of only a few of them, most of them boys between 16 and 20 years of age. We had no way of carrying the rice bags, numbering more than 500, back to the plains. We told those who were in our custody that if they carried the bags downhill to the government-approved rice mills, we would give them 3 or 4 kilograms of rice as wages and allow them to go free. Those who were carrying loads in the capacity of paid carriers readily agreed and conveyed the offer to their companions who were still hiding in the bushes. They, too, agreed and came out of hiding. Even those who were carrying their own loads had to fall in line. By dawn, we were ready for the return trip to Uthamapalayam, which we reached by 10 a.m., with one hundred and 40 people carrying head loads. The paddy was deposited in the rice mills there. The so-called smugglers returned to their respective villages with 4 to 5 kilograms of rice each as their wages. Those who had brought their own rice were allowed to take back a little more than five kilograms. It was more than 20 hours before we could have our first drop of water or cup of tea. We repeated the tiring but rewarding raids thrice a week, each time taking a different path up the hills.

The long and tedious downhill lumber back to the plains established a sense of camaraderie between us and the so-called smugglers. A few of them would even claim to be relatives of my friend and University mate Perumal Thevar, who, at that time, happened to be the Superintendent of Central Prison, Madurai. I had visited his village, Ammapatti, a few times, visits which had apparently come to the notice of some of the smugglers. When I mentioned this to Perumal Thevar, he was nonchalant and said that many of the prisoners in Madurai jail would address him as 'annachi (brother) or machan (brother-in-law)' while on his jail rounds, even though he knew them not!

Name-dropping is not alien to our society. Even decades after my retirement, I get calls from people claiming to be my relatives or close friends when they are about to be booked for some traffic offence. The 'modus operandi' is usually to call my number and, once connected, to hand the phone over to the officer concerned. But I, on my part, do not think it fair or right to embarrass the policeman concerned. It is also possible that just the mention of my name could save many an offender from the situation. However, it is of concern that many people, known and even unknown, have my number stored on their mobiles 'just in case!'

Our success in intercepting the smugglers made them change their tactics, routes, and timings. It was becoming increasingly difficult to reach the interception points on the hills without being noticed by the "look-outs" posted by the smugglers at various vantage points. Sometimes, we would have to enter Kerala by road, either from the Bodi-Bodimettu side or the Cumbum-Cumbummettu side and walk down the smugglers' routes to surprise them. The unauthorised wages we paid to them made them co-operative and reasonably content. It also created a rift between the agencies and organisers on the one hand and the load carriers on the other.

The smuggler syndicate then gave up their traditional routes and paths leading from the villages in and around Thevaram and switched to the cardamom estates that were located on either side of the state border. These routes were longer, so they hired donkeys with handlers to smuggle the rice. It was becoming increasingly difficult for us to reach the interception points. The process after intercepting the animal convoy was even more daunting. Unlike the load carriers, the donkeys stood rock-still while their handlers scurried for cover. Taking the loaded donkeys back along downward slopes was a tedious process because the bags weighed them down and occasionally toppled them. The handlers struggled to lead the heavily laden animals to the centres 2 to 3 thousand feet below, with policemen accompanying them. The downhill process took more than 6 hours. In all, the entire operation—from our getting to the interception point, lying in wait for the convoy, and taking the loaded donkeys to the mills—was a tedious process lasting 2 days and a night.

On one of those raids, I inadvertently strayed away from the team, lost my way back, and found myself in one of the border settlements in Kerala. I was amazed to find a well-organised reception centre, complete with counters, weighing machines, and ready cash to pay the smugglers. The reception I received was not unlike the one that would be meted out to an enemy intruder from across an international border. It was my fluent Malayalam that saved me, but not before being berated for working against and starving my 'fellow Malayalees.' I learnt that day never to stray into hill settlements and reception centres set up in Kerala to receive smuggled rice.

Our reception back in Tamil Nadu, when we returned with the seized donkeys and rice, was equally hostile. On two occasions, we were gheraoed while entering Thevaram, and I was berated for working against the people of my 'own' village. They believed that I was originally from their village, Thevaram and that my name, Davaram, was an anglicised version of Thevaram. They had even been told erroneously that my ancestors had moved out of their village and settled down in Munnar, high up in the hills past Bodinaickanur and Devikulam. We could break through the cordon only after firing a couple of rifle shots over the heads of the protesters. However, the raids and their effect on the poorly paid carriers of paddy were very satisfying. We paid them in paddy to carry the load from the hills to the rice mills in Thevaram, Periyakulam, and other centres. None of them was ever remanded. The only losers were the big-time smugglers who carried out this trade using the needy villagers.

In spite of several successful raids on donkey-borne smuggling, the menace continued. This made me wonder about the never-ending availability of donkeys for smugglers to use. The explanation turned out to be quite simple. The Village Administrative Officers (VAOs), to whom we handed over the donkeys after unloading the bags of paddy at the government-approved rice mills, promptly auctioned them back to the same smugglers at a ridiculously low price of Rs. 5/- per animal! Both men and animals were back in business the very next day.

Something had to be done urgently to break this cycle of the seizure of the animals by us and their prompt return to the same smugglers by 'public auction.' After a particularly large and successful raid in which 78 loaded donkeys were seized, we unloaded the rice in the mills and took the animals back on the same route. We lined them up on the smugglers' path at intervals of 20 to 25 feet and shot them all in the head with a.22 rifle. Death was instantaneous and painless. The rotting carcasses ruled out the use of the path by the smugglers, even on foot, for over a month. No doubt, animal lovers would be appalled by our action, but we took comfort from the fact that, apart from the painless death, the poor animals were spared the agony of carrying such heavy loads uphill day after day. Furthermore, we had achieved our objective of stopping large-scale smuggling from the Bodi-Thevaram plains to the reception centres that had sprung up all along the Tamil Nadu-Kerala border, 3 or 4 thousand feet above sea level.

The other theatres of smuggling were in the districts of Tirunelveli, Ramanathapuram, and Kanyakumari. In Tirunelveli district, the ghats were much higher than those of Madurai district and villages on either side of the border were set too far apart to facilitate smuggling. A few successful raids on the routes leading from the Iyanar Falls near Srivilliputhur and Pilavakkal Dam near Vathirayiruppu put an end to the smuggling activities in Ramnad and Kanyakumari districts. The main smuggling route in Tirunelveli district was the railway line between Sengottai in Tirunelveli district and Punalur in the Kollam district of Kerala. Frustrated by our checking of the trains, the smugglers, carrying head loads of rice, started walking their way through a railway tunnel which conveniently straddled the border, one end in Tamil Nadu and the other in Kerala. We put an end to this by blocking the entry to the tunnel after a line of smugglers had entered it from the Tamil Nadu side and relieving the trapped smugglers of their head-loads at the other end.

Reconnoitring the hills to study and anticipate the smugglers' change of tactics, routes, and timings gave me the opportunity to explore segments of the Western Ghats that formed the border between Kerala and Tamil Nadu. One such climb took me to the source of the river Vaigai, in Velimalai estate in the Pachaikumachi (Chinnamanur) Hills. But Vaigai actually gets its main supply from the Mullaiperiyar Dam after the production of electricity in the Lower Anaicut Power House.

Another trip from Surulipatti along the Suruli Falls and Suruli Power House took me to the Mangaladevi Temple atop a beautiful hill feature on the Kerala side of the border abutting Thekkady Wildlife Sanctuary. The Temple, a stone structure, is believed to have been built by Chera King Cheran Senguttuvan to mark the spot from where the legendary 'Kannagi' ascended into heaven. The annual festival at the Temple has now become a popular event, leading to needless friction between the large number of devotees from Tamil Nadu and the local authorities. It was near this Temple that I found a human skeleton washed white by rain and sun. On my return to Gudalur, I sent a note to the Kumuli Police Station in Kerala about my find. I was pleasantly surprised when, in due course, I received a reply from the police station that the identity of the person could not be established and that no foul play was suspected. On another occasion, I climbed up to 7,000 ft. from the "lower" Ropeway station in Kurangani Village in Tamil Nadu to the "top Ropeway Station" on the Kodaikanal–Munnar Road, the highest road South of the Himalayas. Incidentally, this road had been constructed by the British during the Second World War as an escape route in the event of the Japanese landing on the East Coast. But the Japanese had already reached India from Burma and had been stopped there.

I was gratified that I could tread the path that the first and second generations of plantation staff and workers had used to reach the jungle, which they cleared for the tea plantations. I also went up the jungle trail that led from the Kumbakarai Falls near Periakulam to Kodaikanal via the tribal village of Vellagevi, perched precariously on a mountain slope. It was during one of these climbs that we confronted rice smugglers from Tamil Nadu returning from Kerala with stocks of arrack and Indian-made foreign liquor (IMFL), bought in Kerala where there was no prohibition, with the money they had made by selling rice smuggled out from Tamil Nadu—a two-way profit. Similar two-way smuggling—rice from Tamil Nadu to Kerala and liquor from Kerala to Tamil Nadu—was going on, on a much larger scale between the Kanyakumari and Trivandrum districts. Such is the bane of imposing conditions and restrictions on people's needs and preferences.

The next major area of smuggling lay in the erstwhile South Travancore, which had been bifurcated in the year 1956 into the Kanyakumari district of Tamil Nadu and the Neyyatinkara district of Kerala. The smugglers' routes lay through the coffee, cardamom, and rubber plantations and the thick jungle that lay on either side of the non-existent imaginary borders created by the States Re-organisation Committee. Smuggling rice by sea and through the canals that ran along the border was yet another mode of operation. But the most common form of smuggling was through the densely populated villages that lay interlinked on either side of a boundary that never was. There were houses that were sandwiched between the two states, the front yard in one state and the backyard in the other. In some places, one side of the road belonged to Kerala, and the other to Tamil Nadu, and the people living on either side of the Southern border were closely related to each other: the parents in Kerala and their grown-up children in Tamil Nadu and vice versa.

In such a situation, all that the smugglers had to do when confronted by the police was cross over to the other side of the road or enter one of the houses through the front door and escape through the back into

Kerala territory. We tackled this problem by raiding the markets and godowns on the Tamil Nadu side of the border and confiscating the stock set aside to be smuggled across. My first raid in the Marthandam market yielded 30,000 kgs of rice and earned me the undying hatred of the residents of the border villages like Kaliyakavilai, Padanthalmvoodu, and Samiyarmadam of Kanyakumari district. The raid, however, put an end to open smuggling. On the other hand, we ignored small quantities being taken across to their kin on the other side.

The problem of smuggling rice by Vallams (country boats) called for careful planning and precise timing. The AVM (Ananda Victoria Marthandam) canal, connecting Thengaipattinam in Kanyakumari district and Poovar in Kerala, had been so named by the Maharaja of Travancore to show his loyalty to the Empress Queen Victoria. It ran for 15 km in Kanyakumari district before entering Kerala. The smugglers undertook the trip across only after getting clearance from the look-outs stationed all along the canal. Our difficulties were further compounded by the need to commandeer boats for interception work without the smugglers getting wind of it. Meanwhile, DSP Sadayappan and Inspector Antonysamy had built up a good network of informants to counter the moves of smugglers.

We began our operation by carrying our boat to the canal by an unfrequented route, sailing up quietly, mooring the boat beneath a canopy of coconut trees, and starting the chase only after the smugglers' boat got close enough. Very rarely did the confronted boat have time to pull away. We then escorted the seized boats to the nearest road, where the bags were loaded onto vehicles and taken to the government-approved rice mills.

During one such raid on a moonless night in July 1974, the crew of the challenged boat, instead of stopping, tried to pull away. When it was about to cross into Kerala, I fired a warning shot over the heads of the boatmen. Instead of stopping, they tried to speed away. I fired another round into the water in the wake of the boat. The men on the boat jumped into the canal and swam away, leaving their boat behind. In the boat, we found and seized 18 bags, each containing 60 kgs of rice. As required by the Police Standing Orders, I reported the firing of warning shots to the District Collector Thangaraj, who also happened to be my IAS batchmate. I then returned to my headquarters in Madurai. It was nearly 6 months later, when I was Superintendent of Police, North Arcot district, that I received a summons from the RDO of Thuckalai in Kanyakumari district for an enquiry into the 'Firing on the Boat' because one of the smugglers had died of a bullet injury. Presumably, the shot I had fired into the water had ricocheted and hit him. The RDO thanked me for my presence and for putting an end to the doubts raised by the smugglers.

The only other incident of interest was the interception of a dozen smugglers just before they loaded the rice onto a boat waiting at the far end of the water spread of the Neyyar Dam in Kerala. They had carried their loads over a distance of 22 kilometres through leech-infested jungle. We had started out the previous night, walked all night and half of the next day, to reach the point where a motorboat was awaiting the arrival of the smugglers, to take the load across the ten-kilometre water spread of the Neyyar Dam to Neyyatinkara in Kerala. We had to keep walking without slackening our pace because of the omnipresent leeches. Even so, when we stopped on sighting the reservoir, each one of us was covered with leeches, head to foot. We lay in wait for the boat from our jungle cover and rushed out just before the load carriers reached it. We felt a sense of camaraderie with the smugglers because of the similar leech-ridden ordeal they had gone through to get there. The problem that now faced us was that the bags could not be carried back all the way to the nearest human settlement in Tamil Nadu. Neither could we ferry the rice by the intercepted boat back to Neyyar Dam, which was well inside Kerala territory. As such, we allowed the boatmen to take the paddy after paying the load carriers their well-deserved wages. We started back with the smugglers leading the way through the terrain they knew so well and which took only half the time we had taken for the outward journey. The smugglers were let off after getting an undertaking from them that they would not work for the inter-state smuggling syndicate anymore. That was the last of the inter-state smuggling through dense forest cover on the Tamil Nadu side of the border across the dam in Kerala.

Smuggling of rice from the stretch of the coast between Vedaranyam in the north and Dhanushkodi in the South to the northern parts of Sri Lanka was brought to an end by a few successful interceptions of the fishing boats. These boats also carried, besides rice, other articles like lungis (sarongs) and sarees in a well-established pattern of smuggling between India and Sri Lanka, a practice that had been prevalent for over 100 years.

I have not mentioned the numerous de-hoarding operations we carried out in bazaars and rice godowns all over the state because they would not make interesting reading, though they did ruffle the feathers of well-connected merchants. But I must admit that there was never any interference from the government or the Ministers of the districts concerned. By the end of the year, the rice situation had returned to normal and smuggling came to an end. I was then posted as Superintendent of Police, North Arcot district. My only regret is that I could not get an accelerated promotion for Inspector Fazulludin, who was a master of the forest routes and an invaluable asset to our team.

I thoroughly enjoyed my tenure as Superintendent of Police, Food Cell, a period marked by field operations, long walks, days and nights spent at ambush points, playing hide and seek with smugglers in extremely difficult and hostile terrain, and finally, beating them at their own game. I lived up to the expectations of the government and my superiors in the Police and Civil Supplies Department. Above all, I forged a memorable and lasting partnership with the subordinate staff by living and working with them day and night and by sharing in their difficulties and hardships.

The smugglers, I must say, had also developed a sort of fellowship with us. After all, they were our less fortunate fellow citizens; had they some means of livelihood, they would definitely have led honest lives. In my opinion, it is those who become prosperous by indulging in white-collar crime who should be detained and punished.

Officer on the Spot

A policeman's job is not much fun.
He must stick to his post, come rain or sun;
That man on the spot has decisions to take,
Decisions that might him mar or make.
If that man on the spot happens to be you,
Hold your head high; what's right you must do.

30th Oct 1977 – The Madras City Police stood mobilised to deal with the black flag demonstration announced by the DMK, DK, and the CPI(M) against Indira Gandhi, the former Prime Minister of India, on her arrival in Madras. It was to be her first visit to Tamil Nadu after her defeat in the Lok Sabha elections.

The black flag demonstration by the DMK was to mark the party's disapproval of what they thought had been the "arbitrary" dismissal of the DMK government the previous year. This decision was taken at the party's executive committee meeting held on 27.10.1977 after Indira Gandhi's visit to Tamil Nadu had been announced by the Congress Party. The DK decided to follow suit. The CPI(M), on their part, decided to show their disapproval of "several atrocities that she had committed in the guise of Emergency."

As required by the provisions of Sec. 41 of the Madras City Police Act, all three parties applied for permission to show black flags. They had also indicated the places of their choice. According to the permission granted by the Commissioner of Police, the DMK was assigned the stretch of the Grand Southern Trunk (GST) Road at the Halda Junction, the DK, further on at Guindy and the CPI(M), near the Labour Statue on the Marina, which also happened to be the venue of the evening's public meeting to be addressed by Indira Gandhi.

At that time, all of Madras City was divided into just two law-and-order districts, North and South, each under a Deputy Commissioner of Police. Apart from these 2 DCs, there was one Deputy Commissioner of Police each for Crime, Traffic, Headquarters, and Armed Reserve. As such, there were just six Deputy Commissioners under one Commissioner of Police, who was of the rank of a Deputy Inspector General of Police. Of course, this was much before the proliferation of ranks and the creation of the posts of several Directors General and an equally large number of Additional Directors General and Inspectors General of Police.

All three locations of the black flag demonstrations, as well as the public meeting on the Marina, fell within the jurisdiction of the DC, Law & Order, South. As the then incumbent of this post, I set to work with the Assistant Commissioners of Police concerned. While the barricading at the meeting place followed a set pattern, the black flag venues needed specialised attention, taking into account the location of public offices, residential complexes, hospitals, and educational institutions in the vicinity, as well as the bus and train routes passing through the area. Wooden barricades were erected on both sides of the road to contain the demonstrators when the VIP's convoy drove past. The area was cleared of stones, bricks, sticks, and anything else that might come in handy for the demonstrators to pelt at the convoy. After completing these preliminaries, the party representatives were shown the places earmarked for their demonstrations and advised to mark their protest in a peaceful manner.

According to the tour programme released by the Congress Party, Indira Gandhi was to arrive at Meenambakkam Airport at 9 a.m. on the

29th of October, proceed by air to Madurai, address a public meeting there, and leave for Trichy by road. After addressing a meeting at Trichy, she was to board the Pandian Express at 10.40 p.m. and arrive in Madras at 6.30 a.m. on the 30th. She was to go to the State Guest House and leave immediately by road for Kancheepuram, address a meeting there, and get back to Madras for the final meeting at the Marina that evening. She was to fly back to Delhi on the 31st morning.

Indira Gandhi arrived at Meenambakkam Airport as scheduled. After meeting the party leaders and representatives, she flew out at 11.45 a.m. and reached Madurai at 1.00 p.m. Both in Madurai and in Trichy, specific places were assigned to the black flag demonstrations. But from the time of her arrival in Madurai, everything went amiss. It became clear that the DMK was determined not to allow her to travel anywhere in Tamil Nadu. Apart from the black flag demonstrators who had assembled in their assigned places, large crowds of unruly demonstrators had gathered along her intended route from the airport to the city, attacking shops and torching vehicles. The VIP convoy, and especially the car in which Indira Gandhi was travelling, was attacked with stones, bricks, sticks, and soda bottles. In fact, her car was attacked so violently that she might have been seriously injured or even killed had it not been for the protection given to her by Congress leader Nedumaran, who acted as a human shield against the missiles aimed at her. She could not even enter Madurai City.

Her car was whisked away to Trichy via the highway. On the outskirts of Trichy, the same scenario as in Madurai was repeated; the reception she received was hostile. She did, however, manage to enter the town, but the public meeting could not last more than half an hour. Also, she could not board the Pandian Express as planned and could board only the Kanyakumari Express 2 hours later, arriving at Egmore station at 10.00 a.m. the following morning instead of at 6.30 a.m. as had been scheduled.

The violent incidents in Madurai and Trichy on the 29th compelled the Government to cancel the permissions granted for the black flag demonstrations on the 30th in Madras and Kancheepuram. The DMK, DK, and the CPI(M) were informed of the cancellation. It was also announced over All-India Radio and in all the newspapers. The cancellation orders were received by R.D. Seethapathy of the DMK, K. Veeramani of the DK, and V.P. Chinthan of the CPI(M). But the DMK, in its party organ "Murasoli," published the same day, announced its decision to violate the ban and, in the event of the demonstrators getting arrested in advance, the party leader and other senior members of the party would take their place.

On the 30th, I was at Egmore Station by 5.00 a.m., supervising the bandobust arrangements for Indira Gandhi's arrival, although her arrival had been delayed. As the morning wore on, I found, to my consternation, that every Chennai-bound train was bringing in hordes of demonstrators, all armed with flags tied to long poles. As they came out of the station, we arrested them in batches, preventing them from going into the city. But all was not under control. At 6.45 a.m., I received a call from the Inspector of Police, Saidapet, informing me that, in defiance of the ban order, over a thousand demonstrators were on their way towards Halda Junction from the Guindy Railway Station. I directed V.N. Srinivasan, the Assistant Commissioner of Police, Saidapet, who was at the Government Guest House reserved for Indira Gandhi's stay, to rush to Halda Junction with whatever strength he could muster. DC Crime Jaffer Ali remained at the guest house to provide protection for her from arrival up to her departure from Madras. By then, information was pouring in from many parts of the city that violent crowds were attacking vehicles on the road and forcing shops to close.

I reached Halda Junction at 7.10 a.m. and started clearing the area of demonstrators who kept coming back in greater strength and fury. It was obvious that they were determined to violate the prohibitory order and attack Indira Gandhi's convoy on its way from Madras to Kancheepuram in the morning and again in the evening, on its return to Chennai for the public meeting on the Marina. I decided to disperse them by force. I mobilised the officers and men and assembled them in front of Chellammal College at Halda Junction. Riot flags were raised for all to see, and the first warning was given through a megaphone. The warning, "You are an unlawful assembly. You must disperse immediately, or you will be dispersed by the use of force," was repeated in all directions. It was of no use, and the crowd intensified their stone-throwing, injuring all of us, officers and men, and damaging our vehicles.

When the frenzied mob showed no signs of dispersal, I ordered tear gas shells to be fired at them. Between 7.30 and 8.00 a.m., more than a hundred shells were fired. But the crowd kept regrouping and advancing from various directions. It soon swelled to several thousand, with about two thousands of them advancing from the direction of the Women's College opposite Halda Junction, shouting slogans not only against Indira Gandhi but against the police as well. Repeated lathi charges failed to disperse them. The crowd from the Saidapet side, led by DMK MLA Aranganathan, broke through the police cordon at Mariamalai Adigalar Bridge and joined the crowd that was already attacking the heavily outnumbered police at Halda Junction.

I had no option but to resort to firing. A warning to the effect that firing would be resorted to, which would result in loss of life, was repeated several times before I fired one round aiming at the leader of the mob. He fell dead. I watched the crowd's reaction. As there were no signs of dispersal, I fired 2 more rounds, killing 2 local office-bearers of the DMK party. On seeing three of their leaders fall, the other agitators hastily dispersed.

I stopped firing immediately and took stock of the situation. Two rioters, Balu and Deenan, who were local DMK leaders, and one unknown agitator had died of bullet injuries, and 45 others were injured in the lathi charge and tear gas attacks. On the police side, two Assistant Commissioners of Police, nine Inspectors, 40 Sub-Inspectors, one hundred and 23 policemen, and I had been injured. I arranged to send the seriously injured to the hospital and called the City Police Control over the VHF (Very High Frequency) Radio, asking them to alert the government hospitals to receive the injured civilians and policemen. Meanwhile, the DMK party leader M. Karunanidhi and his senior colleagues, who were on their way to Halda Junction in defiance of Sec. 144 in force that day, were arrested and remanded to custody. They were released from prison only on 8th December, 38 days after their arrest, although the original plan was to release them immediately after Indira Gandhi's departure from Chennai.

I then gave a short situation report through a VHF message, which could be heard all over the city through VHF sets in police stations, as well as those fitted in the vehicles of every police officer. Pon. Paramaguru, the Commissioner of Police, immediately came on air and wanted to know in an agitated voice whether the situation really warranted the use of firearms. Before I could answer, the Inspector General of Police, E.L. Stracey, came on his mic and asked the Commissioner of Police whether he was on the spot. When the Commissioner of Police replied that he wasn't but was on his way there, Stracey categorically told him, "In that case, stop giving instructions. The Deputy Commissioner of Police is the officer on the spot. He will decide the type of action to be taken, including the use of firearms." That silenced the Commissioner. By the time the Inspector General and the Commissioner got to Halda Junction, we had cleared the area completely of the rioters.

Although the situation at Halda Junction had been brought under control, violence continued unabated in other parts of the city. The flagged car in which the Minister of Education of the Government of Kerala was going to the airport was attacked and partially damaged. The Minister was rescued and taken to the airport in another vehicle. A vehicle belonging to the National Cadet Corps was totally burnt down, the mob having mistaken it for a police vehicle.

Two hours after the shooting at Halda Junction, over 3 thousand rioters entered Saidapet Railway Station, forcibly stopped electric trains, and set a few of them ablaze. Another mob stopped the Quilon Express at a level crossing nearby, forced the engine driver and passengers to alight, and set fire to the engine and 28 coaches. Three other trains, including the Kanyakumari Express in which Indira Gandhi was travelling, were attacked with stones, injuring more than 40 passengers and 18 railway staff. There was similar violence at the Guindy Railway Station, and the mob there then proceeded along the railway track to Saidapet Railway Station to join the mob that was already there.

Assistant Commissioner of Police Nagappan, who was on duty near the Panagal building in Saidapet, received news of the mob proceeding towards Saidapet Railway Station. Although he was on the verge of retirement, he showed commendable initiative and immediately went there with his small squad of 15 policemen. On seeing the limited number of policemen, the rioters attacked them with iron rods taken from the railway station, and also with stones from the ballast on the railway tracks. The heavily outnumbered police party had no other option but to open fire. Subramanian, a rioter, fell at the very first shot, and the mob fled the scene. It took more than 6 hours for the fire services personnel to put out the fire on the trains and at the railway station. The number of deaths due to police firing that day rose to four. By evening, the situation all over the city had been brought under control.

I had by then prepared an FIR at the Saidapet Police Station on the events leading to the police firing, visited the injured police personnel in three different government hospitals, and got myself treated at the Government Royapettah Hospital.

By 7.00 p.m., I was at the venue of the meeting on the Marina, supervising the bandobust. Indira Gandhi, who had to cancel the meeting in Kanchipuram as well because of the law-and-order situation there, was escorted from the State Guest House to the meeting place on the Marina by DC Jaffer Ali. At the meeting place, Congress leader Karuppaiah Moopanar introduced me to Indira Gandhi, who expressed deep concern over my injuries and the difficulties undergone by the police on account of her visit to Tamil Nadu. She returned to Delhi without further incident after a peaceful, well-attended meeting on the Marina.

I was deeply disturbed by the totally false account of Indira Gandhi's visit to Tamil Nadu that appeared in the autobiography written by Vaikunth. He was, at that time, DIG of Police, Trichy Range. He has recorded in his book (Page No. 193), "MGR stood up and hugged me in appreciation of my strenuous efforts to maintain peace in Trichy during Indira Gandhi's visit." He has also written that MGR had told him, "I do not know why people like Walter Davaram had to resort to the use of firearms, aimlessly killing innocent people. I wish he learns a few lessons from you on planned, preparedness and preventive measures." Then he goes on to say, "But it is the same Davaram whom MGR posted as the Commissioner of Police, Madras City. In that position, he ended his tenure lathi charging the MLAs in the state Assembly premises." I am quite sure that MGR never uttered those comments; that he had even talked to Vaikunth is doubtful because MGR was very happy that at least in Chennai, Indira Gandhi could address a large gathering.

On page 389, he writes, "I was so preoccupied with the other policing problems. I had very little time at my disposal. I wanted to have my own strategy in nabbing Veerappan. Before I got anything concrete, I had to go out of office. It is not as though J Jayalalithaa was not aware of the criticisms of the public against the helplessness of the police in nabbing Veerappan. In fact, she once told Davaram in my presence, 'Mr. Davaram, nab at least Imam Ali, though you have been spinning stories about Veerappan.'" This is a blatant lie, as such a conversation or meeting ever took place. His next sentence, 'It is a different story altogether as to how then he was made the Director General of Police,' says it all. As far as Imam Ali is concerned, he came into the picture much after Vaikunth and I had retired.

On page 388, he writes that Deva Gowda, Chief Minister of Karnataka, in a joint meeting with the Chief Minister of Tamil Nadu, told me, "Mr. Devaram, how do you think we know you sitting in Bangalore except that we see you in the battle dress and holding your AK-47 very often in the photographs that appear in the press. Every time you go to the hills, you go there only to place wreaths on the bodies of policemen killed by Veerappan, and you are not just able to nab Veerappan."

This is a highly imaginative and false observation. I had never attended any meeting in which Deva Gowda was supposed to have made this remark. I was mostly in the forest and have never met him, not even once. It seems to me that Vaikunth has put into the mouth of Deva Gowda the thoughts he himself had longed to express. The only time I met any Chief Minister of Karnataka was when Veerappa Moily, the Chief Minister, and Jayalalithaa held a joint meeting in Chennai at which I was given Joint Command of the Karnataka and Tamil Nadu Police.

On page 390, he claims that he was not given the chance to capture Veerappan. He states, "I had my own secret plans to arrest Veerappan. I had organised my contacts, which I developed as the SP, Coimbatore Rural, to ensure the surrender of Veerappan, and everything was going according to plan when I had to retire." Veerappan could not have been arrested through the information of the contacts he had developed as SP, Coimbatore Rural more than 30 years earlier; contacts who might have never even gone anywhere near the jungle that sheltered Veerappan. It was easy for him, who might not have even seen the jungle, to belittle the efforts of my officers, men, and myself; we who had spent several days and nights in the 4000 sq. km deep forest, suffering hunger, rain, shine, and leech bites, braving elephants, bison, and other wild animals. If Vaikunth did have 'secret' plans to nab Veerappan, he could have 'secretly' gone into the forest, captured him, and walked out with him hand-in-hand, putting the STF to shame. He could have done the 'secret' job even after retirement! This claim is as ridiculous as his other claims. If he really did have a 'secret' plan to arrest Veerappan, ought he not have taken steps to pass on such "vital" information to the Government for necessary action?

In yet another instance (Page No. 452) relating to the caste-related rioting in Kodiyankulam in Tirunelveli District, he writes, "This is one event where, for the fault of officials, J. Jayalalithaa got a bad name which cost her heavily in the elections in the year 1996. J Jayalalithaa felt, and correctly so, that Davaram, who was sent to Tirunelveli, should have given proper directions to the police officers at the grassroots level. Some respectable elders of the district had also alleged that in the name of being firm, the police went berserk, which is solely due to Davaram's lack of direction. That the same Davaram was elevated later as the DGP by J. Jayalalithaa is a different matter altogether. The less said the better." I have no comments to make on this false and preposterous remark. It is enough to say that I did become DGP within 2 months of the Kodiyankulam incident.

However, I must explain what actually happened at Kodiyankulam. On 31.08.1995, the police raided the village to arrest a Dalit accused of having looted property belonging to some Thevars. The Dalits attacked the police party with country-made bombs, seriously injuring an Inspector, 2 SIs, and several constables. The police, after due warning, had to open fire in the air. They arrested 24 rioters and seized 14 country bombs. Protesting against the arrest, the Dalits took out a procession in Ottapidaram, where they attacked the vehicle in which the tahsildar was travelling and also vandalised his house. Again, on 19.09.1995, the Dalits murdered the Thevar Headmaster of the Government High School at Kollankinar. The one-man Commission of Enquiry by retired District Judge, Sri Gomathinayagam, fully justified the police action and ruled out any police excess.

Here is yet another example of his bitterness towards me. On page 459, he writes, "As for me, as the Chief of the Police Force, I had to ensure proper security arrangements at the wedding of Selvi J Jayalalithaa's foster son. All these things I did, in the manner of speaking, with quiet efficiency. After the ceremony on the 6th evening at the Temple near Malar Hospital near Adyar Bridge, I drove back straight to the marriage hall. As for the procession, there were hosts of field officers to attend to it. There was absolutely no need for Walter Davaram, as the Additional DGP, to walk all along the procession. I felt very sad that Davaram should reduce himself to this level. He walked along with the bridal procession as though he was a junior level Sergeant-Major. Professionally, Mr. Davaram brought a bad name to the force. Walter Davaram walking with the procession became a laughing point in the media and in the Force. Whereas, from Mr. Davaram's point of view, that was how he could walk into the post of DGP, succeeding me."

Surely, Vaikunth should have known that my place had always been with my officers and men in any major law-and-order situation, important bandobast, or dangerous operation. In this particular case, the popular Chief Minister was walking on the public road and my place was certainly beside her, not in the company of the DGP and others in the marriage hall.

Other ridiculous claims that he has made in his book are that MGR hugged him, Periyar patted him, Rajaji placed his right palm on his head by way of blessing him, and Indira Gandhi patted him on his back when she visited Trichy. He says Indira Gandhi, when she visited the TSP Bn. in N.E.F.A., addressed him as "Vaikunth Ji" and, after watching the karagam performance of the TSP Bn., told him, "Why don't you join my security staff?" I did not know that a karagattam could be used as the yardstick for selecting the security officer for the Prime Minister of the world's largest democracy.

I had to deviate from my narrative because of the utter lies that Vaikunth has written in his book. His bitterness was due, probably, to his failure to become Commissioner of Police or to get a further extension as DGP. I must mention here that J. Jayalalithaa had told me well in advance that I would be posted as DGP when Sripal retired. Then, when the time drew near, she told me that she was under heavy pressure from prominent people at the Centre to make Vaikunth the DGP. She asked me whether I had any objection to his being given an extension of

6 months after Sripal's retirement so he could have a chance to be the DGP. I replied that I had absolutely no objection and that I could wait as I still had two and a half years of service before I retired.

Regarding the animosity displayed by Vaikunth, I think that he might have developed a grudge against me and my fellow classmates at Madras Christian College, where he was our lecturer in Economics. The year was 1958. At that time, his name was not "Vaikunth" but "Vaikundam," a name which we found worthy of ridicule, and it led to a lot of merriment with the whole class hollering "Vaikundam, Vaikundam" whenever he entered the class. This went on for about a week, by which time his unusual name lost its sheen. Then, to his bad luck, a Tamil movie which had just been released had a song sung by comedian Thangavelu beginning with the words "Vaikunda, Kailasa." To his discomfiture, the class started singing that song every time he entered the classroom! A few months later, he went on leave to write the UPSC examination. On his return to college, I, on behalf of the other students, got up and requested him to tell us about the all-India examination which he had gone to take. He replied, "Why do you want to know about these very difficult examinations? You will never even pass B.A."

The next time I met Vaikunth was at the Rajarathinam Stadium, Madras, during the State Police Sports Meet. The three of us, Raghavan, Hariharan, and I, had reported in the state as the latest batch of IPS officers. We were taken to the stadium where Vaikunth, Rajasekaran Nair, and Rathnakar Rao of the 1961 batch were introduced to us. Both Vaikunth and I had the shock of our lives; he, on seeing me as an IPS Officer and not as a student who would not even pass his B.A., and I, by his being introduced to me as "Vaikunth" and not as "Vaikundam," the name by which he was known in college.

Coming to think of it, Vaikunth was critical of most of his senior officers and colleagues and referred to them as "a coterie presided over by a senior officer in a sensitive wing," "senior officers who had political links," "officers who did not like my professionalism and principles," "senior officers remote-controlled by another functionary in Delhi" or "intriguing colleagues responsible for denying me important posts." But he never mentioned any of them by name. He reserved that honour for me. Was I his bête noire? During the last 3 months of his tenure as DGP, Vaikunth tried his best to get an interview with Jayalalithaa, even though me, but he failed. No doubt, Jayalalithaa did not want to give him the second extension which he so badly wanted.

My first reaction to Vaikunth's book was to shrug it off as just a tissue of lies, not worthy of attention. After all, it was only someone giving vent to his frustration. But then, I decided that such blatantly falsified accounts concerning me should not go unexposed. Besides, my book really needed some comic relief!

Let me now go back to the main theme of this chapter. The most important lesson to emerge from this incident of controlling a violent crowd and the use of firearms is the reiteration of the golden rule: "It is the senior-most police officer on the spot who has to decide on the action to be taken," be it a lathi charge, the use of tear gas, or, as a last resort, firing. It necessarily follows that it is the same officer who has to take credit or blame for his action.

Before the days of HF and VHF communication, and much before the days of the ubiquitous cell phone, this principle worked well, and the officer on the spot, irrespective of whether he was an SP, DSP, Inspector, Sub-Inspector, or even a Head Constable, acted on his own to deal with any situation. He did not consult his superior officer when a situation developed unexpectedly; nor did he have the means to get in touch with him. I have known SIs and even HCs acting on their own to control situations arising in their respective jurisdictions. All they did after the incident was send a telegram to the superior officer concerned. Their initiative was always recognised and rewarded as long as they had acted in good faith. But now, with the availability of a mobile phone for everyone, officers on the spot can consult their superior officer(s) without losing valuable time. In a city setup, the superior officer is also in a position to rush over to the trouble spot to take control of the situation. But there have been several cases of senior officers talking to those on the spot over the phone instead of rushing over to the area of conflict. Such conduct is unbecoming of senior officers like Commissioners, Deputy Commissioners, and Superintendents of Police. In districts that have now shrunk in size and strength, the SP or the ADSP can and should proceed to the spot immediately, thereby taking control of the situation.

I still remember my visit as ASP Tuticorin to Koppampatti outpost attached to Ettayapuram Police Station. There was no motorable road to the village. When I reached the OP, a surprise awaited me. The sentry constable told me that the OP Head Constable had gone to the nearest P&T office to inform the SP and me that he had shot dead a rowdy who was attempting to attack him with a machete. The HC had left the body under the care of the villagers and proceeded to the nearest town that had the facility of a phone, as there was no telegraph office or post office within a 10 km radius of the village. He did exactly what should be done. In appreciation, I sanctioned a substantial reward for him.

Law-and-order situations like flash floods, tsunamis, major fire mishaps, or road, rail, and air accidents call for immediate action. Success depends on the ability of the officer on the spot to assess the situation correctly and act promptly. Many a situation is allowed to drift and deteriorate when the officer hesitates. This hesitation is often due to the officer's fear of the enquiry, judicial or magisterial, that necessarily follows every police firing, death due to police action, or death in police custody. But very rarely does the Commission of Enquiry find fault with the police action, provided, of course, the officer had taken action in good faith and had followed the principles of riot control faithfully. These principles, well-established by past experience and legal acceptance, are:

a. Resorting to firing only when all other methods of crowd control have failed.

b. Controlled and restricted firing, taking care not to hit bystanders and onlookers and directing the shots only towards the ringleaders or the most menacing part of the mob.

c. Studying the effect on the mob after each shot and stopping the firing the moment the crowd shows signs of dispersal.

Once the firing is over, it is the bounden duty of the police to take care of all the injured, give them first aid, and rush them to the nearest hospital. The Hunter Commission that enquired into the Jallianwala Bagh massacre in 1919 found fault with Brigadier Dyer mainly on two counts. First, for not giving adequate and specific warning to the people assembled in the place to disperse, although they were there in defiance of the prohibitory orders in force; and then, leaving the place soon after the firing without tending to the injured, many of whom might have survived had they been rushed to hospital.

Another question that readers of this book may ask is why an officer would personally handle the firearm instead of directing a constable of the Armed Squad to do it. No doubt, it is a valid question. I could definitely have directed the best shot in the squad to get the leader of the mob. That way, I could have studied the effect of the shot and decided on the need or not for further action. But in every one of the instances of firing in which I was involved, no trained marksman was available—one who could be depended on to shoot none but the leader of the mob. Firing by untrained policemen could result in general members of the mob or even casual bystanders being hit. Besides, it is not always feasible to take seasoned shooters like members of the police shooting team to every venue of mob violence, as mob violence could erupt unexpectedly. Shooting down anyone other than the main rioter is an unforgivable sin. I was the champion police marksman in the state. As such, I had always been confident in my ability; confident in hitting the right target—the leader of the mob.

I have faced several judicial and magisterial enquiries right from my early days in the department and even after my retirement, when I was recalled to lead the Veerappan operation. Not once had any Commission disagreed with my decisions, or with the way in which I handled situations. Perhaps I was lucky to have had the experience early in my career and thereby to have learnt the lessons relevant to the use of firearms to control mob violence. I will be only too happy if my experiences, narrated in the pages of this book, serve as a lesson to the present and future generations of police officers and convince them that the most important principle of police leadership is to take full responsibility when they are cast in the role of "Officer on the Spot."

Debauchery Personified - Depraved Abortionist

Perverts are those whom avoid you must,
Those lecherous ones o'ertaken by lust.
Flex your muscles, deal them a blow
'Tis then to behave themselves, they'll know
If you can't manage that, don't stop; just run
Take every precaution under the sun.

The main responsibilities of a DC (L&O) are the maintenance of law-and-order and the prevention of crime in his jurisdiction. However, during my tenure as DC (L&O) South, there were a few investigations of out-of-the-ordinary cases that helped relieve the tedium of my day-to-day law-and-order duties. One such case earned me the appreciation of the Government and that of the Inspector General of Police.

"A golden opportunity for women
who have missed their period
Full success guaranteed"

No passenger on the electric trains could have missed this advertisement displayed in bold letters at every railway station on the Beach-Tambaram stretch. The advertisement also carried the address of a Maternity Home in Saidapet, Madras.

To the everyday commuter, this advertisement would have seemed to offer treatment for pre-natal maladies. But to the unfortunate few who carried with them either the shame or the burden of an unwanted pregnancy, the hidden meaning was clear. With their drooping spirits revived by the ray of hope offered by that advertisement, they made their way to the clinic in Saidapet.

Once there, the patient would be ushered into an inner room marked 'Private.' The doctor, introducing himself as Dr. K.V. Subramaniam, would reel out his record of more than 5,000 abortions in the course of 12 years, with never a failure. If the visitor seemed unconvinced, the doctor would draw aside a screen to reveal rows of glass jars containing foetuses in various stages of development.

The patient would then be admitted. Fees depended not on the stage of the pregnancy but on the ability of the patient to pay. As soon as the relatives accompanying the girl, greatly impressed by the confidence and magnanimity of the doctor, had left, the doctor would order his female assistants to get the room ready and wheel the patient in. The assistants would then shut the door, leaving the patient with the doctor.

The doctor would commence his examination with an assurance of a painless and easy abortion. Any relief that the patient might have felt at this assurance would be rudely shaken when the doctor put forth his price for secrecy. No amount of pleading or threats would move the doctor, who would go on to violate the unfortunate woman. No doubt, some of them might have offered resistance; most others resigned themselves to their fate. The doctor, however, kept his part of the deal to terminate the pregnancy or to kill and dispose of the body of the baby should it be taken out alive.

It was his employing Nirmala Devi as his new receptionist in December 1976 that proved the depraved doctor's undoing. The new receptionist not only fought off the advances of the abortionist but also managed, without arousing his suspicion, to meet me in my office and apprise me of the harrowing goings-on in the clinic.

According to her, the doctor was conducting 2 or 3 abortions every day. If the fetus was taken out dead, it was preserved in a glass jar as proof of the efficacy of his method; if the baby was born alive as a result of induced labour, it was left to die, and the body was either buried in the garden or cut into small pieces and thrown into the drain.

I was quite convinced that the doctor was not only an abortionist but also a rapist and murderer, and above all, a serious menace to society. I was also aware of the difficulty in getting sufficient evidence to trap him. I felt sure that none of his patients, even if they could be traced, nor his assistants would be willing to depose. The evidence of the receptionist alone, without proper corroboration, would be of little use.

The only alternative was to catch him in flagrante delicto. The receptionist was only too willing to help. She decided to take the doctor's chief assistant into her confidence and to inform me of the planned delivery of any baby in the clinic, either by induced labour or any other method. She also gallantly agreed to stay on in the clinic, unmindful of the ever-present threat that she herself was facing.

Meanwhile, I made discreet enquiries about the doctor. He was K.V. Subramaniam, aged 45. He was not a doctor at all but a government livestock assistant who had got a postal diploma in Homeopathy. He had then set up private practice in several parts of the state. He had also developed a method of induced labour which ensured a very high percentage of success. Oblivious to the fact that the net was closing in on him, the livestock assistant-turned-doctor was merrily carrying on with his nefarious activity.

On 5.1.1977, he admitted into his clinic Rani, an unmarried girl in her eighth month of pregnancy. He had agreed to terminate her pregnancy for a fee of Rs.300/-. At about 5.30 a.m. on 7.1.1977, Rani gave birth to a male child as a result of induced labour. Subramaniam, who conducted the delivery, placed the child in a basin and took it away from the mother. The child cried till it fell silent by evening. Fortunately, the mother, who had been confined in a closed room, was in a dazed condition and could not hear the plaintive cry of her child; but it was to haunt Nirmala Devi and her colleagues for days to come.

Subramaniam buried the child in the garden the following morning. It was only on the 9th that Nirmala Devi could slip out of the clinic and inform me of the infanticide that had taken place on the 7th. I immediately raided the clinic and, on the statement of the receptionist, registered a case. Subramaniam was arrested later that evening. 119 glass jars containing more than 750 foetuses ranging in age from 4 weeks to 7 months and bottles of the medicine prepared and used by the abortionist were seized; also, the placenta of the baby born on the 7th, which was still in the basin.

The body of the baby was exhumed from the garden by the II Class Executive Magistrate. During the inquest, the Magistrate examined the mother of the infant and the doctor's four female assistants. All of them spoke of the role played by the abortionist in inducing labour, delivering the child, and killing it.

Dr. Janaki, the Additional Professor of Forensic Medicine at Madras Medical College who conducted the autopsy, opined that the body was that of a live-born viable male child with a 28-week intra-uterine development and that death was possibly due to the failure of the doctor to take proper care of the baby. She also found evidence of recent delivery in Rani.

The investigation of the case was taken up by the Assistant Commissioner of Police V.N. Srinivasan and Inspector of Police M. Venkatachalam. After completing the investigation, Subramaniam was charged under sections 312, 318, and 302 of the IPC, along with Section 6 read with Section 3 of the Indian Medical Degrees Act.

The accused pleaded not guilty and was defended by three leading advocates. However, the prosecution was ably conducted by P.M. Sundaram, the City Public Prosecutor. The evidence of the baby's mother, the lady doctor, the women assistants, and the investigating staff was sufficient to prove the charges under sections 312 and 318 of the IPC. The evidence of whether the child was born dead or alive was most vital to bring home the charge of murder. Dr. Janaki explained in great detail the tests she had conducted to determine this. Her microscopic examination of the baby's lungs had shown definite signs of respiration. The pieces of the lung, when dropped in water, floated, confirming the presence of respirated air. The doctor's deliberate omissions resulting in the baby's death were amply proved by the evidence of the witnesses.

S.T. Ramalingam, the Additional Sessions Judge who tried the case, found the accused guilty of voluntarily causing the pregnant Rani to miscarry and concealing the birth of the child by secretly killing and burying it. While pronouncing the judgement, the judge referred to the moral depravity of the accused in blackmailing and seducing his unfortunate patients and women employees and sentenced him to 5 years Rigorous Imprisonment under Section 312 IPC, 1 year R.I. under Section 318 IPC, and life imprisonment under Section 302 IPC. We could not but admire and be ever thankful to the receptionist Nirmala Devi for her sense of moral responsibility and the courage with which she came forward to expose the dark happenings in the so-called 'clinic' of a so-called 'doctor.'

Operation Ajanta

When Naxalites took over Tirupattur town,
The place was just dead and dark by sun-down.
Landlords, money lenders, all lived in great dread
As they were the targets of the Banner of Red.

It is the 6th of August 2022. More than three thousand people have come together at the Memorial in the compound of Tirupattur Town Police Station. Members of the public constitute more than three-fourths of the gathering. They are from all political parties, all castes and communities, and various strata of society. Among them are the Collector of Tirupattur district, DIG Annie Vijaya and SP Balakrishnan of Tirupattur, district SPs of Ranipet, Tiruvannamalai, and Vellore, and more than 350 retired officers from all over the state and, more importantly, the relatives of the martyrs of the bomb attack that had killed an Inspector and two constables 42 years earlier. Also present are 4 MLAs, two ex-MLAs, the Chairman and Councillors of Tirupattur Municipality, Presidents of several Panchayats, and Chairmen of a few Panchayat Unions from Tirupattur and Dharmapuri districts, heads of the local colleges and schools, all senior Government servants stationed in Tirupattur, representatives of the Wakf Board, Churches, and Temples, and members of the press and the visual media. Among them are relatives of those who had been killed by the Naxalites and those who had survived murderous attacks and who still bear marks of injuries sustained at that time.

I arrive as the clock strikes eight and take up my position at the head of the assembly. The solemn proceedings begin with the Police Guard presenting arms. The Guards then load their rifles and fire 3 volleys into the air. As they lower their rifles, I step forward, lay a wreath at the base of the memorial, and salute. I am followed by the others, special guests, senior government servants, Police Officers, members of the public, and relatives of the dead. More than a hundred wreaths are placed in homage. The guard presents arms once more. All of us bow our heads and observe a two-minute silence. I read out the 'Commemoration Message.' The buglers sound the 'Last Post' in memory of the heroic dead. The guard marches off and the function comes to a close.

The entire congregation then partakes in the breakfast arranged by the Tirupattur Police. They exchange memories of those horrendous days in the seventies and eighties and express their sympathy to the wives and children of policemen who, even today, are being killed by the Naxalites in ever-increasing numbers in other parts of India. The gathering disperses, promising to meet again at the same place, at the same time, the following year. As I leave the hallowed ground, I once again read the words engraved on the memorial pillar:

"In memory of Inspector Palanisamy and Police Constables Murugesan and Yesudas, who were killed in a Naxalite bomb attack in Tirupattur on the 6th of August 1980."

Forty-two years have gone by since their martyrdom. The memorial was consecrated on 6th August 1981, the first anniversary. The first Commemoration Parade was attended by all the police personnel who had volunteered for the daunting and perilous task, the members of the local police force, and members of the public who had come forward to assist the police, unmindful of Naxalite vengeance. Since then, this ceremony has been conducted every year without fail. I am here for the 42nd time, 26 years since my retirement. It is the same with the members of the initial team of officers and men, but sadly, their number is gradually coming down due to age-related disability or death. However, the gratitude and enthusiasm of the succeeding generations of policemen and civilians more than make up for the dwindling numbers. Today, only five of us who were part of the original team, including me, are alive: SP Ashok Kumar, Inspector Vajram, and SIs Dhandapand and Elango.

With Thukiandi, who was with me during the Naxalite operation and who built the memorial. Unfortunately, we could not conduct the parade in the same solemn manner in 2020 due to COVID restrictions. It had to be conducted with only a few officers in attendance. But thanks to modern technology, all those who could not be there were able to be part of the function via a virtual platform. Once again, the pandemic played spoilsport at the 41st anniversary, and many of us who could not attend had to resort to video conferencing. As I watched those laying the wreaths, I was amazed by the vast increase in the number of both relatives of the martyrs and members of the public.

Late Inspector Palaniswamy's brother, Eswaran, who had recently retired as DC-AR, his sister Gomathi, who had also retired as Administrative Officer of the DPO, Tirupur, his older daughter Yuvarani, who was 10 years old at the time of her father's death, and Ajantha, who was just 6, were present. Also at the parade were Eswaran's son, Dr. Kaushik, his wife, Dr. Yogeswari, and Palaniswamy's younger sister, Kamala, her husband, and son; in fact, the entire family was there except for Palaniswamy's widow, Philomina Lotus, who was too ill to travel. It was touching to watch each member of Palaniswamy's family walking up to the monument with a wreath in hand. But when Ajantha took her turn, all I saw in my mind's eye was a six-year-old sobbing as the lid of the coffin was closed on her father.

Going back to 1967, the Naxal movement started in the Naxalbari Taluk of Darjeeling district in West Bengal, in the form of a peasant uprising organised by the disillusioned Marxist leaders Charu Majumdar, Kanu Sanyal, and Jangal Santhal. They decided that the traditional Communist Parties were not revolutionary or aggressive enough to protect the poor, the landless peasants, and the bonded labourers from oppressive landlords, unsympathetic tea-estate owners, and usurious money lenders. The fire that was ignited in Naxalbari found its way to Andhra Pradesh with alarming speed and added intensity. In Andhra Pradesh, the movement took strong roots in the backward and underdeveloped Telangana region and in the neglected tribal areas of Srikakulam district. The co-founder of the organisation, Charu Majumdar, then undertook a journey further South and set up an underground indoctrination centre at Hognekal. It was from here that Naxalism found its way into Tamil Nadu, Karnataka, and Kerala. L. Appu, Nanchil Selvam, Koval Easwaran, A. M. Kothandaraman, Pulavar Kaliaperumal, P. V. Srinivasan, Tamilvanan, and Kannamani were some of the idealists who were inducted into the organisation by Charu Majumdar.

The very first Naxalite attack in Tamil Nadu took place in 1968 in Nellithurai village near Mettupalayam in Coimbatore district. The person whom Naxalite leader Appu had chosen for annihilation was Krishnasamy Gounder, a wealthy landlord. He was attacked by Appu and his 11 recruits and left for dead. He survived the attack but lost all his jewellery, money, land documents, and a licensed double-barrel gun. More than jewels and money, it was firearms that the attackers were keen on acquiring to build up their own armoury. The first successful elimination by the Naxalites of a so-called "class enemy" also took place in Coimbatore district. The literature found near the body of the murdered farmer, Ramasamy

Gounder of Manpatty village in Udumalpet Taluk, confirmed the Naxal hand behind the murder. In both cases, all the accused, except the leader Appu, were apprehended and prosecuted. But no serious thought was given to the onset of this new phenomenon because murders due to land disputes were not uncommon in this district.

The Naxalites in Kerala opened their account in a spectacular manner. Veteran Communist leader Kunnikal Narayanan and his fiery daughter Ajitha carried out a daring attack on Pulpally Police Station in the hilly Wayanad district, killing a head constable, injuring another, and making off with all of the station's weapons as well as a police wireless set. The attackers left the station shouting Naxalite slogans and leaving behind Naxalite literature. This was in the year 1968. At that time, I was the Superintendent of Police in the neighbouring Nilgiris district of Tamil Nadu, and led a search party for the killers into the jungles bordering the two states. I took the opportunity to alert the tribals and the settlers from the plains about the emergence of the new danger and requested their help in watching out for the movement of strangers in and around their settlements. However, at that time, not much attention was paid in these 2 states to the emergence of this new threat to public safety and to the lives of policemen. The police in both states were totally unaware of the indoctrination classes conducted by Charu Majumdar in Hogenakal the previous year, which had brought the movement from distant West Bengal right to our doorstep. In Kerala, however, the movement died a natural death when the educated and unemployed youth found employment opportunities in the Middle East. Soon, the very same people who were opposed to private property returned home as petty capitalists. Houses began to replace huts, and those once unemployed were now in a position to give employment to others. The exodus to the Middle East and the newfound prosperity tolled the death knell of extremism in Kerala. Of course, the Kerala police force also played its part in putting down Naxalism.

I did not have to wait much longer to deal with the Naxalite problem myself. Within a year of the Pulpally police station attack in Wayanad district, bordering The Nilgiris, I was posted as Superintendent of Police, Thanjavur district, a Communist stronghold where Kisan unrest was at its peak. Even from the early sixties, a regular war on wages had been raging between the Caste Hindu landlords and the landless Harijan agricultural workers. It was no surprise, then, that it was in Thanjavur district that the most sensational Naxalite murder took place. On 21st September 1970, Muthu Thangappa, the Chairman of the Tiruvonam Panchayat Union, who happened to be a leading landlord of the area, was hacked to death in his paddy field. A Naxalite notice was found on his body. The police search parties apprehended one of the executioners who, unable to keep up with his fleeing associates, had been hiding under a culvert not far from the scene of the murder. He was Thyagarajan, a young graduate and a highly motivated Naxalite, weak in body but strong of will. He and his 6 colleagues had zeroed in on the Chairman because of his exploitation of agricultural workers and his penchant for taking liberties with the female farmhands. They openly gave all these details in court during their trial and declined to defend themselves, saying they had no faith in the legal system of the capitalist country. This used to be the standard practice of all accused Naxalites of those early days. They would shout slogans against the Constitution and declare that they did not consider it wrong to enforce social justice by eliminating class enemies. Thyagarajan and his colleagues were sentenced to life imprisonment.

A classic example of such defiance was that of one of the original Naxalites, Pulavar Kaliaperumal of Pennadam, in South Arcot district. Under his leadership, a landlord was killed in Srimushnam in December 1970, along with a so-called "police informer" in Sundaracholapuram and another landlord in Kodalikaruppur. Meanwhile, the bodies of three engineering students from Annamalai University were recovered from a paddy field. They had been killed by an accidental blast while they, at the instance of Kaliaperumal, were experimenting with a chemical bomb. When the police finally caught up with Kaliaperumal, they found to their surprise that most of his associates were his relatives: his brother Masilamani, his sister-in-law and former MLA Anandanayaki, his sons Valluvan and Nambiar, and two nephews. All of them were arraigned in three ritualistic murders and for the death of the engineering students. They refused to contest the cases and were sentenced to multiple life terms.

By 1973, the Naxalite movement had fizzled out, leaving no trace in the pioneering districts of Coimbatore, Thanjavur, and South Arcot, with their leaders safely behind bars, serving life terms. But it was by no means the end of Naxalism. It reared its head again in the backward and poor districts of Dharmapuri and North Arcot. By 1974, the Hogenekal coterie of Tamilvanan, Ramanan, Kodhandaraman, Sivalingam, and Seeralan had managed to convert a large number of unemployed youth from the impoverished and underdeveloped areas of both districts. They also created an excellent underground network extending across both sides of the district border, covering the Dharmapuri, Krishnagiri, and Burgur taluks of Dharmapuri district and the Tirupattur and Vaniyambadi taluks of North Arcot district.

The murder of landlord Palanichamy Gounder of Naickenkottai village (1973), as well as those of moneylenders Dharmalingam Chettiar of Nagarasampatti (1973), Perianna Chettiyar of Nallampalli (1974), and Appachamy Chettiar of Athipallam (1976), all in Dharmapuri district, were typical operations personally led by Tamilvanan. The pattern was the same in all of these execution-type murders. The Naxalites entered the village selected for their operation in the dead of night, woke up all the villagers, and assembled them in the village square. They then dragged the person marked for 'trial' by the 'people's court' from his house and commenced 'judicial' proceedings. The details of the exorbitant interest he had been collecting from the villagers, the confiscation of land in lieu of unpaid interest, and the fraudulent transfer of documents and properties to his name were read out. The impounded documents were returned to the rightful owners. If the intended target happened to be a landlord, details of his exploitation of the landless workers were read out. In some cases, the affected villagers were also made to testify against him. The verdict of the "People's court" was then read out. The exploiter of the poor was declared a "class enemy" and was executed in full view of all the villagers. The executioners then left the village as nonchalantly as they had entered it. The villagers withheld vital information from the police, either out of gratitude to or fear of the Naxalites. There was, however, little or no sympathy for the victims. It is also relevant to note that the very first execution was announced over a Chinese radio channel under the heading "Red Star over Naickenkottai."

The Naxalites then turned their attention to villagers, especially village officials, who helped the police with much-needed information about their whereabouts. These individuals were branded "police stooges" and eliminated brutally. Although the local police and, in some cases, the Crime Branch CID were able to make a few arrests, the top leaders remained at large. They continued their recruitment drive and brought more unemployed youth and poorly paid workers under their control.

By 1976, the Naxalites had extended their terror network over large areas of both North Arcot and Dharmapuri districts. Classes on Naxalite philosophy were conducted by Tamilvanan and Sivalingam, a dismissed railway worker from Jolarpet. In addition to the selective elimination of class enemies and police informants, the Naxalites took up local issues affecting the landless and instigated agitations for higher wages. The prevailing economic condition in the affected taluks was ideal for the growth of Naxalism. The total absence of industries, the prevalence of extremely low wages for agricultural workers, and the general backward nature of the area greatly facilitated the Naxalite drive for recruitment. Unlike in Thanjavur district, where the "Minimum Wages Act" had already come into force, the field workers in Tirupattur and Burgur Taluks were being paid only 2 or 3 rupees for a day's labour. This drove many of them to the nearby hills to fell trees to sell on the plains. The government's efforts to counter this, to save the fast-disappearing forests covering the Jawadhu, Yelagiri, and Madhakadappa hills, further alienated the villagers from the government agencies, especially the Forest Department; this, in turn, drove them into the Naxalite fold.

The Naxalite leaders lost no time in drawing the affected villagers further away from the Government and the existing social order. By the end of 1979 and the beginning of 1980, the law-and-order situation had deteriorated. The Naxalites, instead of moving stealthily in threes and fours, were beginning to resemble small armies on the move. On 14th January 1980, as many as 30 of them, under "Nondi" Palani, invaded Madavalam village and threw bombs at a textile shop, killing one person and seriously injuring many others. On 16th May 1980, about 35 Naxalites led by Sivalingam marched into Ponneri village near Jolarpet, and while the villagers froze in fear, killed landlord Kesava Reddiar, his wife, and their 1½-year-old granddaughter. The fact that he was a well-connected and wealthy landlord made him a perfect target for the Naxalites. The days of Naxalites stealing into the villages at night had given way to their entering them in broad daylight, openly flaunting their identity.

The infiltration of criminal elements, rowdies, wagon-lifters, petty thieves, and illicit distillers into the ranks of the Naxalites added yet another dimension to their outlook and activities. The movement that started with the high idealism of equality was fast turning into a crime mafia, with its new members settling personal scores and indulging in the intimidation and forcible collection of protection money from merchants, shopkeepers, and agriculturists.

Unable to bear the atrocities of the extremists, the villagers started organising themselves into village resistance groups, their members taking turns at guarding their crops, cattle, and houses on a voluntary basis, and helping the police with information on the movement of the Naxalites. This led to the Naxalites targeting the leaders of such resistance groups. Vellaya Gounder of Pochampalli in Dharmapuri district, who headed one such group, was murdered on 19th May 1980 while he was waiting to board a bus. A note, signed by Naxalites Jeevagan, Karnel, Panneerselvam, and Ramalingam, was left at the site warning of a similar fate to anyone who worked against the Naxalites. Five other leaders of similar resistance groups were murdered in quick succession in the Tirupattur Taluk of North Arcot district. That spelled the end of the village vigilance organisations. Villagers were even afraid to talk to policemen because anyone suspected of helping the police with information was killed.

The Naxalites also started attacking solitary policemen on village visits and those on beat duties. People's representatives were also marked for elimination. Anbalagan, the ruling AIADMK MLA of Natrampalli, Annamalai Gounder, the DMK Chairman of Tirupattur Municipality, and Govindasamy Naiker, a leading member of the DMK and the President of Kakkanampalayam Panchayat, narrowly survived murder attempts. A leading money lender of Pachur village on the Andhra Pradesh border survived 2 attempts on his life.

In the first half of 1980, more than two hundred cases of murders, attempted murders, dacoity, robbery, and destruction of property were reported in the two districts. Panic and a sense of helplessness pervaded the entire countryside. Streets were deserted after dusk. Business establishments downed shutters. Public transport went off the road. People shut themselves up behind closed doors. Attendance in schools dropped drastically. Life came to a standstill in Tirupattur and Thiruvannamalai taluks of North Arcot District and almost the whole of Dharmapuri district.

It was then that I was posted as Deputy Inspector General of Police, Vellore Range, with jurisdiction over the two Naxalite-affected districts and over Salem district, which had a large tribal population and several hill features, both factors favourable to the spread of Naxalism.

Devaram – Rendu Varam (2 Weeks)

'Devaram – Rendu Varam', the posters all screamed,
The menace to blot out, not easy, it seemed;
The odds were against us, but determined were we
To wipe out the menace and from fear, set folks free;
To scare us away the Naxalites tried;
But we held on fast till that grim movement died.

The immediate reaction of the Naxalites to the Anti-Naxalite operation in the year 1981 was to put out the warning, 'Devaram – Rendu Varam (2 weeks),' in several places in the town and villages, and most strikingly outside the government guest houses in Tirupathur, Dharmapuri, and Yelagiri, where I used to stop over between search operations. They even exploded a bomb by way of warning outside the guest house in Athiyamankottai, damaging one of its walls. I was, at that time, away on a raid, but Prema was there by herself.

Before I took charge of the Range, I was called to Madras by Mohandas, Deputy Inspector General of Police, CID, Intelligence, and briefed on the priorities and objectives as envisaged by Chief Minister MGR. The task was clear: eradicate the Naxalite movement in Tamil Nadu, and more specifically from the Tirupattur-Dharmapuri areas, where it had grown to alarming proportions since 1973. A special wing of the CID called the "Q" Branch was created to collect "Naxalite" intelligence. ADSP Jagannathan, a bold and resourceful officer, was posted to Tirupattur on Naxalite special duty, and Shanmuganathan, another capable officer, was posted to Tirupattur as its DSP. S. Kumarasamy, SP, "Q" Branch, also set up his temporary headquarters in Tirupattur. Ramalingam, SP, North Arcot district, and K.G. Paulraj, SP, Dharmapuri district, were the other core members of the team that set out to deal with the Naxalite problem and to end it once and for all. I had the twin tasks of motivating the police force and restoring confidence in the minds of the public. My visit to Tirupattur town, which I had known so well as SP, North Arcot district, in the years 1975-76, gave me a rude shock. It presented the look of a ghost town. Even citizens who knew me well did not want to be seen with me or with any other police officer. Such was the hold the Naxalites had over that key town. It was the same in the villages around.

The situation on the ground was very discouraging. The police force stood demoralised due to their inability to contain the marauding Naxalites. Policemen were afraid to go about their routine duties of patrolling, village visits, petition enquiry, and serving summons, because they were easy targets. The villagers were too scared to give us information about the Naxalites, their clandestine meetings, and recruitment drives in the villages.

The murder of one of the leaders of the village resistance group, instead of dampening the spirit of the police, acted as an impetus for action. I asked for volunteers from among the subordinate staff for the special drive to be launched against the extremists. Several of them volunteered and were posted to the most sensitive and dangerous stations. Foremost among them were Inspectors Palanisamy, Purushothaman, Sivaguru, Vellaiya Gounder, and Palani Batcha, and SIs Ashok Kumar, Sudhakaran, Panneerselvam, and Mahendran. They, in turn, brought with them Head Constables and Constables of proven courage and dedication. They were sent out in twos and threes to collect intelligence. Columns of armed patrols were marched to the affected villages, each under a senior officer, both to show our determination to tackle the problem and to gain the confidence of the villagers. I visited 10 to 15 villages at the head of a column every day to get to know the villagers and the problems they faced. With both the police and the Naxalites redoubling their efforts, a showdown seemed imminent.

Of the number of police parties sent on the trail of the killers, the one led by Inspector Palanisamy stumbled upon one of the nocturnal meeting places of the Naxalites at the foothills of Yelagiri. Leaving the car 2 km away, he and the four constables with him crept silently up to the Naxalite rendezvous and surprised three underground Naxalites: Perumal, Rajappa, and Selvan. Suspecting that they were waiting for the arrival of their leader Sivalingam, he handcuffed them after searching them for hidden weapons and sent them to the car with two of the four constables. With the remaining 2 constables, he waited in ambush, which leaders Sivalingam and Chinnathambi walked into around midnight.

For the journey back to Tirupattur, 15 km away, Sivalingam and Chinnathambi were made to sit in the back seat of the car, guarded by two constables of the Tamil Nadu Special Police. The other 3 Naxalites were made to sit in the leg-space of the front seat, occupied by the Inspector, constables Yesudoss and Murugesan of the Tamil Nadu Special Police, and the driver of the car. In their anxiety to reach the police station at the earliest, they seemed to have not subjected the arrested men to a thorough body search. When the car was nearing the Tirupattur Town Police station, one of them, who had kept a country bomb hidden in his underclothes, took it out and tossed it into the front seat, resulting in a devastating blast. It killed all three seated on the floor of the car and two constables, besides causing severe injuries to Inspector Palanisamy. In the ensuing confusion, Sivalingam and Chinnathambi made good their escape. The Inspector died on the way to the hospital, bringing the total number of dead to three police personnel and three Naxalites. The Inspector's funeral in Vellore was attended by Chief Minister MGR, DGP TTP Abdullah, and IGP (L&O) Pon Paramaguru.

The death of the Inspector and two Constables turned out to be a blessing in disguise. Instead of demoralising the police and the already terrified members of the public, it ushered in an era of enormous police-public understanding, goodwill, and cooperation. It also intensified my resolve to stamp out the menace once and for all. It was out of this determination that "Operation Ajantha," named after the 6-year-old daughter of the slain Inspector Palanisamy, was launched. In the difficult days that followed, whenever failures and frustration threatened to sap my energy and zeal, I pictured the little girl crying next to her father's lifeless body, and that gave me the strength to go on.

As a first step towards the launch of "Operation Ajantha," Prema and I moved into the PWD Guest House adjoining the Tirupattur Railway Station. I was buoyed with renewed vigour and resolve to put an end to the Naxalite problem, and Prema, armed with her "Que Sera, Sera; what will be, will be" attitude, crossword books, needlework kit, and her love of trains, of which there was no dearth on the platforms of Tirupattur station. It was here that Prema spent many a day and sleepless night, alone with her thoughts and anxieties. At times, when the raids were centred around Dharmapuri, we moved into the Travellers Bungalow (or TB in government jargon) in Dharmapuri. It was while we were camping there on one occasion that the Naxalites exploded a bomb close to the building. The Naxalites had even pasted on the rear walls of our Tirupattur abode warning notices in Tamil which read (in Tamil) "Thevaram two Varam." They were generous enough to give me 2 weeks of life. Through all of this, I refused to be unnerved. In fact, it fired my determination even more to rid the district of the menace.

The 3 months that followed were strenuous and full of hardship. Each one of us covered 25 to 30 km on foot each day. I was able to visit all the villages in the affected parts of the two districts and also the numerous tribal settlements located in the mountains and hill ranges of the Eastern Ghats, enabling us to expose several training camps and indoctrination centres of the Naxalites. In terms of arrests of wanted extremists, it was a very rewarding period. Although I could not set a deadline for the liquidation of the Naxalites, I was determined to complete the operation within 6 months.

In the very first raid in the Yelagiri Hills, 18 wanted Naxalites and 12 of their collaborators were arrested from their secret camp. Three days later, 22 Naxalites were arrested from their stronghold in Naickenkottai village in Dharmapuri district. At Kaveripattinam in the same district, 17 of the 23 extremists who were wanted in a dacoity case were picked up by Inspectors Sivaguru and Vellaiya Gounder. I shuttled between the two districts, often leading raids into the bordering villages in Andhra Pradesh in pursuit of wanted accused who had been given shelter there by their extremist counterparts. To facilitate my interaction with the border villagers, I had to learn Telugu.

On the 11th of October, Naxalites Subramanian and Shanmugam, who were wanted in several cases of annihilation, murders, and dacoities, were killed in a brief operation in Bommikuppam village. The very next day, Samraj and Krishnan, who were responsible for two murders and three dacoities, were killed in the Chandragiri hills, close to the Madras-Bangalore highway.

In Dharmapuri district, Balan, a graduate from Presidency College, Madras, and a close associate of Tamilvannan, was arrested after a violent confrontation. Balan sustained fractures in both his legs and was taken to Government Hospital, Dharmapuri, for treatment. When his condition turned serious, it was decided to shift him to Chennai. But he died en route. Other important arrests were those of Siddhanadan and Jeevagan, both of whom were wanted in many cases, including the murder of CPI leader Muruganand and the attempted murder of an SI of Police.

On the 12th of October, underground cadres Chinnadurai and Perumal were killed by the party led by DSP Shanmuganathan. The two Naxalites were wanted in more than 20 cases of murder and dacoity. Two days later, Jayapal, one of the Principal killers of Kesava Reddiar of Ponneri village, his wife, and their one-and-a-half-year-old granddaughter, was killed by the party led by ADSP Jaganathan. Another prominent leader, "Kurivikara" Kanagaraj, was accounted for by the 'Q' branch led by SP S. Kumarasamy.

When the Anti-Naxalite operation was in full swing and the Naxalite leaders were retreating deeper into underground shelters, the task force was confronted by a serious dampener. It came in the form of a fact-finding mission that descended upon the operational area on the 14th of October. It was headed by Claude Alvares of the "Committee of Civil Liberties and Human Rights." The members belonged to various Human Rights Organisations and included three women activists and a couple of journalists. The mission first visited Advocate P.V. Bhakthavatchalam in his house in Tirupattur. Bhakthavatchalam, the President of the People's Union of Civil Liberties (PUCL), along with his brother P.V. Ramanujam, supported the Naxalites both directly and indirectly. It turned out that he had prepared the itinerary of the mission in North Arcot and Dharmapuri districts; he had even booked their accommodation in a hotel in Tirupattur town.

Meanwhile, the citizens of Tirupattur, especially those who had suffered grievously at the hands of the extremists, got wind of the mission's plan to visit the relatives of the Naxalites who were either killed or arrested by the police over the previous 2 months. They were incensed that they had visited Bhakthavatsalam, who had been hampering police efforts by filing civil-rights-violation suits in various courts, including the Supreme Court of India and the Madras High Court. They assembled in front of the hotel where the members of the mission were staying and raised slogans against them. Fearing a clash between the public and the members of the fact-finding mission, Natesan, Inspector of Police, Tirupattur Town, proceeded to the lodge and tried to persuade the crowd to disperse. But the agitated crowd refused to leave until the mission gave up its plan and left the town. They also manhandled a few members of the mission, calling them 'Friends of the Naxalites.' I was informed of the situation while in Angur village, where a much-wanted Naxalite had been killed by the police that day. On my arrival at the lodge, I tried to pacify the people. But they would not relent, saying that the mission and the PUCL had not raised even a little finger to question the Naxalite atrocities against them over the past 4 years; therefore, they had no right to interfere with the police operation against the killers. By then, some of the agitators had entered the lodge through the rear entrance and roughed up a few members of the mission, causing injuries to Imran Qureshi of the Deccan Herald, Antonysamy, a journalist from Bombay, and local Advocate K.P. Ibrahim, who was representing P.V. Bhakthavatsalam.

By then, more policemen had arrived on the scene, and we succeeded in keeping the crowd away from the members of the mission. I went into the lodge and persuaded the leader, Claude Alvares, and Professor Brindavan Moses, who incidentally happened to be my classmate at Madras Christian College, to leave Tirupattur for their own safety. I also dissuaded them from visiting other places in the two districts. By then, they themselves realised that the people who had suffered badly at the hands of the Naxalites for so long would not tolerate their interference with the police operation. It was with great difficulty that I managed to get them away from the menacing crowd that had besieged the hotel and escort them to the Jolarpet Railway Station in police vehicles. Realising the mood of the long-suffering public, the mission never returned to the area of operation. Their meeting with the DIG, CID Mohandas, also did not help, and they went back to where they came from, leaving us to continue with the operation without interference. The day the mission left Tirupattur, MGR revealed to the press the shocking fact that the mission had pre-determined its 'finding' and that the government was in possession of a copy of its "report" even before the mission had reached Tirupattur.

The mission had grossly misjudged the mood of the people of Tirupattur, who had suffered the atrocities of the Naxalites for four long years. Almost every one of them who had laid siege to the lodge that day had either lost relatives or sustained personal loss in agriculture and business. Some of them had even had to abandon their farms and move to the comparative safety of Tirupattur town. 'Cho' Ramasamy, the celebrated Editor of the Tamil magazine 'Thughlak,' who was supposed to accompany the Fact-Finding Mission at Tirupattur, resigned from the PUCL because of its unqualified support for the activities of the Naxalites.

I have had more than my share of confrontations with civil rights activists but have come out unscathed every time. It is unfortunate that activists straightaway conclude that the police use high-handed and illegal methods and misuse their powers to harass innocent people during operations against extremists; the police, on their part, think human rights organisations are out to frustrate their efforts to track down members of banned outfits. My own thinking on this issue is that both groups are indispensable to society—the activists to rein in the enthusiasm of the police and keep them within legal bounds, and the police to protect society from extremists and terrorists. Both should function within their limits and be complementary to each other.

The interference by the mission and the frequent petitions filed in the Supreme Court of India and the Madras High Court by Advocates Bhakthavatsalam of Tamil Nadu and Kannapiran of Andhra Pradesh did not, in any way, affect our field operation. On the contrary, they inspired us to redouble our efforts to ferret out the remaining extremists so as to complete our mission at the earliest.

The team led by SI Ashok Kumar succeeded in following the trail of Kannamani, one of the original Naxalite leaders. Kannamani had played a leading role in all the 'eliminations,' starting with the killing of moneylender Dharmalingam Chettiyar of Nagarasampatty on 8th February 1973. After falling out with Tamilvanan, he formed his own group and committed a few more murders and dacoities. He also moved to a new shelter at the foothills of the Madakadappa Hills in Vaniyambadi Taluk. These hills formed the boundary between Tamil Nadu and Andhra Pradesh. There, he conducted indoctrination classes for a new crop of converts from the villages that lay between Vaniyambadi Town and the 4500-foot-high hill range. His followers also kept him informed of every police movement in the area. If the police moved near his shelter, he would slip away across the state border into Kuppam in Andhra Pradesh. He had successfully eluded the police for over 12 years since his first meeting with Charu Majumdar.

On 28th December 1980, we entered Andhra Pradesh in private vehicles, crossed the hill range on foot, and approached Kannamani's reported hideout from the opposite side. Deprived of information from his followers in the villages on the Tamil Nadu side of the border, he was taken by surprise. He was killed in the exchange of fire that followed. Incidentally, he was the first Naxalite in Tamil Nadu to use a firearm against the police instead of the usual country-made bombs. His death left his followers in total disarray, resulting in their large-scale surrender to the police over the next few days. The year-end saw the police gaining the upper hand in the fight against the Naxalites. In the 4 months following the martyrdom of the policemen, 18 hardcore Naxalites had been killed and two hundred and 31 arrested.

The year 1981 started with the death of "Iruttu" Pachaiappan, a "criminal in Naxalite clothing." He succeeded in shooting and injuring HC Vajram, who stormed into the hut where he was hiding before falling to the injured brave Head Constable's bullets. The HC soon recovered and rejoined the hunt within a month. He was awarded the 'Chief Minister's Medal for Gallantry,' which he richly deserved.

The recovery of pistols, revolvers, and other firearms in the armoury of the Naxalites was cause for grave concern. We realised that the weapons were finding their way far into the South through the "Red Corridor" originating on the border of West Bengal and Bihar with Nepal. This discovery urged us to speed up our efforts to complete the operation.

On the 23rd of August 1981, Inspector Purushothaman brought information that some Naxalites were sighted in the Naickaneri hills near

Ambur, well away from their usual field of operation. We immediately proceeded to the hills in two jeeps. I was in the first one along with the Inspector, SIs Ashok Kumar and Pannerselvam, and two constables. SI Sudhakaran and four constables travelled in the second jeep. We took the only motorable path into the hills. After traversing the hills and finding no trace of any human movement, we decided to turn around and return to Ambur by the same route. Around 3:45 a.m., while driving back, we found the road blocked by boulders. They had not been there when we had driven up. As soon as the jeep came to a halt, a shot rang out, hitting one of its headlights. As we jumped out of the jeep and took up positions on either side of the path, more shots rang out, one of them shattering the windscreen of the jeep. By then, the policemen travelling in the second jeep had alighted and moved to the flank, cutting off the retreat of the assailants. We kept shooting and advancing in the direction from which the shots were being fired, and country bombs hurled. The shooting died down after about half an hour, and we heard shuffling in the bushes; someone was escaping into the darkness. When we closed in on the clump of trees, we found 3 men with bullet injuries, two already dead and one lingering with a bullet injury in his abdomen. The Naxal, Saravanan, who was still alive, gave us the names of the other 2 as Anbu and Dhanapal before he died. We removed the bodies and recovered 2 shotguns, a Chinese pistol much more powerful than the pistols we carried, two more guns, a bag containing gunpowder and percussion caps, eight empty cartridges, five used, and three live bullets still in the chamber of the pistol.

All three dead were wanted for several murders, dating back to 1974, both in North Arcot and Dharmapuri districts. Of those who had escaped, two were believed to have been Sivalingam and 'Nondi' Palani who, along with Tamilvanan, Saminathan, and Sundaramoorthy, were the only Naxalite leaders yet to be apprehended. This turned out to be the last major encounter since the launch of 'Operation Ajantha' a year earlier.

With the Naickaneri hill encounter, 28 hardcore Naxalites had been killed and more than three hundred arrested. The main credit for the successful operation goes to the dedicated and fearless officers and men who joined 'Operation Ajantha' voluntarily with no expectation of any reward. They underwent untold suffering and faced constant threats to their lives and to the lives of their families. They never took a day off during the year-long operation and lived true to their vow to not rest until the last of the wanted Naxalites had been accounted for. Neither death threats nor prosecutions by the Human Rights Organisation could deter them. As many as 25 of them received the Tamil Nadu Chief Minister's medal for Gallantry, and five of us, the fearless Inspector Purushothaman, SIs Ashok Kumar, A. Panneerselvam, Sudhakaran, and I, received the Indian Police Medal for Gallantry. Never before in the history of Tamil Nadu Police were so many gallantry medals awarded to police personnel for a single field operation. When the Government restricted the number to only ten as per the G.O. on the subject, I took the matter up with the Chief Minister, who readily agreed with my reasoning that the G.O. was for normal times and extraordinary times called for extraordinary measures. He personally presented the medals to each of the 30 recipients.

The presentation of the Indian Police Medal for Gallantry to the five of us for the Naickaneri encounter was delayed because of the numerous cases of Human Rights Violation that had been filed against me and my counterpart, D.I.G D. Vyas of Andhra Pradesh. Both of us used to meet in the Supreme Court where the petitions filed by Advocate Kannapiran of Andhra Pradesh and Advocate Bhakthavatsalam of Tamil Nadu were being heard. Justice Bhagwati finally dismissed the petitions as unsustainable.

It is a well-known fact that Naxalites never forgive or forget; Vyas was killed by Naxalites on 27th January 1993 while on his morning constitutional in the JN stadium in Hyderabad. AIG Umesh Chandra of Hyderabad, SP Ajay Kumar Singh of Jharkhand, SP Surendra Babu of

Bihar, SP V K Chaubey of Chhattisgarh (along with 11 policemen), 24 CRPF men, and local police in Chhattisgarh were all victims of Naxalite retaliation. Incidentally, I too used to get warnings from central and state intelligence Units that I was also on the hit list of the Naxalites.

Thiru. W. I. DAVARAM, I.P.S. D. I.G.
Thiru. R. N. PURUSHOTHAMAN, INSPECTOR OF POLICE.
Thiru. K. N. SUDHAKARAN, S.I.
Thiru. S. PANNEERSELVAN, S.I.
Thiru. ASHOKKUMAR, S. I.

On the 23rd August, 1981, an information was received that a gang of armed anti-social elements responsible for various crimes was seen in the Nayakkaneri Hills, North Arcot district. Immediately Thiru-Walter Issac Davaram, Dy. Inspector-General of Police, with a Police Party consisting of one Inspector, three Sub-Inspectors, six Constables and two LNKs. proceeded to the spot. When the Police jeeps were about 3.5 kms. from Ambur Thiru. Davaram noticed that the road was blocked by boulders' Suspecting foul play, he directed the occupants to jump down and take cover. As soon as the Police Party stopped, the front of the jeep came under heavy gun fire. Due to pitch dark in the night, it was not possible to judge the gang's position and strength. However making use of the flashes from assailant's guns, he roughly assessed the position and directed Inspector R. N. Purushothaman and Sub-Inspectors S. Panneerselvam and K. N. Sudhakaran to take position and keep firing at the assailants to prevent their escape in the leftside of the ambush point. Followed by Sub-Inspector Ashokkumar, he himself took position on the right flank. In addition to firing, the assailants also hurled country made bombs from behind the barricade of boulders. The gun battle lasted for about half-an hour. The assailants, however escaped during the shoot-out leaving three of their dead colleagues behind. The police party was able to capture one foreign made semi-automatic pistol, one SBBL gun and one SBML gun, two other guns, several spent shells, a large quantity of gun powder and catridges.

In this encounter, Thiru. Walter Issac Davaram, Deputy Inspector General of Police, Shri R. N. Purushothaman, Inspector, Shri K.N. Sudhakaran, Sub-Inspector, Shri S. Paneerselvan, Sub-Inspector and Shri Ashokkumar, Sub-Inspector displayed conspicuous gallantry, courage, and devotion to duty of a high order.

1

230-3—2

The Way Forward - Rehabilitation

Often, over the last several years, governments of the affected states and heads of their police forces have sought my advice in dealing with the 'Maoists.' They have also asked me the inevitable question: "How did the Tamil Nadu Police tackle the problem successfully and put an end to it?" My answer, if not advice, to them is as follows:

i. Be ruthless in eliminating hardcore Maoists. They should be apprehended or killed. There should be no compromise, no truce, no talks, and no let-up in the drive.

ii. Be compassionate and considerate to the marginal ones, even if they were members of the banned organisation; rehabilitate them, give them employment or other means of honourable livelihood.

iii. Take up 'Area Development Work' in a big way in the form of industrialisation, co-operative farming, and distribution of generous loans, thereby bridging the gap between the rich and the poor, the landed and the landless, tribals and non-tribals.

iv. Enlist public support through vigilant groups, but never involve them in fighting the Naxalites as has been done in some states because members of such groups invariably abuse their powers and drive more people into the arms of the extremists.

I have based these guidelines on the remarkable success that the Tamil Nadu government and the Tamil Nadu Police have achieved not only in eradicating Naxalism in 1980-81 but also in putting it down every time it raised its head. Even during the very active phase of Operation Ajantha, we did our best to alleviate the sufferings of the poor. We ensured reasonable wages for the farmhands by talking to the landlords. We put an end to kangaroo courts and usurious money lenders who used to impose their will on the poor. Our efforts to find employment for unemployed youth met with reasonable success. During the operation, on my own initiative and at my own risk, I recruited 40 borderline Naxalites into the police force as constables and 43 more over the next 3 years. I am proud to say that all these so-called Naxalites, who had even attended indoctrination classes, are doing well in the department, with some of them having reached the rank of Inspector of Police. After all, unemployment of educated youth has been the main cause for the growth of Naxalism.

My letter to the government to expedite the implementation of the Area Development Programme estimated at Rs. 2.4 crores and to start agro-based industrial complexes in Tirupattur, Burgur, and Dharmapuri Taluks received a positive response. The government also accelerated the 'Food for Work' programme in the drought-affected villages and extended free-meal and free medical aid schemes to the inaccessible hamlets and tribal settlements in the hills.

The greatest lesson I learnt from the Anti-Naxalite operation was the need to narrow the gap between the tribals and villagers and the need for total public support. Realising that public support for the police operation cannot be demanded or taken for granted, we decided to conduct a Police-Tribal Sports and Cultural Meet in Jawadhu Hills, the core of the Naxalite operation.

The Jawadhu Hills occupy an area of 2500 sq. km in North Arcot district with a tribal population of about 50 thousand, spread out in 350 hamlets, most of them inaccessible. Jamunamaruthur, the most important village in the hills, is the social and cultural headquarters of the tribals. The meet, held on the 9th and 10th of January 1982, evoked considerable interest among the tribals, many of whom had trekked more than 40 km to be there. According to the elders, never before had there been such a large tribal gathering in the Jawadhu Hills.

The two-day meet was remarkable for the variety of events that were conducted. Apart from conventional events like athletics, football, and kabaddi, competitions were also held in traditional tribal sports. Archery turned out to be the most popular event. The forest school in Jamunamaruthur had already made a mark when B. Raman, a 14-year-old tribal boy, won a bronze medal in archery in the all-India Rural Sports Meet held in Amritsar in 1982. The credit for that achievement should go to Alagarsamy, the P.E.T. of the school where Raman was a student.

In almost all the endurance events, the tribals left their rivals from the plains and the policemen far behind. Every competitor completed the gruelling '20 km cross-country run' as well as the '10 km walk carrying a weight of 50 kg.' Even in tug-of-war, the tribal youth defeated the sub-divisional police team.

The tribal women took part in the tribal dance and music competitions. Their initial amazement on seeing the trouser-clad policewomen gradually gave way to friendly curiosity, and towards the close of the meet, they were on very cordial terms with their uniformed sisters.

The police had set up a large community kitchen for over 5000 people. Nothing could have brought the tribals closer to the police than partaking of a feast. The tribals also got to see the police in an altogether different light and openly came out with requests for roads, schools, hospitals, and financial aid for their agricultural projects. The policemen, on the other hand, realised that the policing requirements of the tribals were not the same as those of the people in the cities and towns. A number of talented youngsters were also spotted, and 15 of them were straightaway enlisted as constables. K. Vadivelu, SP North Arcot, and Letika Saran, JSP Tirupattur, were mainly responsible for the great success of the meet. It is no wonder then that Letika began to be referred to as "Jawadu Rani" by the tribals.

We followed it up by conducting several other meets in the tribal areas of North Arcot, Dharmapuri, Krishnagiri, and Salem districts. This was during my 5-year stint as DIG Vellore Range and Vadivelu's 4 ½ year stint as SP and Tukkiandi's 4-year tenure as ADSP North Arcot District.

I was not new to these hills. As SP, North Arcot district, I had lived with the policemen in an improvised hut in Melpet, the highest point in the hills, to construct a radio tower and a connecting road, a task which no PWD contractor was willing to take up because of the difficulties involved in transporting equipment by head loads. The construction work by the police was a remarkable achievement. I must record that the policemen of the North Arcot and Krishnagiri districts are highly skilled as masons, carpenters, road builders, and construction workers; even as tailors and cooks. It was such versatility and skill that were responsible for the origin in the 19th century of the Madras Engineering Group (MEG) and the Kolar Gold Fields in nearby Bengaluru and Kolar, respectively.

Anyone who has the stamina and will to climb to Melpet, the highest point in the Jawadhu Hills, would be astounded to see a 'Wireless Repeater Station' at an altitude of 1100 metres (3782 feet).

The stone plaque at the Wireless Tower reads;

"This is to commemorate the valiant efforts of the men of North Arcot Armed Reserve who surmounted innumerable obstacles to construct this building, a task considered impossible by all the professional builders of the district and also the PWD."

Date of commencement: 10.10.1975
Date of completion: 29.02.1976

Tr. W.I. Davaram, IPS
Superintendent of Police

North Arcot District

Three years later, when the Naxalites dominated the area, it was this wireless repeater that proved to be a boon to the Police during "Operation Ajantha." The tribals of Jamunamaruthur owe much of what they are today to the selfless dedication of Fr. Angelo Codello, an Italian priest who lived with them in that rural setting all his adult life and tirelessly worked for their upliftment. I must mention here that, on his retirement, we saw him off to Italy. But he was back in his beloved hills within 3 months. Such was his attachment to his second home. I attended his funeral 2 years later. He is buried alongside his other colleagues from Italy in the cemetery in Yelagiri. Yelagiri was the missionary as well as the revenue headquarters of the Jawadhu Hills. Thanks to the Naxalite infiltration, a Police Station has also been commissioned there.

My efforts to improve our relationship with the tribal population resulted in an interesting revelation. While visiting one of the newly opened police stations 6 months after the operation, the station staff admitted to the prevalence of arrack distillation in their limits but added that when caught by the Police, the distillers would tell them that the DIG of Police had permitted them to carry on with the distillation as an alternative to extremist activities and also as a means of livelihood. I redoubled my efforts with the government to provide employment to the tribals but continued to go slow on controlling the lesser evil, bootlegging. Apart from recruiting eligible candidates into the police force, I also helped the tribals in getting suitable jobs in the private sector.

It is this combination of extreme vigilance and positive rehabilitation programmes in areas susceptible to Naxalite propaganda and infiltration that has saved Tamil Nadu from the fate that many other states such as Andhra Pradesh, Orissa, Chhattisgarh, Jharkhand, and even Maharashtra have succumbed to. It is not that there have been no attempts to revive Naxalite activities in Tamil Nadu from time to time. But the Special Task Force (STF) and the "Q" Branch have been successful in nabbing the kingpin and their followers every time any such revival has been attempted. To their credit, the "Q" Branch has kept its pursuit of the wanted Naxalites alive for over 36 years, although the government, the public, and even the police have forgotten about them and their acts of terrorism.

The original Naxalites, who went underground after committing ritual murders of 'class enemies' and who had succeeded in evading the police for 36 to 40 years, were tracked down by the efforts of the "Q" Branch and brought before the courts of law as recently as in 2016. The most prominent of those arrested between 2007 and 2016 are Sivalingam, who was responsible for the death of Inspector Palanisamy and two Constables on 6.8.1980, and Tamilvanan, who masterminded all the killings in Dharmapuri and North Arcot districts between 1973 and 1980, including the murder of Appasamy Chettiyar. They were all original Naxalites.

The saga of 'Nondi' Palani is of special interest. After fleeing from Tirupattur in the year 1980, he had worked on the tea estates of Kerala under an assumed name for over 20 years. Assuming that the Tamil Nadu Police would have forgotten him, he moved to the Varusanadu Hills in Theni district, got married, and started life afresh. But he had not bargained for the persistence of the 'Q' Branch and the expertise of the Special Task Force. The Special Task Force, after its successful completion of the operation against jungle-bandit Veerappan and his formidable gang in the year 2004, has been kept under constant training and readiness to undertake any difficult and dangerous assignment in the jungles, thanks to the efforts of SP Karuppasamy, who has had the distinction of being in almost every operation against Veerappan's gang. The combine of these 2 elite Units, the "Q" Branch and the Special Task Force, has flushed out the newly formed Naxalite Units from Varusanadu, The Nilgiris, Kodaikanal hills, Meghamalai, Bodi Hills, and Kalakadu hills and other parts of the Western Ghats. 'Nondi' Palani was apprehended during one such raid in Varusanadu, a part of Kadamalaikundu forests in Theni district. People in Tirupathur Taluk and Dharmapuri district still remember with gratitude how our teams, in the face of extreme danger, freed them from the dreaded Naxalites.

More recently, a doctor who performed my cataract surgery in Chennai told me that he was from Dharmapuri and that his family was ever grateful to me and my team for saving the district from the Naxalites. His father's brother had been one of the victims of the Naxalites. I was pleasantly surprised to receive this compliment from an unexpected quarter, almost 4 decades after Operation Ajantha.

The government giving me a free hand in dealing with the extremists, the total dedication and unswerving loyalty of my subordinates, public cooperation, and the implementation of several welfare schemes were the factors that contributed to the successful completion of 'Operation Ajantha' and the equally successful prevention of Naxalite revival since then.

The Forgotten Villages of Anchetty Forest

Although I have traversed a sizeable portion of the riverine forests in Kollegal, Mettur, and Hosur Taluks, I shall confine my observation to the area bound by the River Cauvery on the west and one of its tributaries, the Sanatkumara Nadhi, on the east and to the inaccessible villages that lie hidden and half-forgotten therein. The entire area falls under the jurisdiction of the Denkanicotta P.S. of Dharmapuri District.

Sanathkumara Nadhi, locally known as Chinnar, rises in the Javalagiri hills near Thali. It follows the eastern ridge of a massive mountain range running northeast to southwest before joining the Cauvery at Hogenakkal.

Kodikare, a hill-top village 5 km away from Kembakare, is the only habitation in the vicinity. It is inhabited by Kannada-speaking Sivachars, a sect of the Lingayats, who have been cultivating a small extent of terraced land for over 300 years.

The valley immediately to the west of Anne Bidda-Halla is Anchetty, through which flows the Dotta Halla River. This river flows through a deep ravine for 10 km before joining the Cauvery. Anchetty village, 25 km away from Denkanicotta, is the commercial and social centre for the entire area.

Bethamugalalam village has a mixed population of the Tamil-speaking Vellikai Vellalars, Padayachis, and Kannada-speaking Lingayats. It has a secondary school that functions at the will and convenience of the teachers. There is nothing left of the coffee plantation (Glanshaw Estate) experimentally started by Col. F.G. Shaw 125 years earlier, as it has been parcelled out to the local ryots for kharif cultivation.

My account would be incomplete without a description of my climb to Guttirayan Peak, which at 4,579 ft above MSL, is the highest peak in the district. I started the climb from Kempakare village at 7 AM on 19.6.1982 and reached the saddle that connects the peak with the thickly wooded Kodikare plateau at 9.45 AM. A steady climb of another 4 km from the saddle took me to the summit of Guttirayan Peak. The northern slope was much gentler but heavily wooded. There was evidence of elephants here and at the top, but no longer of the Naxalites.

Another of my solitary treks took me to the famous 'Mekadatu' (in Kannada) and 'Aadu Thandum Cauveri' (in Tamil), where a goat is supposed to be able to jump across the River Cauveri. Of course, the river had been narrowed down by the huge rocks on the shores and riverbed, but certainly, no goat could jump from shore to shore. The phrase was to indicate the narrowness of the otherwise wide river and the close relationship of the people living on either side.

When I visited the villages on the Karnataka side, I was told in Kanakapura village that one of their students, H.M. Jayaram, had been selected in the IPS, allotted the Tamil Nadu cadre, and was undergoing training in the academy. Later, I met him on several occasions. He was an honest, bold, and efficient officer who left his mark in many important posts. At present, he is in charge of the 12,500-strong Tamil Nadu Armed Police. Under his supervision, the Tamil Nadu Police continues to be the leading state in the All-India Police Duty Meet and All-India Police Meet. Oh! To be able to visit these villages and hills again!

At the Command Post

The senior-most officer's chair is no fun;
You just can't sit there to rock in the sun.
Your officers and men look to you to be led;
They'll follow you surely, if you are ahead.

'I too was there' was the heading of my article that appeared in the Police 'Souvenir' in the year 2006 on the occasion of the 150th year of the Madras Police Commissionerate. Lt. Col. J.C. Boulderson was its first Commissioner under the City Police Act XIII in the year 1856. I was the 77th one (1985-1987). The souvenir was the brain-child of Letika Saran, Commissioner of Police in the 150th year of the Commissionerate.

I was not new to Chennai City Police. I'd had a tenure as Deputy Commissioner of Police, Law-and-Order, South, which had been marked by my opening fire at Halda Junction on DK, DMK, and CPM agitators protesting against the visit of Indira Gandhi. Much water had flowed under the bridge since that tenure and my return to the same complex years later as Commissioner of Police.

Within a month of my assuming charge, the Chief Minister took a drastic decision relating to the fishermen of the Marina. The Marina, while enjoying the distinction of being the second-longest beach in the world, also happens to be one of the best known and most alluring landmarks in the city. At the same time, the Marina is also home to the ancient fishing settlements of Ayodhyakuppam, Mattankuppam, Nadukuppam, and Nochikuppam, all of them located on the coast between the River Cooum in the north and the River Adyar in the South. From time immemorial, the fishermen had been carrying on their fishing operations from the stretches of the coastline in front of their respective Kuppams. When not out at sea, their boats, kattamarams, fishing nets, and other accessories would be left near the waterline while they lived in the multi-storeyed flats that had been built for them close to their areas of operation. They would go out to sea at night and return with their catch at dawn. Local merchants would wait at assembly points on the shore to buy the fish to sell in the city. In short, the entire life of the fisherfolk revolves around that part of the Marina in front of their Kuppams and the sea beyond.

There had been demands occasionally to enhance the beauty and attraction of the beach by clearing it of the fishing operations, but nothing had been done because it would have affected the lives and livelihood of thousands of families who had been plying this trade for thousands of years. The Chief Minister's order out of the blue to the Chief Secretary on the 1st of January 1985 was to clear the Marina of the fisherfolk, lock, stock, and barrel. The Chief Secretary and I were aghast at this pre-emptive order. Aware of the immense human suffering it would cause, we decided to meet the Chief Minister in person and persuade him to rescind the order or at least defer it until alternate sites were prepared for the displaced fishermen.

Here, I must digress a little. It is the bounden duty of every senior officer to study and assess the effect of Government Orders, especially those with far-reaching consequences, and advise the Chief Minister or the Minister concerned on the desirability or otherwise of implementing such an order. Many officers simply carry out orders because they do not have the courage to question anything that is issued from a Chief Minister's or even a Minister's desk. But T.V. Antony, IAS, a second-generation Chief Secretary, and his father T.A. Varghese, ICS, having occupied the same chair earlier, was of a different calibre. Disagreeing with the Chief Minister on sensitive matters was not new to him or to me. I recall one incident when we had worked together in Tanjore District, he as the District Collector and I as Superintendent of Police of the composite Tanjore district during the peak of the kisan unrest in the years 1969 to 1973 following the Keel Venmani tragedy.

The occasion was the Dravida Kazhagam's conference and proposed procession in Tiruvarur town. The exhibition at the conference hall and the floats for the procession carried scenes from the two great epics, the Ramayana and the Mahabharata, as well as from other legends, tailored to show the Hindu divinity in an obscene light. Such exhibitions and processions had already been held by the D.K. in Salem and in one or two smaller towns in the state. The country-wide press, including the Illustrated Weekly of India, which enjoyed all-India circulation, were full of pictures of the venerated Gods and Goddesses indulging in lewd, licentious, and immoral acts like incest, bestiality, drunkenness, and outright debauchery, which sent shockwaves across the country and deeply hurt the feelings of the Hindus. The conference pandal in Tiruvarur was drawing large crowds of visitors who were mostly the D.K. die-hards and seasoned atheists. But if the floats were taken out through Tiruvarur town and, what's more, past the thousand-year-old Thyagarajaswamy Temple, the general public, including women and children, would be exposed to the pornographic depictions that would definitely have hurt Hindu sentiments and outraged the sensitivity of the common man.

The Collector and I decided on the morning of the proposed procession not to allow it on grounds of public decency. We posted a large contingent of police at the entrance to the conference hall to stop the procession. When the C.M. drew his attention to the conduct of similar processions in other places, the Collector reminded him that it was different in Tiruvarur, which was the C.M.'s hometown, and that it would definitely create a very bad impression about him and the Government he headed. After considerable persuasion, the C.M.

permitted the Collector and me to personally meet Periyar and request him to cancel the procession. He was, however, not pleased when he was told that if Periyar did not agree to the request, the procession would have to be physically prevented and the organisers and those attempting to violate the ban, including the D.K. leader, would have to be arrested. The C.M. could not even imagine the arrest of Periyar when the D.M.K, the offshoot of the D.K., was in power.

We called on Periyar at the Government Guest House, Tiruvarur. That was the first time that I, and perhaps also the Collector, had come face to face with the formidable leader. He received us very hospitably and gave us a patient hearing. However, he expressed his reluctance to cancel the procession on the grounds that it was not the first time that such a procession had been taken out in Tamil Nadu. But when we re-emphasised that such a procession down the streets of Tiruvarur would cause great embarrassment to the C.M., he relented and agreed to call off the procession. We thanked him and came out, congratulating ourselves for not having had to arrest or detain the patriarch who was revered all over the state as the saviour of the lower castes and communities of Tamil Nadu from religious orthodoxy and Brahmin domination.

However, with M.G.R., it was different. After listening to our reasoning, he told us with a smile that the entire beach had to be cleared in 2 days. Thinking back, even today, I cannot fathom the reason behind the Chief Minister's decision. He was, as all his welfare measures and personal conduct indicated, genuinely sympathetic towards the poor. He was one of the few leaders who had given away all his wealth to the cause of the poor and the downtrodden, thereby receiving the unconditional love and affection of the common man, especially the working classes, the peasants, the daily-wage earners, and certainly, the fisherfolk. Besides, he could ill afford to antagonise the important fisherman community spread over the entire 1076 km long coast of Tamil Nadu, from the border of Andhra Pradesh in the North to the border of Kerala in the southwest. It could not have been just the beautification of the Marina, to make it the showpiece of the capital city; nor could it have been occasional drowning accidents, chain-snatching, or molestation of young couples on the deserted beach. Whatever his reason for this unpopular move, we had no choice but to carry out the Government's—or rather M.G.R.'s—order.

Operation Clean-Up started at the first light of day on 4th November 1985. About three thousand workers, under the dynamic, duty-conscious Commissioner of the Corporation, Shantha Sheela Nair, IAS, descended on the beach and started clearing it of the fishermen's possessions. About a thousand policemen stood by to give them protection, should the need arise. Realising that the Government would not go back on its decision, the fisherfolk moved their possessions to their houses and their boats from the shore to the edge of the main road. By evening, an ominous silence had descended on the deserted beach.

Although the entire operation had been completed without any incident, the atmosphere was charged with perceptible tension. The civil rights activists moved the High Court and the Supreme Court to revoke the Government order and to restore the fishing rights to the deprived fishermen; but the intervening Deepavali holidays delayed legal relief, if any was forthcoming. The affected fisherfolk, refusing to shift their areas of operation, stayed home, sulked, and starved. On the ninth day, one of the fishermen committed self-immolation in protest against the injustice done to the community. Police pickets were immediately posted all along the beach and at the Kuppams.

Eventually, the dam of pent-up feelings and frustration burst on 4th December, exactly a month after the clean-up operation. An emergency call through the wireless system from a small picket brought Ramanujam, the Deputy Commissioner (L&O) South, to Mattankuppam, where he found a large body of angry fishermen attacking the police pickets and the Slum Clearance Board office, shattering all its windows. They also set fire to vehicles on the road. Soon, the entire stretch of the beach road from the Labour Statue to the Lighthouse was a seething mass of agitating fishermen.

Upon being informed of the sudden development, I ordered reinforcements to be rushed to the Marina and prepared to go there myself. As I was getting into the vehicle, the A.D.C. and A.C. Intelligence pleaded with me to stay back and monitor the situation from my office. They pointed out the advantage of such an arrangement; it would give me an overall view of the situation without getting involved in the operational details. The other argument always used on such occasions was, "Who would support the subordinates in the event of a judicial or magisterial enquiry, which would necessarily follow police action, if the senior-most officer himself were to land in the dock?"

I was not new to those arguments or to the precedents cited in support of such a course of action or rather, inaction. I knew from earlier experience that, in judicial or magisterial enquiries that necessarily follow any police firing, the word of a senior officer carried more weight and authority than that of half a dozen subordinates acting on their own, or on orders communicated by senior officers from the safety of their office.

By the time I reached the Marina facing the DGP's office, the situation had gone beyond control. The police parties, led by the D.C. and a couple of ACs, were in headlong retreat along the Marina towards the DGP's office, with a crowd of fishermen attacking them with stones, bricks, soda bottles, fish hooks, and paddles from their boats. Unfortunately, all three officers were unarmed, as was the practice in those days, before the onset of terrorism and the bomb culture. I was also unarmed.

I did not have much time to decide on my course of action. The armed party I had directed to the Marina before leaving my office would take time to reach the place as they were in a bigger and slower vehicle. There was no time to follow the procedure for mob operations as laid down in the Police Drill Manual or the Criminal Procedure Code. I took the rifle and a magazine of ten rounds from the police guard stationed at the entrance to the DGP's office and returned to the road. By that time, the small unarmed police party had run past me, hotly pursued by the violent fishermen. Pointing the rifle at the mob, I ordered them to stop. The crowd, already enjoying the chase, continued to advance. I shot the leader dead. I fired 3 more rounds, bringing down three more leaders. It was only then that the mob realised that the police meant business. It staggered to a halt and then started retreating into the Kuppams.

The following eye-witness account by a journalist on the action on the Marina appeared in the newspapers the next morning: "As the police were concentrating on Nadukuppam, the fishermen ran along the banks of the Buckingham Canal, regrouped themselves, and launched a fresh onslaught on the handful of policemen. Two jeeps had already been set ablaze on either side of the bridge on Lloyds Road. The regrouped policemen were pushed back by the relentless missile throwing by the violent mob. Commissioner Davaram rushed to the spot with a rifle slung over his shoulder and ordered his men to fall in line. The attack did come, but this time, the policemen held ground, the Commissioner personally leading the shooting. By 1.30 PM, a lull settled down with both sides nursing their injuries. The Chairman of the Slum Clearance Board, who had been trapped inside the besieged building for over 2 hours, was rescued."

Meanwhile, the sentry constable at the Marina Police Station, further to the South near the Lighthouse, had fired one round at a mob that had attacked the police station, killing one. The picket on Lloyds Road had also opened fire at the mob attacking it. Altogether, 5 people were killed and six injured in the police firing. Besides me, 88 police personnel were injured, and 48 vehicles, including 18 belonging to the Police Department, had been damaged.

When I walked into the DGP's office to brief DGP Lakshminarayan and IGP Sripal on the day's events, I found them returning to their offices after having watched the entire 'Action Thriller on the Beach' from the terrace of the building. They informed me that the Supreme

Court had restored fishing rights to the fishermen. If only that order had come an hour earlier, all those deaths could have been avoided. On the positive side, however, we had faithfully and effectively carried out the Government Order. We had established the supremacy of the police in a riot situation, regardless of the cause of the rioting. I, for my part, had reaffirmed the principle, 'The senior-most officer in the thick of battle.'

Of the several police personnel injured, Inspector Kothandaraman had to be admitted to and remain in hospital, with doctors labouring to extract pieces of his splintered cheekbone.

Soon, everything returned to normal, and once again, I started riding out with the Mounted Branch on its beach patrol duty. As for the fishermen, all was forgotten, and they started greeting me as they had done before. MGR, who had learnt of my riding out on the Marina, advised me to avoid the area for some time at least. Such was his concern for his officers.

The magisterial enquiry into the firing was conducted by the PA to the Collector of Madras. He justified all three instances of police firing. A special award was presented to the lone constable who single-handedly saved the Marina Police Station from destruction. Looking back, it was a human tragedy that need not have happened at all; an inexplicable exercise of governmental powers.

Six months later, the same sands witnessed another memorable event, a calm and peaceful one; an event that those fortunate enough to be part of would cherish all their lives. It was the first-ever visit of a Pope to Madras; the visit of the peregrinating Pontiff, the head of the Roman Catholic Church, His Holiness, Pope John Paul II.

This event required elaborate safety and security arrangements. A special bullet-proof, see-through vehicle had to be prepared for his drive from the airport to the Bishop's residence in Santhome via St. Thomas Mount, where he addressed a gathering, down Anna Salai (Mount Road).

The vehicle, which we named the 'Pope-mobile,' was prepared in record time, thanks to the resourcefulness of DC N. Balachandran, popularly known as 'Bobby Nair.'

I have no words to describe the awed hush that descended on the chattering crowd that had lined both sides of the papal route as the Pope-mobile carrying His Holiness cruised past. The Holy Father stood all the way, so immaculate and serene, blessing the crowds that had lined both sides of the entire route; crowds comprised not just of Christians, but of people with mixed religious beliefs. I must mention here that I had the awesome and divine opportunity of reverently holding his outstretched hand and kissing his hallowed ring.

Beyond the Call of Duty

A policeman's duty is not policing alone;
He is the guardian of people, known and unknown;
For rescue from calamities, fires, floods and more,
The police force is there, steadfast to the core.
Twenty-four hours, seven days of the week,
They are there to keep watch while the rest of us sleep.

Protection of life and property has been, and will always be, the prime responsibility of the Police, whether it be from petty thieves, professional criminals, burglars, robbers, blackmailers, kidnappers, contract killers, confidence tricksters, or the modern-day terrorists, extremists, and members of the Mafia. Apart from this day-to-day responsibility, the Police are often called upon to play a much bigger role. It is the police, the largest body of trained and disciplined men and women, that people look up to for help in times of major calamities, both natural and man-made. Floods, cyclones, landslides, major fires, earthquakes, and the more recent phenomenon, the tsunami, come under the category of "Natural Calamities."

During my service, I have been called upon to play the role of life-saver on several occasions. The major fire that destroyed the market in Thanjavur on Deepavali day in 1970; the collapse of a building in Gudiyatham Town in 1975, its terrace weighed down with onlookers watching a religious procession; and the collision of two express trains near Vaniyambadi railway station in 1980, resulting in the death of more than 45 passengers and injury to many more, are some of them. On all of these occasions, I was on hand to marshal the available strength for the rescue and rehabilitation of the victims. Although the train accident was, as established later, due to human error, at the time it happened, it was thought to be the handiwork of Naxalites, who were an everyday menace in that area. As a result, the public, who otherwise would have rushed to the rescue, were reluctant to go near the accident site, fearing explosions and bomb attacks. It was left to the railway authorities and the police to carry out the difficult task of extricating the passengers who were trapped inside the mangled compartments and taking them to hospitals in Vaniyambadi, Tirupattur, Ambur, and Vellore. On the day of the train accident, I was in Tirupattur leading an Anti-Naxalite operation and was able to reach the accident spot within half an hour. The Government of India, the Government of Tamil Nadu, and the general public acknowledged and appreciated our role on that fateful day.

I have also personally experienced two major floods in Madras, both involving the River Adyar and the sea, which on each occasion claimed the lives of more than 500 people. The first was in 1976 when I was Deputy Commissioner of Police, Law-and-Order (South), and the second, in 1985 when I was the Commissioner of Police, Madras City.

On the night of 24-11-1976, Madras City experienced the heaviest rainfall in its history, 45.2 cms in 24 hours. This, by itself, was not the cause of the ordeal the city had to face over the next 48 hours because, at the same time, equally heavy rains lashing the hinterland had caused all the major irrigation tanks to overflow. It was not long before the water level in Chembarambakkam, the biggest tank in Chengalpet District, crossed the danger level and threatened to breach its bund, posing grave danger to the city and the numerous villages that lay between the tank and the sea. There was no alternative but to release the excess water. This overflow, in turn, flooded the River Adyar, which traversed the city on its way to the sea. The Cooum, the other river flowing through the city, was also in space. To add to the seriousness of the situation, a high tidal wave blocked the absorption of the river waters by the sea.

The water level rose rapidly, and by midnight, both rivers had broken their banks, and their waters had gushed into the low-lying areas on either side. By dawn, almost all the huts had been washed away, and all the single-storeyed buildings were underwater.

Although no one anticipated floods of such magnitude, the Madras City Police had swung into action the previous evening itself. On receipt of a cyclone warning issued by the "Area Cyclone Warning Centre" of the Meteorological Department, police messengers fanned out all over the city, warning people, especially those living in areas adjoining the watercourses, of the possibility of floods and of a cyclone striking the city the following morning. Save for a few, none vacated their houses, thinking the river, even if it did overflow its banks, would soon recede, and the danger would pass.

However, by midnight, the City Police Control Room had become a beehive of activity, receiving distress calls and directing rescue work, which, in the beginning, was confined to rescuing people from under collapsed walls and helping to shift the old and disabled to places of safety. A party of one Sub-Inspector and ten Police Constables worked in total darkness and in chest-deep water for more than 3 hours to move the inmates of a Home for the aged from the flooded ground floor to the upper floor of that building. In another operation, the debris of a collapsed building was cleared in a frantic attempt to rescue a 4-year-old child buried underneath. Police lorries worked non-stop to tow out submerged cars, the tops of which alone could be seen above the water.

It was not until daybreak that the real gravity of the situation revealed itself. The city had become one vast sheet of water, dotted with tree-tops, lamp-posts, Temple towers, and roofs with people clinging to whatever they could. More than five lakh people had been rendered homeless in a matter of hours. Communication had been completely disrupted, with water flowing 5 to 10 feet above the road surface. Power supply and telephone connections had broken down in several parts of the city.

Kotturpuram, a low-lying area on the Southern banks of the river Adyar, was the worst affected. Here, almost 2 thousand 5 hundred families were housed in 72 single-storeyed buildings and 83 multi-storeyed blocks of flats built by the state Slum Clearance Board. When the water level rose and submerged the single-storeyed buildings and the ground floors of the multi-storeyed ones, the occupants managed to move up to the rooftops or to the upper floors. The old and crippled who could not climb onto the roofs clung to the rafters. Many of them were washed away before help could reach them.

The challenge that awaited the police party that reached Kotturpuram was the rescue of about 15 thousand marooned people, three thousands of whom were perched precariously on the gabled asbestos roofs of the single-storeyed houses and on the upper floors of the multi-storeyed buildings, some of which had begun to develop dangerous cracks and were in imminent danger of collapsing.

I decided that no time should be lost in reaching the marooned people and bringing them to safety. When I called for volunteers to make the hazardous trips, Om. Ramamurthy, the Additional Deputy Commissioner of the Armed Reserve, who was to retire in a year's time, Reserve Sub-Inspector Sarveswaran, three Head Constables, and eight Constables of the Armed Reserve readily came forward, and a Task Force was immediately formed. Soon, two parties, one led by Om. Ramamurthy and the other by me, got onto the boats and set out, overruling the apprehension of the boatmen.

Battling the turbulent current and unseen dangers like fences and compound walls that lay beneath the surface, the boats reached the buildings. We climbed onto the roofs, calmed the people, and started rescue operations. At first, we swam or jumped across from one roof to the other, forced our way into each house by breaking open the door or the roof, and brought out 56 old men and women who were clinging to the rafters in the narrow space between the water and the roofs. They were lowered onto the boats and taken ashore.

At about 2 p.m., one of the two boats was washed away. However, Ramamurthy and his men managed to save all the occupants. The remaining boat was joined by six catamarans and their crew of fishermen-volunteers at about 3 p.m., and rescue work was stepped up. Each member of the police party not only made as many as 30 trips across the treacherous waters but also kept up the morale of the panic-stricken people on the rooftops by clambering up to them and reassuring them, transferring them from one roof to another by ropes, and fishing out children who kept slipping into the water from the roofs of buildings that were fast giving way to the fury of the deluge.

By dusk, another horror was added to the ordeal: snakes had begun to climb onto the roofs from the water. These were killed, and the strained nerves of the people were calmed. The operation became even more hazardous as darkness fell. The boat and the catamarans often lost their way, and the lowering of the people from the rooftops onto the perilously rocking craft became a nightmare.

Even as this rescue operation was in progress, the heart-rending cry of 26 people, including women and children, on the damaged four-storeyed building nearby continued to assail the rescue team. Most of the ground floor had sunk, and the tall building was tottering dangerously on a shaky foundation. But repeated efforts by catamarans and the boat to reach the building ended in failure as the current was too swift. Three catamarans were lost to a whirlpool. These failures only added to the panic of the people on the building, who continued to wave pieces of cloth, imploring the rescuers not to give up their attempts. By nightfall, a mechanised boat belonging to the Marine Department of the Madras Port Trust joined in the effort and, after several abortive attempts, reached the building at midnight and rescued the people just as they had all but given up hope. At half past midnight, the huge building collapsed with a thunderous crash that sent a shudder through the hearts of those rescued as well as those of the rescuers.

By 2 a.m., in a non-stop operation, all three thousand people from the rooftops had been brought to safety. These included two women and the babies they had delivered atop the roofs that day. During this risky operation, five catamarans and one boat were lost to the fury of the floods.

A night-long vigil was kept on the shores by K. Chenthamarai, the Commissioner of Police, who had arranged to have the area floodlit with generators collected from various places and brought over with great difficulty. He kept up the morale of the people who were yet to be rescued with his continuous presence on the shore and reassurances through a megaphone throughout the night.

The operation resumed on the morning of the 26th. The river continued to flow in unabated fury. In yet another non-stop operation lasting from 6 a.m. to 10 p.m., 12 thousand people were brought ashore. Even at the start of the first day of operation, I had been badly injured in a fall while jumping from one roof to another in a bid to save a child. But I carried on and made more than 30 trips to reach the marooned. Om. Ramamurthy defied his age and performed miracles with his flimsy boat. The others, with single-minded determination, carried on with the arduous and perilous task.

Meanwhile, more policemen, boats, catamarans, ropes, generators, and scores of fishermen were rushed to the other points where similar rescue work was being carried out. Where the marooned people were not in imminent danger, food, drinking water, and medical supplies were taken to them on catamarans. Altogether, more than 50 thousand people had been rescued.

Never in living memory had Madras faced such an ordeal, and never in the history of the Tamil Nadu Police had such a massive rescue and relief operation been undertaken. As the city limped back to normalcy, praise and gratitude for the magnificent job by the police came pouring in. In appreciation of the services rendered during the flood, the Government granted a sum of Rs.1,00,000/- to the Tamil Nadu Police, which bore the brunt of the rescue operation. In a splendid thanksgiving function on the Marina, the Governor of Tamil Nadu praised the magnificent efforts of the police during the floods and distributed commendation letters to the gazetted officers and cash awards to the Sub-Inspectors, Head Constables, and Constables. It was a fitting finale to the whole episode.

To sum up, I quote the words of Harry Miller of the Indian Express in his article, "After the Deluge in Madras":

"…… then again, over and above the call of duty, the Police were magnificent. It was Deputy Commissioner of Police W.I. Davaram who courageously took the first boat across when the current was at its dangerous height before anyone else had dared. I was on the spot for the best part of 10 hours and so was the Commissioner Mr. K. Chenthamarai and his men and throughout the time I never saw them relieved. I never saw anyone bring them so much as a cup of hot coffee."

All 13 of us, the Constables, the Head Constables, the Reserve Sub-Inspector, ADSP Om. Ramamurthy, and I were awarded the Prime Minister's "Life Saving Medal." The medals were presented to us by the Governor of Punjab at the closing function of the All-India Police Duty Meet in Jalandhar in November 1977.

Nine years later, I was back in Madras as Commissioner of Police when floods hit the city again. Once again, the banks of the river Adyar were the most affected. Even the construction of retainer walls from Ashok Nagar to Saidapet could not save the houses on the banks. The two major lakes that fed the river Adyar overflowed, and the river rose several feet, submerging the Guindy-Poonamallee Road as well as Chief Minister MGR's residence in Ramapuram. The bridge on the river Adyar near Ramapuram was also underwater. It was with great difficulty that V.C. Perumal, then DC-Headquarters, and Reserve Inspector Adaikalam reached Ramapuram, rescued MGR, and took him to safety by boat. MGR was accommodated in Hotel Connemara, where he remained over the next 21 days. After ensuring the safety of MGR, Adaikalam joined me in Kotturpuram, the worst affected area in the city, where we continued with the rescue work.

This time, the onset of a cyclonic storm forced the sea up the mouth of the river, preventing its flow into the sea. This, in turn, caused the water level of the river to rise several feet higher than it had in 1976. The Navy brought in a rubber dinghy to supplement the boats and catamarans that the police had marshalled. Even though motorised, the dinghy was unstable in the swirling waters. As someone familiar with the layout of the basin, I offered to guide the dinghy operator to the people stranded in the buildings. Adaikalam volunteered to go with me. The rising water had already submerged the ground floors and was steadily rising to the first floor. The occupants of the apartments on the ground floor were clinging to the half-submerged balconies of the first floor.

We made several trips to the buildings, carrying food packets to those stranded and taking the sick, the injured, and children to shore. After 2 hours of non-stop operation, the cyclonic wind stopped abruptly. This resulted in the river waters, which had been held in check by the inflow of the sea, surging seaward. The dinghy went out of control and, despite the frantic efforts of the crew, started hurtling towards the open sea. We were unable to grasp the ropes that people were throwing out to us from the upper floors of the nearby buildings. All seemed lost as we were almost past the last block of apartments. Beyond that, there was nothing to stop the dinghy from being washed out to sea. But, as luck would have it, it got entangled in a bush that was half submerged in the water. A 45-minute struggle ensued to keep the dinghy from getting loose. Finally, we managed to grasp one of the ropes thrown out to us from the nearest building and fastened it to the dinghy. We then hauled ourselves onto the balcony of the second floor of that building.

After securing a foothold, we resumed evacuation with the help of another rope tied to the Kotturpuram bridge over the Adyar. We made several trips and saved more than five thousand people. Meanwhile, catamarans joined us in the rescue operation, which continued through the night until all the marooned were brought to safety.

Writing about the cyclonic rains that resulted in the loss of hundreds of lives, Harry Miller, in the Madras Musings dated December 16-31, 1995, said, "The Slum Clearance Board had ignored repeated warnings that it was in the river's natural floodplain. Had it not been for the heroism of a single young police officer, and the Additional Director General of Police, Walter Davaram who worked through the night in total darkness against the terrifying forces of nature, many more families would have been swept away by the unbelievable and unprecedented torrent."

Reserve Inspector Adaikalam and I (for the 2nd time) were awarded the Prime Minister's Life Saving Medal. Corresponding Naval honours were awarded to the Naval personnel who operated the dinghy. Our medals were presented to us by the Vice President of India at the valedictory function of the All-India Police Duty Meet in Bhopal in December of the following year.

The year 1986 witnessed several bomb blasts; but when the terrorists turned their focus on the railways, it was of serious concern. A bomb had been planted on the rail track near Singanallur Station in Coimbatore district; another had been planted near Madurai junction. Luckily, both bombs went off before the targeted trains arrived; however, a bomb planted in a compartment of the Trichy-Erode passenger claimed one life and injured 25. Of greater concern was when they turned their attention to the suburban railway system of Chennai, which criss-crossed the distance between the Beach Railway Station and Tambaram and served several thousands of commuters in both directions.

It was with a sense of anxious urgency that I rushed to the level crossing near Pachaiyappa's College Hostel on 29th December 1986 when

I was informed of a bomb blast on the rail track there. Luckily, the blast had occurred after the train had passed over it but had been so powerful that it had created a cavernous crater on the track and had sent the ballast flying into the houses nearby. The residents of the area rushed to the level crossing and noticed another bomb lying on the track and a train bound for Tambaram approaching it. They managed to stop the train, but two compartments had already crossed it. I rushed up to the train and, ignoring the efforts of the public to keep me away from the bomb, I crawled under the train, retrieved the bomb, and defused it. People often ask me why I was not awarded a gallantry medal or a life-saving medal for that daring act. It was up to the DGP to take the initiative. I couldn't recommend a medal for myself, could I? But then, all the appreciation that I got from the press was worth more than a medal.

i.   News Item No. 1: News Today – "Thousand passengers have brushed with death in City."

"Commissioner of Police W. I. Davaram showed daring and enterprise to defuse an unexploded gelignite bundle attached to a device and thereby averted what could have been a major catastrophe to a suburban train last evening. Earlier in the day, Davaram had attended a class on diffusing bombs. He put to the test what he had observed and learnt."

ii. News Item No. 2 - The Week "The Tamil Nadu Police had never faced a situation like this before."

"The Police Commissioner W. I. Davaram, an expert in firearms, is now catching up on his studies on explosives. He, who headed the Anti-Naxalite operation in the early 1980s, was familiar with crude impact bombs. In the present case, they are very powerful, and an explosion on the track when the train was passing could cause considerable damage and loss of human lives."

iii. News Item No. 3 The Indian Express - "Big explosion."

"A big explosion was caused by four sticks of gelignite (a powerful explosive containing nitroglycerine and sodium nitrate used to blow up huge rocks). The unexploded bomb had a 60 cm long wire connected to the detonator. As a result of the bomb explosion, train services were disrupted for 2 hours. Police Commissioner W. I. Davaram arrived at the spot and removed the unexploded bomb himself, declaring the area safe."

iv. Makkal Kural – "After a bomb exploded, the public warned the train to stop because one more unexploded bomb was still on the track. Very soon, Commissioner W. I. Davaram rushed to the spot. Though the unexploded bomb could burst at any time, Davaram bravely removed the bomb by hand and was appreciated by the entire public."

Surely, I could not have asked for more. Similarly, when I single-handedly disarmed a group of EPRLF militants in Choolaimedu, Chennai, I ought to have been considered for a gallantry medal. But again, the recommendation ought to have come from my superiors. My only regret is not having got a medal for Inspector Babu for his courage in following me to the terrace, totally unarmed. He collected the surrendered weapons and also dressed the injuries that the Sri Lankans had received in the clash with the local residents.

Their Pensions Found them

'Impossible!' Can there be such a word?
If you think there is, it's quite absurd.
'Cos where there's a will, there is a way,
You'll find your goal. Yes! Come what may.

My greatest satisfaction as Commissioner of Police was the sanctioning of pensions to 117 police widows 40 to 60 years after their husbands had died. The press highlighted this unusual service to the forgotten widows. I'd like to share a press note dated 7.11.1986 about the granting of pensions to several police widows on the basis of obituary notices published more than 60 years ago.

i. 'Lakshmikutty Amma became a widow at the age of 22. The 'obit' said, 'Mr. M.S. Krishnan Nair, B.A., prosecuting sub-inspector, Madras City Police, died at the General Hospital on Tuesday afternoon of jaundice. The deceased was a young officer and quite popular in the force. The funeral took place yesterday morning at the Barber's Bridge crematorium with police honours.'

ii. 'At that time, there was no pension scheme for widows of government servants who died in harness. By the time the scheme was introduced by the Tamil Nadu Government in 1975, Lakshmikutty Amma had moved to Kerala and did not apply.'

iii. 'Only when she heard about the sanctioning of a pension to Narayani Ammal, widow of a City Police constable, 42 years after her husband's death, did she choose to apply for the pension.'

iv. 'The City Police, which processed the application, soon ran into difficulties. There was no record of the employment or death of the SI.'

v. 'The old lady had no documentary evidence either but still had a good memory, leading to the location of the newspaper obituary.'

vi. 'Though the news had no evidence to directly prove that the SI had completed one year in service, the Commissioner of Police sanctioned the pension on the presumption that the SI must have undergone a minimum of one year of training before becoming a 'prosecuting SI.' The widow will now get Rs.235 plus admissible DA every month for the rest of her life, besides pension arrears of Rs.15,000/-. Interestingly, even her sons have since retired from government service and have been receiving pensions.'

vii. "Swaminatha Iyer has been described as a Sub-Inspector of Police in a land sale deed dated May 11, 1919, and this entitled his wife, 82-year-old Parvathi Ammal, to claim her pension."

viii. "C.P. Reddy had served Madras Police as a Motor Vehicles Inspector in the forties before he died. Pension has been sanctioned to his wife Sarojini (71) on the basis of a condolence message from the Deputy Commissioner (Traffic) dated May 29, 1947, to the bereaved family."

Widows of the 53 policemen who had died were sanctioned family pensions, thanks to the efforts of the Pension Section of the City Police Commissionerate. I sanctioned special cash rewards to Section Superintendents Nagamani and Padmavathi and 11 staff members working under them. This departmental reward motivated the staff to process 64 more pension applications within a month.

The pension section of the Madras City Police relentlessly pursued each case and enabled 53 widows to get lump sum arrears of Rs.17,000/- each besides a monthly pension. I had relied upon even condolence messages and obituary notices to sanction the pensions. Narayanammal was sanctioned a pension 44 years after the death in 1942 of her SI husband on the basis of a postcard received by him.

i.   A cash bill dated October 16, 1935, from a City Fancy Store in the name of constable Narayanasami Pillai enabled his wife, aged 76, to draw a pension.

ii. Constable Md. Hussain had been awarded the King's Police Medal for gallantry in the year 1931. A Gazette Notification came in handy 56 years later to enable his 82-year-old wife to draw her pension.

iii. The 82-year-old widow of an SI of Police getting a family pension 62 years after the death of her husband deserves special mention here. All that the widow knew was that her husband's death was on February 3, 1924. 'The Hindu' obliged me with a copy of 'The Hindu' dated February 4, 1924, which carried the obituary.

iv. In another case of a newspaper reference to an SI by his name, and on the presumption that the SI should have completed a minimum of one year of service, I sanctioned the pension, granting the widow Rs.235/- plus admissible DA per month and a lump sum of Rs.15,000/- as the pension arrears accrued since April 1, 1979, when the pension scheme was introduced by the Government.

While on the subject of pensions, it might interest readers to know of the longest period of pension in history recorded in the Guinness Book of World Records. Neither the beneficiary nor her father belonged to the Police but to the Madras Regiment of the British Army. The entry reads:

"Miss Millicent Barclay, daughter of Col. William Barclay, was born on 10.7.1872 and became eligible for a Madras military fund pension till her marriage. She died unmarried on 26.10.1969, having drawn the pension for every day of her life of 97 years 3 months."

Curtains on a Legend

The first time I met the renowned MGR
'Twas in Ooty; he was with another star
I knew not then that they both would be
CM's of Tamil Nadu; and both served by me
But MGR was in a class of his own;
As the State's CM, in stature, he'd grown
His fans even thought, immortal was he,
and thought that with them, for e'er he would be;
That no harm nor ill would their hero befall;
When the end did come, could they believe it at all?

I have written about the management of unlawful assemblies in other chapters. It was only on the occasion of Indira Gandhi's visit to Tamil Nadu that the assembly started out as a pre-planned, unlawful one, with the crowds gathering in public places in defiance of the regulatory orders proclaimed by the City Police.

On the other hand, the violence on the Marina started out as a peaceful congregation of fishermen who wished to voice their grievance against the ban on their traditional fishing rights, which had deprived them of their livelihood, leaving them and their families to a month of hardship and stress. It was no surprise then that the peaceful protest soon turned violent. The clashes in the Assembly also started with opposing groups merely trying to establish their respective majorities in the house but later turned violent.

The violence that mars the funeral of a popular celebrity is due mainly to the anxiety of the people to get one last glimpse of their beloved hero. The situation often deteriorates when rowdy elements mingle with the mourners and try to take advantage of the circumstances to settle private scores. Criminals also take advantage of the situation to loot shops, burn vehicles, and indulge in other acts of violence. Additionally, problems arise from deaths in road and rail accidents, with people anxious to get to the place where the body of their leader has been laid for viewing, and later, to where it is to be cremated or interred. When Annadurai died, several mourners travelling to Madras atop railway carriages were swept off by girders when the train crossed a railway bridge, and others were crushed to death when a portion of the ceiling of Rajaji Hall caved in with the weight of mourners who had clambered onto the roof to get a better view of their leader whose body lay in state in the hall below. Similar scenes were witnessed at the funerals of DK leader EVR and of Congress leader and Ex-CM of the erstwhile Madras State, K. Kamaraj. In Tamil Nadu and neighbouring Andhra Pradesh, it is not unusual for a spate of suicides to follow the death of any popular leader.

I was away in the districts as Superintendent of Police when the leaders mentioned earlier breathed their last. All I had to do was control the demonstrations of grief in the district and regulate the movement of mourners rushing to Madras by public transport and private vehicles. But when former Chief Minister M. Bakthavatchalam died on 13th February 1987, I was Commissioner of Police, Madras. There was hardly a crowd in the house where his body had been laid for public viewing, or at the cremation ground. His major shortcoming was his failure, while in power, to get close to the people. I remember accompanying the Chief Secretary, Home Secretary, and the DGP to select a place between Gandhi Mandapam and Kamaraj Memorial in Guindy for a monument to be erected in his memory. Similarly, when Rajaji, the former Chief Minister of Madras and the last Governor General of India, passed away, there was hardly a ripple, the reason being the same as in Bakthavatchalam's case: aloofness from the public.

But M.G.R., whose end came on the night of 24th December 1987, was of a totally different calibre. No leader, either before him or after, had his charisma or the power to attract the common man. When 4 years earlier he had fallen seriously ill and had been admitted into Apollo Hospital, people simply could not believe that what befalls every mortal could also befall their hero. The total disbelief among the public resulted in a spate of suicides and self-sacrifices in every part of the state for his early recovery. Had anything untoward befallen him at that time, Apollo Hospital would have found itself at the mercy of his devastated followers. His winning the General Election in absentia while under treatment in the United States only reaffirmed his popularity and mass following. But then, except for his die-hard followers, everyone else was aware that he was not immortal and had survived only by divine intervention and the proficiency of the doctors, mainly Dr. Kono of Japan. When M.G.R. returned to Madras on 31.10.1987 after his second spell of treatment in the United States, he appeared to be in excellent health. He transacted government business just as he had done before he fell ill. On 05.11.1987, he attended R.M. Veerappan's swearing-in as Cabinet Minister and made kind enquiries of the officers he met there. I met him again on the 21st and 22nd December.

So, it was that when, in the early hours of 24th December 1987, the news of his death came in, it was totally unexpected, and neither the government nor the public was prepared for it. Our immediate concern was to shift his body to Rajaji Hall, ten kilometres away, before the public could get wind of the tragic news and block all roads leading to and from his residence in Ramavaram. As the DGP and IGP were conferring with the senior ministers at MGR's house, I, as Commissioner of Police, mobilised the City Police as well as the Tamil Nadu Special Police from Avadi and summoned all Police officers who were available in and around the city for emergency duty. Meanwhile, a set of Police officers and PWD officials got down to work at the Government Estate, preparing the portico of Rajaji Hall where the body was to lie in state and erecting barricades from St. George Gate in the North to the portico, and from the portico to the Walajah Gate in the South.

A short note on this historical edifice will not be out of place here. It had been built during the tenure of Governor Lord Edward Clive, the son of Lord Robert Clive, the founder of the British Indian Empire. It came up on the campus of the Admiralty Building, now known as the Government Estate, and was raised to commemorate Robert Clive's victory in the Battle of Plassey in 1757 and the final defeat of Tippu Sultan in 1799. Mr. Goldingham, the architect, had it constructed in the year 1802-1803 at a cost of Rs.2.2 lakhs. It took the form of a Greek Temple with an imposing frontage and a soaring flight of steps. It was opened on 17.10.1802 and was known as the 'Banqueting Hall,' used by governors to hold public events. It was renamed 'Rajaji Hall' on 9.4.1948 in honour of C. Rajagopalachari, Chief Minister of the erstwhile Madras State. It became well-known all over the country when it became the site for the funerals of four Chief Ministers of Tamil Nadu – Annadurai, MGR, Jayalalithaa, and more recently, Karunanidhi.

K. Subbaiah, SP, Chengalpet East, and K. Vadivelu, DC L&O, managed to bring the body of MGR to Rajaji Hall by dawn, but not without having to battle their way through the sea of humanity that had choked all the roads, the news of his death having got around even before it was officially released. Both officers stayed with the body till it was interred. As the day advanced, thousands of people, mainly youngsters, started roaming the streets, attacking vehicles and forcing shops to turn down shutters. Shops that were slow to close were ransacked, with the most affected being liquor shops. Several buses were set on fire in various parts of the city.

With public transport off the roads, the genuine mourners, as distinct from rowdies and hooligans, were arriving at Rajaji Hall in lorries and private vehicles. Trains from the South, West, and North were packed and running behind schedule, having had to make several unscheduled stops along the way to pick up mourners. The Police had to open fire in several places to discourage looters and the rabble. While such scenes were being enacted in several parts of the city, the main action drama was taking place at the Government Estate.

Although the surging crowd was being directed to the North gate of the Government Estate and from there to Rajaji Hall in queues between barricades, it was well-nigh impossible to plug every entry point. So, it was inevitable that force had to be used on all the roads leading to the Government Estate - Walajah Road, Anna Salai, Chindadripet Road, Pallavan Salai, and the Beach Road. All around, pitched battles were being fought between the mobs and the heavily outnumbered Police. The police had to fire tear gas shells several times to prevent the unruly crowd from gate-crashing. By noon, almost all of us, officers and men alike, were injured, hit by stones, soda bottles, and other missiles. While the more severely injured policemen were sent to hospital, those not too badly injured remained at their posts continuously for over 38 hours, without food or water. Meanwhile, a mob had started damaging former Chief Minister Karunanidhi's statue at the Wellington Theatre junction. Before the Police could reach that junction from the Government Estate, a distance of only one-and-a-half kilometres, it had been completely demolished. DC Crime Dharmarajan, who was in charge of Chintadripet Road leading to the North Gate, had to open fire on many occasions. A couple of bodies were found on the banks of River Cooum the following day. It is also possible that some injured might have been taken back by their associates and treated privately. It is only on such occasions that there would be no outcry against the police and demand for judicial inquiries. My own estimate of those who were killed due to police firing and resultant stampede was 12, a number that could have toppled the government at any other time.

Despite the turmoil outside the Government Estate, at Rajaji Hall itself, everything was going on peacefully, as mourners filed past the body. The never-ending queue kept growing longer and thicker with the arrival of mourners from the mofussil areas. They had to be urged by policemen and the AIADMK volunteers to keep moving. Keeping vigil at the head of the platform bearing MGR's body were several ladies, including his wife Janaki Ramachandran, and the party's Propaganda Secretary Jayalalithaa. While most of them took turns to rest awhile inside the hall, Jayalalithaa did not move from the place she had taken up at the very start of the vigil. Efforts by well-wishers and women police personnel to persuade her to rest awhile, or at least drink some water, failed to move her, and she stood steadfast all the 38 hours that the body lay in state, setting an example of fortitude and single-minded devotion. Apparently, not everyone took kindly to this. Policewomen on duty near her reported to me that she was being physically harassed by women who were probably sympathisers of Janaki Ramachandran. I had to post policewomen in mufti to mingle with the crowd and protect her. MGR's niece Leelavathi, who was beside the body, was inconsolable. She was the one who had donated her kidney to MGR, giving him borrowed time.

By 11 am on 25ᵗʰ December, it was decided to close the gates and prepare for the journey to the final resting place on the Marina. We were anxious to finish the burial before dark. By that time, more than a million people had filed past the body. Also, most of the dignitaries had paid their last respects to the departed leader. They included the President of India, N. Sanjeeva Reddy, Governor of Kerala P. Ramachandran, Chief Ministers of Andhra Pradesh N. T. Rama Rao and of Jammu and Kashmir Farooq Abdullah, Sri Lankan Minister Thondaiman, union Ministers P. V. Narasimma Rao, Buta Singh, M. L. Fotedar, P. Chidambaram, R. Prabhu, and N. Arunachalam, all the Tamil Nadu Ministers, and AICC General Secretaries G. K. Moopanar and K. N. Singh. Most of them then left for the burial site when the body was taken into the hall to prepare it for the last journey.

Meanwhile, the gun carriage had arrived and was positioned at the foot of the steps. When the body was placed on it, Jayalalithaa got onto it and sat next to the body. As it was against army regulations, the army personnel explained this to her and helped her get onto the pick-up truck which had been attached to the gun-carriage. Immediately, M.L.A. Dr. K. P. Ramalingam, belonging to the R. M. Veerappan group, tried to pull her down from the truck. The policeman standing nearby pushed him away. But Deepan, a nephew of Tmt. Janaki Ramachandran, jumped onto the pick-up truck and managed to get her down. Even as the police formed a protective cordon around her, she got into her car and drove away in a rage.

Lakhs of people lined the 10 km route from the Government Estate to the Labour Statue on the Marina via Anna Salai, Cathedral Road, Dr. Radhakrishnan Salai, and the Marina. As was my practice, I took my place at the head of the convoy and covered the entire distance on foot. The two-hour journey was a continuous struggle between the police and the crowd trying to get close to the gun-carriage. The scent of marigold being showered on the hearse from a helicopter above blended with the pungent smell of tear gas. When the crowd defied the tear gas and got closer to the gun carriage, lathis were used to keep them away. People had occupied all vantage points en route: buildings, hoardings, scaffoldings, compound walls, bus shelters, trees, and even transformer frames, in order to get one last glimpse of their 'Puratchi Thalaivar.'

Our anxiety increased as the cortege reached Radhakrishnan Salai. Over the last 2 km, tear gas grenades had to be lobbed at the crowd almost continuously, severely affecting those of us who formed the inner cordon. With our eyes watering from the effects of the tear gas, we walked with our backs to the gun-carriage, aiming our rifles and revolvers at the crowd closing in from all four directions. Progress on the Beach Road, however, was comparatively smooth, although scores of wailing mourners, some of them tearing their hair and beating their breasts, tried to follow the gun carriage to its destination. Others stood silent, too stunned to say or do anything.

It is pertinent to add here the remarks of correspondent Ravi Shankar in "The Week" magazine dated 10-16 January 1988. He wrote, "The Police Commissioner Davaram walked in front like Rambo. Davaram is a policeman with a vision. Later he was shooting people on the beach when everything went mad."

Again, at the burial place on the Marina, the crowd of mourners became uncontrollable. When tear gas failed to keep them at a reasonable distance, we had to resort to selective and restricted firing, especially on the crowd surging in from the direction of the sea.

A last burst of frenzy overtook the mourners as the coffin was taken down from the gun carriage. The close relatives and the senior members of the party could not reach the burial place. I had to lend my hand in lowering the coffin into the grave, holding a rifle in my other hand. The grave was closed to the sound of volley fire by the police party and the strains of the 'Last Post' sounded by the army buglers.

Our job, however, was not over. It took another 2 hours to clear the crowd. We had to open fire on a crowd that was intent on reopening the coffin for one last look. One group of 5 or 6 policemen was isolated and attacked by some of the crowd near the River Cooum, north of the burial place. I set off with a small party to rescue them and was soon joined by the young police officer Narendra Pal Singh, who was at that time on the staff of the DGP's office. We chased the miscreants across the river with a few shots and rescued the policemen.

Finally, all was quiet as the last rays of the sun faded away. Altogether eight people had been killed and 19 injured in the police firing. More than three hundred and 50 people had been treated at the various hospitals for injuries sustained during the two eventful days. On the police side, over a hundred officers and men and nine horses of the City Police Mounted

Branch were injured. It was well past midnight when I eventually stepped into the Government Hospital to have my injuries attended to, and to visit those who had been admitted there, including DIG Saravana Perumal, who had been set on by a mob while on his way to Rajaji Hall to assist the City Police. Unlike on other occasions of police firing, those during the funerals of popular leaders, especially in Tamil Nadu, evoked no protest or demand for inquiries. Still, the deaths due to shooting were subjected to magisterial inquiries. For the first time, I lost count of the number of rounds I had fired to warn the crowd and to protect the body of the legend.

I made special mention of Narendra Pal Singh because he was a headquarters officer and not part of the bandobust team and therefore not obliged to join me or the City Police in pursuit of the frenzied mourners. But he was a true policeman, on or off-duty. That is the spirit expected of every police officer whether on duty or off, in uniform or not, in office or at home, or on vacation elsewhere.

The City Police officers K. Vadivelu, Kalimuthu, Dharmarajan, and other officers D. Manoharan, V.C. Perumal, R. Rajamanickam, R.V. Gopalan, and K. Ramalingam, who voluntarily came forward to help, deserve the highest praise for their indefatigable work for 48 hours with no rest or even a cup of tea.

As I wound up the bandobust, I could already sense the rumblings of the power struggle within the party which eventually led to the imposition of President's Rule.

The Sanctity of the Assembly

Sanctity of the Assembly? What a misnomer it is!
Doesn't 'sanctity' describe a state of pure bliss?
But when unruly MLAs do enter therein,
Then sanctity's out and its chaos within.
When violence gets dangerously out of hand,
And the watch-and-ward staff only stare and stand,
Should not the police just outside the hall,
Respond to the Speaker's distress call?

The unexpected death of MGR on Christmas Eve 1987 led to equally unexpected developments. It threw the existing socio-political structure in the state into total disarray. Even as his body lay in state in Rajaji Hall, the senior party leaders had plunged themselves into a power struggle that was to alter the profile of the monolithic AIADMK party significantly.

Senior Minister V.R. Nedunchezhiyan was appointed acting Chief Minister by the then-Governor Khurana, who also gave the official yet-to-be-elected AIADMK nominee time till the end of the mourning period, just 4 days away, to prove his majority. However, the very next day, Minister R.M. Veerappan projected MGR's apolitical widow, Janaki Ramachandran, as the next Chief Minister. The idea behind this move was obviously to cash in on the sympathy factor that would favour the late leader's widow; and, more importantly, by installing her, she would be a dummy Chief Minister while he would become virtually the de facto Chief Minister of the State. Further, such a move would frustrate plans, if any, of other senior party leaders, including Nedunchezhiyan, staking their respective claims to the Chief Minister's chair.

3rd January was the deadline set by the Governor for the nomination of the leader of the AIADMK legislative party. S. Raghavanandam, the deputy general Secretary of the party, had already called for a general body meeting to elect the party nominee. The legality of this announcement was immediately challenged by Nedunchezhiyan on the grounds that the general body meeting could be convened only by him as the party's general Secretary or by Jayalalithaa in her capacity as the party's propaganda Secretary.

In a dramatic move on New Year's Day, 15 of the 20 district secretaries met in Madras and elected Jayalalithaa as the general Secretary of the party. In her newly acquired capacity, she announced that the general council meeting of the party would be held on 2nd January, followed by the legislators' meeting. It happened to be the same day on which the deputy general Secretary S. Raghavanandam had called for the legislators' meeting.

In mounting tension, both meetings were held on 2nd January. Ninety-seven MLAs arrived in three buses at the meeting convened by the deputy Secretary just minutes before the scheduled time. Without wasting any time, they elected Janaki Ramachandran as the party's nominee. The other meeting called for by general Secretary Nedunchezhiyan had to be conducted in a marriage hall, as the party office had been locked up by the rival faction headed by R.M. Veerappan. Nedunchezhiyan was named the leader of the legislative party by the 34 MLAs who attended this meeting.

Both groups then presented their nominations to the Governor. The Governor informed them that he required time to study their respective claims. His decision was not expected before Monday, the

5th of January. However, when Janaki Ramachandran called on the Governor late in the afternoon of Sunday, the 4th, he informed her of his decision to invite her to form the ministry on the condition that she proved her majority on the floor of the assembly no later than 3 weeks from the date of her assuming office. She chose 7th January for the swearing-in, thereby gaining maximum time to strengthen her questionable and dubious claim by 28th January.

The Governor, who had given the acting Chief Minister Nedunchezhiyan only 4 days to prove his majority, gave an over-generous 21 days to the new claimant, Janaki Ramachandran. He had also failed to question the legality of the meeting called for by the deputy general Secretary, as against the meeting called for by the newly elected general Secretary Jayalalithaa. Although 97 of the one hundred and 31 MLAs had pledged their support to MGR's widow, who had never taken any interest in politics, public life, or party affairs, it was quite apparent that the majority of the party cadre was solidly behind the high-profile, extremely popular, and politically active Jayalalithaa.

The following days saw an intense struggle by the rival groups to rope in the MLAs sitting on the fence. Nedunchezhiyan was the choice of the general body for no reason other than that he was the senior-most member of the legislative assembly, a fact that not only he but everyone else acknowledged. The obvious choice, however, would have been Jayalalithaa, the propaganda Secretary of the party and the well-known confidante of MGR. She had the unqualified support of the rank and file throughout the state. Everyone, party members and others alike, saw her as the true successor of MGR.

With the final trial of strength set for 28th January, both groups began to frantically try to increase their respective strengths. The police were not involved except on 16th January, when the group led by Nedunchezhiyan and Jayalalithaa tried to break into the party office, which had been locked by the rival Janaki group. I reached the spot and advised the leaders to seek a remedy in a civil court. But they refused to leave the place, and I ordered the arrest of the leaders, including Nedunchezhiyan and Jayalalithaa, and made them get into a police van. By then, the followers called off the siege, and Nedunchezhiyan got down from the van to talk to them. But Jayalalithaa refused to leave the vehicle, and I told the van driver to drive her down to Poes Garden. After the van reached her house, I got the message that she was refusing to get off the vehicle. I reached the spot and told her that there was no case against anyone and requested her to go home. She obliged with a smile.

28th January was the deadline fixed by the Governor for Janaki Ramachandran to prove her majority. Sufficient police strength had been deployed at the Fort. But security within the Assembly itself was, as was customary, left to the Watch-and-Ward Staff, who worked under the authority of the Speaker. I had asked the Deputy Commissioner (Law & Order) North, who was the jurisdiction officer, to remain in the Police Control Room in the Secretariat to watch out for any developments outside the Assembly. I remained in my office in Egmore, keeping track of the events as they unfolded.

At 10:00 a.m., the House assembled for voting on the confidence motion. The Speaker, P.H. Pandian, took his seat, recited a couplet from the Thirukural, and announced that five Congress (I) members had informed him 15 minutes earlier that they had resigned from the party and that they were on their way to the Assembly to take part in the election. As such, he announced that the voting would take place only at 12 noon and adjourned the House. Loud protests from the Congress (I) and pro-Jayalalithaa members filled the house. Shortly after, the five Congress (I) members who had resigned entered the house and were set upon by the other Congress MLAs. They freed themselves with difficulty and took cover in the Speaker's chamber. A lull set in with the MLAs waiting for the all-important mid-day session.

As soon as the House reassembled, the Speaker announced the disqualification of six pro-Jayalalithaa members and adjourned the House a second time till 3:00 p.m. Protest from the MLAs of the Jayalalithaa faction, the Congress (I), and the Communist Party was followed by the first bout of violence. Slippers, paperweights, and microphones wrenched from the desks were hurled at each other. After initial resistance, the outnumbered pro-Janaki members beat a hasty retreat from the House.

The opposition group then held its own assembly session and elected MLA S. Sivaraman as its Speaker. They also prevented the Watch-and-Ward Staff from entering the house in order to ensure the confidentiality of their deliberations. After passing a No-Confidence Motion against the Janaki Government and a resolution removing P.H. Pandian from the post of Speaker, Sivaraman adjourned the House sine die.

By then, I had reached the Secretariat to deal with the legislators' violence should it spill out of the Assembly. The AIADMK MLAs belonging to the Jayalalithaa faction were at that time leaving the House. On seeing me outside the Assembly, they told me that my presence there would not be necessary, as they were going to the Raj Bhavan to request the Governor to dismiss the Government that had lost its majority. They also told me that they would not be returning to the Assembly till the Governor announced his decision.

The Home Secretary suggested that I could return to my office as there would be no trouble during the afternoon session, which would be attended only by the Janaki faction. Besides, whatever happened inside the Assembly had to be dealt with only by the Speaker with the help of the Watch-and-Ward Staff, not by the police. But having gone to the Secretariat, I decided to stay on at the police outpost. I had asked for my lunch to be brought there and told the officers and men on bandobust to have their lunch and be ready when the Assembly met again at 3:00 p.m. I also arranged to keep the supporters of both groups, who were hovering around, well away from the Assembly building.

At 3:00 p.m., the session opened with the MLAs of only the Janaki faction of the AIADMK, the DMK, and Independents in attendance. The Confidence Motion was promptly passed with 99 MLAs voting for and eight against. Twenty-seven MLAs belonging to the Jayalalithaa faction were disqualified on the grounds that they had defied the Party Whip by absenting themselves from the Assembly. But within half an hour, the situation changed dramatically. The MLAs who had gone to meet the Governor returned to the Assembly en masse. A few of them pushed the Speaker out of his chair and installed in his place, Sivaraman, as the rival Speaker. The tussle for the Speaker's chair was the signal for an all-out fight between the rival groups. Once again, chairs and paperweights flew across the hall. Anything that came to hand became a missile. The rival MLAs had taken up battle positions inside the hall, trading missiles and abuses. Many MLAs were injured, and one or two had slumped to the floor. The Speaker appealed frantically for police protection.

When I reached the gate of the Assembly, I found the Home Secretary and the Assembly Secretary debating the legality of the Speaker's appeal for police assistance. Never in the history of legislatures anywhere in India had the police entered the Assembly, the myth of the "Sanctity of the Assembly" having been ingrained in everybody's mind. Boisterous yelling and the sound of tables, fans, and microphones being broken and flung around rose in a crescendo, drowning Speaker P.H. Pandian's frantic call for help.

There was no time to be lost. I had to decide immediately whether to follow the convention that kept the Assembly out of bounds for the police or to act on the primary responsibilities of the police, namely maintenance of law-and-order and protection of life and property. As in times of earlier crises, I followed my basic instinct and entered the Assembly Hall through the door nearest the Speaker's chair. Most of the senior officers, including the jurisdiction officer, the DCP (L&O) North, and some mid-level officers, hastily made themselves scarce to stay clear of possible entanglement with the elected representatives of the people, worried about the legality or otherwise of the police entering the exclusive domain of the People's Representatives. But ADC-IS Hirudaya Doss, who was there more as an adviser and moderator, entered the hallowed premises with me, as did the members of the lower subordinate staff, Inspectors, Sub-Inspectors, Head Constables, and Constables, who were not conditioned by any such concerns. They followed me as they had always done, without hesitation. Incidentally, I had known Hirudaya Doss from my training days in Madurai, and later in my service, whenever I was involved in any law-and-order situation, such as during confrontation with the fishermen, he would be there with me; and he was there with me throughout the police action in the Assembly. I am grateful to him not only for his initiatives but also for his concern for me throughout my service, from my training days in Madurai till my retirement.

On entering the Assembly, I found some MLAs who had occupied the visitors' galleries above, hurling chairs from there. One of the chairs grazed my back. That was the signal for the constables to swing into action. As the policemen closed in on them, the MLAs jumped over the desks and ran towards the exit to escape their lathis. The press representatives were asked to take shelter in the press Room. In less than 5 minutes, the hall was cleared, and the Speaker was escorted to his chamber. The fleeing MLAs joined their supporters outside the hall to nurse their injuries and plan their next move.

The opposition demanded a judicial inquiry into the violence, the police lathi-charge, the improprieties committed by the Speaker in reassembling the loyal MLAs while the rest were away at the Raj Bhavan, and above all, in summoning the police into the house. The following day, the Congress Party organised a demonstration outside the Assembly premises. A few MLAs, swathed in bandages, were among the demonstrators who demanded the dismissal of the minority Government that had the support of only 97 MLAs in a House of two hundred and 35, and action against the Speaker and the Commissioner of Police, both of whom had violated the "Sanctity of the Assembly," the former by summoning the police into the house and the latter by entering the forbidden premises.

On 30th January, 2 days after the Assembly incident, President R. Venkatraman dissolved the Tamil Nadu Assembly and placed the state under President's Rule. His decision was based on Governor Khurana's report that the constitutional machinery in the state had broken down. The Governor had also made adverse remarks on the manner in which the Janaki Government had secured the confidence votes of 99 members. That, however, did not save him from being replaced by Governor P.C. Alexander. The state soon settled down to President's Rule.

But that was not the end of the challenges for the police, definitely not for me. A 'quo-warranto' petition questioning my continuing as the Commissioner of Police after I had "illegally" entered the Assembly was filed by a Congress (I) member of the dissolved Assembly. It said that the Commissioner of Police had acted beyond his executive powers, forgetting the fact that he was an executive under the state and not under the Speaker. Justice Mohan, before whom the petition was filed, said in his finding, "The petition was misconceived as it was the Speaker who controlled the proceedings with the request. There was no violation of Article 21 or Article 166 (3) of the Constitution. To quell a riot and restore order, the Commissioner could act in a manner best known to him as the circumstances might demand, and there was no question of any written order from the Speaker to act. The circumstances might vary and, depending upon the gravity of such circumstances, it was for the Commissioner of Police to act." With this observation, he dismissed the petition.

The landmark judgement of Justice Mohan made it clear that no premises were beyond the reach of the police if it was for the purpose of maintaining law-and-order or for preventing crime. The Police Department should be grateful to the learnt Justice for reminding it of its inherent responsibility and inalienable duty. It fully supported my belief and conviction backed by my past record of entering even mosques,

Temples, and churches to prevent clashes and to maintain law-and-order. The Assembly could be no different, more sacred, or more sanctified.

In spite of such a clear court order, it is painful to see the police remaining mere spectators when violence is unleashed in their very presence. The hour-long clash between two groups of students in the Madras Law College a few years ago was one such incident. That such an incident could take place right in the capital where the Commissioner of Police could reach the spot within minutes is certainly a black mark on the police. True leadership does not take shelter in negative precedents but acts on positive thinking; not on personal safety but on the department's reputation.

Had someone died or been grievously injured during the clashes within the Assembly while the police stood by outside in spite of distress calls for help from the Speaker, I could never have forgiven myself; and the same people and the members of the media who condemned my entry, unprecedented though it had been, would have been the first to blame me for my inaction.

"Any police officer who succumbs to external pressure and fails in his duty is not worth his salt. He might as well quit."

I must also mention my entry into another premises, which was considered beyond the reach of the police. This was the Secretariat located inside Fort St. George. The occasion was the sudden decision of the lower secretarial staff to strike work, demanding higher wages and allowances. All of them had come out of their offices and congregated in front of the newly built Namakkal Kavignar Maligai. Shouting slogans against the government, they walked out of the main gate of the Fort onto the main road, blocking traffic. I reached the place with a small squad of officers and men and warned the demonstrators to restrict their activities to within the Fort. They did not listen to me, and I had to chase them away from the road. They ran inside the Fort and took shelter in the eleven-storeyed Namakkal Kavignar Maligai. I ensured accessibility to the old building where the offices of the Chief Minister, the Chief Secretary, and other important ministers and secretaries were located. I then proceeded to the new building from the verandas of which the striking staff was raising slogans. As I walked alongside the building, the demonstrators started throwing flower pots at me. Luckily, nothing fell on me, and within a few minutes, we cleared them from the verandas and warned them either to go into their offices or leave the building. They did go in but continued with their protest. Cries of 'Down! Down! Police,' complemented by an occasional 'Down! Down! Walter' chanted by my erstwhile college mates who were also members of the secretarial staff, filled the air. But soon, normalcy was restored. The entire secretarial staff put the incident behind them. Cordiality reigned once more.

When I look back, I am proud of my action in entering the Assembly as well as the Secretariat. I am prouder still of my constabulary, which followed me without hesitation into the so-called "Sanctified" areas where many of their senior officers had feared to tread. I still consider my transfer from the post of Commissioner of Police after the dismissal of the Government an acknowledgement of my correct and bold action.

Serendib

'Tear-drop of India' is what she looks to be,
Because of her shape and her place upon the sea.
'Serendib' was how she earlier had been known
And then, on world maps, as 'Ceylon' she was shown.
As days went by, they again changed her name,
And to the world, Sri Lanka she became.
That peaceful isle, that jewel on the sea
Became the battle-ground of the LTTE.

Sri Lanka, the island separated from India by the Gulf of Mannar, was originally known as Serendib, a name given to it by the Arabs and Persians. After colonisation by the Portuguese, Dutch, and English, it came to be called 'Ceylon.' Even after its independence in 1948, it continued to be called Ceylon. It was only in the year 1972 that it came to be known as Sri Lanka. The island, because of its shape and position near the South of India, is also known as the 'Tear-drop of India.'

The major ethnic groups in Sri Lanka are the Sinhalese, Tamils, Muslims, and Burghers. However, I will confine myself to only two of those groups – the Sinhalese, who form the majority of the population, and the Sri Lankan or the Eelam Tamils, who are the descendants of the Tamils of the old Jaffna Kingdom, occupying the northern and eastern parts of the island. The Muslims were late arrivals from India, and the Burghers, descendants of the Portuguese and Dutch who had married

Ceylonese women. The two last-named communities are too small to influence Sri Lankan politics.

The Tamil population in the hilly areas of Nuwara Eliya is of a totally different origin. They had been recruited from the old Madras State by the agents of the British-owned tea estates in the mid-19th century and taken to work on the tea estates in Ceylon. When I started my service as ASP Tuticorin in the year 1966, I found that one of the police stations, Thattaparai, was housed in what had been the quarantine camp for the migrant labourers before they embarked upon the Dhanushkodi-Talaimannar voyage. The camp had been in existence from the year 1880. It was, at that time, controlled by an official from the Ceylonese government. By the year 1916, migration of workers from India had stopped altogether, as by then, the tea estates in Nuwara Eliya had acquired all the Indian labour that they needed. Although the Tamil labourers on the plantation did not get involved in the freedom struggle of the Sri Lankan Tamils, the Ceylonese government decided to gradually repatriate them. It is sad that the South Indian Tamil labourers who were responsible for raising the export-oriented and highly profitable plantations of tea, coffee, and rubber in Ceylon were given a raw deal. But the Government of Tamil Nadu opened up new tea estates in The Nilgiris to accommodate them.

When the influx of Sri Lankan Tamils was at its peak, there were 107 settlements in Tamil Nadu accommodating 59,345 refugees who received assistance, including existence allowance, from the government. 34,000 more had registered their names at the local police stations but were on their own, without much help from either the government or their leaders.

Students from Sri Lanka, both Sinhalese and Tamils, used to study in various colleges in Tamil Nadu. I had both groups as my classmates in the YMCA College of Physical Education in the year 1956 and in the Madras Christian College in the year 1957. But the enmity between the two ethnic groups had grown to such an extent that they rarely spoke to each other. However, I do remember the very friendly demeanour of the Sinhalese students. This congeniality can be seen even today, with large groups of them coming to Tamil Nadu to visit places of religious importance, both Hindu and Buddhist, and of course, for shopping. They are safe in their Mahabodhi Temple Guest House on Kennet Lane, Egmore. In 1999, as President of the Tamil Nadu Athletic Association (TNAA), I took a team of four athletes to participate in the Sri Lanka National Games in the Sugathadasa stadium in Colombo. All of them— Anju George, Latha, Ramachandran, and Shankar—won gold in their respective events, the last named winning two gold medals. On the special invitation of Yashodhara De Silva, President of the Puttalam District Athletic Association, Secretary Latha, Coach Pugalendhi, and I took another athletic team of four boys and four girls to Puttalam in the year 2012. All of them won gold medals in their respective events. We were hosted by the office-bearers in their homes as their personal guests and experienced the warmth of Sinhalese hospitality. Again, as President of John Memorial Volleyball Club, I took a team to Colombo. We have, on our part, hosted their athletes and volleyball players in Chennai even while hostilities between the two linguistic groups were going on unabated on the island. Isn't it true then that sports alone can foster camaraderie?

The uneasy calm that prevailed in Sri Lanka between the Sinhalese majority and the Tamil minority from the time of Sri Lankan independence in the year 1948 finally broke out into open conflict. The terrorist attacks by militant Tamil outfits in the northern and eastern parts of the country and retaliatory attacks by the Sinhalese elsewhere on the island resulted in the large-scale exodus in the early 1980s of the Tamil population to Tamil Nadu across the narrow strip of the sea between the two nations. With them, also arrived the Tamil militants. The first indication of the presence of militants in Tamil Nadu was the shoot-out on 2.4.1984 between Velupillai Prabakaran and Raghavan, leaders of the LTTE (Liberation Tigers of Tamil Eelam), and Uma Maheswaran and Jothiswaran of the PLOTE (People's Liberation Organisation of Tamil

Eelam) in Chennai's busy Pondy Bazaar. In the shoot-out, the first of its kind in Tamil Nadu, Jothiswaran was injured. Prabakaran and Raghavan were arrested and taken into judicial custody. Uma Maheswaran, who escaped, was arrested 4 days later near Gummidipoondi Railway Station after a brief exchange of fire with the police. The gun culture had entered Tamil Nadu.

It became a very complex situation when all the Sri Lankan militant groups, LTTE, PLOTE, EROS, and EPRLF, made Tamil Nadu their training ground. We, the police, were very uneasy because all of these groups had the latest automatic firearms. We, with our outdated weapons—.410 muskets for the local police and.303 rifles for the Armed Police—stood no chance against them in the event of an armed conflict.

But the Government of India and the Government of Tamil Nadu, not to mention the people of Tamil Nadu, were very benevolent towards the refugees as well as towards the militant groups. As many as a hundred thousand refugees and militants were accommodated in camps set up in various districts of Tamil Nadu. There were 30 refugee camps spread out across nine border districts, mainly Ramanathapuram, Pudukottai, and Thanjavur, which were close to the Jaffna Peninsula. The leaders of all the groups were in Madras City, liaising with their local contacts. Although most of the militant groups were concentrating on their training, some of them abused the hospitality they were enjoying in Tamil Nadu, and in doing so, embarrassed the host country. One such instance was the explosion at Meenambakkam Airport on 2nd April 1984, in which 30 air passengers were killed and extensive damage was caused to the air terminal. The militants' plan was to set the time-bomb to go off on a Colombo-bound Air Lanka flight either during the flight or upon landing at Colombo Airport. The plan went awry when the conspirators failed to get customs clearance for their lethal baggage. They did try to alert the airport officials, but it was too late, and the bomb ripped through the customs office and the nearby passengers' hall, taking the lives of several people.

Inspector Vellingiri of CB-CID, who took up the investigation, skilfully reconstructed the events. Three of the accused, Karthikesan, Vigneswara, and Thambi Raja, jumped bail and absconded. The remaining 5 were sentenced to life imprisonment by the Sessions Judge, Chengalpet.

Support, both direct and indirect, for the Tamil freedom struggle in Sri Lanka was one of the reasons for the emergence of Tamil extremist groups in Tamil Nadu. The 'Tamilar Viduthalai Padai' had many proclaimed and unproclaimed items on their agenda apart from the creation of Tamil Eelam. This only went to prove their clouded and confused thinking. As a result, all the victims of their violence were their fellow Tamilians in Tamil Nadu.

Another powerful blast ripped the railway line at Maruthiyar Bridge on 15th March 1987, causing seven bogies of the Rockfort Express to plunge into the dry riverbed below, killing 26 passengers and seriously injuring 140. The CB-CID that took up the investigation found 11 hardcore extremists functioning under R. Aranganathan, a school teacher in Karai Village in Padalur in Thanjavur district, who also was found to be in possession of a sten-gun and ammunition. But before the police could close in on those accused, 12 of them, in their abortive bid to loot a bank in Ponparapi Village, were lynched by the villagers. That, we thought, was almost the end of Tamil extremism in Tamil Nadu, but it wasn't to be. There was a bomb blast in the Botanical Gardens in Ooty on 18th May 1988, more as a warning to the government. The CB-CID arrested Pandiarajan and eight others of the Tamilar Viduthalai Padai. All of them were convicted and sentenced to 7 years RI. On 6th April 1991, in another of their attacks, in Pudur police station in Cuddalore district, one constable was killed and one SI and three constables injured. I visited the station the same day along with S.R. Jangid, Superintendent of Police, who later arranged to bring down from Rajasthan a marble bust of the martyred constable and have it installed in the District Police Office, Cuddalore. Another attempt to loot the Indian Bank at

Pennagaram in Dharmapuri district on 4th July 1991 failed. Inspector Mohammed Basheer and Karunakaran arrested 12 of the 29 accused. While the case was pending trial, ten of the other accused were killed in various encounters with the STF.

The CB-CID had always proved its competence in investigating perplexing and complicated cases. When extremism and terrorism challenged it with their combined might, it rose to the occasion by successfully investigating all the cases and arresting almost all the accused.

I was not directly involved in the intelligence work relating to the activities of the militant groups. As DIG of Police, Vellore Range from 1980 to 1985, I was only aware of the settlement of more than a hundred thousand refugees in several camps all over the state and the support extended to them by the Governments of India and Tamil Nadu. The training centres of the militants were also functioning with the tacit support of the two governments.

When I assumed charge of Madras City Police in 1985, I made an inventory of the militant leaders and their followers in the city. However, I had no way of monitoring their activities. Mohandas, DGP-CID, was in touch with MGR, who at that time, was undergoing treatment in the USA. The Tamil militants had the full support of MGR, who, incidentally, was born in the Sri Lankan town of Kandy.

On Deepavali day, 1st November 1986, a 24-year-old resident of Chennai was killed and two others were injured when, following an altercation, the militants belonging to the EPRLF opened fire on a holiday crowd in Choolaimedu. They retreated into their rented house and, armed with their automatic weapons, took up position on their terrace. It all began at 2.15 pm when 4 of the EPRLF (Eelam People's Revolutionary Liberation Front) group were returning to their house. Apparently, a Deepavali reveller had accidentally brushed against one of them, leading to a fracas. Three local youngsters sustained bullet injuries, resulting in the death of one of them. The local crowd, numbering more than a thousand, surrounded the house and continued to throw stones at the Sri Lankan militants.

As it was a holiday, I had not asked for my vehicle. When I heard about the shooting, I called Control Room over the wireless and asked them for a vehicle. G. Babu, Inspector of Sembium Police Station, on hearing my call, hurried to my residence with his vehicle and took me to the place of the incident. This he did, although the incident occurred well outside his jurisdiction. When we reached the spot, IGP S. Sripal was already there trying to pacify the locals but did not take steps to disarm the militants.

I directed the militants to lay down their arms. However, they were reluctant to do so, fearing reprisal by the large number of local residents who had surrounded their house. Armed with only a pistol, I went up to the terrace and secured their surrender. I was followed closely by the unarmed Inspector G. Babu. We seized 6 automatic guns, two revolvers, one pistol, and 350 rounds of live ammunition. In a commendable show of compassion, Inspector Babu bandaged the wounds of the militants who had been injured by the stone hits. After the crowd dispersed, we arrested all ten militants, including their leader, Douglas Devananda. It was this same Devananda who later became a minister in the Sri Lankan government. The murder case against him and others, however, is still pending in Chennai. The Inspector's gallant act was not recognised by a medal because of the complex nature of the relationship between the Government of Tamil Nadu and the Sri Lankan militants. I refrained from initiating a proposal for the grant of gallantry medals because I myself was involved in the incident. Looking back, I regret that I could not get Inspector Babu a gallantry medal or an accelerated promotion, a process I had successfully initiated for subordinates on several occasions.

On 8.11.1986, a week after the Choolaimedu shooting, Mohandas, DGP-CID, ordered a massive operation to disarm all the Sri Lankan militants. "Operation Tiger" was launched, and midnight raids were conducted simultaneously in all the camps in nine districts and in Madras

City. All the militants were rounded up and their weapons seized. In Chennai, as the Commissioner of Police, it was my responsibility to disarm the LTTE, the most powerful of the militant groups. With a small team, I surrounded the residence of Prabhakaran in Indira Nagar, disarmed him and his followers numbering over 30, and took them to the office of the DIG, CID. Prabhakaran, who was kept waiting in the corridor of the CID office, maintained total silence. It was only his associate, Anton Balasingham, who raised an objection to the arrest. The following day, all the arrested militants were released but without their weapons. However, the LTTE were allowed to keep theirs. The process benefitted none but the LTTE.

The simultaneous disarming of all the militants caused much confusion in the department. The disarming itself had no parallel in history. Even an accidental firing by one of the militants in any of the camps could have developed into a major conflagration. I shudder to think of a battle between militants armed with the most modern weapons and the Tamil Nadu police armed with prehistoric firearms fit only to control unlawful and unarmed assemblies. As Commissioner of Police, I arrested all the leaders, including Prabhakaran and Anton Balasingham of the LTTE, but we were asked to release all of them and also to return the weapons seized from them. I learnt that the operation had been ordered by MGR while he was in Delhi, as was the order to return the weapons to the LTTE. The Government of India also endorsed MGR's view because it needed Prabhakaran's cooperation at the proposed SAARC meeting in Bangalore, where Prime Minister Rajiv Gandhi and the Sri Lankan President were supposed to discuss the Sri Lankan-Tamil issue with Prabhakaran.

However, Prabhakaran refused to attend the Bangalore meeting, although a special flight had been arranged to take him there. I was on my way to attend a wedding reception with Prema and my daughter Anita when I received a frantic call from Mohandas to somehow ensure that Prabhakaran attended the Bangalore meeting the following day. I was in mufti and unarmed. I stopped by the City Police armoury, took a pistol, and rushed to Prabhakaran's house. I told Prema and Anita to wait in the car and to duck down below the seat if they heard the sound of gunfire. When I met Prabhakaran and Anton Balasingham and told them of the importance of their presence in Bangalore, Prabhakaran was quiet, but his spokesman Balasingham said that they had decided not to attend the meeting. I then told them in clear terms that they were in our country as our guests, and when our Prime Minister wanted them to meet the Sri Lankan delegation, they had no choice but to obey. Reluctantly, they agreed, and I took them to the airport and put them in the special aircraft that was waiting for them. Anita was disappointed at not being able to watch a gunfight like in a cowboy movie!

Nothing came of the meeting in Bangalore, and soon after, Prabhakaran left for Sri Lanka and resumed his armed conflict with the Sri Lankan Army. However, his close followers, one-eyed Sivarajan, Shoba, Dhanu, and many others, remained in Tamil Nadu. It was they who played a major role in the assassination of Rajiv Gandhi in Sriperumbudur on 21.05.1991.

The general public opinion on "Operation Tiger" was that it was timely, well planned, and well executed. F.V. Arul, former IGP Madras and Director CBI, and many other administrative chiefs said in a joint press statement, "We wish to convey our high appreciation of the professional excellence displayed by the Tamil Nadu police in organising and executing 'Operation Tiger.' The wide-ranging character of the operation, which ended in complete success and without a single untoward incident, and the split-second timing speaks highly of the discipline of the operational force. This is a splendid achievement on the part of the Tamil Nadu police in contrast to what has been happening in other terrorist-infested areas in India." But in sharp contrast, Claude Alvarez, the civil rights activist, described Tamil Nadu as a police state and Walter Davaram, DIG, as a Frankenstein created by Mohandas.

MGR's response to his remarks was, "There cannot be Mahatma Gandhis in the Police Force."

My own reading of the order to disarm all the Sri Lankan Tamil militants is that it was the brain-child of DGP-CID Mohandas, a brilliant, self-willed, and capable officer who had the capacity to influence the Chief Minister and even the Prime Minister on matters relating to Sri Lanka. The lack of direction, the inconsistency of both the Government of India and that of Tamil Nadu, and above all, the prolonged illness of MGR complicated the whole situation and also marked the end of the brilliant career of Mohandas. He served the rest of his years in unimportant posts, finally retiring as Chairman of Pallavan Transport Corporation.

India, by its fluctuating stance, further confused the Sri Lankan issue. The number of refugees had by then grown to nearly 2 lakhs. There was no way of separating the refugees from the militants. I always felt that the local police of Tamil Nadu were placed in a perilous position in dealing with the LTTE, who were equipped with highly sophisticated arms.

In May-June 1987, the Sri Lankan Army launched an offensive called 'Operation Liberation.' Many Tamilians were massacred in the course of the conflict. This offensive marked the Sri Lankan Army's first conventional warfare. Leaders Prabakaran and Thillai Ambalam Srinivasan narrowly escaped death. The key military officers involved in the operation were Brig. Denzil Kobbekaduwa and Lt. Col. Gotabaya Rajapaksa, the brother of the former President of Sri Lanka, Mahinda Rajapaksa. Under the Indo-Sri Lankan Peace Accord signed on 29th July 1987, a few concessions were given to the Sri Lankan Tamils, including the merger of the Northern and Eastern Provinces into a single province and the granting of official status to the Tamil language. Needless to say, the agreement was honoured more in its breach than in its implementation.

Under the mandate of the same Peace Accord, India agreed to ensure peace in the Tamil area of Sri Lanka through an army unit called the

Indian Peace Keeping Force (IPKF). Although the LTTE initially agreed to surrender their arms to the IPKF, they reneged on their agreement and started a guerrilla warfare against them, resulting in a conflict that lasted 3 long years. In April 1989, President Ranasinghe Premadasa clandestinely handed over seized arms to the LTTE to fight the IPKF. Although the IPKF suffered heavy casualties in the guerrilla attacks by the LTTE, Rajiv Gandhi refused to withdraw the forces from Sri Lanka. However, following his defeat in the Indian Parliamentary elections in December 1989, the new Prime Minister V.P. Singh ordered the withdrawal of the IPKF. The last ship with soldiers of the IPKF arrived in Chennai Harbour on 24th March 1990. Karunanidhi, the then Chief Minister of Tamil Nadu, declined to receive them, thereby indicating his opposition to India's interference in the hostility between the Sri Lankan Government and the LTTE. As many as 1,200 soldiers of the IPKF had lost their lives to the guerrilla tactics of the LTTE during its 32-month stay in Sri Lanka, a high casualty rate compared to India's wars with Pakistan in 1965 and 1971. It was a needless war that India was unwittingly drawn into and referred to as India's Vietnam. As a regional superpower, India had no need to undergo such humiliation. History will remember India's involvement in the Sri Lanka Crisis as a catastrophic error that led to the loss of numerous lives without achieving the desired result. The only matter of pride was the award of the Param Vir Chakra, though posthumously, to Major Ramaswamy Parameshwaran of the Mahar Regiment. However, it is a pity he has not been honoured in Tamil Nadu, no doubt a decision taken to placate the Sri Lankan Tamil militants.

Meanwhile, 72 militants from Madurai and 70 from Chennai City were repatriated to Sri Lanka. Thukkiandi SP-Q branch and I accompanied them to Jaffna and returned to India by the same flight. I still have the poignant memory of the children fondly clutching the toys given to them in India, with their future in Sri Lanka so uncertain.

Earlier, K. Padmanabha, Secretary-General of EPRLF, and 13 others of his group had been massacred by the LTTE in Madras. The LTTE's murder spree did not spare even Indian citizens. One local resident was killed by LTTE bullets, and another lost his eye. The whole operation took place in the heart of the city, which only pointed to the utter contempt the militants had for the host nation.

This massacre was not an isolated incident. Even from 1984, the LTTE had been transporting arms and explosives to their base in Sri Lanka. Following the seizure of a large cache of arms and ammunition from Durgavalasai Village in Ramanathapuram District on 20.1.1990, check posts were set up at Pattanamkathan on the Ramanathapuram-Mandapam Road and Koperimadam on the Ramanathapuram-Devipattinam Road.

At 22:25 hrs on 18.2.1990, a white Maruti Gypsy and a white Ambassador car were stopped at the Pattinamkathan check post located near the District Police Office in Ramanathapuram. The vehicles were heading towards Rameswaram. The occupants of the car informed the check post HC that they were carrying medicines and should be allowed to proceed without being checked. They also told the HC that another car was following and that it too should not be stopped and checked. When the HC approached the vehicle, the occupants brandished automatic weapons, lifted the check post bar, and sped towards Rameswaram. Immediately upon receiving this information, K. Radhakrishnan, Superintendent of Police, Ramanathapuram, left his headquarters in Madurai in pursuit of the vehicles, after alerting all check posts and police stations en route and the refugee camp in Mandapam. At 12:30 a.m., as he reached Pirappanavalasai, 22 km beyond Ramanathapuram, he noticed three vehicles, 2 of them bearing the number plates noted at the Pattinamkathan check post earlier. He turned around and gave chase. He was joined by a police patrol party consisting of one Inspector of Police and 11 police constables of the Tamil Nadu Special Police. At 12:45 a.m., the vehicles were stopped at the Ramanathapuram check post. The Superintendent of Police and his team stood right in front of the vehicles and asked the occupants to identify themselves. Immediately, the occupants opened fire from all three vehicles. In the first volley, a constable of the Tamil Nadu Special Police was killed. The miscreants fired nearly 150 rounds from 5 or 6 automatic weapons, injuring 17 other policemen and two civilians. Another constable, Subramani, later died of gunshot injuries. The police van had received as many as 30 direct hits.

In the mayhem that followed the murderous firing, the occupants of the vehicles lifted the check post bar and escaped. All three vehicles passed the Kenikarai police station, 3 km away, where the local police tried to stop them. However, the terrorists broke through the barricades, killing one civilian and injuring 2.

Meanwhile, the SP took control of the situation and gave instructions on his car radio to all the check posts. He was ably assisted by DSP S.N. Seshasai and Inspector Sethurajan. He also sent the injured to the hospital. While this was happening, I, in the capacity of IGP (Prohibition), was in the midst of a distillation raid in Thanjavur. I was asked by the DGP to rush to Ramanathapuram and take charge of the situation there, which I did, covering over 250 km in my raid-soiled fatigues. Such was the faith the department had in me, irrespective of the post I held.

My last dealing with the Sri Lankan militants was when 43 of them escaped from Tipu Mahal in Vellore Fort through a 150-foot-long tunnel they had dug. This happened on 15th August 1995, India's Independence Day. Referring to the escapees as prisoners or even detainees was a misnomer because they were not treated as detainees. There were no security arrangements in the Mahal. While the militants were kept in Tipu Mahal, their families were housed in the adjoining Hyder Mahal. More importantly, the management of the detention centre was with a tahsildar, not with the Police or the Prison Department. Of course, there were police guards outside the Mahal, but they had no authority to enter it. It was therefore unfortunate that the 'short-term' DGP Vaikunth recommended the suspension of Superintendent of Police Ashutosh Shukla over the incident.

When I took over as DGP, I explained to the Chief Minister that the police in Vellore, headed by Ashutosh Shukla, were not in charge of the Sri Lankan refugees. She immediately cancelled the suspension and posted SP Shukla as AIG (Administration). Later on, as DIG, Coimbatore, Shukla did outstanding work by leading a team to the hideout of Muslim terrorist Imam Ali in Bengaluru and eliminating him and four other Muslim terrorists. For this, he was awarded the Police Medal for Gallantry. What a far cry from the needless and vindictive suspension he had suffered.

Meanwhile, SP Radhakrishnan, who succeeded Shukla in Vellore district, lived up to his reputation and arrested 9 of the 43 escapees at Egmore Railway Station the next day. For this, the SP was awarded the Tamil Nadu CM's Medal for Outstanding Devotion to Duty. Nine more were arrested by Inspector Karuppasamy of the STF from the Sathyamangalam forest, where they were trying to join Veerapan's gang. No alliance could have been more ridiculous than that of freedom fighters with forest brigands. Inspector Karuppasamy and others were given accelerated promotions for their remarkable work. While the promotions of SIs, HCs, and PCs were sanctioned, Karuppasamy's promotion was not approved as promotion to the gazetted rank of DSP had to be sanctioned by the TNPSC.

The dauntless Inspector Karupuswamy

Within a year, SP K. Radhakrishnan, then posted to Chengalpet East district, again proved his courage by arresting six crew members of the ship "Tongo Nova," who had escaped from the Central Prison, Chennai. Their ship, carrying Rs. 18 crores worth of arms and ammunition to the LTTE in Jaffna, was intercepted in Indian territorial waters on 8.11.1991 by the Indian Navy. The police throughout the state reacted brilliantly to the red alert issued by the SP. All the check posts were alerted and strengthened. Within 2 hours of their escape, five of the escapees were found travelling in a bus bound for Andhra Pradesh by the Arambakkam border check post staff. Three of them, including the Captain of the ship, Philendren, committed suicide by swallowing cyanide capsules. The remaining 2 were arrested. The Chief Minister promptly recognised the brilliant work of the check post staff by announcing accelerated promotions for SI Purushothaman, HC Kuppan, Gr.1 PCs Bhagvan Doss, Karthikeyan, and Subramaniam, and Gr.II PCs Karikalan, Sekar, and Manivannan, and TSP constable Velmurugan. Probationary Inspector K. Kumar of Gummidipoondi, who led the interception, was brought to the top of the 1979 batch to facilitate his future promotion.

The Assassination of Rajiv Gandhi

The stage was set, with all in place;
I, at the airport met him face to face;
He greeted me as my hand he shook;
He waved; then the road to his fate he took.

The total and unconditional freedom and support given to the Sri Lankan
Tamil militants and refugees in Tamil Nadu were not honourably
respected by all of them. The rival militant groups, all of whom had
shifted their headquarters to Tamil Nadu, continued their attacks on

each other. Furthermore, their large-scale arms-smuggling by sea into the state made Tamil Nadu a haven of illicit firearms. In Tamil Nadu, they even attempted to build a submarine. Thanks to the efforts of IGP Amalraj, this half-finished submarine, along with many of their other modern weapons, wireless equipment, and even a rocket launcher, can be seen in the Police Museum in Coimbatore.

The Sinhalese, on their part, were also not sure of India's stance on the situation. Was India taking a fair view of the dispute? Was India supporting the militants? Surely, the Sinhalese must have been resentful; but that did not stop their regular shopping visits to Chennai.

It was in the year 1987 that the India-Sri Lanka agreement on the Sri Lankan Tamil issue was signed in Colombo by Rajiv Gandhi and the Sri Lankan President Jayawardhane. Rajiv Gandhi was given a Guard of Honour after signing the agreement. At that parade, one of the naval guards hit him with the butt of his rifle, just as he walked past him. Rajiv Gandhi managed to duck, receiving the blow on his shoulder instead of on his head. Had the attack been more serious, the agreement would have come to nought.

Later, not much attention was paid to the assault. However, I did manage to get further details about the assailant, Vijayamuni, who had been sentenced to 6 years of rigorous imprisonment by the Sri Lankan court. 2 years later, he was pardoned by the new President Premadasa. Vijayamuni contested the provincial council election, but not only did he not win, but he also lost his deposit. Nothing more has been heard of him since. In spite of the serious attack, the general goodwill between the two nations continued.

Rajiv Gandhi was no longer the Prime Minister of India when he visited Tamil Nadu on 21.5.1991 to canvass for the Congress Party candidates in the forthcoming general elections. For the purpose of the election and pre-election bandobust, the whole state had been divided into groups of 4 or 5 districts, each one under an ADGP or

IGP. Kancheepuram, Vellore, and Chengalpet were allotted to R.K. Raghavan, the then IGP-Forest Cell. As IGP (Law-and-Order), I was in overall charge of the election campaign and of the maintenance of law-and-order in the state.

I received Rajiv Gandhi at the airport. He shook hands with me and followed me out of the airport. I still retain the photograph taken on that occasion. I accompanied him from the airport on his way to Sriperumbudur. All along the way, he threw caution to the wind, crossing barricades to meet the people who were anxious to greet him. We found it difficult to keep the crowd away from him or him from the crowd. At several points en route, I had to pull him away from the crowd behind the barricades. But no thought of any threat to his life crossed my mind. After stopping at several places along the way, we reached Poonamallee, when Raghavan informed me that he was already in Sriperumbudur, the meeting place, and that everything was in order. He had with him, on bandobust duty, Kancheepuram district SP Md. Iqbal, ASP Pradeep V. Philip, and other district staff. I handed over charge and returned home.

I had just reached home when I heard over the microphone that there had been a bomb blast at the meeting place. I left for Sriperumbudur at once; I called Raghavan over wireless and was told that "the worst had happened." As I drove towards Sriperumbudur, I saw DIG Mathur, SP SB-CID Nanjil Kumaran, and many other officers going in the opposite direction to hospitals to have their injuries, simple or serious, attended to. Further down the road, I saw a police van that stopped on seeing me, and ADSP Ramakrishnan of Kancheepuram came over to tell me that he was carrying the bodies of Rajiv Gandhi and his PSO Inspector Gupta of Delhi to the General Hospital for post-mortem. I turned around and accompanied the bodies to the GH to organise a speedy post-mortem so as to be able to send the bodies back to Delhi before people could hear of the tragedy and hold up the departure. At that time, nobody, not even the hospital authorities, knew about the tragedy. However, it was not long before the word of the blast spread, and people started congregating in anxious groups. On reaching the airport, we loaded both bodies onto the special aircraft that had brought Sonia Gandhi from Delhi. As she had been told that the flight would leave Chennai only in the morning, she had retired for the night. As the senior officers at the airport were reluctant to disturb her, I went up to her room and explained to her the need to leave Chennai at the earliest. She accompanied me to the aircraft. The flight left without delay.

The chaotic scene that prevailed in Sriperumbudur after the blast defied description. All the injured officers and men were rushed to the hospitals by whatever transport was available. The Congress workers attacked the police officers and men who had stayed back simply because their leader had been killed. Even though R.K. Raghavan had been badly assaulted, he remained at his post till 11:00 a.m. the following morning for the sole purpose of preserving the scene of the crime. It was to his credit that the most valuable evidence, that of the damaged camera used to record the incident by an Indian LTTE sympathiser Hari Babu, had been safeguarded. The ten snaps that had been taken before the blast gave a clear insight into the sequence of events and also the identity of the actual accused. Hari Babu, the photographer, had also died in the blast. But the valuable photos showed the presence of LTTE sympathisers Dhanu and Shuba, and also of one-eyed Sivarasan, the mastermind behind the assassination. Yet another photograph showed SI Anusuya trying to keep the crowd, and even the assassin Dhanu and her companion Subha, away from the VIP. But Rajiv Gandhi did not want anyone to be kept away from him. 'Relax,' he told the SI. It was the last word that he spoke.

Dhanu, who had landed in India 10 days earlier along with Sivarajan and Subha, was wearing a lethal suicide-waistcoat under her salwar kameez as she approached the VIP. While garlanding him, she pulled the fuse to set off the deadly jacket. Rajiv Gandhi, his security officer, seven civilians including Dhanu and Hari Babu, and nine police personnel including the SP were killed in the blast. The martyred policemen were Rajiv Gandhi's Security Officer P.K. Gupta, SP Md. Iqbal, Inspectors of

Police Edward Joseph and Rajaguru, S.I. Ethiraj, and PCs Ravi, Dharman, Murugan, and WPC Chandra. Pradeep V. Philip, ASP, Kancheepuram, was seriously injured while trying to hold back the crowd pushing its way towards Rajiv Gandhi.

Sadly, Tamil Nadu was not yet in the know of the latest and advanced techniques of camouflage and disguise that Sri Lankan militants employed so successfully. They were even enjoying our facilities without rousing the slightest suspicion. In fact, Sivarasan, who had lost an eye in a conflict with the Sri Lankan Army in 1997, had even been treated at Aravind Hospital in Chennai, posing as an Indian citizen.

Of the 41 accused listed by the prosecution, one-eyed Sivarasan and Subha led the police on a wild goose chase and finally committed suicide in Bangalore. So also did LTTE sympathisers Dixon, Vickey, Guna, and Sivaraj, and those who manufactured the explosives.

After Rajiv Gandhi's body had been removed, there was nobody to guide or direct the supporting bandobust staff. As a result, most of them left the place. R.K. Raghavan's evidence and the camera he managed to save exposed the role of the LTTE in the assassination. The presence of one-eyed Sivarasan, Dhanu, Subha, and Nalini, wife of Murugan, near the scene of the blast was clearly proved, although the LTTE continued to deny their role in the assassination, asserting they had a cordial relationship with Rajiv Gandhi.

The Government of India appointed a single-member Commission of Inquiry, headed by Justice M.C. Jain, on 23rd August 1991 to enquire into the sequence of events leading to the assassination of Rajiv Gandhi. In its final report, the Jain Commission categorically stated that there was tacit support to the LTTE by the DMK government. On the basis of this report, the DMK government was dismissed.

Retired CBI officer Karthikeyan was chosen to handle the case of the assassination. He was assisted by DIGs S. Ramani, R. Srikumar, Amod

Kanth, and Radha Vinod Raju, all from the CBI, 8 SPs, 14 DSPs, and a large team of Inspectors. It was DIG S. Ramani's documentation, which ran into several thousand pages, that greatly helped the investigation. Ramani also met the Chief Justice of the Madras High Court and asked for the appointment of a special judge to try the case. Justice Siddique was then appointed. Ramani also formed four teams to investigate the case, personally headed one of them, and looked after the administrative needs of the large team of officers, advocates, and others. Simultaneously, he continued to head the Madras Branch of the CBI and retired as DGP Training in 2009.

On 28th May 1992, Karthikeyan laid charge sheets before the TADA Trial Court against 41 accused, including 12 who were already dead, and three absconders. On 28th June 1998, the court sentenced 26 of them to death. On appeal, the Supreme Court upheld the death sentence of Murugan, Santhan, Perarivalan, and Nalini, sentenced Jayakumar, Fayz, and Ravindran to life terms, and freed 19 others.

The claims of the Government of India that it took strong action against the LTTE were not supported by facts. The Indian Peace Keeping Force (IPKF), as the name itself indicates, was not a combat force. By sending the IPKF, India lost her reputation as well as the lives of 1,200 soldiers. After the DMK government's dismissal on the basis of the findings of the Jain Commission, the Congress and the AIADMK derived tremendous electoral mileage, sweeping all 39 seats in the 1991 Parliamentary elections.

It is unfortunate that R.K. Raghavan, who stayed on at the spot till 11:00 a.m. the following day to preserve the crime scene and safeguard the all-important camera and photographs, was not honoured. Instead, he and many of his subordinates, including the seriously injured SI Anusuya, were charged with 'Dereliction of Duty.' This was a serious miscarriage of justice, although subsequently, all of them were cleared by the Trial Court.

I tried in vain to get R.K. Raghavan, Pradeep V. Philip, and WSI Anusuya the Indian Police Medal for gallantry. But the controversy over the involvement of the LTTE did not support my proposal.

I do not see any reason for releasing Rajiv Gandhi's murderers whose death sentences were later commuted to life terms. I can still see in my mind's eye the tear-stained face of Sonia Gandhi at Chennai Airport that night when I escorted her to the aircraft which carried the body of her husband to Delhi. I also remember visiting the grieving families of the eight Tamil Nadu police personnel who lost their lives that night. There was no way I could console them. The government job given to one member of each of the martyr's families is only a small compensation for the irreparable loss. I am also in touch with the family of Rajiv Gandhi's PSO Inspector Gupta of the Delhi police.

In April 2000, the Governor of Tamil Nadu commuted Nalini's death sentence to life. On 11th August 2011, the President of India rejected the mercy pleas of the others carrying death sentences. On 21st January 2014, the Supreme Court commuted the death sentence of the three on grounds of inordinate delay in disposing of their mercy petitions. This order was issued just 10 days before the day marked for their hanging. On 15th September, the Supreme Court issued a notice to the Government of India to shift the convicts' petitions out of Tamil Nadu. On 21st January 2014, the Supreme Court commuted the death penalty of 15 of them, including four aides of forest brigand Veerappan and three of Rajiv Gandhi's assassins, to life sentences, citing inordinate delay in disposing of the mercy petitions as the reason.

31 years have gone by, but DGP Pradeep V. Philip and Inspector Albert Dayakaran still carry numerous pellets embedded in their bodies. Albert Dayakaran says, "I am still suffering physically and emotionally, but the accused made use of the delay in the process of clearing their mercy petitions by successive Presidents." Karthikeyan, the head of the CBI's Special Investigation Team, said, "The verdict will be a lesson to governments that they cannot delay decisions. The assassins have waited

long and have gone through mental agony, knowing they could be executed any day. To execute them now would be a double punishment."

I conclude this chapter with the remarks I made much earlier in my visiting notes at Ramnathapuram PS on 19th February 1990, the day after the Pattinamkathan check-post incident in which the LTTE armed smugglers opened fire at the check-post, killing one policeman and one civilian before escaping with a huge cache of explosives and firearms: "The most important work at hand is to apprehend or kill the culprits who dared to raise their hands against the people who had given them shelter in their darkest hour and who received them with open arms every time they crossed the sea with real or imaginary threats to their lives."

Tamil Nadu Special Police

Oh, what a joy it was for me
To be posted in charge of the TSP;
The TSP, ever a force dear to me
Just like the army where I once yearned to be.
Of all police forces, they are the elite;
Such a never-fail team, elsewhere you won't meet.

My two short tenures with the Armed Police, once as DIG (1985-1986) and once as IGP (Oct 1990 to Jan 1991), gave me immense joy and great satisfaction. They partly fulfilled my desire for my first choice, the army. The Tamil Nadu Armed Police is in no way inferior to the army. It has now grown into a formidable force with 15 battalions from the original single one of the Malabar Special Police raised in 1921 to deal with the Moplas, who had massacred a large number of Hindus and 24 police officers, including two British ASPs, Lancaster and Rowley. Martial Law was proclaimed and after many days of bitter fighting, the Moplas were subdued by Richard Hitchcock, the District Superintendent of Police, with the help of the newly raised MSP, with its strength of six British officers, six Subedars, 16 Jamedars, 16 Havildars, and 600 Constables.

The Moplas had misunderstood Gandhiji's support for the Khilafat Movement and, in a frenzy, started killing Hindus. The British Government was caught off-guard, and not even Units of the army, including the Gurkha Regiment, could contain them. The only answer to the problem was to have an army-model police force drawn from the Hindu Nair population. Thus was born the MSP. It was trained and commanded by specially selected British officers. After the hanging of Mopla leader Ali Musaliar in Coimbatore on 2nd April 1922, their movement came to an end, but not before 70 of the 100 Mopla prisoners being transported from Malabar to Coimbatore in a goods wagon had died of suffocation. The MSP was considered more efficient than army Units in dealing with rebellions, like the Fituri in the Godavari district, and uprisings in the Minicoy Islands, Nagaland, West Bengal, and Arunachal Pradesh. The MSP's standard of drill, fitness, and smartness was such that Lt. Gen. Sir Archibald Nye, the Governor of Madras, declared it to be as good as that of the Buckingham Palace Guards.

But it was not enough to cover all of Madras Presidency, consisting of present-day Tamil Nadu (minus Kanyakumari district), Andhra Pradesh, Malabar, Palghat, and South Canara, so a new wing of Armed Police, the Special Armed Police (SAP), was raised in 1948. Soon after the SAP was formed, it was sent to deal with the Razakars in Hyderabad. Two more battalions were raised and stationed in Trichy and Palani respectively. At the time of the state re-organisation in 1956, the Malabar Special Police had been divided equally into 2, with one-half retained in Tamil Nadu and the other sent to Kerala. In 1962, the MSP and SAP were merged to form the Tamil Nadu Special Police (TSP), which became the most sought-after team to deal with any uprisings.

No doubt, then, it was the TSP that was chosen for the perilous job of escorting convoys of vehicles and public buses between Kohima, the capital of Nagaland, and Imphal, the capital of Manipur, from 1962 to 1965. These convoys would often be ambushed by Naga militants. Within a week of my stay in Imphal, a convoy was fired upon by a group of Nagas, killing 2 passengers. However, the escort party under Hav. Edward of MSP-II repulsed the Nagas and brought the convoy safely to Imphal. He was awarded the Police Medal for Gallantry for his initiative and courage. It is quite relevant to mention here that the same Edward's daughter, Inspector Rajeswari of Chennai City Police, is renowned for her courage and initiative.

The MSP drill instructors were much in demand all over the country. When I was a trainee at the Central Police Training College, Mount Abu, in 1964, most of the drill staff, from the Chief Drill Instructor DSP S.P. Spadigam to the Havildar instructors of each squad, were from the MSP, as were those in the Police Training Colleges of Tamil Nadu and Kerala.

Charles Sobhraj, an international criminal and murderer, and his associate David Hall were undergoing 12 years' rigorous imprisonment in Tihar Jail, in Delhi. Before the Indian government could hand Sobhraj over to Thailand, where his death sentence was pending execution, he managed to escape from the highly-guarded Tihar Jail by offering sweets laced with sedatives to the guards under the pretext of it being his birthday. After several escapades, Sobhraj was arrested in Nepal, where he was shifted to death row for a couple of murders.

The Tamil Nadu Special Police was the automatic choice to prevent such escapes, and Tihar Jail was placed under its charge on a temporary basis. The TSP's assignment was made permanent when 2 of Indira Gandhi's assassins, Satwant Singh and Kehar Singh, were detained there. The Government of India could not trust even the para-military forces because of the Sikh element in their composition. After its first posting 38 years ago, in 1985, the TSP continues to guard the sensitive jail, establishing its superiority and dependability over all other state Armed Police and para-military forces.

As DIG Armed Police, I would often visit Manimuthar, the headquarters of TSP II Bn. My morning walks would take me across Manjolai Estate to Manimuthar Dam and back, following a different path each time. One of those walks took me to the Sorimuthu Ayyanar Temple deep in the jungle. It was on this walk that I came upon an imposing figure on his morning walk. He was the Raja of Singampatti. I came to know from him that he happened to be the youngest proclaimed prince in India at the time of India's independence, having been crowned on 14th January 1936 at the age of four. He had been schooled at Trinity College in erstwhile Ceylon. Trinity College was at that time the preserve of the children of Indian royal families and was headed by a British scholar. This chance meeting heralded a period of letter-writing, his in English of such high standard that I needed a dictionary to understand and savour its contents, and mine, a string of simple words. Our letters criss-crossed until he passed away 3 years ago.

After independence, all the landed property that belonged to the Rajas and Zamindars was nationalised. The Raja of Singampatti lost more than 80,000 acres of forest land, which had been presented by Raja Marthanda Varma of Travancore to one of his ancestors for his assistance in defeating his rivals, the 'Ettu Veetu Pillaimars.' Even today, an area near the Armed Reserve in Nagercoil is called 'Maravan Kudiyiruppu,' where the Singampatti Marava Army had been stationed.

I would accompany the battalions whenever they went on sensitive and difficult duties. In 1985, as IGP Armed Police, I accompanied a TSP Bn on election duty to Ferozepur and Ludhiana in riot-torn Punjab, much to the disapproval of the top brass. But none could stop me from accompanying my officers and men on vital duties within the state or beyond. While supervising the election in Ferozepur, I visited the burial place of martyrs Bhagat Singh, Shivaram Rajguru, and Sukhdev Thappar, who had been hanged by the British in Lahore on 23rd March 1931 for killing a British officer, J.P. Saunders.

General Niazi, the Governor of East Bengal and Commandant of the Eastern Sector, surrendered before the Indian Army and East Bengal's Mukti Bahini in the 1971 war with the combined West and East Pakistani armies. The number of those surrendered was 93,000, and after an initial tussle between the newly created Bangladesh and the Government of India over the control of the Prisoners of War (PoWs), India took over the entire responsibility of guarding them. The aim of the newly created

Bangladesh was to return the captured army in exchange for Pakistan's recognition of the new country. However, India retained control of the captured Pakistani soldiers and held them in several camps. When the question of guarding the most dangerous Pathan prisoners, who nearly lynched General Niazi for surrendering instead of fighting to the end, arose, the choice was TSP V, which was already on sensitive border duty in NEFA, presently Arunachal Pradesh.

The battalion headquarters was in Teju, in Lohitpur district, and the Rear Headquarters was in Mohanbari, the northernmost airport in the Eastern Himalayas. Assistant Commandants Vadivelu, Dinamani, and Appadurai, along with Inspectors Pichaimuthu and Vanniyan, would brave the biting cold and walk several kilometres from camp to camp to keep up the morale of the men. Some of the detachments could only be reached after a walk of 25 to 30 days. Even army Units had not been in such isolation and with such limited resources to face the challenges of high altitude and extreme cold.

Perumalswami did a commendable job of closing down the various detachments and transporting them in special trains to Rae Bareli, the major Prisoners of War (PoW) camp. The only attempt by the prisoners to escape was effectively foiled. In the non-stop firing from all the LMG positions, 15 PoWs were killed, and the rest were driven back within the barbed wire fence. Tamil Nadu Police continued to guard them until 1975, when, in accordance with the Warsaw Pact, the detained soldiers were returned to Pakistan. The excellent work done by the Tamil Nadu Special Police is still remembered both in Bangladesh and in Pakistan.

The TSP continues to maintain its reputation for smart turnout and high standard of drill at major parades, such as the Medal Parade, Farewell Parades, and the all-important Republic Day Parade. The TSP battalions are deployed all over the country on important assignments. However, it is a pity that the rate of promotion in the TSP remains far behind that of their counterparts in the local police. For instance, during the recruitment of SIs in 1987, 137 of them were allotted to the Special

Armed Police; one of them, Johnson Jayapaul, son of the famous athlete Royappan, has remained a battalion commandant for 15 years with no chance of further promotions, whereas their counterparts in the local police have risen to the rank of DSP and even SP; a couple of them have even been conferred with the IPS. Here, I must mention the rare case of retired commandant J. Gunasekaran. He joined the force as a constable in the TSP and served in that capacity for 11 years. He then passed his BA and MA, took his selection examination for the post of Sub-Inspector, and passed. His next promotion took him through the ranks of Inspector, Assistant Commandant, to finally a battalion commandant, a remarkable journey. Meanwhile, he was awarded D.Lit (USA). He was also one of the few commandants to be awarded the selection grade, which entitled him to wear two stars and the Ashok Chakra, the insignia of a selection grade SP. After retirement, he has been looking after the interests of retired policemen and officers as President of the Tamil Nadu Retired Police Welfare Association.

TSP battalions have been posted all over the country. As such, my second recommendation is that Area Medals or Service Medals should be given to all those who serve in places outside their home states. Just as the army staff are given Sena Medals for serving in other states, including the border areas, the TSP officers and men should also be given similar medals for being posted to sensitive posts outside of Tamil Nadu.

I cherish the time I spent with the officers and men of the TSP, both in the fields of action, shooting ranges, and on the playfields. They were always dependable and added to the prestige of the department.

The All-India Police Duty Meet

The All-India Police Duty Meet is a test
To see which police force is truly the best.
The tech-savvy criminals they deal with these days,
Pose a challenge to the police force to out-wit their ways.
The Tamil Nadu Police manages this and much more;
They out-do the other teams and stand to the fore.

The Madras (Tamil Nadu) police force has always been referred to as the 'Second-Best Police Force in the World,' second only to Scotland Yard. Obviously, only crime prevention and detection would have been taken as the criteria for this assessment. Scotland Yard may be as good as or even better than Tamil Nadu in this aspect; but when it comes to maintaining law-and-order, especially when hordes of rioters indulge in unexpected violence, Scotland Yard would certainly be totally lost. Again, crowd management during religious festivals would leave Scotland Yard out of its depth, whereas in India, it is nothing out of the ordinary, our forces being conditioned to dealing with lakhs of pilgrims at short notice. As such, it is proper that a competitive comparison is made only among the state police forces in India. The All-India Police Duty Meet does just that.

With V.K Pell who led the team to the All-India Duty Meet

The first All-India Police Duty Meet was held in Nagpur in 1953 and the second one in Madras the following year. Since then, the meet has been an annual event with competitions conducted in the following major disciplines:

1. Scientific aid to investigation

2. Photography

3. The Dog Squad

4. Cyber-Crime

5. Computer Applications

6. Rifle and Pistol Shooting

7. Mounted Branch

8. Commando Competition

Now, with modern technology readily available to all and sundry, criminals have become a force to be reckoned with. As such, disciplines like videography, computer applications, anti-sabotage systems, and more advanced systems of crime and cyber-crime detection have become an inseparable part of crime investigation and have been included in the All-India Police Duty Meet curriculum. The Tamil Nadu Police continues to maintain its supremacy over all the other teams and has been winning the overall championship every year.

The inclusion of the highly trained para-military forces in the All-India Police Duty Meet has taken the competition to Asian and international levels, especially in shooting. The CRPF, started in 1939, is the only pre-Independence para-military force. After independence, the Indo-Tibetan Border Police, the Sashastra Seema Bal, the Border Security Force, the Railway Protection Force, and the Assam and Manipur Rifles have been included in the list of competitors, thereby raising the standard of shooting to international levels. It would be in order to mention here that DGP TamilSelvan, SP Ashwin M. Kotnis, S. R. Jangid, and R. P. Ilango are medal winners and have done much to promote the sport in various districts.

In 1991, the Tamil Nadu Police hosted the meet in Madras. Excellent arrangements for the meet were made by the Manager of the Tamil Nadu team, IGP Letika Saran. The host emerged victorious and won a record number of individual medals and the overall Champions Trophy. I won a gold medal in revolver shooting, the third in my service. Although we had conducted the meet in 1991, we were requested by the All-India Police Control Board to conduct the meet once again in 1994. I won my fourth gold medal, beating India's best marksmen from the BSF, CRPF, ITBP, and other para-military forces. Again, the Tamil Nadu Police won the overall team championship, and I had the privilege of receiving my individual medal as well as the team championship trophy from the CM, J. Jayalalithaa. I continued with my shooting practice until the end of my service and won the Champions Trophy for the 26th time, 20 days before my retirement in 1997. Altogether, I won 92 medals (61 gold, 24 silver, and seven bronze), a record that stands unbroken to date.

Shooting star

A dashing cop's passion for the trigger

HE is Tamil Nadu's top gun. Walter Issac Davaram, the IG of police in charge of law and order has been winning the top spot in state police shooting championships with relative ease for more than two decades now. To be precise, the 52-year-old Davaram has won the title 24 times.

Give him a revolver, point a target and Davaram is sure to hit the bull's eye without batting an eyelid. Such is his skill that he has no peers in the revolver shooting event in the state. Davaram began calling the shots from 1966 when he was the assistant superintendent of police in Tuticorin. The winning streak did not come easy. He used to be up at 3 in the morning, drive down to Tirunelveli, where there was a shooting range, practice for a few hours and then report to his office by 8 a.m.

"It used to be a little strenuous, but I was keen on shooting. I lost the top prize three times. In 1973, I had gone to Japan for training. In 1976 I lost to Padmanabhan, DSP in the armed reserve and in 1977 to Kuppuswamy, a reserve inspector," says Davaram.

Davaram's passion for the trigger was kindled when he was a kid. He was born in the tea estates of Munnar, situated on the high ranges of Kerala bordering Tamil Nadu. His father Henry Davaram, a retired Major who saw action during World War II, was working in the plantations there. And in Munnar one had always to be close to a gun to keep away wild animals that prowled around menacingly at night.

The familiarity with a gun came in handy when he went for training in Mount Abu after being selected for the IPS in 1963. "That was where I took part in a shooting competition for the first time. I got the 'best shot' and 'best all-rounder cadet' awards", said he recalling his early days in the force.

The mustachioed Davaram has also taken part in the National Duty meets. "It is very difficult to perform in the national meet without practice. You have to compete with participants from the BSF, CRPF, Indo-Tibetan Border Police and even the Black Cats. They are practising day in and day out while, with postings in the administrative side I hardly get time to practice regularly. You are allowed to participate only five times in your entire career in the nationals and I have so far taken part three times and won a gold in 1980 and a silver in 1967. I intend to take part in this year's national duty meet at the Madhukarai range in December," said the hot-shot officer.

Davaram's sharp eye has served him well while on duty on many an occasion. One instance he recalled was in 1980 when he was in charge of the anti-Naxalite operations in North Arcot

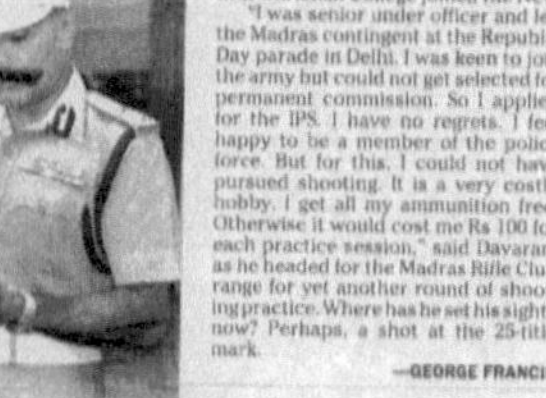

Aiming for perfection. *Walter Davaram at target practice*

district. "We left in two jeeps as two parties but could not find the Naxalites and so returned by the same route we went. But we were surprised to find our path blocked by the Naxals and there was no escape route. Suddenly the Naxals started firing. We returned the fire and killed three of the five attackers."

For snuffing out the Naxal menace, Davaram was honoured with the President's medal for gallantry. He also won the Prime Minister's Life Saving Medal twice, in 1976 and in 1985.

The 'trigger-happy' policeman is a strict disciplinarian. He is always dressed smartly and has a trim and fit physique. What is the secret of his fitness? "I get up at 4 in the morning and walk for 90 minutes."

He has climbed almost all the hills in the regions he has been posted. Horse-riding is another of his interests. But shooting will remain his first love. "This is one sport where age does not count. Your nerves have to be good and by God's grace I have reasonably good eyesight," says he.

Davaram comes from a family which has been serving the armed forces for two generations. His grandfather was a subedar-major who saw action in World War I. His father too was an armyman and his brother is a retired air force sergeant. Davaram continued in the great tradition and while in Madras Christian College joined the NCC.

"I was senior under officer and led the Madras contingent at the Republic Day parade in Delhi. I was keen to join the army but could not get selected for permanent commission. So I applied for the IPS. I have no regrets. I feel happy to be a member of the police force. But for this, I could not have pursued shooting. It is a very costly hobby. I get all my ammunition free. Otherwise it would cost me Rs 100 for each practice session," said Davaram as he headed for the Madras Rifle Club range for yet another round of shooting practice. Where has he set his sights now? Perhaps, a shot at the 25-title mark.

—GEORGE FRANCIS

I may be permitted to record the inconveniences that I had to suffer at the start of my shooting career. Shooting used to be the preserve of the weapon-toting constabulary, SIs and Inspectors of the district Armed Reserve and the state Armed Police. Having won the national shooting competition in the NCC and also the Champions' Trophy in the Central Police Training College, I continued to nurture my interest in this discipline. After joining the Tuticorin Sub-Division as ASP, I competed in the district meet and was selected to represent Tamil Nadu police in the All-India Duty Meet; as such, I would leave Tuticorin at 4 a.m., drive up to the district headquarters in Tirunelveli, a distance of 40 km, join the district team in the shooting range, and return to Tuticorin and be in my office by 9 a.m. I would mention this in my weekly report that went to the DIG, through the SP and District Collector. The District Collector once made the following remarks in my weekly report: "The ASP has been visiting the district headquarters quite often. He will do well to call on the Collector." The following week, I reached the Collector's bungalow at 5.15 a.m. and told the guard to inform the Collector that I was there to call on him. He told me that the Collector was not up yet and asked me to come after 9.00 a.m. I told him that I couldn't wait that long as I had to be back in my sub-divisional headquarters by then. I went back to Tuticorin after half an hour of practice at the Range. That was the last time the Collector made any remark in my weekly report. What a pity; he had not bothered to check on why I was at his headquarters and, more importantly, when!

In the year 2010, yet another competition called the Commando Competition was introduced. Apart from shooting, obstacle races, jungle, and other commando operations were included under this head. When the meet was conducted in Chennai in 2014, under the supervision of IGP Sanjay Arora, Tamil Nadu won the championship, beating all the para-military forces and the States. The Chief Minister, Jayalalithaa, in appreciation, introduced the prize scheme to encourage the winners.

Our latest achievement is in the field of Horse Riding, which had been introduced a few years ago. In the All-India Police Equestrian Meet held in Gurgaon, Haryana in 2020, our team took part against the top teams from the BSF, CISF, and ITBP and won one gold, one silver, and one bronze medal. The gold medal winner, SP Deshmukh Shekhar Sanjay, is an ardent rider and had also won the Equestrian Cup at the Police Academy, Hyderabad; this, although he had taken to riding only after joining the Academy. It is sad that as an SP, a DIG, or even an IGP, he will not get a chance to pursue his passion for riding because, apart from the Police Mounted Branch in Chennai and a few horses in Coimbatore and Madurai, no other district has a Mounted Branch. I had to wait 8 long years until I was posted to Chennai as DC L&O to ride again.

The achievements of the male members of the City Police Mounted Branch have been overshadowed by that of WPC Suganya, a girl of slight build who volunteered to join the Mounted Branch with its demanding responsibility of taking care of the horse allotted to her besides riding it. She was also a member of the State Police Equestrian team that took part in the All-India Police Meet in Haryana in 2020.

Tamil Nadu has been winning the overall championship from the inception of the All-India Police Duty Meet 68 years ago. It has not fallen back even after the introduction of new disciplines like computer awareness and narcotics detection. What better criterion can there be to decide on the 'Best police force in the country?'

Police Medal for Gallantry

Those metal discs that are valued so much,
Tell of the wearers' achievements and such;
Some are for valour in times of great stress,
Or for acts of courage and deeds of prowess;
Life-saving ones are won at great personal risk;
The service medal? You must merit that disc!

Recognising 'acts of gallantry' by medals, extra allowances, and even accelerated promotions is an age-old tradition in the armed forces and in the police. The first-ever Police Gallantry Medal in the Madras Presidency was awarded to a constable in the year 1828. The awards depend largely on the goodwill and promptitude of the senior officers in initiating and forwarding proposals to the sanctioning authorities both in the state and at the Centre. Indifference and delay have cost many a deserving person his rightful award.

The members of the Indian Police force are eligible for the Government of India's gallantry medals, life-saving, and service medals. The Government of Tamil Nadu sanctions its own gallantry medal for Outstanding Devotion to Duty and the CM's Medal of Excellence.

The earliest case of trivialising a gallant act was that of HC Mariappan, who was alone in Vellakoil Police Station in Coimbatore district when it was attacked by anti-Hindi agitators in 1965. The HC locked the building from inside, but the rioters broke open the roof to enter the building. The HC single-handedly repelled their attack, shot one of the rioters dead, and injured 6 others. The DIG of Police, Coimbatore Range, who visited the Police Station soon after, promoted him on the spot to the rank of SI of Police. He also recommended his name for the Indian Police Medal for Gallantry, which was duly awarded. But the DMK government that came to power in 1967 on the embers of the Anti-Hindi agitation, which had claimed 50 lives including those of 2 SIs and 2 HCs, stripped him of his promotion. The proud and valiant SI refused to accept the insult and resigned from his job.

In most cases of not recognising merit or gallantry, the fault lies with the senior officers concerned. The Chief Office also has to share the blame for not sending recommendations to the Government of India in time. Whenever I came across deserving cases, I would send proposals on my own, even if the deserving act happened outside of my jurisdiction. I have been doing the same even after my retirement, either through the Chief Minister or through the DGP, who is often kept in the dark about the gallant acts of their subordinates.

One such case relates to retired IPS officer K.V.S. Gopalakrishnan. After serving as SP in four districts, he opted for the Intelligence Bureau (IB) for a change. The departmental heads there also realised his efficiency and gave him important postings in Mizoram and Himachal Pradesh. He also served in Berlin, Germany for 4 years as Special Director of the IB. He retired from the IB, settled down in Chennai, and is now looking after the management of the famous Pennathur Subramaniyam

Iyer Group of Schools and also helping retired and serving officers in the matter of school and college admissions. I happened to see his badly scarred forearm when he was SP of the Nilgiris. He told me that he had been injured a year earlier when he was serving as Joint Superintendent of Police, Dindigul.

On 13.10.1980, he had accompanied V.R. Chitrapoo, the District Forest Officer, to a village near Gujiliamparai to enquire into the movement of a panther in and around the village. The panther charged out of the woods, sprang on Chitrapoo, and brought him down. As it was trying to bite his head, the JSP hit the panther with the butt of his rifle and also fired a shot. Thereupon, the animal turned its attention on him and caused him serious injuries to his hand before escaping into the forest. Later on, it was killed by the Police as a potential man-eater. V.R. Chitrapoo retired as the Principal Chief Conservator of Forests.

I was surprised that none had bothered to recommend a Gallantry or a Life-Saving Medal for the JSP. I took up the issue and sent a proposal to the Chief Minister, although it was much delayed, and also, the incident had happened outside my jurisdiction. The Government of Tamil Nadu forwarded it to the Government of India, which promptly granted him the Prime Minister's Life Saving Medal. He received it from the Governor of West Bengal at the All-India Police Duty Meet in Barrackpur.

I may mention here that I have received 5 Gallantry medals (2 for the operation against Naxalites and three for the Veerappan operation). There were two other instances that warranted the award of gallantry medals: one for disarming an armed gang of EPRLF militants single-handedly after one of them had killed a local Deepavali reveller, and another for removing a live bomb from the railway track. I was at that time the Commissioner of Police. Though both incidents made the headlines in the papers and received the appreciation of the public and the police, my superior officers, the IGP L&O and the DGP, did not care to make the necessary recommendations. But then, one does not live by medals alone.

About to pick up an unexploded device from the railway track, between Chetpet and Nungambakkam stations in Madras yesterday, is the Police Commissioner, Mr. W. I. Davaram. The suburban electric train in the photograph had stopped right above the device. Had the train reached the spot minutes earlier, disaster would have followed since another bomb had gone off at the same spot. None was injured.
— Another photograph on Page 12

The series of bomb attacks in Coimbatore perpetrated by Muslim extremists in 1998 was handled with great courage and perseverance by SP Thamaraikannan and his hand-picked team of volunteers. They traced the accused from numerous hideouts all over India. The main accused was caught alive in Rajamundry in Andhra Pradesh. As many as 181 accused were prosecuted under the brilliant leadership of IGP Paramvir Singh. Thamaraikannan, Inspectors Lakshmanaswamy and Gandhi, and two constables from Andhra were awarded the Police Medal for Gallantry.

IGP R. Sudhakar's right to a gallantry medal has been ignored not once, but twice. On the first occasion, as SP of Theni district, he led a party to a Naxalite hideout and, after an exchange of fire, arrested 5 of them, including 'Nondi Palani' of Tirupathur, who had been evading arrest for over 37 years, and another notorious Naxalite from Maharashtra. The second instance was an equally risky confrontation. On 23.1.2012, 4 men entered the Bank of Baroda at mid-day, threatened the bank officials and customers, and decamped with Rs. 19 lakhs. The same gang committed another dacoity in the Indian Overseas Bank, Kilkattalai, on 20.2.2012 and decamped with Rs. 14 lakhs after locking up all the officials. On doubts expressed by a house owner about his North Indian tenants, Sudhakar surrounded the house with his team; the dacoits opened fire, injuring 2 Inspectors. The police returned fire and killed all five dacoits. Five pistols, one revolver, one shotgun, and cash amounting to Rs. 14,01,020 were seized from them. It is very unfair that the gallantry displayed by Sudhakar and his team has not been recognised.

Another case of repeated injustice relates to DGP K Radhakrishnan, who was denied a gallantry medal after he faced indiscriminate shooting by a group of LTTE militants carrying firearms and explosives past the Pattinamkathan check-post in the Ramnathapuram district in 1990. Although I was not his superior officer, my recommendation for a gallantry medal for him was somehow delayed in the Chief Office. Another commendable action of his was the recapture of Sri Lankan militants who escaped from the Vellore Fort, for which he was recognised by the Anna Medal for Outstanding Devotion to Duty. Again, it was he who was chosen to bring about peace to Coimbatore City after it was devastated by the Hindu-Muslim clashes in 1998. He lived up to the expectations of the government and the public by arresting and prosecuting all those involved in the riots and restoring peace to the city. But sadly, he was denied the post of DGP L&O despite his eligibility, seniority, and excellent record.

The inter-state gang of dacoits that had been successfully carrying out their operations from Uttar Pradesh to Kerala for over 12 years belonged to the 'Bawaria' gang of criminals. After initial investigation of each case, the total lack of evidence connecting it to the Bawarias left the case undetected. But on 9.1.2005, when Sudarsanam, a city MLA and former minister, was shot dead by the dacoits and his son and daughter-in-law grievously injured in Thiruvallur district and their property looted, the government and the public pointed an accusing finger at the Police.

On the whole, 24 such cases along the national highway from Andhra Pradesh to Krishnagiri, resulting in the death of 13 villagers, injuries to

63 people, and loss of property worth more than a crore between 1995 and 2005, were reported. The state government chose S.R. Jangid to personally lead the team of investigators. Jangid, who was then DIG, set aside all other responsibilities and formed a team of 150 officers and men, including Dy. SPs Jayakumar, Sudhakar, and Arul Arasu. After extensive investigation of the migrant criminal gangs Sansis, Shekh, Bangalas, and Bawarias, the investigation narrowed down to the Bawarias.

Jangid's team scoured the country and arrested 13 of the 15 criminals. He personally led the search, and in an armed encounter, leaders Bhoora Bawaria and Rajendra Bawaria were shot dead near Meerut. The rest of the gang was brought in for trial to the Fast Track court, Ranipet. The operative portion of the verdict dated 24.6.2006 complimented the leadership of S.R. Jangid in having detected the cases which had remained unsolved for over 11 years. In a sensational judgement, the court sentenced 2 leaders to death by hanging and the rest to extended jail terms. For their outstanding work for over a year, Jangid, Dy. SP Lakshmanan, and SI Alwyn Sudhakar were awarded gallantry medals.

Karuppusamy, IPS, is yet another officer who volunteered for every dangerous assignment, including the search for Veerappan and the hunt for LTTE jail escapees. He spent as many as 18 years with the Special Task Force, turning his back on posts that were much in demand for questionable reasons. He is the only police officer to have received 2 accelerated promotions. He was conferred with the IPS in 2010. Mention must also be made of Periaiah, who also volunteered for dangerous assignments. He has been awarded a gallantry medal and two service medals.

The very idea of this chapter is for the present and future generations of officers to lead from the front while facing dangerous situations and, more importantly, to recognise acts of courage by their subordinates by initiating necessary proposals for appropriate awards.

My belief is:

'The honour, welfare, and comfort of the men you command
come first, always and every time.'

'Your own ease, comfort, and safety come last,
always and every time.'

Police Sports Meet and Medal Parade

The State Duty Meet was an annual event
To which, teams from every district were sent.
The closing function was a treat for all,
The multi-talented force stood out tall.
After spectacular mass-drill, karagam et al,
The police bands took over, the audience to enthral.
As darkness fell and hid the sun's rays,
The bands switched on lights upon their berets.
They marched in formation, their berets aglow,
Bringing to a close, an enchanting show.
Whose brain-child, this pageant? I surely must tell
'Twas of dear old commandant, Vincent K Pell.
Once the show was over, we all had to stay
For the IG's Bada Khana which ended the day.

1965! The year I became a part of the elite Madras Police force. At that time, much importance was given to sports, which was an integral part of police activities. Every district and battalion conducted annual sports and selected the team for the state's Sports Meet, which was conducted in Madras every year along with the Police Medal Parade. Both these events were conducted in the Rajaratnam stadium, which took on the appearance of an Olympic village. After 2 days of athletics, the stadium would be prepared for the Police Medal Parade when the Governor would present the medals. The prize distribution was followed by a spectacular cultural show by the police, which included 'Karagam,' stunt riding, and mass-drill by the participants carrying flaming torches. When night fell, it was time for the mass bands to march in formation with little lights aglow on their berets.

The eagerly awaited week would come to an end with the dinner hosted by the IGP in his official residence, 'The Grange,' with its large compound beautifully illuminated. The IGP R.M. Mahadevan was the last to occupy 'The Grange.' It was later renamed 'Kanchi' and allotted to one of the ministers, depriving the future Heads of the Police Force of their right to quarters. As a result, during my term as DC L&O (1976-1977), we had to stay in a room in the police guest house in the city AR complex. Later, as Commissioner of Police (1985-1987), we stayed on the first floor of the Chennai North Beach police station, and for the remaining period of my service (1988-1997), including 3 years as DGP, we stayed in various rented houses. What an insult to the office of the Head of the State Police Force. This also spelled the end of the much-anticipated yearly bada khana.

It will not be amiss to mention in this chapter the world-class achievements of some of the members of the police force. Let me begin with the greatest of them all, Francis:

> Francis, the greatest goal-keeper of yore,
> Of Olympic gold medals, three was his score
> The Olympic great was a policeman too,
> Who got not the recognition to him that was due!
> Policemen and women now are doing rather well;
> Francis up above will be pleased I can tell.

I need not tell the readers how difficult it is to represent the country in the Olympic Games, not to speak of winning a medal, gold, silver, or bronze. India had won the gold in hockey in 1928, 1932, 1936 (no

Olympic Games in 1940 and 1944 because of World War II), and again in 1948 (London), 1952 (Helsinki), 1956 (Melbourne), 1964 (Tokyo), and 1980 (Moscow). Since then, India's only podium finish in hockey was in the Tokyo Olympics 2021, and that too only a bronze.

Francis's achievement is unique and nearly impossible to be equalled by anyone else in the world. However, it is surprising that he was given no departmental award, prize money, promotion, or any recognition each time he returned to Madras with an Olympic gold. This is clearly a failure on the part of the government and the Police Department.

Although I had read much about his unique achievement, Francis was a nobody when I met him in Madras in 1966. He was just a Reserve Inspector of the City Armed Police, on the verge of retirement. He was living in abject poverty, and I was told that he had even sold his gold medals to keep his home fires burning. I helped his son, Christy Roy, join the force as a constable. Recently, I learnt that he had died young, aged 45. Realising our failure to honour a triple Olympic gold medallist, V. Baskaran, the Captain of the gold-winning Indian hockey team in the Moscow Olympics (1980), and I tried our best to name the newly constructed hockey stadium for the SAF Games after him. But as the stadium belonged to the Corporation of Madras, it had to be named after the Mayor, Radhakrishna Pillai, a leading congressman, senator, and freedom fighter. Fresh hope has risen now with the sanctioned construction of an Astro-Turf Hockey Stadium in the Veerapuram Armed Police Campus.

I have also taken steps to help Francis's impoverished family. His grandson, Francis Rajini Roy, was still without a job, although he had been on the list of candidates to be recruited as a 'data-entry assistant' since 2007. DGP J.K. Tripathy was kind enough to appoint him early this year on a priority basis.

I must also mention Olympian Ivan Jacob of the Madras City Police, who represented India in the Helsinki Olympics (1952) and was also specially selected to carry the Olympic Torch at the Sydney Olympics (2000). J.B. Joseph, who had represented India in two Asian Games, Tokyo (1964) and Manila (1968), won silver medals in both meets. He was unbeaten in the All-India Police Meets before he decided to call it a day. He was given the honour of running an exhibition race in Rajarathinam Stadium with the all-time great Olympic Champion Jesse Owens of the USA when the latter visited Madras in 1956. I remember going from Tambaram to Rajarathinam Stadium to watch the two champions. Little did I think that in 1958 J.B. Joseph would join the department as an SI and that I would meet him as my Sports Instructor in Central Police Training College, Mount Abu (1964). He returned to the state in 1972 and retired as a Commandant TSP in 1988. He was one of the few people to join the department as an SI and retire as an IPS officer.

Deputy Commissioner, Armed Reserve, and Superintendent, Tamil Nadu Commando School, N. Dakshinamoorthy, has won a record number of gold medals in the All-India Police Meets. His record in the triple jump (15.55 metres) stands unbroken today. In the open National Meets, he also won 3 gold and three silver medals for Tamil Nadu.

The longest-standing police record belongs to retired Commandant Pichai Muthu of the TSP. He was unbeaten in pole-vault for 32 years, almost until he retired. His record, set with the rigid pole of the time, was beaten only after the fibreglass pole was introduced.

There have been police officers who have played a major role in promoting sports. Commandant V.K. Pell, ADSP P.V.R. Reddiyar, ADSP Robson, DSP Veeranan, and Inspectors R. Veerasekaran, Soundararajan, and Fernandes are the most prominent among them.

Inspector R. Veerasekaran had the distinction of having led the state hockey team at the All-India Police Meet and narrowly missed the gold medal to the star-studded Punjab Police team led by Olympian Ajith Pal Singh. Veerasekaran also acted as Principal of the temporary Police

Training College for 6 years, training a large number of Category-1 SI cadets.

Another long-standing police athlete was Reserve Inspector Royappan of Tirunelveli district. He had won several gold medals in the All-India Police National Meets. I remember him overtaking me thrice in the 10,000 metres run in a state Meet. I was then 17 years old and a student of the YMCA College of Physical Education.

The second Olympian from the Tamil Nadu Police is athlete Reserve Sub-Inspector P. Subramaniam. He represented India in the Moscow Olympics (1980) and did commendably well by finishing the 200 metres race in 21.2 seconds. He also won both the 100 and 200 metres in the Asian Invitation Meet held in Pakistan in 1979 and the Asian Track and Field Meet held in Tokyo in 1981. The first policeman to receive Rs. 5 lakh from the present Chief Minister of Tamil Nadu is Naganathan Pandi, who represented India in the Tokyo Olympics 2020.

Before independence and for several years after, the Police Hockey Team comprised mostly of Anglo-Indians, including Robson, Fernandez, Huggins, Dubier, Harry Hart, Cunningham, and Louis, to name a few. F.V. Arul, Francis, Haridoss, and Rangadoss were the top non-Anglo-Indian players. The exodus of the Anglo-Indians to Australia was a big loss to the Police, Railways, the state, and the country. Australia owes its initial supremacy in Hockey to the immigrant Anglo-Indians who introduced the game there.

Another police athlete who has won international honours is Inspector S. Raghunath of the 2008 batch. He won a gold medal in the 5000 metres, a silver in the 10000 metres, and a bronze in the 3000 metres in the World Police Games held in New York in 2011. His All-India Police record in the 10000 metres and State Police record in the 5000 and 10000 metres are unbroken. SI Raghunath, now promoted to Inspector, won the gold medal in the National Cross-Country Championship representing Indian Police.

Among the senior officers who continue their physical fitness schedule despite the burden of office, ADGP Dr. Jayant K Murali stands foremost. He has run as many as 30 full marathons and is the current holder of the Asia Book of Records for both full and half-marathons. I am amazed at his stamina, physical ability, and determination alongside his highly demanding departmental commitments, besides contributing lengthy and highly technical articles to a leading English daily once a week.

Another police officer who undertakes long runs, swims long distances, and leads cycle tours to create awareness in the public mind on important current issues is DGP Dr. C. Sylendra Babu, whose achievements include a 4500 km cycling trip from Kashmir to Kanyakumari.

The only IPS officer from Tamil Nadu to win the all-India Badminton Singles Championship in the all-India IPS Officers' Meet is ADGP Dr. M. Ravi.

There are also sports-minded police officers whose children have achieved national and even international honours. The most prominent among them is Roopa, daughter of Unnikrishnan, a Tamil Nadu cadre IPS officer. She won her first national medal in shooting at the age of 13. Since then, she has won several medals in international meets. The other girls who brought glory to the department are Valli, daughter of DGP Tamil Selvan, and Hastna, daughter of DGP Jaffar Sait. Both have won silver medals in the Mowlankar Trophy Championship and gold medals in the national junior shooting championships. ADGP K. Thukkaiandi's daughters Yuba and Yamini have made their mark in international tennis tournaments.

I have been keen on sports since my school days. Football was the only outdoor game played in Munnar, and I played it for my college and University. I also competed in the 100 metres, Shot-put, and Hammer Throw in Inter-Collegiate and Inter-University Meets. I was declared the best athlete at Annamalai University and also at the Central Police Training College, Mount Abu.

Horse riding has always been one of my passions. In the National Administrative Academy in Mussoorie, I would ride all four periods: 2 in the morning and two in the evening. In Mount Abu, in the Riders Cup competition, I was beaten by a born rider and Polo Player, Damodhar Singh of the Manipur Rifles.

Back in Tamil Nadu, I had no opportunity to ride except in Madras. I had to wait 8 years until I was posted to Madras as DC, Law-and-Order. It was only then that I could ride again. I made full use of the Mounted Branch, and my wife Prema and daughter Anita also took to riding. To our amusement, the horse given to Prema was also called Prema! Prema says her trainer's stern "toe up, heel down" command still rings in her ears!

During the annual State Police sports at Rajarathinam Stadium, I performed the difficult tent-pegging event to the appreciation of the spectators and Chief Minister MGR. A short description of tent-pegging would be appropriate here. The rider on horseback takes up his position at one end of the 100-metre stretch. Midway, a wooden peg, 9 inches by 6 inches, is driven into the ground with only the top half visible. The rider, carrying a lance, rides at great speed and picks up the peg with his lance. If by chance the rider misses the peg and his lance hits the ground, he would be thrown off his horse, presenting a rather ungainly spectacle.

Oh, for those good old days!

Citius, Altius, Fortius

(Faster, Higher, Stronger)

'Citius, Altius, Fortius;' is the Olympic motto, we know;
Years of preparation go into that 'Ready, get-set, go!'
A place upon that podium, is every athlete's dream,
From every corner of the world, they come with hopes agleam,
Rivals when competing, and friends when all's done;
To nurture camaraderie, sports stand second to none.

The catchphrase 'Citius, Altius, Fortius' was coined by Fr. Henry Martin and adopted by Baron Pierre de Coubertin as the Olympic motto. He also built the Olympic heritage on five pillars: i. Joy in Efforts, ii. Fair Play, iii. Respect for Others, iv. Pursuit of Excellence, and v. Harmony of Body, Will, and Mind.

Apart from my police work in the District, Range, and state, I kept alive my interest in the various sports disciplines that had been part of my life through my school and college days. Although athletics, football, riding, and shooting were my major interests, I had to accept the leadership of a record number of sports organisations, compelled by sports lovers who were keen on preventing the factionalism that was plaguing sports bodies.

Padmashree Dr Sivanthi Adityan, the most prominent person in the Indian sports arena, President of the Indian Olympic Association for a record number of years, and Life President of the State Association, also persuaded me to look after the welfare of the state Sports. After his death, I took over the Tamil Nadu Athletic Association as President. It also fell to my lot to promote the Paralympics for the physically disabled, world-level competitions for the mentally disabled, and the fast-growing veteran (masters) sports.

I have held honorary posts of President or Vice President of several national and international associations like Athletics, Tamil Nadu Olympics, Veterans, Judo, Volleyball, Sports Development Authority of Tamil Nadu (SDAT), and The Kerala Sports Persons Association (KESPA) over the past four decades with reasonable success.

Sports never came in the way of my carrying out my police duties. On the contrary, it helped foster police-public affability. As President and Vice President of the Athletic Federation of India, I have led Indian teams to various World, Asian, and Commonwealth meets held in Japan, South Korea, China, Vietnam, Indonesia, Italy, Kazakhstan, and Sri Lanka. Whenever I accompanied the Indian teams as Manager, I would have absolutely no time to spare except for an early morning walk. Two walks that stand out in my memory are one on the Great Wall of China and the other over the beautiful Alpine meadows in northern Italy bordering Switzerland, dotted with grazing sheep and surrounded by the awesome Dolomites. International sports meets foster friendship among athletes, overriding political enmity. The amity between the athletes of Pakistan and India deserves special mention. Perhaps the shared history and linguistic similarity between Urdu and Hindi are the unifying factors. Sports are a never-fail source of camaraderie, overcoming political, linguistic, and cultural barriers.

Although I have been President of the Athletic Association for 35 years, the actual fieldwork used to be done by the Secretary of the Association, Neela Sivalinga Swamy, a former national champion who also produced several international athletes. It was he who introduced the popular Kanyakumari-Nagercoil Marathon. After his unexpected death in 2011, his wife Jayanthi, a state volleyball player, and his nephew Ramesh continue to render every help to the Association, she as one of the Vice Presidents and he as a committee member of the Association.

International athlete C. Latha took over the Secretaryship after Neela's untimely death.

With C. Latha

Tamil Nadu has made good progress in athletics and holds the top position in India. Of the five athletes who went to the Tokyo Olympics in 2021, 2 of them, Naganathan Pandi and Arokia Rajiv, belong to the Tamil Nadu police. By way of encouragement, the Chief Minister, M.K. Stalin, granted Rs. 5 lakhs to each of the 12 state participants in the last Olympics.

The police department plays a major role in promoting sports by recruiting talented sportspersons as constables and SIs. The district, range, and state-level competitions conducted regularly in Tamil Nadu have made the Tamil Nadu police the No. 1 sports organisation in the state. IGP F.V. Arul himself was a state hockey player, and R.M. Mahadevan, a top tennis player, RI Royappan, and SI Ganesan were national-level athletes. International athletes Santhi and Inspector Pappathi (Francis Merry) have brought glory to the country at several international meets. Other officers who have worked to promote sports in the department were P.V.R. Reddiyar, Veeranan, Dakshinamoorthy, Joseph, Ivan Jacob, and V.K. Pell; and more recently DSP Raghunath, IGPs Amalraj and K. Rajendran, and SP Kapil Kumar C Saratkar.

More than clubs and colleges, it is the schools that should take up the responsibility of identifying and training sports-oriented children. I had the opportunity of interacting with the Gabriel Brothers of the Montfort Schools, who encouraged and produced several good athletes.

Nehru stadium in Coimbatore is always full of life, with several coaches, athletes, juniors, seniors, and veterans making full use of the facility. I find parents and grandparents who bring their wards to the stadium gradually taking to running and competing in the veteran athletic meets with encouraging results. The top coaches who never miss a day of training are S. Srinivasan, Nandakumar, Nizamuddin, and Narayanan. Murali, a veritable sports encyclopaedia, is an all-important part of the sports arena.

*Nizamuddin, Mujetha Begum and
Mohammed Salahuddin- A family of athletes*

Palanisamy, Secretary of the Tamil Nadu Masters (Veterans) Association and a native of Munnar, has been doing great service to youngsters, training them to clear the physical efficiency tests required for selection as SIs and constables. He trains them free of charge at Tharuvai Maidan in Tuticorin. So far, hundreds of his trainees have been selected into the police and other sports-oriented departments. The Association owes its phenomenal growth to the former secretaries Subbaiah, Anbananandan, P.V. Parthasarathy, and the highly efficient treasurer Radhamani, as well as senior members like Shenbaga Murthy, Balasundaram, and Rukmini. Anbanandam of Trichy and the involvement of his entire family in athletics are praiseworthy. The family's national medal winners include himself, his wife Anthoniammal, his sister-in-law Elizabeth, father Savari Nayagam, and above all, his father-in-law Savariyar, who won gold at the age of 98. Octogenarians Daisy

Victor and John Devasir, who won several medals at state, national, and international meets, are no longer with us.

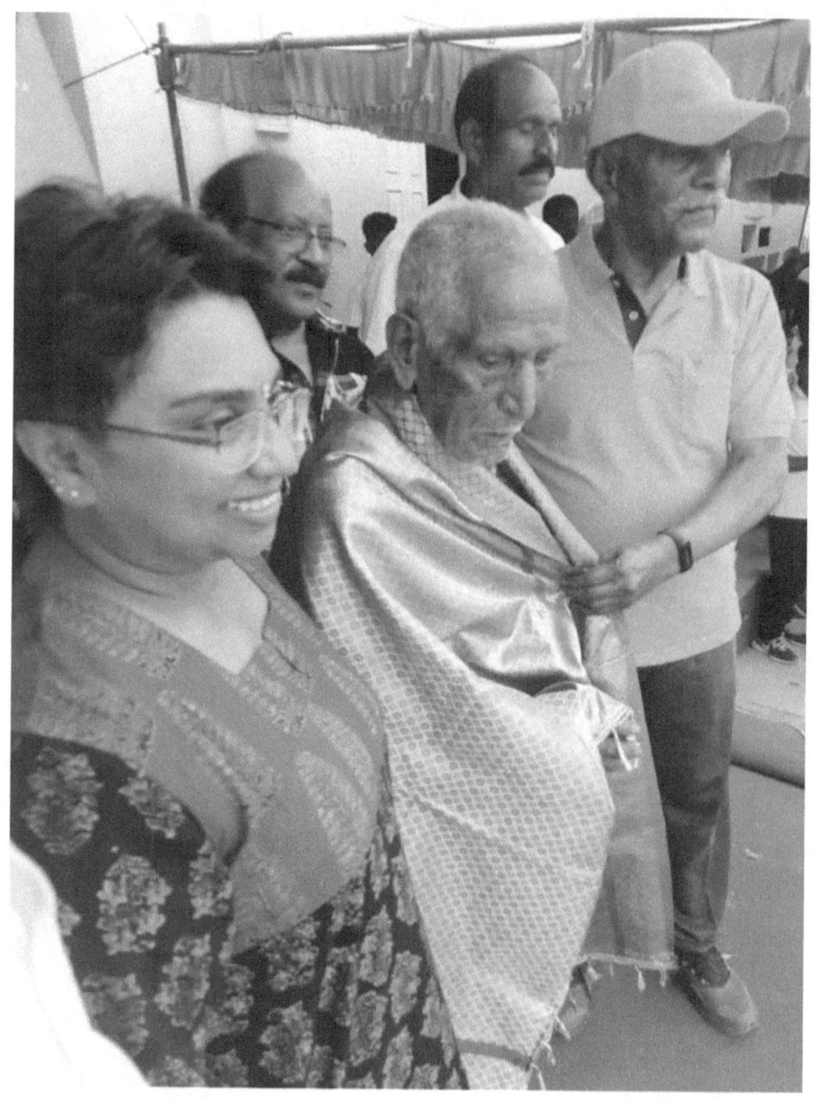

Savariyar who won gold at the age of 98

The Masters (veterans) athletics is not part of the Olympics or the Asian Games. However, it has assumed great importance at national and international levels because of the enthusiasm of the veteran athletes, who are grouped into five-year categories starting from age 35. Under my presidentship, Tamil Nadu has been winning the National Team Championships year after year.

My presidentship of the state Judo Association is yet another story of success. Judo in Tamil Nadu owes its growth to the efforts of C.S. Rajagopal, Black Belt Second Degree, Kodokan, Japan 5th Degree, known to everyone as 'Master.' At the age of 82, he continues to take part in the anniversary functions of the Japanese Embassy and thrills the audience with his breathtaking Judo demonstrations. Secretary Sadish and experts Srinivasan, Mathivanan, Bhaskar, Manikumar, and woman judoka R. Kani are responsible for many young judokas becoming national and All-India Police champions. In the last 5 years, as many as 254 men and 45 women judokas have been recruited into the police department under the sports quota.

The Nellai Volleyball Club, started 60 years ago, was the brain-child of the late Police Inspector V. John. On his personal initiative, he laid three volleyball and two basketball courts on the campus of the Egmore stadium and trained youngsters, both boys and girls. He also conducted several national and state-level tournaments. I took over as President of the Club after his death in 1996; national volleyball players Chitirai Pandian, Dinakar, Jagadeesan, Kesavan, and Srividya looked after the club and coached new players. Among them, Asha Rani played for India, and Zahira Begum, Jennifer, Fernando, and Jothi played for Junior India. Hema Malini and Rosy represented India in beach volleyball. The entire women's police volleyball team comprises past members of the Club.

Nellai club state volley ball champions

As President of 'Special Olympics,' I have conducted several national-level meets and some international ones for the intellectually disabled, the deaf (Deaflympics), the physically handicapped (Paralympics), and the visually handicapped. The actual credit for conducting these international meets goes to Professor Dr Nagarajan, Founder of the Para-Olympics Committee of Tamil Nadu. Two women, Juliya Vasanth and Geetha, with remarkable managerial ability and wholehearted sympathy for mentally and physically handicapped persons, train and send the special athletes to international meets.

The Sports Development Authority of Tamil Nadu (SDAT) is responsible for the state's outstanding performance in most disciplines. I have been closely associated with the organisation over the past 35 years and have also served as its Vice President after my retirement.

I have been the patron of the Kerala Ex-Sportspersons Association (KESPA) since its inception 18 years ago. With its headquarters in Chennai, it is a unique organisation because most of its members are international sportspersons. Some of the active members of KESPA are Jaishankar Menon and his wife Prasanna, both Indian basketball captains;

their daughter Krishna, who is currently undergoing training for discus throw in the USA and has won honours in a couple of international meets to be ready for the world junior athletic meet; Padma Shri Shiny Wilson and her husband Wilson Cherian, both Arjuna Awardees; J.P. Jossy Mathew and his wife Saramma; Roy K Mani and his wife Lekha Roy; swimmers Arjuna Awardee Sebastian and his wife Molly Chacko; footballer Ranjith and his wife Sherley; Olympian Ranjith Maheswari, national record holder in triple jump, and his pole-vault national record-holder wife Surekha; volleyball player Jose Varghese; and football ace Abraham Varghese.

Jaishanker Menon, Prasanna, Archana and Krishna

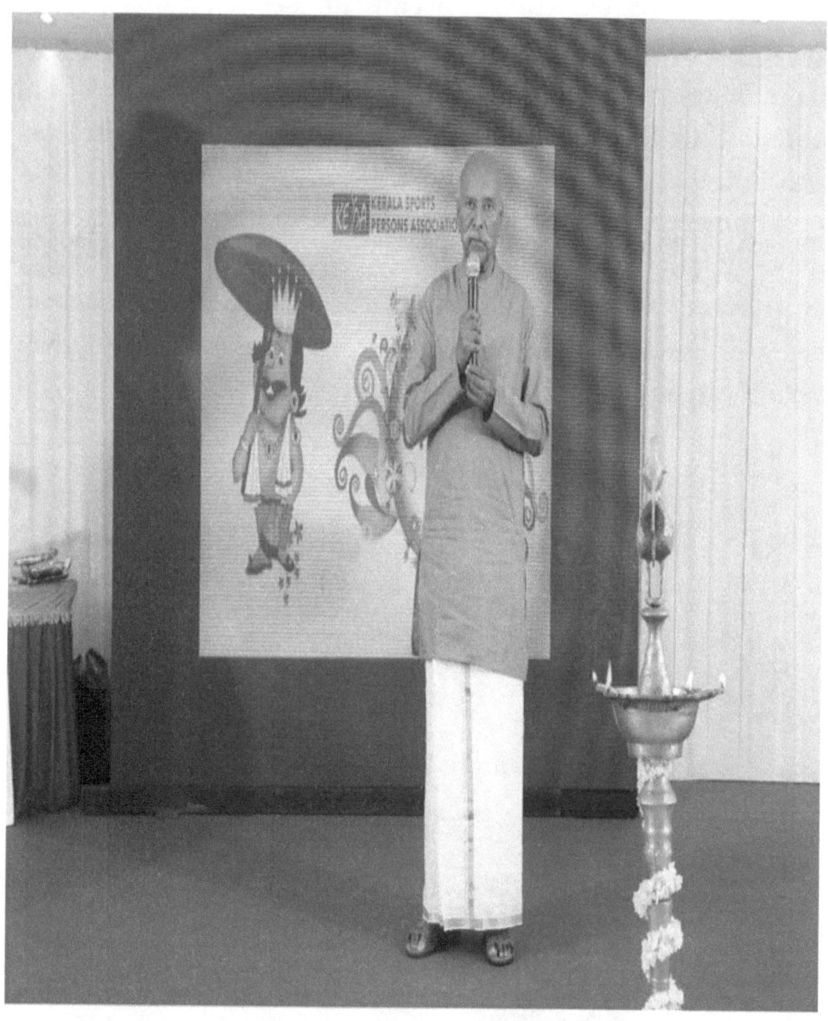

At the KESPA Onam celebrations

Anju Bobby George

It is time now for me to move from centre-stage to the spectators' gallery. I hope the present generation of officers will take a similar interest in sports and produce national and international champions. If every police officer could save one potential delinquent from poverty and crime, this concept could be considered to have achieved substantial success. Was it not a Louisville policeman, Pat Brown, who took Cassius Clay out of a ghetto to mould him into the greatest boxer of all-time?

A Patron of Police and Sports

A Patron of the Police force and of sports was she,
Anything for them, would straight sanctioned be.
For the welfare of the force, she was second to none;
Because of that, I could get ever so much done,
Anything I asked for, she'd readily agree
As she knew very well, I wanted nothing for me.

As mentioned earlier in my book, I first met Jayalalithaa in Ooty in the year 1968. Twenty-three years were to pass before my second meeting with her. I had been posted as Commissioner of Police, Chennai City. The day I took charge, I received a bouquet from her, brought to me by Public Relations Officer Natarajan. I thanked her and asked for an appointment, which she readily gave. I called on her at her residence and was overwhelmed by her hospitality. The next time I saw her was from a distance, at MGR's funeral.

I was fortunate in that I was able to serve her as IGP (Armed Police), IGP (L&O), ADGP (L&O), and as DGP, Tamil Nadu. I found in her a multi-faceted person who could keep anyone's attention riveted with her engaging and well-informed conversation. As Chief Minister, she was a brilliant administrator and an uncompromising disciplinarian; as a leader, she was sympathetic and generous.

Another trait of hers was that whatever she did had to be better than the best. This was showcased when the South Asian Federation Championship Athletic Meet was allotted to Chennai by the International Body. She took a personal interest in the infrastructure for the games, including the indoor and outdoor stadia, the Hockey Stadium, the Aquatic Complex, the Velodrome, and the practice venues.

The magnificent Jawaharlal Nehru Stadium was constructed based on the directives of FIFA (Fédération Internationale de Football Association). It cost Rs. 40 crore and had a seating capacity of 40,000. What set it apart from other stadia was that all the 40,000 seats were individual plastic-moulded seats, unlike in other stadia where concrete galleries provided the seating accommodation. The eight-lane athletic track was on par with international standards. The Russian delegate Yuri Semine was full of praise for the facility. He said, "This is an excellent stadium, and I would rate it as the finest in the world!" The stadium was inaugurated by the Prime Minister of India. The inaugural function, the brain-child of Chief Minister J. Jayalalithaa, was one of the grandest and best-organised events in recent memory. More than ten thousand school children and hundreds of police personnel took part in the cultural programmes, including the spine-chilling motorbike stunts by teams of policemen and policewomen. Music directors Shankar-Ganesh provided the music.

As the Organising Secretary of the Athletic Meet, I witnessed the praise from the visiting teams for the arrangements and the conduct of the meet. The Chief Minister was at the stadium every day of the meet and displayed exceptional knowledge of each discipline and each sportsperson. It was at this meet that Shiny Wilson, an international athlete, lived up to everyone's expectations and set a new record in the 800 metres. She became the first Asian woman to run the distance in under 2 minutes. The Chief Minister, watching the event, asked me to find out from Shiny what she would like as a reward—a house or a car? I told her that Shiny and her husband were both Arjuna Awardees and had a house of their own in Chennai. A car would, therefore, be a better choice. She then asked me to find out from Shiny the colour of the car she would like. Hearing that, the then Chief Secretary pointed out that Shiny was not from Tamil Nadu. Her succinct retort, "Is she not an Indian?" silenced him. Although Shiny was from Kerala, she was working in Chennai and representing Tamil Nadu in the National Meet. I met her on the track and asked her for her colour preference for the car. Understandably, she was perplexed by the question until I told her that the CM was planning to present her with a car for her record-breaking performance. She chose white. The next day, an expensive white car stood by the victory stand, suitably festooned. The CM personally handed over the keys of the car to Shiny, who was there with her husband and parents.

Shiny Wilson and Wilson Cherian

The inauguration of the stadium also signalled the start of the 10th Jawaharlal Nehru Gold Cup Football Tournament, with eight foreign teams participating. North Korea won the championship, beating Romania in the finals. Conducting a tournament for top football nations in Chennai was the brain-child of C.R. Viswanathan of Coimbatore, who also played a major role in promoting football in the state. As I write this, sad news comes in of his passing away. Earlier, football had been nurtured by stalwarts like Nelson Issac and T.R. Govindarajan. Those were the days when the football league matches between top teams like Wimco, the Southern Railway, ICF, and Sporting Youngsters were grand affairs attracting thousands of spectators. I can still picture the stadium in those days when the Southern Railways played. It would be awash with red, with railway porters in their red shirts filling all the galleries. The porter tradition is now almost lost with the arrival of convenient wheeled suitcases. No longer do we see a red line systematically falling into place along the edge of the platform as a train steams in.

The Chief Minister was keen on kindling interest in and promoting sports and was generous in rewarding achievements. She presented Rs. 25 lakhs to Anju George for winning a bronze medal in the World Athletic Meet in France. It was an impressive array of prizes and promotions that the CM awarded after every major sports meet. She enhanced the amounts of the awards to winners of medals in major meets. She increased the sports quota in police recruitment from 2 per cent to 10 per cent. No other state or even the Government of India had ever contemplated a hike like this. She also recruited 15 women volleyball players into the police without their having to go through any selection process. The team, named 'Jaya's Spikers,' brought great honour and glory to the state by winning most of the national-level trophies. One of the players, Asha Rani, even went on to represent India. Two others, Hemamalini and HC Rosi, represented India in the World Beach Volleyball Tournament.

Once, her tendency to give much more than what was requested almost caused an administrative imbroglio. Of the two sports hostels in Chennai, one was for the junior sportsmen selected by the Sports Development Authority of Tamil Nadu (SDAT) and the other run by the Sports Authority of India (SAI). The dietary allowance for the inmates of the SDAT Sports Hostel was Rs. 75 per day per athlete, while for SAI inmates, it was Rs. 150 per day. In my capacity as the honorary Vice President of the SDAT, I requested her to increase the dietary allowance of the SDAT Sports Hostel inmates to bring it up to par with that of the SAI Hostel. Promptly came the order raising the dietary allowance from Rs. 75 to Rs. 250 per day per athlete, with instructions to give the hostellers the very best and most nutritious food. The SDAT staff were dumbfounded by the order and found it difficult to spend Rs. 250 per day on a school student. With this unparalleled hike, the daily dietary allowance worked out to Rs. 7,500 per athlete per month, which is unthinkable even today. Such was her generosity.

Following the transfer of SP Tamilselvan, 2 SIs, and two constables who were seriously injured in an ambush by the Veerappan gang from a hospital in Mysore to Malar Hospital in Chennai, the Chief Minister visited them and announced accelerated promotion for all except the SP, who, being an IPS officer, was not eligible. PC Selvaraj, who was killed in the shoot-out, was also honoured posthumously with a medal, Rs. 50,000, and jobs for his son and daughter.

In the space of one year, the Chief Minister opened as many as 57 All Women Police Stations, increased the women police strength by 30%, recruited 12,000 constables including 2,000 women constables, and 2,500 SIs including 200 women SIs. By a special procedure, 22,000 policemen were promoted to the rank of SI. Additional posts of 31 ADSPs, 36 DSPs, and 750 Inspectors were created. She also sanctioned Rs. 10 lakhs to the families of policemen who die in harness. She raised the prize money for medal winners in the All-India Police Duty Meet to an astounding Rs. 5 lakhs for gold, Rs. 3 lakhs for silver, and Rs. 2 lakhs for bronze; Rs. 50,000 to every member in a team event and to medallists in the All-India Police Games.

The high point of her generosity was her acknowledgement and recognition of the hardship faced by those who took an active part in the Veerappan operation. They spent days walking tirelessly through the thick jungles, often going hungry and thirsty, and always conscious of being stalked and of the possibility of getting killed by the bandit. Each participant was granted a cash prize of Rs. 3 lakhs, a one-stage promotion, and a house site.

With Best Wishes

To Mr. W. I. Davaram, I.P.S.,
Addl. D.G.P. (L & O) Tamil Nadu,
One of the finest, bravest and
most outstanding Police Officers
India has ever known.

J. Jayalalitha:
6/4/1994

Chief Minister.

She was, indeed, a patron of the police department and of sports.

Horse Racing and Jallikattu

Horses just like to gallop or run;
Who would think they don't find it such fun?
Racing, for horses, isn't torture at all;
The torture's for spectators when tote windows call.
The Jallikattu thrill is not quite the same;
A bull charges out, and you have to him, tame;
The thrill that it offers is spine-chilling I find;
Draws spectators too, but of a different kind.

Animal welfare is of high priority even in countries where meat is an integral part of people's diet. The slightest harm to animals, especially to house pets like dogs and cats, evokes universal protest, and quite often the related law is invoked against the perpetrators. But horse racing has been accepted as a sport from time immemorial; the horses enjoy a gallop as much as their riders enjoy the ride. Horse racing in Madras dates back to the year 1777, making the Guindy Race Course the oldest in India. Boasting such heritage, it was surprising that the government of Tamil Nadu abolished races in Madras and Ooty in 1974. Was it aimed at the wealthy horse owners, or could it have been to protect the members of the poorer sections of society from the evils of betting?

The government's decision came as an unexpected shock to the racing fraternity. The Race Club obtained a stay from the Supreme Court, and racing continued under the supervision of the government through two government-appointed stewards—one, an IAS officer, and the other, the DC (L&O South), who, at that time, happened to be me. Our duty was to ensure the proper conduct of the races and to settle any disputes that might arise. The Supreme Court appointed a committee under Dr. Nataraj to assess the social outcome of the races. Meanwhile, the races went on as usual. Finally, in 1996, the Supreme Court ruled that racing was a game of skill and, as such, could not be banned. Thus, a needless measure by the government proved futile, and racing continues to be a popular pastime both in Madras and in Ooty.

Horse racing by the English and Scottish managers was a regular Saturday feature in Munnar, except during the monsoon. How I longed to ride in those races! I got my chance when I was posted to Madras as DC L&O South. I took part in the Gymkhana Races held at the end of the racing season, in which amateur riders from the Army and the Police participated. As a Gymkhana rider, I remember winning a race on the police horse 'Adayar' and receiving a trophy from CM M.G. Ramachandran. Prema still has the 'Jockey Colours' that I wore that day.

From time immemorial, 'Jallikattu,' the sport of subduing bulls bred and specially trained to defy the efforts of adventurous 'bull-tamers,' has been a popular event, especially in Pandiyanadu and parts of Cholanadu (Southern districts of Tamil Nadu). Several places in Madurai, Ramnad, Trichy, and Pudukottai districts are known to conduct the event every year, particularly during the 'Pongal' holidays. Bulls are specially fed and trained throughout the year for the single day's show. Jallikattu in Alanganallur, Palamedu, and Avaniapuram in Madurai district has become world-famous, drawing a large number of foreign tourists. However, Animal Welfare Associations have been agitating against the use of the bulls and the accidental deaths of the bulls, bull-tamers, and even spectators. They took the matter to the Supreme Court and obtained an order on 7th May 2014 banning Jallikattu. But all of Tamil Nadu protested against the Supreme Court order. In Chennai alone, more than 30,000 students assembled on the Marina, protesting against the SC order that had put an end to the 2000-year-old traditional sport of the Tamilians. The agitation continued peacefully for 7 days before turning violent, resulting in the burning of police vans and jeeps.

Finally, the government of Tamil Nadu passed an act legalising 'Jallikattu.' After a gap of 3 years, 'Jallikattu' returned to the old centres with renewed enthusiasm. On the positive side, several improvements have been made to ensure the safety of spectators, competitors, and also the bulls. It was also ensured that the bulls were not fed any alcohol, as had been reported earlier.

I, for one, am glad that one of the most ancient sports of skill and courage has come back in all its splendour. Similar bull fights are conducted in countries like Spain, Mexico, and other South American countries. They are gory events in which the bulls are killed by picks. But in Tamil Nadu, great care is taken to protect the bulls.

My mind goes back to the day my friends and I took part in a major Jallikattu event in Madurai district. Perumal Thevar, Ramakrishnan, Gopal, and I were University-mates involved in sports. The three of them hailed from Gudalur and Theni taluks of Madurai district bordering Kerala, and I, from the other side of the border, Idukki district in Kerala. 2 of us held onto the hump of the bull, and the other 2 tried to get hold of the prize tied to its horns. The bull had no time at all to throw all of us off and ran to the exit, and so ended our adventure with Jallikattu. We received minor injuries, mostly from the bull trampling our feet; luckily, there were no fractures. But the crowd appreciated our effort as we were just students.

On another occasion, we took my parents-in-law to the world-famous Jallikattu in Avaniyapuram. On seeing my mother-in-law, the organisers gave me a disapproving 'how-could-you' look. But she surprised everyone by deftly climbing up the rickety ladder and ensconcing herself comfortably on the makeshift gallery. That was when I understood where Prema, who had no qualms about climbing over fences and shinning up walls, got her adventurous streak from.

We Can, Too

Had little Miss Muffet a lady-cop been,
A different scenario, we all would have seen;
No spider could ever have scared her, I'd say
Boldly she'd have faced it, come what may;
Her boots she'd have stomped to scare it away,
Or used her lathi to keep it at bay.

When I joined the Police Force in the year 1963, there were no women police. For that matter, there were no women in the Army, Air Force, or Navy, other than those in the medical services. But, in 1973, when I went to the Central Police Training College, Mount Abu, for my Senior Officers' Course, there she was – India's first woman IPS officer, Kiran Bedi. There had been much opposition to accepting a woman in the force that had, over the years, been a male preserve. Braving all that and ignoring 'well-meant' advice suggesting she choose some other All-India Service, she did not just invade the male bastion but conquered it, proving that she was as good as any efficient male officer.

A former Asian Tennis Champion, she was superior to most of her male colleagues in outdoor activities and finished high in the year's IPS seniority list. Later on, she created history as Deputy Commissioner of Traffic, Delhi, where she earned the moniker 'Crane Bedi' because of her ruthlessness in towing away any vehicles parked in unauthorised places. The picture of her charging an unlawful assembly of 'Nirankaris,' a radical

Sikh sect, all by herself and armed with only a long lathi, while her male colleagues merely stood by watching the confrontation, hit the headlines. Later, the other side of her personality surfaced when she revolutionised the working of Tihar Jail in her capacity as DGP Prisons, Delhi. She was awarded the prestigious "Ramon Magsaysay Award" for her excellent prison reforms. She also acted as the Lt. Governor of Puducherry.

Coincidentally, in Tamil Nadu, an All-Women Police Station (AWPS) was established in Madras City in 1973 with one SI, one HC, and 21 PCs. It might have been only the second of its kind in India, with Kerala having experimented with an All-Women Police Station earlier. It had the privilege of being led by the smart, sophisticated, and dynamic SI, A.V. Usha. Under her leadership, the station carried out all its responsibilities with utmost efficiency. Also, the women police became the cynosure of all eyes at parades and major government functions. They dominated the CM's medal parade in Vellore in 1975 and won the appreciation of Chief Minister M. Karunanidhi and also that of the large number of spectators who had never seen women in khaki, let alone women in khaki stomping past them in their service boots. I was, at that time, the Superintendent of Police, Vellore. I vividly remember the Catholic Nuns and staff of Auxilium College, Katpadi, who were there to watch their illustrious past student leading the parade. A.V. Usha is still cited as the model for all her successors in Tamil Nadu and was recently personally honoured by CM M.K. Stalin when he inaugurated the police museum in Chennai.

The success of the experiment with the All-Women Police Station led to the creation of similar stations in the headquarters towns of the three Police ranges: Trichy, Madurai, and Coimbatore, in 1978. As DIG, Vellore Range, I sent a detailed proposal to MGR spelling out the need for women police throughout the State. The most important reasons I gave the Chief Minister were:

i. They would be sympathetic while dealing with complaints by women.

ii.   They would look after the safety of women accused in the police station until they were remanded.

iii. They would settle family and civil disputes sincerely, sympathetically, and impartially, looking after the interests of the women involved, whether complainant or witness.

iv.   Finally, they would be honest and incorrupt.

On this basis, MGR created the posts of 60 SIs, 60 HCs, and 600 PCs, which were filled in a single recruitment drive in 1981. He entrusted me with the recruitment of the HCs and PCs in Vellore. But I now realise how wrong I was regarding the honesty of women police, especially women Inspectors. They are as competent in their duties as their male counterparts and equally competent in corrupt practices. I am dismayed that in the last 2 years, as many as ten women Inspectors and SIs have been caught red-handed and are facing departmental charges or prosecution for corruption. On the very last day of the year, 31.12.2020, the woman Inspector of the Narcotics Intelligence Bureau, Coimbatore, was caught demanding Rs.1 lakh for allowing an opium dealer to carry on with his trade. Hardly 10 days later, two more women Inspectors were caught receiving bribes.

Bribe-taking was made an insignificant crime compared to the role of a dacoit played by a woman Inspector on 5th August 2021. Inspector Vasanthi, her brother Pandiarajan, and three others waylaid a vehicle on the Madurai-Theni Road and robbed the driver, Arshad, of Rs.10 lakh. A case was registered in this connection, and three associates were arrested by a Special Team, and Rs.2.26 lakhs were recovered from them. Inspector Vasanthi, who was suspended, absconded, and after a vigorous search, was found along with her brother in a lodge in Kotagiri in The Nilgiris and jailed. What a sad and deplorable reflection on women police.

As I write this chapter on women police, my mind goes back to the very first recruitment drive. It was the sad story of a divorcee whose recruitment was cancelled based on a letter sent by her ex-husband stating that she was already married. According to the recruitment rules prevailing then, married women were not eligible to be recruited as constables or SIs. However, as she was already divorced, she was a single woman. All I had to record was that 'at the time of recruitment, she was not married,' thus giving her a chance to rebuild her life. The condition that women candidates should not be married at the time of recruitment has since been removed. I was also liberal regarding the height requirement, provided all other conditions were fulfilled.

Realising that we have been recruiting women SIs and constables for several years, with the IPS providing the higher ranks, the Government of Tamil Nadu and the Tamil Nadu Public Service Commission started recruiting women DSPs from 1991 onwards. Two women DSPs were selected in the first year, one of whom left the force, leaving Vanitha as the first woman DSP in Tamil Nadu. She has already reached the rank of IGP and is likely to achieve greater heights.

Later on, as Commissioner of Police, Madras City, I recruited 45 more women PCs for the City Police. All of them have since risen to the rank of Inspectors of Police. The women police have now become an integral part of the police force, not only in dealing with women-related crimes and complaints but also in performing every police duty that their male counterparts perform. Apart from police work, they have proved their worth in parade, sports, stunt riding, shooting, and even horse riding and band display. As of now, Tamil Nadu has 58 women IPS officers, including those in the IPS promotion list, 22 women DSPs, 1086 Inspectors, 1600 SIs, and 17,778 other ranks. Altogether, women police total 20,544 out of the total police strength of 113,724. This is the highest percentage of women police in any state police force. Currently, as many as 267 women SIs are under training at the police academy, certainly a world record. I met them twice at the academy and introduced them to gallantry medal winners SP Ashok Kumar, Woman Inspector Rajeshwari, and also the first woman SI, A.V. Usha, hoping they would be an inspiration to the trainees.

Another first by our women police was the formation of a Commando Force trained in escort duties, shooting, martial arts, and physical fitness. All 130 of them were trained by ADSP Damodaran at the Tamil Nadu Commando School. As part of their challenging training, they ran a relay from Kanyakumari to Chennai (750 KM) and at the end of the final leg handed the baton to the Chief Minister at the Secretariat. They completed the relay in 72 hours. Para-military Units, including the National Security Guard, have sent their observers to study the training process and the performance of the Tamil Nadu Women Commandos. It's worth mentioning that even the Indian Army trained its Women Commando Force only in 2021, 15 years after the Tamil Nadu police formed theirs.

Women are often referred to as the weaker sex, but ADSP Anusuya is one who disproved this belief. She was on bandobust duty in Sriperumbudur on the day of Rajiv Gandhi's assassination. It was she who tried to stop Dhanu, the assassin, from getting close to the VIP. Her efforts to hold Dhanu back were thwarted by Rajiv Gandhi himself, who told her to 'relax' and motioned Dhanu to get closer to garland him. The rest is history. SI Anusuya survived the blast but was grievously injured. She lost two of her fingers and spent several months in the hospital for rehabilitation and removal of numerous pellets embedded in her body. Shockingly, instead of being considered for an award, she had to face a charge of 'dereliction of duty.' Although she was later cleared of the charges, she did not receive any recognition for her display of courage.

The failure to recognise deserving acts of gallantry by women was partially set right after Kalpana Chawla, an astronaut of Indian origin, died along with seven others when the space shuttle in which she was carrying out experiments malfunctioned and crashed in Louisiana, USA, on 1st February 2003. I had by then retired but took the liberty of writing to the Chief Minister suggesting the institution of a gallantry medal exclusively for women in the name of Kalpana Chawla. The government order was issued the very next day, installing the medal and a cash award of Rs.5 lakh for one woman awardee every year.

R. Ponni, a 2008 batch IPS officer, is the only woman police officer to have been conferred with the Kalpana Chawla award to date. This was in recognition of not one, but several acts of courage displayed by her in a single year. She seized 200 lorry loads of illegally mined river sand, 26 of them in one day, all by herself with only her driver to assist her. She also recovered 70 sovereigns of jewellery from a notorious thief. Above all, she was responsible for the arrest of a much-wanted Maoist.

The multi-talented Inspector Rajeswari is someone the police force should be proud of. She is the daughter of Hav. Edward of MSP-II, who had been awarded the Police Medal for Gallantry for saving the lives of a convoy of bus passengers travelling from Kohima in Nagaland to Imphal in Manipur in 1962. Several years down the line, the same Havildar's daring daughter, Rajeswari, was awarded the Police Medal for Gallantry for overpowering an armed criminal in Periamet in Chennai despite being repeatedly stabbed by him. This could possibly be the only instance of both father and daughter receiving the Indian Police Medal for Gallantry. In 2014, Rajeswari was adjudged the "Best Inspector of Police" by the Bureau of Police Research and Development, New Delhi. She is also into sports and has won several prizes at the International Masters Athletic Meets held in Taiwan, Thailand, and Finland. She has also been awarded the Chief Minister's Medal for Good Service at the Independence Day Parade 2020.

She is known for helping several underprivileged children complete their schooling, getting them admission to colleges, and also paying their fees. Her most recent achievement is arresting a shopkeeper for storing and selling gutka and in the process, unearthing a series of serious offences involving minor girls. He has since been charged under the provisions of the POCSO Act. I fully approve of her physical treatment of the despicable paedophile.

She was again in the limelight when she carried a man presumed dead on her powerful shoulders while even his associates and the policemen who accompanied her were scared to touch him, fearing Covid-19 infection. This effort of hers is a combination of mental courage, physical strength, empathy, departmental loyalty, and obligation to society.

Rajeshwari

The only policewoman in Tamil Nadu to have won the Prime Minister's Life Saving Medal is WHC Catharine Daria Hepsin of Tamil Nadu Special Police. She was in Colachel, a coastal town in Kanyakumari District, spending Christmas 2004 with her family. What started as a joyous family get-together on Christmas Eve turned into a nightmare. The coast was struck by the devastating tsunami, which washed away all the buildings, including her house, and took the lives of 386 people. Battling her way against the raging sea, which first came rushing in and receded with equal fury, she saved the lives of nine children, carrying them one at a time to the safety of higher ground. This happened in 2004, but it was only in 2007 that she received the Prime Minister's Life Saving Medal, due to the efforts of Assistant Commandant Siva Jayaprakash, who has since retired.

As I write these paragraphs highlighting the achievements of women police, comes the heartening news of a Woman Head Constable defying her high-handed senior officers and colleagues by giving a statement against their brutality—HC Revathi of Sattankulam Police Station in Tuticorin district. While on night duty at the station, she witnessed the night-long thrashing of a father and son duo, owners of a mobile phone shop, which they had kept open beyond the regulation time. Needless to say, this violation demanded no more than a warning or a fine. One cannot fathom the real reason for the night-long torture meted out to them by the Inspector, 2 SIs, and seven other police personnel, resulting in their death.

As details of the night's horror unfolded through the bold statement of WHC Revathi, the whole state, nay the whole country, was aghast at this police excess. Revathi, who exposed her seniors' brutality, deserves not just approbation but an out-of-turn promotion. Meanwhile, all the accused, including one Inspector, two of the 3 SIs (one having died of Covid-19), and nine constables, are still in prison.

Turning to the positive side of the picture depicting the extraordinary achievements of our policewomen, let me begin with the expertise of our women stunt bike-riders, "Jaya's Flaming Arrows." Their spectacular repertoire includes 15 of them riding seven bikes while performing various stunts like climbing ladders, reading newspapers, and having a ball game. The most dazzling performance was that of a single rider, WHC Raleena, supporting six others on her shoulders in Lotus formation. Another stunt perfected by Raleena was to ride up to the VIP dais, dismount, run alongside the bike, jump onto the right pedal of the bike, and salute the VIP as the bike moved past the VIP's dais. After watching their first public performance, CM J. Jayalalithaa told the press that she was 'on edge watching the dare-devilry of the policewomen.' She also awarded each biker Rs.5,000/- and a medal in appreciation of their remarkable and death-defying performance. The bike squad became a major attraction at all-important parades and functions. Although this chapter is dedicated to our women achievers, it would be amiss not to mention the men who trained the women bikers. They are constables Parthiban, Chandramohan, Ravi, Pandian, and Kamaludhin, who, along with the first batch of stunt riders, were trained by the Military Police in Bangalore, thanks to the initiative of DGP Jagan Seshadri.

The women police are also doing very well in sports. With 10 per cent of the total recruitment reserved for sportspersons, the police teams get young blood once every 2 or 3 years. The Tamil Nadu state Women Police Volleyball Team was unbeatable in India for several years. Our women athletic team has also won several gold, silver, and bronze medals in All-India Police Sports Meets and National Meets.

The best performance of the Tamil Nadu Women Police was in the World Police and Fire Services Games in Chengdu, China, in 2019. Those who won medals in Chengdu are Woman Inspector Papathi alias Francis Merry, WPCs Tamil Selvi, Krishna Rekha, Parimala, and Uma Maheswari. Inspector Francis Merry of Pudukottai district won 4 gold, 2 silver, and two bronze individual medals. This world-level achievement by the Tamil Nadu policewomen has brought great credit to the state.

The greatest achievement of one of our policewomen is winning a shooting gold medal in the All-India Police Duty Meet in 2017, long after my retirement. P. Radhika, Woman Gr.1 constable, won the gold medal in the difficult three-position (standing, kneeling, and prone) shooting with a modern.506 rifle; what's more, she was the only woman competing against national and international shooters (men) from the ITBP, CRPF, BSF, and SSB.

The tsunami of 2004 marked the beginning of the glory of women footballers in Tamil Nadu. Girls who had been orphaned by the tsunami were taken care of by coach Mariappan of St. Joseph's School, Cuddalore, and formed into a team that won the National Football Championship. Natarajan, my fellow football player at Annamalai University, and Fr. Ratchagar of St. Joseph's High School helped each one of them graduate. Nine of those orphans were recruited by the police. One of them, SI Indhumathi, has created history by captaining the Indian Women's Football Team on its pre-Olympic tour of several countries. It is worth mentioning that, so far, no one from Tamil Nadu police, man or woman, has ever captained a national team.

There is no doubt that Tamil Nadu Police has no equal in investigative skills, as proven by them year after year in 'Scientific Aid and Investigation' at the All-India Duty Meet. We have been winning the overall trophy ever since the competition was launched in 1953. Since 2018, the union Home Ministry has been awarding the 'union Minister's Award for Excellence in Investigation' to the best investigator of the year. No doubt, we top the list. Of the six Tamil Nadu Inspectors of Police who have received the award, five are women – G. Jhansi Rani, M. Kavitha, A. Ponnammal, C. Chandrakala, and A. Kala. There is no need for any further proof of the superiority of Tamil Nadu women police in almost every aspect of police work.

I must also introduce N. Gomathi of the In-Service Training Centre of the Madras City Police, a woman HC who is an outstanding commentator, easily the best in the state, as proved by the fact that she is the automatic choice for all government functions, including the Republic and Independence Day Parades, all police functions, and sports meets. She has been discharging this responsibility over the past several years and has won many accolades and awards.

HC Gomathi is not only a talented commentator but also a fearless woman. During her daily early morning walks, she noticed a man stalking her. She put an end to it by slippering him on the road itself. Instead of complimenting her, she was given a charge u/r 3(b) by S. George, the Commissioner of Police, for 'assaulting a member of the public.' I intervened and allowed the charge to die a natural death. Our society, not only the police, needs such 'brave-hearts.' Does being in government service deprive a woman employee of her right to defend herself?

15th August 2020 was a special day for the Tamil Nadu Women Police. Outstanding performances by two of them made headlines in the newspapers. One was the picture of Inspector Allirani of Thellar Police Station, Thiruvannamalai District, carrying a corona victim to the ambulance when even his relatives dared not touch him. This courageous act was recognised by Collector K. S. Kandasamy, IAS, of Thiruvannamalai district. At the Independence Day parade, he invited her to take his place on the stage, stepped down, and saluted her. This was in recognition of her courageous work, which was appreciated by all who attended the parade or read about it in the papers. I personally thanked him for his noble gesture.

Another noteworthy and courageous act was that of Inspector Maheswari, who commanded the 2020 Independence Day parade in Tirunelveli. What was not known to others was that her father had passed away on the night of August 14th. Knowing that it would be difficult to find a last-minute substitute, Maheswari kept her grief to herself and commanded the parade the next morning. This truly is a remarkable act of courage and fortitude. I have commanded several parades, including the Republic Day, NCC Parade in New Delhi, the Passing-Out Parade at the Police Academy, and many more. But I would not have had the fortitude to command a parade under similar circumstances, because it requires a mind free of all other thoughts, especially of grief, to be able to remember the sequence of the parade and the correct words of command.

Letika Saran, one of the first two women IPS officers in the Tamil Nadu cadre, set new standards in professional efficiency and administrative excellence. She was the first woman officer to become the Commissioner of Police, Chennai City, and the first woman DGP of

Tamil Nadu—a twin distinction that no other lady officer in the country has achieved so far. As Joint Superintendent of Police, Tirupathur, she did commendable community service in the Yelagiri and Javadu Hills, which had just been cleared of the Naxalites. In 1982, she, along with Vadivelu, the SP of North Arcot, organised a mega three-day tribal sports meet with the help of Father Codello, an Italian priest who devoted his entire life to the upliftment of the tribals in the area. Letika, who was with the tribals all those 3 days, did not realise that she was being referred to as "Javadu Rani," a title by which she is still remembered. With her Munnar background, she was naturally a great hiker and would climb every hill in her jurisdiction. People in Thiruvannamalai still remember her climbing the 2,668 ft hill where the 'Mahadeepam' is lit to mark the start of the 'Karthikai Deepam' festival. When posted to Coimbatore, she climbed the difficult Lampton Peak, named after the first Surveyor General of India.

Another woman IPS officer who has made a name for herself is the smart and cheerful Archana Ramasundaram. She has proven herself a competent and uncompromising maintainer of law-and-order and an efficient crime investigator. She became the first and only woman IPS officer to head a para-military force, the Sashastra Seema Bal (SSB). As the DGP of the SSB, she established close coordination with the governments of Nepal and Bhutan. At present, she is a member of the Lok Pal and is the only police officer among the four non-judicial members.

Just recently, we received news of the most valuable addition to Tamil Nadu's Women Police Force, Kiran Shruthi of the 2018 batch of the IPS. She was declared the 'Best Cadet' at the National Police Academy, outshining all her male and female colleagues—129 in all—and earning the honour of leading the Passing-out Parade. Her parents, both doctors, named their baby daughter Kiran after India's first woman IPS officer, Kiran Bedi. She grew up not only to live up to their expectations but also to surpass Kiran Bedi by winning the Best Cadet award.

The induction of women into the police force was strongly criticised, nay, opposed by the male bastion, while society kept its fingers crossed. But then, the bold and determined first entrants paved the way for many more to follow. The women police satisfied not only departmental requirements but also proved their worth in times of calamities, both natural and man-made. Their determination to excel resulted in commendable achievements in sports, parades, stunt riding, rescue operations, and every activity that was once thought to be the preserve of the male bastion. As I am about to wind up this chapter, I get the news that M. Malathi, a woman SI trainee, has been declared the best cadet out of 927 trainees (688 men and 259 women).

In this chapter, I have tried to highlight the varied and extraordinary achievements of our women police since they became part of the police family 48 years ago. In conclusion, I would like to say that our women police have indeed done very well and can quite rightfully sing these lines from the old English musical, *Annie Get Your Gun*:

"Anything you can do, I can do better

I can do anything better than you"

Pune – Encore!

A delayed flight did my mind ignite
My random thoughts, as they came, to write
What drew me to Pune, like to none other?
My seventh trip this. Will there be another?

Written on 5.2.2013 at Pune Airport While Waiting for My Delayed Flight to Be Called.

I have long since realised that destiny binds man to certain places for no apparent reason, just as it binds him to certain people and certain ideas. In my case, it was Pune. Today, on 5th February 2013, I am here in Pune airport, at the end of my seventh visit.

Did destiny select Pune out of a myriad of places of historical significance and plant it on my chart? Or was it a partial answer to my fascination for the Maratha country, nurtured by the history of the great Shivaji, Tantia Tope, and Rani Lakshmi Bai; or to my secret desire for a pilgrimage to the historical forts of the Sahyadris that gave birth to those legends of heroism; or to my attachment to Pune itself, from where the Peshwas and their intrepid generals, Scindia, Holkar, Bhonsle, and Gaekwad set out to raise the Maratha flag on the ramparts of the Red Fort? The popular saying that Maratha rule extended from Attock (in present-day Pakistan) to Cuttack (Odisha) is an understatement. Their rule actually extended from the River Indus in the north to the River

Cauvery in the South, from the Arabian Sea in the west to the Bay of Bengal in the east. The Maratha Kingdom in Thanjavur, founded by Venkoji, brother of Shivaji, lasted until the British takeover in the 19th century. By then, the Marathas and the local people had merged into one race without any problems of language or race. Today, one cannot distinguish the Maratha from the Tamil; so seamless has been the fusion. All the monuments built by the Marathas, especially Temples, tanks, and numerous cultural edifices, including the Saraswathy Mahal Library, have been well preserved and have stood the test of time.

My first visit to Pune was in July 1964 when my group, one of the four from the Central Police Training College, Mount Abu, was sent to Maharashtra on a study tour. The tour ended in Pune, then 'Poona.' All my batchmates took advantage of the 10-day break given to us to go home, but I chose to visit the mountain forts of the Sahyadris—by bus, train, and even on foot. Sinhagad was one of them. It was here that Tanaji Malusure, Shivaji's most trusted general, lost his life in the war to take possession of Fort Kondhana. Shivaji mourned his loss with the immortal words, "Gadh Aala, Pan Simha Gela" (Won the fort but lost the lion). The fort has been rightly named 'Sinhagad' (Lion's Fort).

On my way to the fort, I visited the National Defence Academy, Khadakwasla, which had once been the destination of my dreams. Had I been selected for the NDA in 1957, I would have been commissioned in 1962, just in time for the Chinese War, perhaps to face defeat, retreat, being taken prisoner of war, or even death. But here I was, an IPS trainee wistfully looking at the shut gates of my once intended destination.

At that time, there was no proper road to the fort. I took a goat track from Khadakvasla Dam and reached the fort in pouring rain, walked on the rampart, slipped, fell backwards, hit my head on a rock, and lay unconscious for how long I knew not; it was the rain that revived me. The silver lining to this dark cloud was the hospitality of a poor family whose hut I staggered into. The members of the family happily shared their simple meal of makki-ka-roti with me, a total stranger who could not even communicate with them in their language. When I took out my purse to pay them, I found that all the notes had been totally soaked by the rain. I forced the family to accept my purse along with its rain-soaked contents. I walked back to Pune, 30 km away. I had survived 2 calamities in unfamiliar terrain: a fall that could have killed me and the loss of all the money I had.

In Pune, I borrowed just enough money from the hotel where we were lodged, reached Palanpur, and went on to Bhuj in Kutch to meet my Mussoorie IAS roommate, Sohan Lal Varma. I was disappointed to find him away on a study tour as part of his IAS probation. I left Bhuj after visiting the fort, the last one in the desert bordering Pakistan. I borrowed more money from Sohan Lal's office staff, which enabled me to visit a few more of the famous and formidable forts of Rajasthan—Rana Pratap's Chittor, Amber, Udaipur, and Ranthambore—before returning to Mount Abu to complete the second half of my training.

My second trip to Pune was in 1968 when I was Superintendent of Police, The Nilgiris. The occasion was the All-India Police Duty Meet. MSP S.I. Panickar, who had been my instructor in Mount Abu, RI Dennyson, and I formed the state Revolver Team. Commandant V.K. Pell was the Manager, and Vetrivel, AC/AR, was the coach. We did not win any medals, as the standard of the State Police Teams was nowhere near that of the Para-Military teams of the BSF, CRPF, CISF, and ITBP. On the other hand, as always, the Tamil Nadu Police team won the overall trophy for scientific aid and investigation, fingerprints, first aid, photography, and the dog show. After returning home, I involved myself in continuous and regular practice with both rifle and revolver. I won my first of three all-India gold medals in Nasik, again in Maharashtra. Incidentally, that was the only one of the three times I could be spared for the all-India competitions. The second time I won the gold was in Jalandhar. My last participation was in 1991 when the Meet was conducted in Chennai, where once again I won the gold in pistol shooting and led Tamil Nadu to its first team shooting championship.

My third visit to Pune was in 1993. The city had changed beyond recognition. All the actors mentioned above had left the stage. The new entrant was my brother-in-law, who had settled in Pune after retiring from the Air Force. From him, I learnt that two of my batchmates who were allotted the Maharashtra cadre were in Pune: Narayanasamy, the Commissioner of Police, Pune, and Satish Sahney, IGP, Crime, with headquarters in Pune. I was thrilled to meet both of them after almost 30 years. The only other thing that I remember of the visit is the thrill of the ride on the Deccan Queen, as I watched the light brown escarpments and multi-coloured rock formations rushing past the window, and the table-top mountains in the distance gliding slowly in the opposite direction. Of course, there was the inner vision of the lightly clad Maratha horsemen dodging and harassing the heavily armed Mughal soldiers and drawing them and their cumbersome caravans of camp followers deeper and deeper into the mountains to defeat them.

My fourth visit was on 15.5.1997. The occasion was the wedding of the daughter of Suresh Kalmadi, the Minister of Railways. He was then the President of the Amateur Athletic Federation of India (AAFI), and I was its Vice President and also the President of the Tamil Nadu Athletic Association (TNAA). The marriage itself was a memorable event, with all of us sporting colourful turbans, a Maratha tradition. The brief ceremony was conducted with great dignity to the chanting of Sanskrit mantras. The colonial racecourse, where the pre-wedding cocktail party was held, and the 160-year-old Empress Botanical Garden, where the marriage took place, lent a historical charm to the event. Kalmadi overwhelmed us with his warmth and hospitality.

I took the opportunity to visit the Yerwada prison, where most of India's top freedom fighters, including Gandhiji, Nehru, Netaji Subhas Chandra Bose, and Ambedkar, had once been detained. I also visited the memorial of Kasturba Gandhi, who had died while in detention in Pune. The Sangam of two insignificant rivers near the prison was nothing more than just a confluence. In Tamil Nadu, it would surely have been sanctified by a Temple for Sangameswarar (Lord of the Confluence).

This fourth trip was not wasted—for that matter, no visit is ever wasted. It was on this trip that I visited the Pune University campus with the sundial that had been built on the lines of Maharaja Sawai Jaisingh's Jantar Mantar in Delhi, Jaipur, Mathura, and Varanasi.

The Commissioner of Police, Agarwal, had arranged my accommodation in the Vaikunth Mehta National Institute of Co-operative Management. It was close to the famous Chattushringi Mandir, from where Goddess Parvati stood surveying the sprawling city below with a weapon in each of her four hands (Chattushringi). As I slithered down the slippery river slope of the Temple hill, I thanked God for making me fit enough to walk, climb, and even run as I had done decades ago, despite several fractures, a bypass surgery, an angioplasty, and surgeries on my spine.

My fifth visit was to attend the wedding of my brother-in-law's only son, who is now with his family in China. My brother-in-law, a veteran of the '71 Pakistan war, had retired prematurely as Group Captain from the Indian Air Force due to ill health and had settled down in Mundwa, a suburb of Pune, along with several other retired IAF officers.

My sixth visit was to attend the funeral of my brother-in-law, who passed away a few months after his son's wedding. Incidentally, his wife, Sumi, also comes from my birthplace, Munnar.

My seventh visit was to attend the wedding of the same brother-in-law's adopted daughter, Mona, whose father, a colleague of my brother-in-law, had died in an air crash; her mother had also passed on soon after, leaving their only child to be adopted by my brother-in-law. After the wedding, Prema and I left for Ahmednagar and visited the Ajanta and Ellora Caves, fulfilling a long-cherished dream.

Who knows? I may visit Pune yet again with the same expectation and curiosity, childlike and insatiable; the same anticipation which had marked all my previous visits. Whether it is to a totally unknown place or to an oft-frequented one, is it not the aim of every traveller to arrive at the starting point to find it again for the first time?

Delayed flights are an inconvenience, to say the least; but I thank the flight to Chennai for its three-hour delay, which enabled me to write these reminiscences on paper that I got from the Airport Office. I close this chapter as I hear the boarding call.

Au Revoir Pune.

"When You Are Stood in the Corner"

When Little Jack Horner is stood in the corner,
He gets to eat Christmas pie;
But if you are Jack Horner and Mandabam's the corner,
You just have to sob and sigh.
And if perchance, you've arrived out there,
A miserable victim of spite,
You just have to grin and that misery bear
With no help or succour in sight.
Now Mandapam's again set to become what it was,
Just a village by the azure sea;
No more should it be a 'corner' because
No officer should thus wasted be.

As I start this chapter, what comes to my mind is a punishment all of us would have suffered at some point or another as children when we were made to stand in a corner, made to feel unwanted and not able to look at anything but the corner.

Service in the Police Department could, on the one hand, be one of appreciation, awards, medals, and special postings; and on the other, one of punishments like reduction in rank, suspension, compulsory retirement, and even dismissal. Between the two lies the nondescript zone of unwelcome and humiliating postings, reserved for those who have fallen out of favour but who cannot be punished. The affected officers cannot protest or go to court as their postings do not affect their ranks or salaries. The post of Vigilance Officer in Transport Corporations and other government organisations like Aavin Milk and TNPL (Tamil Nadu Newsprint and Papers Limited) come under this category.

DGP S.R. Jangid and SP Jayasri head the list of officers who spent 8 years of their service in the state Transport Corporation. Many others, including S. George, Shyam Sundar, and Christopher Nelson, served in those demeaning posts for shorter periods. M. Ravi, an outstanding officer, was Vigilance Officer in Aavin Milk Co-operative for 5 years. DGP S. Kumarasamy, who played an important role in eliminating Naxalites in the early eighties as SP Q-Branch and who maintained absolute peace in the whole state as IGP and ADGP L&O, had to spend the last two-and-a-half years of his service in the Transport Corporations. The DMK government has since abolished these posts.

The most degrading of such posts is the important-sounding 'Special Officer, Sri Lankan Refugees Special Camp,' with its headquarters in Mandapam on Rameswaram Island. My mind goes back several years to an episode in the British TV series *Yes Minister* in which the main worry of the civil servants who fall foul of the government is to get posted to the ornamental post of Chairman, 'War Graves Commission.' Perhaps every country has its 'Mandabam' and 'War Graves Commission.'

The most glaring of injustices was suffered by Sunil Kumar. As a second-generation DGP from Uttar Pradesh, he worked in various capacities to the satisfaction of his superior officers and colleagues. He also headed the Tamil Nadu Uniformed Services Recruitment Board (TNUSRB).

As SP Tirunelveli, Sunil Kumar controlled a communal situation by opening fire and killing one of the rioters. His DIG was furious that he had resorted to firing. When I arrived on the scene from Chennai and asked the SP the number of rounds that had been fired, he answered six. Instead of blaming him for shooting only one rioter, I asked him what happened with the other 5 rounds. That silenced the DIG. "Bullets are not crackers. Each one of them must be accounted for by hitting the leaders instead of mere followers or, worse, even casual onlookers." It was not that I was in favour of shooting people down, but I was particular that only the leaders and instigators of unlawful assemblies should be targeted and not their followers, who would usually disappear from the scene when their leaders fell.

As CoP Salem, he refused to include a leading personality in a case of kidnapping. His refusal was followed by his immediate removal from that post. DGP Govind went to his rescue, provided him with a vehicle to take him to Chennai, and allotted him quarters. But he had to wait 54 days for a posting.

Sunil Kumar

Later, as JCP Chennai City, Sunil Kumar refused to arrest the leader of the opposition, M.K. Stalin, who had led the DMK members on a protest march out of the Assembly to sit on the road in symbolic protest. The JCP sent a three-page note explaining the peaceful nature of the dharna, which did not require any arrest. When he got back the note, he found that the second page had been replaced by another, containing a false account that Stalin had physically attacked him. Once again, he refused to act on the false note. As a result, he was immediately brought to the 'Vacancy Reserve.' Not stopping with that, within half an hour of the order, a police van was sent to his house to take away all government properties like wireless sets, phones, vehicles, and even the camp office orderly.

The attempt to deny Sunil Kumar further promotions by grading his work as 'average' in his ACR by the Commissioner of Police on the instructions of the then DGP failed because the DGP did not have the minimum of 3 months in the post to assess the work of the officer concerned. His predecessor, the generous and benevolent DGP I.K. Govind, graded him as 'Outstanding,' thereby ensuring his promotion to the rank of IGP.

It is painful to note that Sunil Kumar was transferred 29 times in his service of 33 years and was also kept in 'vacancy reserve' thrice for a total of 183 days without salary and the usual facilities available to a senior IPS officer. The service-long injustice has since been partially corrected by his appointment as a member of the 'Real Estate Regulatory Authority' after his retirement by the present Chief Minister, M.K. Stalin.

The Annual Confidential Report is a deadly weapon in the armoury of a coward. I have come across a few 'average' and even 'below average' entries and have altered them in the capacity of the Reviewing Authority. One glaring injustice was the entry made on the ACR of N.P. Singh, CoP, Madurai, by K.V.S. Moorthy, ADGP, L&O, on the instructions of the DGP for refusing to transfer an Inspector to please certain elements. To the assessee's good luck, Home Secretary Raina, who knew the whole story, negated the entry. Another such entry made in his ACR by his DIG was cancelled out by IGP B.P. Rangasamy.

The worst misuse of the ACR is the grade 'below average' given by 2 DGPs to D. Mukherjee, one of the most respected, honest, and efficient officers both at the Centre and in the state. However, Home Secretary Nagarajan negated the grading, thereby paving the way for Mukherjee's posting as the DGP of Tamil Nadu.

Another officer of outstanding merit who was adjudged 'below average' was SP D. Manoharan. He was also known for defying the Election Commissioner, who demanded an apology from him for not clearing agitators who prevented his departure from the airport. Knowing the character and conduct of the Reporting Officer, IGP K. Chenthamarai negated it and gave him a good grade. Manoharan was subjected to similar treatment by another DIG, Krishnan, because he refused to toe his line. That time, IGP Stracey came to his assistance and expunged the grading.

Jaffar Ali, who was DC Crime, Chennai, was a highly capable officer who was given the special job of providing security to former PM Indira Gandhi during her visit to Tamil Nadu, a visit strongly opposed by the DMK party, which she had dismissed. Jaffer Ali ensured her safety in the government guest house and at the public meeting on the Marina, despite severe threats to her safety. After serving as the Intelligence Chief to the DMK government, Jaffer Ali was kept under suspension for 20 months without any reason.

The ultimate and most glaring injustice was denying K. Radhakrishnan the post of DGP, although he was the senior-most officer and the lawful successor of the retiring DGP. He had defied the armed Sri Lankan militants, recaptured several Sri Lankan jail escapees, and, above all, brought total normalcy to Coimbatore after the communal mayhem. He remained DGP-Civil Supplies for five-and-a-half years until his retirement. The career-long injustice he suffered has since been corrected by Chief Minister M.K. Stalin, who has appointed him as a Member of the Fourth Police Commission.

There have been cases of senior officers who manipulated the postings of their uncompromising juniors by sending them to Mandabam, only to find themselves forced to drink from the same distasteful brew. One of them, A.X. Alexander, spent more than a year in Mandabam but managed to get back to the top post of DGP in an eyebrow-raising reversal of fortunes, referred to by everyone as the journey from 'Mandabam to Marina' (the Marina being the location of the DGP's Office).

As far as government servants are concerned, corruption is the most dastardly of all offences. Those indulging in it should be stripped of their uniforms. The name and fame of the Tamil Nadu police should not be allowed to be spoiled by the shady activities of a handful of criminals in uniform, men or women.

Stupidity Raised to the Power of Infinity

Born a poor tribal, he rose to great height;
Steadfast in his aim, he set high his sight.
How managed he this? T'was sheer power of his will.
Now, focussed he is, on greater heights still.
Positive thinking, he proved was the key
That could open the door to such victory.

The harrowing story of a boy belonging to the tribal 'Malayalee' community of a remote tribal village in the erstwhile North Arcot District and the ordeal he suffered in the department deserves the attention of the entire police force. Born on March 23, 1980, in the tribal hamlet of Bhimarapatti, a village in North Arcot district, he started his education in the government tribal school where he studied up to standard IV. By then, he had lost both his father and mother but was determined to continue his studies. He was admitted into the CMS Orphanage Children's Home run by the Christian Missionary Service in Cherapathi village in the Kalrayan Hills of South Arcot district. In his 5th standard, he obtained a caste certificate from the RDO declaring him a 'Malayalee tribal' coming under the category of Scheduled Tribes (ST).

He passed his tenth standard with good marks. After that, he worked as a tanker-cleaner for 2 years before joining the police as a Grade II

Constable of the Armed Police. Despite the difficult duties, which gave him very little time for studies, he passed standard XII in the year 2004, B.A. Economics in the year 2007, and M.A. in Public Administration in 2008.

He also passed a few job-oriented examinations conducted by the Staff Selection Commission, a remarkable feat for someone employed in a demanding and active job.

While waiting for the work order after the VAO examination, he wrote the Group-I preliminary exam and qualified for the main. He then took 120 days of accumulated earned leave, prepared for, and cleared the main exam. He appeared for the interview on 29th December 2008 and was selected for the posts of both RDO and DSP. He chose the latter.

His remarkable achievement turned into a matter of distress when he was asked to produce a fresh certificate from Thiruvannamalai district, which had been carved out of North Arcot district in 1989. The authorities refused to accept the certificate issued by the RDO, Thiruvannamalai, when Thiruvannamalai had been part of North Arcot district. He went from pillar to post but could not get the required certificate. Many times, in sheer desperation, he thought it better to remain a constable. The officials responsible for this abominable callousness belong to the TNPSC, the DGP's office, and the Secretariat. They deserve condemnation for withholding his appointment order on an imaginary, non-sustainable, and stupid reason. All they had to do was refer to the age-old caste list of North Arcot district and honour the certificate issued by the RDO of Thiruvannamalai. It is beyond anybody's comprehension how a person born a tribal could become anything else. But the TNPSC required a fresh caste certificate from the newly formed district, which in turn directed him to get it from the TN Archives. Sending him to the archives is the height of stupidity. The staff of the archives told him that they dealt only with ancient records and not with those of recently created districts.

He spent another 2 years running between the archives, TNPSC, Chief Office, and the Secretariat. By then, a new batch of DSPs had joined the Department while he remained a constable. Adding insult to injury, he was told that the certificate had to be issued by the Social Welfare and Nutritious Meal Programme Department. However, when he approached that department, they too directed him to the archives. Finally, he obtained an order from the Government of India through the Right to Information Act. After much delay, he was given a list of tribes living in various states of India since Independence and communicated the same to the TNPSC. But the TNPSC further delayed the decision on the grounds that all 12 members of the Commission should meet and sign the order. The task of getting all 12 members together was as difficult as cleaning the Augean stables. Eventually, it was left to the knowledgeable and practical new Secretary of the TNPSC, Dr. T. Udayachandran, IAS, who saw no necessity for all 12 members to meet and sign the appointment order. Finally, on 21.3.2012, he was given the appointment order after 3 ½ years had gone by. The process might have taken many more years in fixing his salary and seniority due to the absence of rules relating to the creation of new states and districts. The DGP ordered the completion of his probation as a DSP on 31.7.2015.

Meanwhile, the TNPSC, which had woken up from its slumber, wrote to the Home Department on 19.4.2017, fixing his seniority between Sl.No.26 and above Sl.No.27 and promoting him to the post of ADSP. The government approved the placement, but his request dated 13.11.2020 to the DGP to fix his basic pay and salary on a par with that of serial 26 and 27 is yet to be finalised. Meanwhile, he has been promoted to the rank of SP. By not acting on his request for almost a year now, the Police Department has joined the TNPSC, Home, Tamil Nadu Archives, and the Social Welfare and Nutritious Meal Programme Departments in adding insult to injury to a police officer who has risen from the rank of a constable to that of SP through sheer perseverance, sacrifice, and hard work.

While condemning those who have been unthinking and unsympathetic in this unfortunate saga, those who helped him deserve commendation. Inspector Raadhu Raji, who took the first initiative to help him, is still an inspector while he is now an SP, thus reversing the saluting order! Dr. T. Udayachandran, IAS, was the only other person who understood the situation and came to the rescue of the harassed officer. The protagonist in this ridiculous and pointless exercise is the constable turned SP, P. Kumar.

Casteism and Caste Wars

Neither caste nor creed should divide us
For, mankind all are we;
And God above doth provide us
With the same for you and me.
A peaceful world is all for us,
When we are family

Tamil Nadu is known more for clashes between castes than between religious groups. Although there have been a few clashes between castes belonging to the Backward and Most Backward categories and between the coastal fishermen community and people living in the hinterland, most of the clashes feature the Dalits on one side and one or two of the so-called 'High Castes' on the other. The predominance of caste consciousness, even in the 21st century, can be seen from the fact that even fifth and sixth generation Christians continue to identify themselves by the castes that their ancestors belonged to before their conversion, rather than by the religion they had chosen to escape the caste system that deprived them of their basic rights and dignity.

I grew up in Munnar, Kerala, in the casteless atmosphere of the British-owned tea estates of the High Ranges, where people were known and identified by their names as Tamilian or Malayalee, or as Hindu, Muslim, or Christian. However, on the plains, the outlook was very different, with an atmosphere of fierce loyalty to caste. This came as an unsavoury surprise and shock to me when I arrived in Chennai for my college education. Even in the highly cosmopolitan Madras Christian College, where I did my Intermediate and Bachelor's courses and which had students from all over the country and from countries beyond the sea—Sri Lanka, Malaysia, Fiji, Mauritius, Kenya, and Uganda, to name a few—the students from the highly caste-conscious Southern districts of Tamil Nadu bound themselves in caste-based groups and went all-out to find out the castes of newcomers to induct them into their respective groups. Most of us gave such groups a wide berth, preferring to be known by the activities we were involved in, such as N.C.C., sports, drama, music, and social service. The N.C.C. and sports kept me out of the narrow confines of caste, religion, and language and in the casteless atmosphere in which I had grown up.

I did not have to deal with any major caste-based violence during my tenure as Superintendent of Police in The Nilgiris, Thanjavur, and North Arcot districts, Deputy Commissioner of Police (Law-and-Order) in Madras City, DIG of Police in Trichy and Vellore Ranges, and Commissioner of Police in Madras City. From 1968 to 1988, Tamil Nadu was, by and large, free from caste and communal clashes. This is not to say that there were no incidents at all, as the Dalits continued to fight for their basic human rights, which the Caste Hindus continued to deny them.

In 1989, caste violence returned to Tamil Nadu with a vengeance, not in Ramanathapuram or Tirunelveli districts, both of which had a history of inter-caste upheavals, but in the relatively peaceful Western half of Madurai district, the present Theni district.

The memory of the events in Mudukulathur Taluk more than half a century ago is still kept alive today by the Thevar Guru Pooja, performed in Pasumpon Village every year on the 30th of October, the birth and death anniversary of Muthuramalinga Thevar. In recent years, the martyrdom of Immanuel Sekaran is also observed on a massive scale on the 11th of September. Both these emotionally volatile anniversary celebrations necessitate massive police bandobust at their respective venues as well as in the villages that lie along the roads leading to them.

The spark that ignited the Theni riots in 1989 was the highly provocative speech by Dalit leader John Pandian in Meenakshipuram Village near Bodi on the 10th of September that year. The occasion was the 32nd death anniversary of Immanuel Sekaran. When John Pandian reached Theni from Tirunelveli, his native district, he was informed of the murder the previous day of a Dalit woman in Duraisingapuram Village and the irresponsible conduct of the staff of the Bodi Taluk and the Palanichettipatti Police Station in tossing the complaint between the two on a point of jurisdiction. The already agitated Dalits were instigated by John Pandian to picket buses, demanding the immediate arrest of the murderers who were strongly suspected to belong to the Piramalai Kallar community. Order was restored following the assurance given by the RDO and the Deputy Superintendent of Police that the accused would be arrested at the earliest.

While addressing Immanuel Sekaran's Memorial Meeting that night, John Pandian made derogatory remarks not only about the Thevar community but also about all other so-called high castes. He even went to the extent of saying that the lot of Dalits in Meenakshipuram Village would improve if a Dalit married the daughter of the President of the Village, a high caste Pillai. He kept repeating the slogans 'kill the Maravas and marry the Marathies (Marava women).' This indiscriminate speech roused the Caste Hindus, who started picketing buses in Theni, Bodi, and Uthamapalayam areas, demanding the arrest of John Pandian. The Caste Hindus boycotted the conciliation talks led by the Minister, the DIG of Police, Madurai Range, and the Collector of Madurai District.

The violence soon spread over the entire district, and several Dalit houses were burnt down, leading to the Dalits fleeing from villages where they were outnumbered; many of them were killed. The Dalits, on their part, targeted Caste Hindus who were either alone or in small groups. They also attacked a Head Constable in Kandamanur Village. A case of attempted murder was registered, and two Dalits were arrested and held in the lock-up of Kandamanur Police Station. They were to be produced in court the following day.

The market town of Theni, the gateway to Kerala, had been totally paralysed by the Caste Hindus, thereby cutting it off from the rest of the state and the Western corner of the district comprising the taluks of Gudalur, Kambam, Bodi, and Uthamapalayam. Road traffic to Kerala through Kumuli and Bodinayakanur had come to a halt. Rajasekaran Nair, IGP, Law-and-Order, had already left for Theni. I was, at that time, IGP, Armed Police. DGP B.P. Rangasamy directed me to go to Theni to assist Rajasekaran Nair. As I was getting ready to leave for the affected areas, I received a call from the Chief Secretary cautioning me against opening fire. I told him that unless it was absolutely necessary, there would be no use of firearms; but that I could not promise a shooting-free bandobust.

I reached Madurai City by the morning flight and drove down to Theni with a section of Armed Reserve. When we crossed Andipatti, we encountered the first roadblock where we had our first shock, finding two corpses. They were those of Caste Hindus who had been caught unawares by the Dalits the previous day. We cleared the block and entered the Varushanadu area, a thickly forested tract in the Western Ghats. The area had once belonged to the Zamindar of Kandamanur. I was in for a greater shock when I entered the Kandamanur Police Station. The bodies of five Dalits were sprawled on the floor in the building. I learnt from the shell-shocked Sub-Inspector of Police and Sentry PC that at 07:30 that morning, about 300 Dalits had forcibly entered the Police Station, demanding the release of the two Dalits who had been arrested the previous night for the attempted murder of the Head Constable. The heavily outnumbered SI of Police and Constable had no choice but to open fire in self-defence. This had resulted in the deaths of five Dalits and serious injury to one. The others had fled the scene, leaving the injured SI and Constable with the bodies of the dead. The carnage inside the

Police Station made a mockery of the general instructions to refrain from opening fire. I believe such instructions and the reluctance of the Police to resort to firing to contain rioters, arsonists, and killers always lead to the loss of many more lives and greater destruction of property.

I arranged to send all the seven bodies—the five found in the Police Station and the 2 I had found en route—for post-mortem. But the road to the Theni government hospital had been blocked in several places. We cleared the numerous roadblocks and reached Theni, which had been cut off from the rest of the district by burnt and damaged vehicles abandoned across every road leading to it. The Police had already opened fire on the rioters in Allinagaram, the Southern suburb of Theni town, killing one. The IGP, Rajasekaran Nair, was busy clearing the Theni-Periyakulam Road. I went on to clear the Theni-Gudalur Road. The Caste Hindus in the very first village, Palanichettipatti, offered stiff resistance, but we were able to open the road up to Chinnamanur, 15 km away, before darkness forced us to suspend operations. The next morning, we cleared the rest of the road up to the border with Kerala at the Lower Camp. I also visited Bodi Meenakshipuram, where the trouble had started with John Pandian's hate speech. The entire Dalit population had fled from the village, unable to withstand the united opposition of the other castes. Some of their houses had also been burnt down. They had paid a heavy price for John Pandian's indiscretion. After stirring the hornet's nest, John Pandian hastily left for Tirunelveli, his home district, fearing the wrath of the Caste Hindus as well as that of the Dalits who were aware that he had only recently been released from prison after serving time for the contract murder of a youngster in Coimbatore at the instance of his rival in a love triangle in 1992. His humiliating failure in the recently held assembly election had further eroded his hold over the Dalits belonging to the Kshatriya Kula Vellalar (Pallars), the dominant Dalit community in the Southern districts.

We restored the Kerala-bound traffic to Thekkadi and Munnar by the third day, but not without having to resort to lathi charges and tear gas at every roadside village. We also organised the stranded vehicles into convoys and escorted them to the inter-state border. I stayed in the area for the next 15 days, by which time total normalcy had been restored and almost all those involved in the violence had been arrested. Peace Committees were formed in each village, and conciliatory visits were undertaken by Ministers and senior Government officials. I then returned to Chennai by road via 'My Munnar' and Udumalpet, which acted as a soothing balm to my weary, fatigued body and mind.

A mention must be made here of Meenakshipuram Village in Shengottai station limits, which attracted worldwide attention in 1981 when 175 of its 250 Dalit families embraced Islam. It was clear even then that their decision was not due to social discrimination or atrocities against them by the Caste Hindus. What had lured them was an economic proposition offered by the Muslims of neighbouring Panakuzhi and Vadakarai, providing lucrative employment in the Gulf countries.

Although we often hear of Hindus becoming Christians, very rarely do we hear of Hindus becoming Muslims. As such, this proselytisation sent shock waves throughout the country and brought politicians, Hindu theologians, and reformers to the hitherto unknown village. Even A.B. Vajpayee of the BJP, who later became Prime Minister, along with several Central and state Ministers and leaders of the RSS, hastened to visit the village to study the extent of the conversion.

Even after I became the Additional Director General and later, Director General of Police, Law-and-Order, I had to rush to Tuticorin to contain a Nadar-Fisherman clash that had assumed dangerous proportions. There, a group of fishermen entered the campus of the Collector and set fire to a jeep while we were holding Nadars and Fishermen at bay on the main Albert-Victoria Road. When I rushed over with a police party, the miscreants jumped into the sea and dared us to get them. I fired a few shots over their heads, which were bobbing up and down with the waves. The next round of firing sent the bullets closer to them. When I warned them that the third volley would be aimed at them, they swam ashore and surrendered.

The next bout of violence in the Harbour Town took place on the occasion of the general elections in May 1996. For the first time, the fishermen decided to field their own candidate instead of supporting one or another of the contesting candidates as they had always done in the past. They made their areas out of bounds for candidates other than their own. They displayed menacing notices warning others from entering their area and displaying their symbols. The Police had to intervene and remove the offending notices. Despite several Peace Committee Meetings by the DIG of Police, Tirunelveli Range, and the Collector of Tuticorin District, the fishermen remained recalcitrant. On Election Day, all of them cast their votes by 11:00 a.m. and then started preventing others from reaching their respective polling booths. The Police had to use force repeatedly to disperse them and provide protection to the voters. By evening, all other communities had joined hands to oppose the fishermen, resulting in several clashes. The violence continued unabated for nearly a week after the elections. In one incident, the mob hurled country-made bombs at the Police, injuring ADSP Ramasamy, one Sub-Inspector of Police, and seven Police Constables. In the resultant Police firing, one rioter was killed and another injured. After several rounds of talks and a few 'rounds' off a rifle, the situation was brought under control a week after the election. During the pre-election, election, and post-election periods, 67 houses, 66 shops, 34 vehicles, 2 theatres, and six godowns had been vandalised. As many as 227 criminal cases had been registered. Needless to say, the fishermen's candidate failed to disrupt the well-established party system and was drubbed in the election. The District Judge V.K. Thirunavukarasu, who headed the Commission of Enquiry into the caste-based violence, fully justified the Police action, including the opening of fire.

It was in Tuticorin that I had my first experience dealing with caste-based violence. The year was 1966, and I was Assistant Superintendent of Police, Tuticorin. Again, it was in Tuticorin, now called Thootukudi, that I had my last brush with the abominable caste phenomenon. The year was 1996, and I was Director General of Police (Law-and-Order). I had the satisfaction of reporting to the government the return of total normalcy in the district.

I had only 14 months of service left, and I was grateful to the government for giving me the opportunity to return to Thoothukudi, where I started my career. My service in the department had come full circle, encompassing a life of challenges, triumphs, and above all, fulfilment.

Communal Clashes and the Ratha Yatra

Ratha Yatras should, in peace, just pass
Through towns as devotees worship en masse.
But when faiths are so many in our land,
Shouldn't tolerance and harmony go hand in hand?

Religious gatherings and processions pose a serious challenge not only to their organisers but also to the Police, who must regulate the often-frenzied crowd and ensure the safety of the devotees. Matters become much more complicated when communal animosity or group rivalry arises. Tamil Nadu, compared to many other states, is relatively free from communal clashes. However, the police would be living in a fool's paradise if they imagined they would never have to deal with religious clashes, especially Hindu-Muslim ones. The construction of new Temples or mosques in disputed territory or the passing of religious processions through areas predominated by the other religious group or past their places of worship often provides the spark that ignites communal fire.

It was in North Arcot, the present Vellore district, that I first dealt with a serious communal situation. The demographic pattern in this district, the former domain of the Nawab of Arcot, is not the same as in the rest of Tamil Nadu. The towns of Vellore, Ambur, Vaniyambadi, Arcot, Ranipet, Pernambut, and Melvisharam have a sizeable Muslim population, largely Urdu-speaking, unlike the rest of the state where they have remained Tamil-speaking even after their conversion to Islam centuries ago. In the Southern districts of the state, Muslims are still referred to as "Islamanavar" (those who embraced Islam) and Christians as "Vedakarar" (those who took to the Bible). Their common ancestry and years of living together have resulted in total religious harmony, frustrating the efforts of fundamentalist elements to disturb the peace.

The passing of thousands of Kavadis on the auspicious day of Adhi Krithigai from the villages of North Arcot district to Tiruttani in the neighbouring Tiruvallur district, one of the six Padai Veedus of Lord Muruga, had been going on from time immemorial without any problem. This was despite the Kavadis having to pass through several towns and villages with a significant Muslim population, including several mosques and dargahs, en route.

When I was Superintendent of Police, North Arcot district, in 1975-76, Adhi Krithigai was just an event in the religious calendar and nothing to be worried about. Barely 3 years later, in 1979, the festival led to a serious communal clash in Pernambut village, which had a Muslim majority. When the Kavadis from villages to the South of the town were on their way to Tiruttani, the Muslims objected to their going through a street with several mosques, claiming there were no Hindu houses. The Kavadis then avoided the street in question and left the town without any major incident. However, after sunset, the Hindus from villages around Pernambut torched a few godowns where leather goods belonging to the Muslims had been stored. Later, in the Peace Committee meeting arranged by the District Administration, both communities agreed to bury the hatchet. After all, both had been living in harmony till then. Besides, they were mutually dependent on each other, as many Hindus worked in the leather factories owned by the Muslims and patronised their shops and establishments.

I was posted as DIG of Police, Vellore Range, in 1980, mainly to deal with the Naxalite menace. The Range had jurisdiction over the districts of North Arcot (presently Vellore, Thiruvannamalai, Tirupattur, and Ranipet districts), Salem (presently Salem city, Salem, and Namakkal districts), and Dharmapuri (presently Dharmapuri and Krishnagiri districts). From the day I took charge, I was kept busy with the Naxalite problem, which had assumed alarming proportions in the Dharmapuri district and in the Tirupathur Sub-Division of North Arcot district.

When Aadi Krithigai dawned in July 1980, I was leading a police party in the Jawadu Hills in search of the Naxalite killers of Natesa Nainar, the leader of the resistance group in Kathirampatty village. The Collector and the Superintendent of Police were in Pernambut, where the Muslims, as they had done the previous year, were refusing to permit the Kavadis to pass through the Muslim Street where the most important mosque was located. I was kept informed of the developments through the police wireless network. By 4 p.m., it became clear that the district administration would not be able to either persuade the Muslims to allow the Kavadis to go through the traditional route, or the Hindus to take an alternate route. Fearing a repeat of the previous year's spate of arson, I rushed to Pernambut, 45 km away, to resolve the issue before nightfall.

By the time I reached the town, there was barely an hour and a half of daylight left, and both the Hindus and the Muslims were adamant in holding their respective stands. More than 500 Kavadis were being restrained by the Police from entering the street concerned while the Collector and the Superintendent of Police were holding parleys with the leaders of both communities. I got the Kavadis lined up a little away from the entrance to the street in question, which had been blocked by more than 500 Muslims shouting provocative slogans. I walked up to them and tried to reason with their leaders. I told them categorically that the street was a public thoroughfare and therefore could not be closed to the Kavadis. But they refused to relent, calling themselves 'Jehadis' and declared that the Kavadis could enter the street only over their dead bodies.

I gave them 5 minutes to clear the blockade and got the policemen ready for action. Bursting tear gas was ruled out because it would also have affected the families living on the street. At the end of the stipulated time, I led the party in a lathi charge. After initial resistance, the protesters broke rank and fled down the street, pursued by the lathi-wielding policemen. I led the Kavadis down the narrow-cobbled street, which was littered with shoes and slippers of the fleeing protesters. Stones were pelted at us as we passed the first mosque on the disputed street; we entered it and cleared it of the miscreants. All the Kavadis went through the street before day gave way to night. I told the Muslim leaders, in no uncertain terms, that no public street could be made out of bounds for anyone, not even on religious grounds. At the same time, I assured them that the Hindus, as was the practice elsewhere in the state, would not be permitted to take the Kavadis past the mosque at prayer time and would also stop beating drums and playing music.

Two days later, at the instance of the Chief Minister MGR and by way of placating the Muslims, the Director General of Police, T.T.P. Abdullah, paid a visit to Pernambut. The DGP, who was from the Mopla heartland of Malabar, was fluent in English, Malayalam, and Tamil; and also in Arabic, as he had served two terms as Indian Ambassador to Saudi Arabia; but he did not know Urdu. As such, ahead of his visit, I told the Muslim leaders that they should talk to him only in English, Tamil, or Arabic.

To the Muslims of Pernambut, it was inconceivable how a Muslim dignitary would not know Urdu, the language of Muslims in both India and Pakistan. They started voicing their complaints in Urdu, only to be snubbed by the DGP. However, he accepted their request to visit the mosque located on the disputed street. When we entered the mosque, I was taken aback to see about 75 people, including children in arms, with bandaged heads and limbs. The D.G.P. was told that they had sustained the injuries during the lathi charge on the Muslim Street and in the mosque. I was sure that it was a false claim because I never saw any children among the protesters at the time of our entry into the street. Injury to adults was possible because of the lathi charge and their fleeing down the narrow street. I reached out and lightly pulled at the bandage on a child's head. It came off in my hand, and there was no injury whatsoever. That was the end of the D.G.P.'s commiseration. He left the town without waiting for their explanation.

Whatever might have been the justification or effect of the police action, there has never been any communal incident in Pernambut or any other part of the district since then. Kavadis continue to be taken to Tiruttani with brief stops at the important shrines of Rathnagiri and Vallimalai en route. Needless to say, I had the advantage of being neither Hindu nor Muslim.

I recall the murder of a police constable within the Murugan Temple atop Ratnagiri Hill, halfway between Vellore and Arcot. The year was 1975, and I was the Superintendent of Police, North Arcot district. The Rathnagiri Temple, though not as important as the 'Aarupadai Veedukal,' attracted a large number of 'kavadi'-carrying pilgrims on important festive days like 'Adhi Kiruthigai' because of its location on the main road. The Temple was also famous for the Mouna (silent) Swamiyar, otherwise known as 'Bala Murugan Adimai,' who presided over the Temple. After I had visited the Temple with DSP Subbaiah of Ranipet and made enquiries, the rumour spread that during my interrogation, the swamy had broken his silence and spoken. Nothing could have been further from the truth. We treated him very respectfully, and he did not break his silence. The case was soon detected, and a Temple servant admitted to murdering the constable. He was convicted and sentenced to life imprisonment. After that, I became a special guest of the Temple and was treated with much respect during 'Aadi Kiruthigai,' which I attended every year of my five-year tenure as DIG, Vellore Range (1980-1985).

The unfortunate incident of opposing the Kavadi procession was a clear indication that communal animosity had finally entered Tamil Nadu, which had hitherto been a haven of communal harmony. Militant

Hindu outfits had established their foothold in Coimbatore, Tiruppur, Mettupalayam, and Vellore and indulged in provocative speeches resulting in attacks, both verbal and physical, on the Muslims.

Matters came to a head on 15th September 1990 when the B.J.P., led by L.K. Advani, initiated a Ratha Yatra from the famous Somnath Temple to Sri Rama's birthplace in Ayodhya, demanding the establishment of a Temple for Lord Rama on the very site of the Babri Masjid. Hindu outfits all over the country took out similar Ratha Yatras in support of Advani's venture. In Tamil Nadu, the Ratha Yatra was to start from Coimbatore, pass through or halt at important towns en route, and reach the Bay of Bengal at Chennai, where the Ratham would be submerged. Whatever might have been the merits of Advani's Yatra to Ayodhya, the Yatra in Tamil Nadu was a needless exercise, aimed only at rousing communal passion. At that time, I was heading the Armed Police of the State and had been put in charge of the Yatra. Apart from the police party that accompanied me throughout the Yatra, the bandobust itself was left to the jurisdiction Police with instructions to follow my overall command. The armed escort that followed the Ratham was supplemented by the local Police whenever it entered sensitive areas or stopped for night halts.

Contrary to apprehensions, the Yatra had a peaceful start at Coimbatore, which had just witnessed two communal murders. The first night halt was in Tiruppur, where the Hindu opposition was headed by a retired Commissioner of Police, Kuppusamy Gounder, setting an unfortunate precedent. It was followed by a few other senior government servants like DGP Pon Paramaguru, IPS, and the Home Secretary Malaisamy, IAS, heading caste-based organisations after their retirement. It is true that, after retirement, they are not bound by the code of conduct that had regulated the conduct of Government servants. But such associations cast serious doubts on their impartiality and sense of justice in dealing with the public and also with their own subordinates during their service. Senior public servants should set an example, not only during their service but even after their retirement.

I talked to the leaders of both communities before the Ratham entered the textile city and followed it up with a foolproof bandobust. I realised that the most vulnerable time was when the Ratham entered a town or city to a boisterous reception by the Hindus and the sullen acceptance by the Muslims. The departure of the Ratham the following morning from the place of halt was also a sensitive time, as was its passage past Muslim places of worship. We had to ensure that the crowd accompanying the Ratham did not wilfully tarry or beat drums when it went past a mosque. We also frustrated the designs of the Yatris to go past any Mosque at prayer time.

The Ratham passed through Erode, Salem, and Dharmapuri towns without any incident, despite Salem having a history of Hindu-Muslim animosity dating back to 1890, when a Mosque was sought to be constructed near a Temple in the Shevvapet area. The presence of Hindu Munnani leaders in Hosur 2 days prior to the arrival of the Ratham seemed to spell trouble. Hosur was not like other towns through which the procession had to pass because of its dominant Telugu population and an equally aggressive Muslim presence. Apart from Melapalayam in Tirunelveli district, Hosur and nearby Denkanikottai were the only other places in Tamil Nadu where the formation of Pakistan in 1947 and the assassination of Gandhiji in 1948 were celebrated by the Muslims. The Hindu Munnani leaders could expect much more support for the Ratham in Hosur than in any other place on the Ratham's route.

The local police had already prescribed the route and timing of the Ratham within the town to avoid the street on which the major mosque was situated as well as the prayer time. The organisers had accepted the conditions laid down by the Police. But when the Hindu Munnani leaders saw the massive reception being accorded to the Ratham, they insisted on going past the Mosque. When I reminded them of their written consent to the conditions laid down by us, their leader A. Rama Gopalan replied that in India, they had the right to go anywhere, past Mosque or Church. I told him, 'Not when I am in charge.' That was the last I saw of him.

We stopped the procession at the entrance to the street. The crowd had swelled with the arrival of more Hindus, who started bursting crackers and trying to force their way into the street. We had no option but to bar their way and lathi charge them. In a few minutes, the crowd, along with the Hindu Munnani leaders, dispersed, abandoning the Ratham on the road. We carried it with all reverence and left it at the place assigned for its night halt.

The departure of the Ratham from Hosur was an anti-climax. The Hindu Munnani leaders had left the town surreptitiously, and their local supporters had also made themselves scarce. The Yatris quietly carried the Ratham and left the town. Hosur was an important landmark in the passage of the Ratham from Coimbatore to Chennai. Until it reached Hosur, the passage had been smooth and incident-free. After Hosur, it was marked by increasing defiance of police regulations by the Hindus and an equally hostile reception to the Ratham by the Muslims.

The Hindu outfits worked overtime to gather as many people as possible at the subsequent halts, mainly Ambur and Vellore, to overawe the police and provoke the local Muslims. The passage of the Ratham through Vaniyambadi, a predominantly Muslim town, gave us anxious moments, but it went through peacefully. However, trouble erupted in Ambur, another town with a sizeable Urdu-speaking Muslim population. A large Hindu crowd received the Ratham at the entrance to the town with music and bursting of crackers. R.V. Gopal, DIG of Police, Vellore Range, had made elaborate arrangements to ensure its peaceful passage. I accompanied the Ratham to its halting place in a Temple at the other end of the town. A few bricks were thrown at a Mosque by those who carried the Ratham, bricks which were supposed to be symbolic of the proposed construction of the Temple to Lord Rama in Ayodhya. We successfully localised the trouble and maintained full vigil through the night. The aggrieved Muslims were pacified and told to remain calm.

In the morning, an unexpectedly large crowd accompanied the Ratham on its way out of the town. Several youngsters accompanied it on their motorbikes, wantonly raising the noise level, much to the annoyance of Muslims who were on their way to the Mosque for morning prayers. The bikers then threw stones at a Madrasa located 2 km out of the town and tried to force their way into it. We caught up with them before they entered the building and dispersed them by force. They abandoned their bikes and fled back to Ambur. The Rath, now divested of its motorcycle escort, proceeded calmly along the road to Vellore, which it reached shortly after sunset. The abandoned motorcycles, all ten of them, were returned to the owners by the Police after getting an undertaking of good behaviour from them.

In Vellore, both sides were evenly matched. The Muslims had gathered in strength at the mosques along the route of the Ratham. There was mutual stone-throwing, and we had to make repeated lathi charges to separate the antagonists. We also made several preventive arrests before settling down for the night, the penultimate night of the Yatra.

In the morning, the Ratham set out on its way to Madras via the Muslim strongholds of Mel Visharam, Arcot, and Wallajapet. At Mel Visharam, a predominantly Muslim township, the processionists wanted to take the Rath through the town, although the Hindu leaders had earlier agreed to take it via the bypass road, avoiding the numerous mosques lining the main street of the town. When we stood firm on our decision, they put the Rath down by the side of the road and refused to go further. We, on our part, had chairs and benches brought over and settled down in preparation for a long wait. We also had our lunch brought over to us. Exasperated by this move, they quietly took up the Ratham and proceeded to Madras via the bypass.

The Ratha Yatra proved to be a challenging experience in that we had to use every tactic available to us - persuasion and compulsion, restraint and action, patience, as well as on-the-spot decisions, without offending either community and at the same time impressing upon them our commitment to law-and-order and communal harmony. The

Hindu Munnani leaders made a last effort to embarrass the Government and provoke the Muslims by insisting on going past the Big Mosque in Triplicate. But by then, the novelty of the Ratham had lost its charm, and the efforts of the yatris to provoke a last-minute confrontation failed. Finally, it was left to the Chennai City Police to perform the last rites of the Ratham.

Imam Ali – India's Osama Bin Laden

Should thoughts of revenge cloud one's mind,
When we are the world, and we are all one?
All differences let us leave behind;
Aren't we all warmed by the same bright sun?

Of the Muslim extremists who brought the bomb culture into Tamil Nadu in the late 20th century, the most dreaded was Imam Ali, a native of Melur near Madurai. After completing his tenth standard in 1986, he was working as a radio mechanic in Melur when his life underwent a dramatic change. What caused it was the destruction of the Babri Masjid by Hindu fanatics on 6th December 1992.

By way of revenge, Imam Ali wanted to cause similar damage to Hindu Temples. He started studying explosives used for the digging of wells and gradually learnt how to make bombs. He had a close friend, Soundararajan, whom he converted to Islam and renamed Hyder Ali. Both of them met Palani Baba, former President of the outlawed All-India Jihad Committee (AIJC) in Chennai, and joined that organisation. He and four others were experimenting with explosives on a hill near Melur. Based on information given by the public, Imam Ali was detained under the National Security Act. In January 1992, when he was being escorted from Melur court to the bus stand, he requested permission to go to the toilet. Taking advantage of the opportunity, he escaped from police custody. He then travelled all over India, including Kashmir, and into

Bangladesh, where he perfected his training in explosives. He returned to Tamil Nadu on 2nd August 1993 and prepared for the destruction of the RSS office. After an initial failure due to a defective battery, he succeeded in blasting the multi-storeyed building in Chennai on 8th August 1993, a blast that claimed 13 lives.

He spent the next 2 years travelling all over India. In Lalmasia, Bangladesh, he learnt Arabic and Urdu. Upon returning to Tamil Nadu in April 1995, he planned to eliminate Rama Gopalan of the Hindu Munnani and disrupt Vinayagar Chaturthi processions. However, before he could execute his plan, the police arrested him on 29th August 1995 at the Nellithurai Farm near Mettupalayam, along with five of his associates, weapons, and a large quantity of explosives. He was in police custody for the next 6 years, facing several court cases. On 7th March 2002, he and Hyder Ali were being escorted from Palayamkottai Jail to Madurai to have their remand extended in the first bomb-making case. The escort comprised 1 ACP, 1 RI, 1 RSI, and 8 ORs armed with AK-47, SLR, and .303 rifles. The court extended their remand until 28th March 2002. The escort team then left for Kovilpatti to have their remand in another case extended. En route, they stopped at Thirumangalam Taluk Police Station for lunch. The accused were made to have their lunch in the vehicle itself. At that moment, a rescue party consisting of nine Muslim fanatics surrounded the police, opened fire with country-made weapons, and lobbed six country bombs, injuring two PCs. Before the police could react, the rescue party freed the accused and escaped with them. While escaping, they also snatched one AK-47 weapon and damaged the police vehicle. This second escape of the dreaded Imam Ali dealt a severe blow to the police. Shakeel Akther, who was DC, Crime and Traffic, Madurai City, immediately organised a search for the escapees but did not succeed in capturing them. The DGP then formed a special party led by DIG Coimbatore, Ashutosh Shukla, who had earlier dealt with Imam Ali's file in his capacity as SP Special Division-CID and was well-versed with the details of Imam Ali. He took DC Shakeel Akther to assist him in forming and monitoring the search team.

The team's relentless search led them to a three-storeyed residential building in Bangalore. Two Kannada-speaking SIs, pretending to be a couple, went to the suspected house under the pretext of enquiring about its availability for rent. They identified three men on the ground floor from photographs taken earlier. At that time, I had just been recalled from retirement and given the special assignment of tracing Veerappan. I had with me a team of ace shooters under SP Ashok Kumar, a veteran Naxalite hunter. I sent him with his team of sharpshooters to assist Shukla and his team in Bangalore. As the entire action was in another state and since I had already retired, I had to stay back and watch the search and encounter from the sidelines. As the house was part of a three-storeyed building in a crowded area, the Commissioner of Bangalore City did not want to take part in the raid, worried about possible civilian casualties. Ashok Kumar and his team burst into the house through the door and surprised the occupants. In the ensuing exchange of fire, Imam Ali and four of his associates, Basheer alias Anwar of Melapalayam, Md. Ibrahim, Saifulla, and his wife Yasmin, were killed, and 13 policemen sustained injuries.

The President's Gallantry Award was rightly given to IGP Ashutosh Shukla, DIG Md. Shakeel Akther, SP Ashok Kumar, and DSPs Sekar and Kalimuthu. Four Inspectors of Police, four SIs, one HC, and 38 ORs were awarded the CM's Gallantry Medals and a cash prize of Rs. 2 lakh each.

Having personally led several search operations and armed encounters, I can confidently say that the pursuit of Imam Ali and the final shoot-out in a residential area, and in another state without causing injuries to civilians, was a remarkable achievement.

The episode of Osama Bin Laden has several similarities with that of Imam Ali, although on a larger scale. Both started their careers of revenge due to activities of another country/state, another language, and another religion. If the destruction of the twin towers of the World Trade Centre was the reason for the pursuit of Osama Bin Laden, the destruction of the multi-storeyed RSS building in Chennai was the main reason for the pursuit of Imam Ali. It took the pursuers nearly ten years to trace and finally kill the fugitives. Although we do not have the exact details of the pursuit of Bin Laden, we know that he was killed using modern technology. The American Navy submerged his body in the sea so that he would not become an international hero. Although Imam Ali was treated as a common murderer, he continues to be regarded as a religious hero by some.

I must explain the reason behind the heading of the chapter comparing Imam Ali and Osama Bin Laden. Both have had a lot in common throughout their careers. Bin Laden became an enemy of the Christians and carried out several genocidal attacks on them. Similarly, Imam Ali became a bitter enemy of the Hindus after the wanton destruction of the Babri Masjid. Osama Bin Laden is best known for masterminding the destruction of the twin towers of the World Trade Centre on September 11, 2001, resulting in the deaths of 3,000 people. He became the subject of a decade-long manhunt by the USA from 2001 to 2011. The FBI offered 25 million US dollars for information about him. Finally, on 2nd May 2011, he was shot dead by the US Naval Special Warfare Development Group (SEAL Team 6) in Abbottabad, Pakistan. His body was submerged in the sea to avoid sensationalising his death within the Muslim community. The destruction of the RSS building in Chennai on 8th August 1993 earned Imam Ali the sobriquet of "India's Osama Bin Laden." Both of them remained untraceable for nearly a decade despite efforts by the US in Bin Laden's case and by the Tamil Nadu police in the case of Imam Ali.

As I close this chapter, I must admit that I do not see Ashutosh Shukla, Shakeel Akther, Ashok Kumar, and their team simply snuffing out Imam Ali and his associates in a shoot-out. What I do see is the brave team overshadowing the final scene of the Osama Bin Laden saga, in which, surrounded by the US Navy SEALs, the founder of Al-Qaeda met his end.

Religious Festivals and Pilgrims' Safety

When God's in his heaven, all's well here below,
So, turn your eyes heavenwards, your praise to bestow;
The Mahamaham tank, the source of God's power
Be there on that day and, precisely that hour

Four of my earlier chapters dealt with unlawful assemblies. The first was the violation of the code of conduct regulating the election campaign by a revolver-wielding Captain Natarajan leading a group of Congressmen. The second was the unleashing of violence by the unlawful assembly of workers in the Cordite Factory at Aravankadu in The Nilgiris, which eventually led to police firing. The third was the unlawful assembly of the DMK, DK, and Communists to protest against the visit of ex-Prime Minister Indira Gandhi. This confrontation again led to police firing at the Halda Junction at Guindy, resulting in the deaths of three rioters. My entry into the Assembly also followed the rioting between the followers of Jayalalithaa and those of Janaki. Again, the police had to clear both groups out of the Assembly Hall by the use of force.

It is also not unusual for a perfectly peaceful religious function, of which there is no shortage in our country, to get out of control. Stampedes occur due to the anxiety of the pilgrims to be in the right place at the right time. It is the 'auspicious time' that rules the roost and sets the pattern. In a trice, a perfectly orderly procession can become disorderly and throw the well-planned bandobust arrangements into total disarray. Such situations arise at Kumbabishekams, Ratham festivals, and during holy dips in seas, rivers, and sacred tanks.

I had my first experience of such a situation in Tuticorin, where I had just then been posted as the Assistant Superintendent of Police. The year was 1965, and the occasion was the annual Car Festival of the sacred shrine of 'Our Lady of Snow.' This Catholic festival, held in one of the oldest churches in the country, attracted Christians, both Catholic and non-Catholic, as well as Hindus. It was also the occasion for a leadership tussle between two leading families of the prominent fisherfolk community, and the time to establish their respective rights and privileges. The yearly jostle for the right to start pulling the sacred car had been resolved by a convention set by a former ASP, E.L. Stracey, IP, who took the first pull himself. The rival community leaders did not mind a police officer giving the lead.

A similar state of affairs prevailed in many other festivals, whether Hindu, Christian, or Muslim. The best solution was for the senior-most Revenue or Police officer to give the 'Start.' However, there are festivals like the annual feast of Velankanni, attended by Christian and Hindu pilgrims from all over India. The high sense of oneness that prevails among the organisers and the pilgrims relieves the police of the need to settle diverse claims. This leaves them free to concentrate on other aspects like crowd regulation, restoration of lost children, and keeping a watch out for pickpockets, confidence tricksters, and chain-snatchers, thus ensuring the general safety of the pilgrims. I have had the privilege of supervising the bandobust for the annual festival of the Velankanni Church, the Ur's of the equally famous Dargah in Nagoor, and the Car Festival of the 1,000-year-old Thyagaraja Temple in Thiruvarur, as many as six times: twice as the Superintendent of Police, Thanjavur District, twice as Superintendent of Police, Nagapattinam, and twice as the Deputy Inspector General of Police of Trichy Range. It was in Thanjavur District, which has the largest number of Temples, sacred tanks, Adeenams, and Mutts, that I learnt to plan and organise bandobusts for religious festivals.

The most enjoyable pre-festival survey relates to the Karthikai Deepam in Thiruvannamalai because of the elegance of the Temple and the mesmerising view of the Deepam atop the 2,662-foot-high mountain. I was lucky to have attended eight Karthikai Deepams: two as SP, North Arcot District, five as DIG, Vellore Range, and one as ADGP (L&O). I made it a routine to climb up the hill with the men carrying the 'kopparai,' ghee, and the 100-yard-long wick which had to burn for 10 days. I would then go down alone through a different route every time. I remember Superintendent of Police, North Arcot, Vadivelu doing the climb with his wife and children. I must mention here that Laxmi, Vadivelu's wife, was also from Munnar and much junior to me in school. So were her twin brothers, one of whom was the college mate of IGP Vadivelu. The love for mountains and trekking had passed on from Mrs. Vadivelu to her children. Of course, Vadivelu had walked hundreds of miles in the NEFA as an Officer of the TSP Battalion on duty.

Starting with the Kumbabhishekam of Vaideeswaran Koil in the year 1969, I have planned, personally worked out, and supervised the bandobust schemes of as many as 427 Temple Kumbabhishekas. The most memorable and challenging ones were those of Thiruvidaimarudhur, Thirupanandal, Mannargudi, Thanjavur, Swamimalai, and Thirukadayur. My interest from my University days in Temple lore, history, legends, and procedures at festivals peculiar to each Temple stood me in good stead to carry out my responsibilities as a supervisory officer. The 'Sthala Purana' of each pilgrim-centre made fascinating reading. The best and most authentic information on the origin of the Temples and the various festivals and pujas performed there can be found in the police station records called Part IV or Village History. Thanks to the diligence of the Inspectors of yore, this Part IV on each village was a treasure-house of information on the composition of castes and communities, details of factions, festivals and ceremonies, traditions peculiar to each village, and above all, details of places of worship, fairs, and festivals. I used to add to this any information that came my way in the course of my village and Temple visits. Most of the Inspectors and sub-divisional officers down the line satisfied themselves with filing copies of official reports on faction fights, bandobust schemes, and other important developments without making any effort to analyse the effectiveness of their schemes. The officers of today should try to revive the useful, informative, and interesting tradition by making use of the invaluable Part IV.

In spite of every precaution taken, it is always touch and go during the Kumbabhishekas, especially at the exact moment when the Kalasams atop the Temple tower are anointed. Devotees who occupy every available space for miles around the Temple push forward to get a view of the Abhishekam and get a drop or two of the holy water on themselves.

At the 1972 Kumbabhishekam of Swamimalai Temple, one of the six Padaiveedus of Lord Muruga, a sudden rush to view the Abhishekam from a bridge spanning River Kudamuruti resulted in a stampede in which six women devotees were suffocated to death with no external injuries whatsoever. As the Superintendent of Police in overall charge of the preparation and implementation of the bandobust scheme, it was my responsibility to shift the dead to the hospital for post-mortem; this I did with the help of the policemen and devotees nearby. Very rarely are the police blamed for such mishaps. But the acceptance of karma does not absolve the police of its failure to prevent any last-minute rush resulting in loss of life.

I informed the D.I.G. of Police and the Secretary of the Hindu Religious and Endowment Board, who were at the Temple top at the time of the mishap. The Secretary, a Senior IAS Officer, joined me as soon as he could wade through the crowd and helped me organise formalities like conducting the post-mortem and recording the statements of the witnesses.

When both of us tried to contact the DIG, who had been seated near the Kalasam at the time of the Kumbabhishekam, we were told that, as soon as he received my initial message through the police wireless, he went down the specially erected ladder and quickly left for his headquarters in Trichy, 90 km away. Thereafter, he maintained strict radio silence until the dust raised by the multiple deaths had settled down. No marks for guessing who would have taken the credit had the festival gone off without any mishap.

I was, however, thankful to the Secretary of the Hindu and Religious Endowment Board, who remained with me until all the formalities were completed. Later on, he gave the police a clean chit. I have long since lost track of the numerous successful bandobusts. But the death of the six women devotees in Swamimalai still rankles in my mind.

The Mahamaham in Kumbakonam, which takes place once in 12 years, is of a much higher league altogether. Though not comparable to the Kumbh Melas, which are also observed once in 12 years in Allahabad, Ujjain, Nasik, Haridwar, Triumbakeswar, and Benares, where more than a crore of pilgrims gather and where deaths due to stampedes caused by pilgrims rushing to the river at the auspicious moment or while hastily making way for the Trishul-wielding naked Sadhus, the Mahamaham, on the other hand, offers a severe challenge to the police because of the narrow confines of the town, the difficult approaches to the tank, and the very limited surface area of the tank in contrast to the vast expanse of the Gangetic waterfront.

Tradition has it that, during the Mahapralaya (Great Floods) after Dwabara Yugam, a Kumbam containing Amirtham and seeds of creation was set afloat by Lord Shiva, who proclaimed that the place where the pot touched the ground would be the holiest of all places in the world. The place where the Kumbam came to rest was named Kumbakonam after that Kumbam. As soon as it settled down, Lord Shiva appeared in the guise of a hunter and broke the Kumbam of Amirtham with his arrow. The Amirtham spilled out and formed a pool, which became the

Mahamaham tank. Lord Shiva then collected the sand, wet with the remaining Amirtham that had overflowed, and shaped it into the present Mahalingam, known as Sri Adhi Kumbeswara.

Mahamaham is celebrated once in 12 years on a full moon day in the month of Masi, when the Maha Natchathiram is in Rishaba Lagnam, Guru in Simha Rasi, and the Moon in Kumba Rasi. During this auspicious period, all the holy rivers of the world are believed to converge in the Mahamaham tank. It is also believed that those who take a dip in the tank at that auspicious moment would be absolved of all their sins.

The Mahamaham tank covers an area of over six acres and has 16 mandapams spaced out along its sides. The streets around the tank are known as Mahamaham East, West, South, and North. The important roads that lead to it are the Head Post Office Road from the north, the Kamarajar and Lal Bahadur Sastri Roads from the east, the Indira Gandhi Road from the South, and the Gandhi Adigal Road (Kadalangudi Street) from the west.

It is believed that in this tank there are 19 sacred springs or Theerthams to mark the confluence of the many sacred rivers flowing into it. The sacred Theerthams are not wells in the true sense of the word, but spaces, one to three feet in diameter, marked by parapet walls.

The Mahamaham tank is fed by underground springs which have their source in the nearby Arasalar River, a distributary of the river Kaveri. About two months before the Mahamaham festival, the tank is drained of all the water and de-silted. The tank bed is then covered with a layer of sand. On the auspicious day, water is let into the tank and maintained at a height of about two feet.

I had my first Mahamaham bandobust in 1980. As DIG of Police, Trichy Range, it was my responsibility to prepare and implement the massive scheme. Preparing the scheme was not difficult for me, as I had the benefit of the schemes prepared for the previous Mahamahams of

1956 and 1968. I was also quite familiar with the layout of the tank in relation to the Temple town, the railway station, the bus stands, the numerous roads that criss-crossed the town, and the numerous Temples and Temple tanks all around. All I had to keep in mind was the certainty of a much larger turnout of pilgrims, devotees, and visitors with every succeeding Mahamaham.

The auspicious time that year was between 10:15 and 11:15 a.m. But much before dawn, the tank was packed with devotees. The water level, which had been kept at the two-foot level, rose to neck level after the first group of devotees stepped in. Bhajans were being broadcast through loudspeakers. The devotees, those inside the tank and those moving from Temple to Temple, were treated to the awesome celestial display of Jupiter, Venus, and the Moon forming a close-knit triangle.

As the auspicious time approached, all four banks of the tank became packed with people waiting to occupy the places that would be vacated by their luckier counterparts who were already in the tank. On the signal given by firing a very pistol (a pistol used for firing coloured signal flares) at the precise moment, all those in the tank had their dip and started leaving through the northern and Western sides, making room for those waiting to enter through the Southern and eastern banks. Both entry into and exit from the tank were regulated through barricades.

All went well, and the Mahamaham ended peacefully, without a single untoward incident or accident, not even a death due to natural causes. The following day, the Citizens Committee of Kumbakonam honoured us in the Town Hall for the flawless bandobust.

Twelve years later, the Mahamaham fell on 18th February, with the auspicious time for the holy dip calculated to be between 10:40 and 11:45 a.m. Needless to say, the same exercise was repeated, but on a much larger scale, to deal with the greater influx of pilgrims into Kumbakonam for the week-long religious observance and finally the dip in the holy tank. J. Jayalalithaa was at that time the Chief Minister. S. Sripal was the

DGP, and I continued as IGP (L&O) through Governor's Rule over the next six months.

It again fell to me to prepare the bandobust scheme and implement it. But it was to my advantage that the local minister, Alagu Thirunavukarasu, who was also looking after the local self-government, posted one of his most efficient officers, M. S. Sivasamy, as the Municipal Commissioner and also as the Special Officer, Kumbakonam, to attend to all matters relating to the festival. Incidentally, Sivasamy was my classmate in college, which facilitated coordination and the fulfilment of all other requirements. Several new modifications had to be made, taking into account a much larger influx of pilgrims than at the previous Mahamaham. More bus shelters were built outside the town limits; more special trains were organised; more feeding points and field hospitals were set up; and more one-way routes were formed to ensure the smooth flow of human traffic to and from the various Temples and tanks. Policemen and policewomen were formed into 'MAY I HELP YOU' squads and given special training to guide and help the pilgrims. The town was made out of bounds for vehicles. Everything pointed to a more successful festival bandobust than the one in 1980.

A little concern was caused by the identity of the DIG-Trichy, who was the jurisdiction officer in charge of Kumbakonam and therefore the Mahamaham. He was Md. Kasim, who had, on his own, attended to the cleaning of the sacred tank and the repairing of the steps and lamp-posts well in advance. Despite my objection, we were made to bring in DIG V. C. Perumal in his place, supposedly to avoid controversy. The organisers wondered about me as well but answered it themselves: "Davaram is our own, and there can be no better officer to handle a major Temple festival or a large crowd." Who was I? What was I? Could it have been my Hindu-sounding name? The answer is still a mystery.

Now the question of celebrities attending the function came up. At the head of the government was the popular and highly religious Chief Minister J. Jayalalithaa. When the Mahamaham was discussed at a meeting with her, the Chief Secretary, the Home Secretary, the DGP, and other senior government officers, including me, requested her to grace the occasion, as it was the first mega festival after she took charge as the Chief Minister. She was emphatic that she would not like to undertake the visit, as it would put a heavy strain on the police. However, all the officers pressed for her presence as the festival coincided with her birth star, Maham. Finally, she relented and agreed to reach the spot just before the auspicious time and leave immediately after the holy dip. A temporary helipad was then set up 3 km away from the tank, and arrangements were made to drive her car straight from the helipad to the tank and back.

On the all-important day, everything went according to plan. The pilgrims had easy access to various Temples and tanks. The Mahamaham tank started filling up four to five hours before the auspicious time. The pilgrims did not mind standing in neck-deep water during all those hours. The priest was ready to initiate the proceedings. I remained in the Police Control Room, which had been set up in a building on the Southern bank. People who were not lucky enough to get into the tank stood on the eastern and Western banks, ready to occupy places vacated by those already in the tank. The arrangement was for them to enter from the eastern or Western banks and exit through the northern or Southern banks.

An hour before the auspicious time, I took up my position alongside the head priest on the Southern bank, just as I had done in 1980. I was to fire a very pistol as soon as the head priest gave the nod, the flare announcing the auspicious moment to the pilgrims.

When the helicopter arrived with the Chief Minister, DGP Sripal received her and her companion, Sasikala Natarajan, and accompanied them to the tank. A small strip of water, 10 feet by 5 feet, had been enclosed by ropes held in place by policemen and volunteers. The Chief Minister and her companion arrived at the tank ten minutes before the Zero Hour and were escorted by the Archakas down the steps to the cordoned-off area. When the head priest signalled the auspicious time, I fired the very pistol. As the illuminating signal sped skyward, the entire congregation inside the tank took their dip thrice and started going up the steps towards the exit points. Their places were taken by those awaiting their turn at the top of the steps. This process was ongoing when the Chief Minister's entourage left the tank, accompanied by the Chief Secretary and the DGP.

It was a while after the Chief Minister had left the tank that I became aware of the tragedy that had occurred on the northern bank, which was the main exit point. It was caused by the hasty descent of those waiting on the bank getting in the way of those leaving the tank. This had resulted in the drowning of many pilgrims, both those trying to get into the tank and those trying to get out.

By the time DIG V. C. Perumal, SP T. K. Rajendran, and I waded through the water and reached the accident point, the policemen on duty on the northern side of the tank, and the volunteers, had rescued several pilgrims from drowning. I arranged to take the bodies of those who had drowned to the Government Hospital. I also called the DGP on the VHF and informed him of the tragedy. The helicopter was yet to take off, but the DGP decided not to inform the Chief Minister of what had happened, knowing full well that she would insist on returning to the tank to convey her sympathy and supervise the relief operations. Such a move would only have created mayhem, resulting in more deaths.

She was informed of the tragedy only after the helicopter reached Madras, by which time it was too late for her to return to the scene of the tragic mishap. Meanwhile, the process of entering the tank, taking a dip, and leaving it continued uninterrupted, with the pilgrims totally unaware of the great tragedy that had claimed the lives of as many as 48 pilgrims.

Under similar circumstances, heads would have rolled, at least the DGP's and mine; definitely mine, as I was in direct charge of the entire bandobust arrangements. But the Chief Minister, in all her magnanimity, instead of blaming the police, as is often done, took the blame on herself, thereby pacifying the public, silencing the opposition, and moderating the press. She continued to draw flak from various quarters, especially from the atheist forum, but she stuck to the stand she took on that fateful day.

There have been stampedes and loss of life in other religious festivities in the past. The death of over eight hundred pilgrims on Maunya Ammavasai at the Kumbh Mela in Allahabad in 1954, one hundred and 45 pilgrims in Chamundya Temple in Jodhpur in 2008, and one hundred and two pilgrims in Pulmedu on the way to Sabarimalai in 2011 are some of the calamities that come to mind.

For pilgrims, past and present, they have to be at the right place and, most importantly, at precisely the right time. It is this compelling need that makes them throw caution to the winds. If they make it safely, they feel assured of a place in heaven. If they don't, their relatives are gratified that their loved ones have surely and safely reached paradise.

However, the loss of so many lives, and that too of innocent and ardent devotees, along with the flaw in the otherwise foolproof bandobust scheme, dealt a severe blow to my professional esteem and left a permanent scar on my mind.

Hamilton Then, Amalraj Now

Hamilton was a policeman of yore,
The Police clubs he'd built do stand to the fore;
Move over Hamilton! For Amalraj make space;
He's done much better and taken your place
A news item from 'The Hindu' dated 8.7.1993:

i.   "A significant contribution to Indian history and archaeology has been made by the police by retrieving a historic cannon in Dharmapuri district and preserving it for posterity.

ii. This cannon was located by Mr. Walter I Davaram, Deputy Inspector General of Police, Vellore Range, during one of his village visits.

iii. It was part of the siege train of the East India Company when it took Royakotta Fort from Tippu Sultan in 1791. After the successful assault on the fort, it had been abandoned some two km from the fort, where it appeared as if it was positioned to bombard the fort.

iv. On the suggestion of Mr. Davaram, it was decided to shift the cannon to a central place in Royakotta so that the public might be made aware of the historic event connected with Royakotta. Steps were taken by the then Superintendent of Police, Mr. K. Vijaya Kumar, and the Deputy Superintendent of Police, Mr. P. K. Das, to transport the cannon to the Royakotta Police Station. But the cannon, weighing nearly three tonnes, defied their several attempts.

Not even the combined strength of bulldozers, tractors, and several enthusiastic villagers and policemen could dislodge it from the loose soil in which it was embedded.

v.   Finally, Engineering Systems (P) Ltd., Hosur, came to the rescue by fabricating a special harness and brought it to the police station.

vi.   At the police station, it was cleaned by a special chemical process and given a coat of anti-corrosive paint before it was fitted onto a steel swivel.

vii.   Today, the cannon, measuring 3 metres by 1.5 metres, with a British Crown embossed on it, stands on a platform in the compound of the newly constructed police station building at Royakotta."

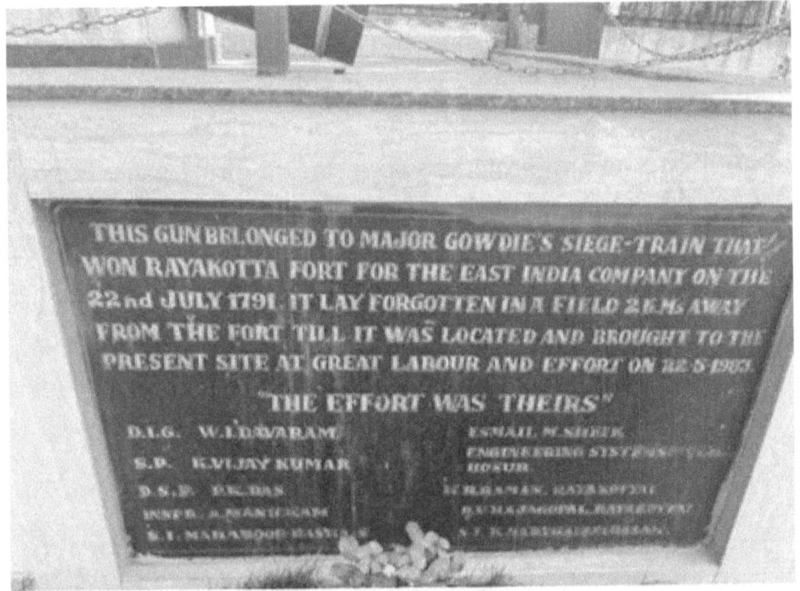

Except for the fact that the 231-year-old cannon has become the proud possession of the Tamil Nadu police, the news has no relevance to police heritage. My habit of visiting police lines and meeting police families went a long way in redressing their day-to-day grievances. Similarly, my visits to the remote and inaccessible tribal villages enabled me to identify and recruit tribal youngsters into the police force. But what have I done by way of improving the infrastructural requirements of the police force, such as playfields, clinics, kalyana mandapams, rest houses, reading rooms, and shooting ranges? The answer is a big 'NOTHING.'

SP Hamilton was the first SP-level officer who took up construction work almost 90 years earlier. He was the one who first thought of providing affordable accommodation for officers and men visiting district headquarters. Later on, these guest houses came to be called Police Clubs. We do not know how many police clubs he constructed apart from the ones in Coimbatore, St. Thomas Mount, and Tirunelveli. It is quite possible that he might have provided similar facilities in districts that were once part of the erstwhile Madras Presidency. He retired as IGP in 1930 and chose to stay on in Bangalore until his death.

The rightful successor to Hamilton is A. Amalraj, IPS, presently Commissioner of Police, Tambaram Commissionerate. Even as ASP, he started out on a developmental spree. He laid basketball and tennis courts, hockey and football fields, and children's parks; he set up bus shelters, police canteens, athletic tracks, and shooting galleries wherever he had been posted. As SP of the newly formed Theni district, he created a model parade ground carved out of a hillside, which has since become the pride of the town.

A. Amalraj

He has converted the dilapidated century-old Hamilton Club, located opposite the Coimbatore Railway Junction, into a police museum with an impressive collection of memorabilia within the building and in the compound.

Amalraj's major contribution to the shooting fraternity includes converting the old shooting range in Coimbatore into a modern Rifle

Club. He has also provided Trichy with a world-class range developed at a cost of Rs.10 crores. This Rifle Club has three shooting ranges—10 metres, 25 metres, and 50 metres—a reception room, a guest room, restrooms, and galleries for spectators. Within a year of its creation, it hosted the 47th Tamil Nadu state Shooting Competition in 2022, which attracted 1,500 competitors, a record number. Amalraj also left his mark in Coimbatore with a Modern Control Room, a police-run restaurant, a Children's Traffic Park, a well-equipped modern gym, and a mineral water plant.

Questions arose about how he found funds for all these projects. He was able to unearth funds lying unknown and unutilised, such as the Local Area Development Fund and the Self-Sufficiency Scheme Fund. Amalraj has proved that there is truth in the saying, 'Where there's a will, there's a way.' He deserves to be crowned 'Hamilton II,' although his contribution to the department far exceeds that of his British predecessor of days gone by.

Amalraj's latest focus of attention has been the old City Police Commissionerate in Egmore. The Commissionerate moved into that building on 1st May 1842 on a monthly rent of Rs.165/-. In 1856, Lt. Col. Boulderson, who took over as the city's first Police Commissioner, bought the property for the government for Rs.21,000/-. It served as the Commissionerate until 10th November 2013, when it moved into the newly built modern multi-storeyed building in Vepery.

Amalraj wasted no time in taking over the old building to work his magic. He converted it into the best Police Museum in the country. The 181-year-old building, sprawling over 36,000 sq. ft. with its mind-blowing display of artefacts, was opened to the public by Chief Minister M. K. Stalin in 2021, who appreciated the efforts of the officers. When Amalraj asked me if I would consider gifting the Prime Minister's Revolver that I had won as the 'best cadet' of the 1963 batch of IPS officers to the museum, I was elated. I readily agreed, hoping it would inspire present and future generations.

With the best cadet revolver which I donated to the police museum.

I must mention here that the master developer is also a very efficient and dedicated police officer. He has been awarded the Police Medal for Meritorious Service. He is also an outstanding shooter, having won several medals in the State Police Duty Meets. At present, he has been given the dual responsibilities of Commissioner, Tambaram Commissionerate, as well as that of Director of the Police Academy. How do I classify him? A builder? A welfare-oriented person? A professional police officer? He is all of these and more. I heard that his wife once jokingly asked him, 'Are you a policeman or a mason?' Either way, the department will be forever indebted to him.

Odd Man Out

Standing tall among shrubs, those cypress trees
Swaying gracefully in the gentle breeze;
How like those trees is that odd man out,
Of whom, I here, do write about.

There are officers who have minds of their own. They meet all the requirements of the posts they hold and carry out their duties efficiently, but in their own honest and unconventional ways. One such officer is Anoop Jaiswal, who was an outstanding probationer at the National Police Academy, where his tendency to put his instructors on the spot by asking tricky but legitimate questions landed him in hot water. Once, he questioned the DGP-Director of the Academy about the logic behind the Indian Penal Code prescribing 7 years RI for stealing an article from a tent or a vessel, but only 3 years RI for stealing the entire tent or the vessel along with the article in it. The Director was stumped and, as a result, developed a grouse against him, as did the other teaching staff. Consequently, 15 days before the passing-out parade, he received an order from the Ministry of Home Affairs stating that 'he was discharged from service on account of unsuitability.' However, he was not one to give up his rights without a fight. The Delhi High Court, to which he appealed against the order, would not even admit it on the grounds that, as a trainee, he had been found unsuitable by the authority concerned, the Police Training Academy. But the Supreme Court, to which he appealed and where he fought his case without any legal aid, reinstated

"

him, restored his original seniority, and sanctioned the salary he had lost along with all other benefits. The Supreme Court concluded its order with the following observation: "The Government took away your job; the law of the land and the Court of Law have restored it. This case must have affected the morale of the petitioner. Now, the court's order makes him a public servant in the true sense of the expression. It is a lease given by the law to you. Your loyalty should ever remain to the law of the land and not to any individual, party, or government." A year later, Jaiswal became part of the Tamil Nadu Police family and remained true to the Supreme Court's exhortation. He has held important posts, including that of Commissioner of Police, Chennai, during the general elections. He also spent 14 years in the IB before returning to the state. Throughout all this, he never gave up his habit of asking logical and complex questions, putting his superiors on the spot. Throughout his service, he remained a highly misunderstood free-thinker. As ADGP/CB-CID, Jaiswal had been directed to register a case against Vaikundarajan, a rich industrialist of Thoothukudi who enjoyed a monopoly over granite quarrying and sand mining. But no case had been pending against him, and Jaiswal was not prepared to fabricate one. A month later, at a meeting of senior officers with the Chief Secretary, he was again asked whether a case had been registered against Vaikundarajan. When he answered in the negative, he was asked whether he was 'afraid' of the man. He replied, 'yes' to a stunned gathering and, pointing his finger heavenward, he said, 'of Him,' Vaikunda Raja, the God above; and pointing his other finger downwards, 'but not of the one down here below.' The officers present broke into laughter, much to the embarrassment of the Chief Secretary. Jaiswal stood his ground. He brought in an element of equality and compassion in treating subordinates. He treated even the lowest-ranked constable with respect, insisting that he take a seat while presenting his grievance or petition.

Jaiswal's free-thinking and honest interpretation of rules and regulations attracted the attention of all senior officers and even the judges. When the lawyers and a section of the public clashed on the premises of the High Court, the CJ appointed him as investigating officer, although he was at that time IGP Administration and had nothing to do with investigations or case studies. He completed the investigation and sent the report to the CJ through the Advocate General. As his report put the blame mainly on the lawyers, the AG requested him to modify it in favour of the lawyers. However, he re-sent the same report to the CJ without modification. This time, the CJ accepted it without reservation. Such was the respect the top-level judiciary had for Jaiswal.

But even perfectionists like him could make mistakes. One of the papers he had signed in a hurry while handing over charge to his successor was the ACR of the lady Dy. SP, who was on the verge of being conferred with the IPS. The Reporting Officer and the Reviewing Officer graded her as 'average' in each column of the ACR, thereby making her ineligible to be conferred with the IPS. When the affected officer approached him, he realised his mistake and sent a modified ACR to the Government, which the Government refused to accept. Jaiswal, who was no stranger to the courts, took up the matter with the High Court, which accepted his corrected ACR, leading to the affected officer getting into the IPS cadre. I too have gone to the High Court and Supreme Court on several occasions but have never questioned their decisions.

He also broke my near-Guinness record of working out pensions for 100 widows of policemen who had died 40 to 60 years ago. The earliest death I had recorded was in the year 1924. However, Jaiswal, as ASP Tuticorin, worked out a pension for a widow whose husband had died 65 years earlier, in the year 1923.

After his retirement, he decided to settle down in Tamil Nadu to offer his services and expertise to the younger generations, especially school children. He took innovative classes in 139 schools until COVID-19 stepped in.

Jaiswal is definitely of a totally different calibre, a rarity among government servants.

Our Pole Stars

Twinkle, Twinkle, big bright star,
Show the world how great you are!
Your integrity just has no par,
Your courage of conviction's exemplar.
Hold your head high, you big bright star;
The world must know how great you are!

There may be only one pole star in the sky, but I am proud to note that there are several pole stars in our police firmament. This chapter traces their exemplary character and remarkable service to the state, the Department, and the public.

The prestige of the police depends on three factors. The first is the government's policy and the manner in which it is implemented and safeguarded. The second is the bold, honest, and unbiased leadership provided by the senior officers. The third is the day-to-day performance of the subordinate staff and field officers, policemen and women.

Of the three factors, the role of senior officers is foremost for the proper functioning of the department, for it is their responsibility to give the government correct and practical advice and then to follow the government's lawful instructions faithfully. It is also their responsibility to motivate and lead the subordinates, who constitute 85 per cent of the force, and to look after their welfare.

I must first mention the officers who shaped the post-independence police force. They are IGPs R.M. Mahadevan, F.V. Arul, and E.L. Stracey of the Indian Police (IP), and DGPs K.R. Shenoy, S.M. Diaz, both belonging to the British Indian Armed Forces, T.T.P. Abdullah (twice Indian Ambassador to Saudi Arabia), and Singaravel, later IGP, Kerala.

After them came the early IPS officers C.V. Narasiman, K.V. Subramanyam, V.R. Lakshminarayan, K. Raveendran, and K. Mohandoss, who took Tamil Nadu police to the top of the ladder by their integrity, professional efficiency, and above all, their concern for the department. More than their professional efficiency, it is their concern for the subordinates, leniency towards their minor mistakes, and awards for their good work that I modelled my man-management on.

One incident that comes to mind may appear a violation of rules but was actually a life-giving act. The HC working under DGP V.R. Lakshminarayan complained to him that his son did not get selected as a constable. The DGP asked DIG-Administration Guruvaiah to show him the answer paper concerned. According to the answer paper, his mark was '9/100.' The DGP put in a four before the 9, making his marks 49, enabling him to be selected as a constable. No one can question me for following his example in the matter of selecting constables and SIs, taking into consideration the loyalty of their parents to the department, but who fell short of height and physical fitness requirements despite fulfilling the other criteria. Rules and regulations are man-made. Compassion is God's command.

Century-long poverty drove some members of the tribal communities to join the Naxalite (Maoists) organisation. Certain physical requirements, like height, defy candidates from these communities who are inherently short.

After dealing with the active Naxalites, I made special arrangements giving exemption from physical requirements. I was proved right, as not one of the tribal recruits has been disloyal to the department.

D. Mukherjee was an outstanding officer who left his mark both in Tamil Nadu and in Central Police organisations. He succeeded in tracking down notorious serial murderer and jail escapee Auto Shankar to his hideout in Rourkela and bringing him back to Chennai to be hanged.

I.K. Govind is another brilliant officer whose capacity and ability could not be fully appreciated in the state because of his long tenure on deputation with the Intelligence Bureau (1973-1984) and RAW (1989-1997). He also has the rare distinction of having been a counsellor in the Indian Embassy of Myanmar for four years. Back in Tamil Nadu, he left his mark as Director, Vigilance and Anti-Corruption, and as DGP.

Letika Saran, the first lady Commissioner of Chennai and also DGP, Tamil Nadu, proved that she was as competent, compassionate, and physically fit as most of her male colleagues.

K.K. Rajasekaran Nair filled the gaps left by the frequent change of governments with his straight-forwardness, total impartiality, and professional efficiency.

J.K. Tripathy took the reins of the department at the time of the dreaded COVID-19. His monumental efforts in utilising the entire police force to ensure rules and regulations imposed by the government were strictly followed. It is but natural that the largest number of casualties, next to the medical staff, were in the police department. He also increased the remuneration for working on rest days from Rs. 200/- to Rs. 500/- and the fuel allowance of the staff.

P. Kandasamy, IPS, recently retired after holding the top position in the state as Director of Vigilance and Anti-Corruption, and had a glorious career both in the state and in the CBI. The death of Sister Abaya, a 21-year-old Catholic nun on 27.3.1992 in the premises of a Convent in

Kottayam, had defied the efforts of the State Police, CBI, ACB Cochin, and SIC II, New Delhi for over seven years. Finally, the High Court of Kerala handed the investigation over to the CBI. Kandasamy, who at that time was with the CBI, took up the investigation on 18.11.2009. He made use of the latest scientific methods such as brain mapping, brain fingerprinting, and narco-testing on the three suspects, Fr. Thomas Kottoor, Fr. Jose Poothrikkayil, and Sister Sephy. All the tests led to the conclusion that the crime had been committed by the suspects. The trial commenced on 5.8.2019 and concluded on 10.12.2020. As many as 49 witnesses were examined, of whom nine turned hostile. The Special Judge for CBI cases delivered the judgement, convicting Accused No. 1, Fr. Thomas Kottoor, to double life imprisonment, 7 years RI, and a fine of Rs. 6,50,000/-. Accused No. 3, Sister Sephy, was sentenced to life imprisonment, 7 years RI, and a fine of Rs. 5,50,000/-. Accused No. 2, Father Jose, was discharged for lack of evidence. The court appreciated the efforts of the CBI in ensuring justice in a sensational case even though 28 years had gone by since the incident.

In another sensational case of the rape and murder of a foreigner on a beach in Goa, both the accused were acquitted. Kandasamy took up the case as a challenge, proved the charges, and obtained 10 years RI for both of them. The verdict brought great relief to the thousands of tourists who throng Goa's beaches.

It is to the credit of Amresh Pujari, Commissioner of Police, Coimbatore, that the "Neighbourhood Police System" was launched successfully. His greatest gift to the department is the "Handbook of Investigation," a veritable Bible for investigators. His most noteworthy achievement, however, was the detection of the "Great Indian Train Heist" on 9th August 2016. The culprits had zeroed in on the particular compartment carrying 343 crores in currency notes belonging to the RBI. They got onto the roof of that compartment and entered it by cutting open the roof while the train was in motion, decamping with Rs. 5.78 crores. After considerable fieldwork all over the country, Pujari identified the culprits as members of a notorious criminal tribe in Madhya Pradesh. In a well-planned and daring raid, he arrested Mohar Singh, the leader of the 'Pandi' criminal gang, and four other members, recovering all the stolen currency. Further inquiries resulted in the arrest of a few other members of the inter-state criminal gang.

An IPS couple that has made history by rivalling each other in their respective assignments is A.K. Viswanathan and his wife Seema Agrawal. Viswanathan is an expert in urban policing, with records of 2 ½ years as DC L&O Madurai and 3 ½ years as Commissioner of Police, Coimbatore. As the 106th Commissioner of Police, Greater Chennai, he is best remembered for the efficient and humane running of the Commissionerate, including the installation of cameras to detect traffic violations. Seema Agrawal, as ADGP Headquarters, has contributed greatly to the modernisation of the police organisation. She has also been entrusted with the challenging job of dealing with cyber-crime.

As DC L&O, Coimbatore, Sandeep Rai Rathore played a major role in containing the Muslim fundamentalists who caused considerable damage to life and property in Coimbatore because they failed in their main objective to kill L.K. Advani in the year 1998. He has been chosen to be the first Commissioner of Police of the newly created Avadi Commissionerate, a timely recognition of his capacity.

ADGP Davidson Devasirvatham, one of the top-ranking IPS officers of his batch, has made a mark for himself in dealing with several major problems in the state. When Coimbatore was paralysed by Muslim violence, he was hand-picked to assist the Commissioner of Police, Radhakrishnan. He arrested most of the wanted members of the fanatic Muslim organisation and the equally aggressive members of the Hindu community, restoring normalcy to the city. During his tenure in the state Intelligence Bureau, he busted a secret Al-Qaeda cell and rounded up more than two dozen accused who were conspiring to set off a series of bomb blasts. He also unearthed more than 100 kg of explosives from an LTTE boat berthed in Chennai Harbour. He is the only Indian Police

Officer from Tamil Nadu to have been selected by the U.N.O. to bring peace between the Albanian Muslims and Yugoslavian Christians in Kosovo.

Once, while waiting at Chennai Airport for my flight to Delhi, I encountered DSP K. Bhavaneeswari, the third woman DSP in the state. She told me she was taking her parents on an annual holiday and introduced them to me. I remarked that they were fortunate to have such a caring daughter. I couldn't help but think of the couplet praising daughters:

> "A daughter is a daughter all her life;
> A son is a son till he finds him a wife."

Apart from being a devoted daughter, she has also proved herself a brilliant investigator, as demonstrated by her brilliant detection of the 'Kulithalai Meenakshi' case. This case established K. Bhavaneeswari as an able, honest, intelligent, and fearless investigator. Upon her promotion to the rank of IGP Vigilance and Anti-Corruption, she, along with DGP Kandasamy, successfully organised massive search operations that unearthed enormous caches of unaccounted wealth held by politicians.

Among senior officers who maintain their physical fitness regimen despite the burden of office, ADGP Dr. Jayant K. Murali stands foremost. He has run as many as 30 full marathons and holds records for both full marathons and half-marathons, earning a place in the Asia Book of Records. He also contributes highly technical articles to a leading English newspaper once a week. I received living proof of his extraordinary physical and mental capacity when, after reading his article in 'DT Next' one morning, I rang him up to get the meaning of a few words and phrases in the article like 'algorithmic policing' and 'cloud computing.' As he explained each word, I realised he was breathing hard and asked him whether he was running. He said 'yes' and that he was preparing for a 46 km run the following week. He starts his day at 3:30 AM, gets ready and reaches the starting point of the marathon and other road races at

5:30 AM, wins the 42 km race in the veteran category, and is at his desk in time to deal with his official duties.

DGP Dr. C. Sylendra Babu undertakes ultra-marathons, swims long distances, and leads cycle tours to raise public awareness of important current issues. He has also been awarded the title of Randoneur for cycling 200 km, 300 km, 400 km, and 600 km in one cycling season. He has published several books for the benefit of the younger generation.

Former DGP Kumaraswamy has also left his mark in all the posts he occupied, from his Anti-Naxalite work in the capacity of SP, Q-Branch. He has served in all branches of police work with distinction, proving himself to be a worthy son of the brilliant SP Subbarayan.

As I bring this chapter to a close, I hope to find many other stars dotting our vast police sky.

Other Stars in Our Sky

The stars in a galaxy, big and small,
They serve their purpose, one and all,
All of them twinkle in the nightly sky
Alongside the brighter ones nearby
From the starry sky, they shine down bright
With their achievements set our hearts alight

I first met Perumalswamy, a Group-1 officer, in Ooty. He was ADC to the Governor, selected no doubt for his impressive personality, impeccable social manners, and fluent English; and I, the newly promoted SP of the State's smallest but most beautiful district, The Nilgiris. Later on, we worked together in Chennai City, he as DC L&O North and I as DC L&O South. As the only two law-and-order officers, we were kept busy with the maintenance of law-and-order in the entire city. Our wives, Sowdha and Prema, referred to by the constabulary as 'North-amma' and 'South-amma,' were left to their own devices to keep themselves entertained as best as they could in a 'Madras' of yesteryear, devoid of the diversions available in the 'Chennai' of today.

S.K. Dogra of the 1982 batch has become more of a Tamilian than a Tamilian! He started learning Tamil even while he was at the National Police Academy, and by the time he reached Tamil Nadu, he was able not only to deliver lectures in Tamil but also to sing Tamil songs at functions. His stories in Tamil have appeared in the Tamil daily 'Dinamalar,' and he has been a regular contributor to other Tamil papers and magazines, as well as to programmes of All-India Radio. He was of great assistance to me in handling the serious Bodi-Theni communal outbreak in the year 1989. Now, as a retired officer settled in Chennai, he produces videos on spirituality and self-development for the benefit of the people of Tamil Nadu.

M. Balachandran, who retired as ADGP, left behind a glorious record of service. He started his career assisting me in dealing with the Kisan problem in the Thanjavur district. Later, he detected the case of the murder of the watchman of the Tharamangalam Temple and the theft of priceless Panchloka idols from there. In less than a fortnight, all of the 13 accused were arrested, and all the idols were recovered from Shanmuga Sundaram, the owner of several medical colleges and other institutions in Salem and Puducherry. As DC L&O in Chennai, he appeared before the Privilege Committee in Parliament for arresting an MP. As DC, Chennai Central, he arrested most of the accused wanted in the sensational 'Tarasu' magazine case. Later, as DIG, Tirunelveli, he brought under control the serious Kodiyankulam riots and other instances of communal violence, opening fire on several occasions. The judicial Commission applauded and justified his actions. Post-retirement, he became a part of Reliance Industries Limited and rose to the position of Group President, a rare case of distinction both while in service and after. The induction of ex-service officers who had served in the Indo-Pak wars of 1965 or 1971 was a welcome boost to the prestige of the Tamil Nadu police. This reservation held good for four years. The first officer to be recruited was Captain D. Radhakrishna Raja, who had fought in the 1965 war against Pakistan in the Baramullah-Uri sector. He is the recipient of the 'Samar Seva' and 'Raksha Seva' medals. Balachandran was known for his effective management of unlawful assemblies and major bandobust. As an officer of the Directorate of Vigilance and Anti-Corruption, he has the rare distinction of having arrested two CMs, M. Karunanidhi and J. Jayalalithaa.

Captains Md. Iqbal and V.N. Srinivasan were recruited in the second batch. Iqbal, who was SP Kancheepuram, was killed in the bomb blast along with Rajiv Gandhi. Srinivasan, as AC Saidapet, dealt with the widespread rioting during Indira Gandhi's visit to Chennai. Captains Habibullah and Dharmarajan were the other two ex-army officers who also rendered commendable service to the department. Unfortunately, none of these four is alive today. Unlike the above-mentioned officers, Captain S.G. Rajendran of the Indian Artillery was selected through the regular Group-1 exam. He had fought in the Western Sector (Ferozepur) and had received the 'Sangram Medal,' 'Western Star,' and two other medals for serving in Jammu & Kashmir. He is remembered especially for suppressing a major Vanniya agitation in the then South Arcot district.

Rajamanickam, a Category-1 officer, is another officer who had his practical training under me. He had the courage to refuse to carry out MGR's order to arrest an important leader of the opposition in a case of attempted murder. MGR soon realised that the facts were not as presented to him and that the DSP had been right in his decision. He retained Rajamanickam in the same post of DSP St. Thomas Mount for 2½ years. During that tenure, Rajamanickam played a major role in the funeral arrangements for MGR. Another officer who was inseparably associated with his job was Guruviah, who practically ran the Chief Office for over seven years, first as AIG, then as DIG-HQ, and finally as DIG Admn. As a competent administrator, he looked after the grievances of the staff as well as the demands of the government.

Indispensability for a particular post also applies to the post of Special Branch Inspectors in headquarters. They are held in high esteem because of their ability to give correct intelligence and advice to their SPs and Commissioners. I can name a few who literally ran my office when I was busy with numerous law-and-order duties and prolonged jungle operations. Krishnaswamy of Coimbatore was SB Inspector for four years and AC, Intelligence for four years. SB Inspector Sivasubramaniam of Dharmapuri was our main adviser in the operation against the Naxalites.

Inspector Jayasingh spent four years as SB-SI, four years as Inspector, and finally as AC-IS, Madurai. Hirudayadoss, who had been a highly competent law-and-order officer in Madurai city for ten years, was brought to Chennai by SSB Sripal. He stayed on in Chennai and was in charge of Chennai City IS for nearly 13 years.

SP A. Jawahar Chandrasekaran, who began his career as an SI, was much in demand throughout his service as a reliable and capable Aide-De-Camp to senior officers, SPs, Commissioners, IGPs, and finally the Chief Minister MGR, especially during the latter's year-long declining health. In a dramatic finale, he hurt himself badly while protecting MGR's body on its final journey from Rajaji Hall to the Marina. He had to spend nearly two months in the hospital to have his broken ankles set. He was one of the few SIs who retired as an SP. He was SP, Dindigul, for a period of 2½ years but narrowly missed being conferred IPS.

A. Kaliamurthy is an outstanding all-rounder. He is the only police officer to have won gold medals in the All-India Duty Meet in both Scientific Aids to Investigation and Revolver Shooting, disciplines requiring dissimilar talents. He was also awarded the state Medal for Gallantry for arresting two LTTE personnel, Varadhan and Siva, in 1991. Again, in 2001, he killed two Naxalite extremists and, in the process, received a bullet injury. He was given accelerated promotion for his heroic action, which gave him eight years as Superintendent of Police, a rare achievement for one who had entered the department as a Sub-Inspector. He was bestowed with a "Lifetime Achievement Award" by P. Sadhasivam, former Chief Justice of India and Governor of Kerala, for delivering motivational speeches on more than 1000 platforms, 21 of them in foreign countries like Canada, USA, Malaysia, Singapore, Saudi Arabia, and Kuwait.

An officer who made headlines wherever he was posted still lives in the memory of the public. He is K.K. Muthusamy, who was called 'Terror' or 'Simha Swapnam' wherever he was posted. He changed the total image of Palani town within two months of his assuming charge as DSP. All elements of crime that thrived in the popular Temple town (sale of drugs and hooch, gambling, pick-pocketing, prostitution, and the nefarious activities of sadhus) were totally eradicated. After cleansing Palani, he was posted to Coimbatore as DSP/L&O, a more onerous job because his charge covered the entire city, which at present is being policed by a Commissioner of Police, three DCs, and their corresponding staff. Muthusamy's ruthless elimination of all criminal elements in the entire city is still being talked about. The political bigwigs who tried to have him moved out of their way failed in their endeavour. He received the Indian Police Medal for meritorious service in 1980 and the Chief Minister's Medal in 1996. After 20 months of ruthless law enforcement in Coimbatore, he was posted to Flower Bazaar Range in Chennai City, which needed a bold and honest officer to eliminate the sale of narcotic substances like opium, cocaine, heroin, and gutkha. Within a month, numerous lodges which were promoting liquor sales, gambling, heroin distribution, and prostitution closed down on their own. I still remember him openly challenging a magazine which condemned the entire police force as a corrupt organisation, with the words "I have never taken a bribe nor will I ever take one. I challenge anyone to contradict me"; this assertion should be the guiding principle for posterity. When he was transferred out on promotion, all the affected hoteliers and merchants heaved a sigh of relief and returned to their old ways. Muthusamy retired as an ADSP and is now back in his village, enjoying a simple farm life.

R. Chinnaraj, who retired as DCP, joined the police in 1970 as an SI. He ranked first in the Homicide Investigation Exam conducted by CB-CID and was awarded a 'Merit Certificate' by the then IGP F.V. Arul, IP. That set him up as a 'Master Investigator' of complicated cases. He spent as many as 30 years of his service in Chennai City. One of the notable arrests he made was that of an inter-state criminal gang consisting of a husband and wife team and their two associates from Karnataka. In Chennai alone, the gang had been involved in three cases of murder and robbery. Chinnaraj successfully investigated the cases and recovered the entire stolen jewellery from their disposal points in Karnataka, Andhra

Pradesh, and Maharashtra. In recognition of his commendable work, Chinnaraj was awarded the Chief Minister's Medal for Excellence.

N. Damodharan, who began his service under me as SI, Armed Police in North Arcot district, was with me in the Anti-Naxalite operation. He was a regular member of the State Police Shooting Team and won several medals in the Duty Meets. As DSP and later as ADSP, Tamil Nadu Commando School, he trained more than 2500 SIs and 3000 constables in counter-terrorism, riot control, and the escorting of dangerous criminals. He trained 150 policewomen as commandos in 2003. The State Police Shooting Team that won the overall championship in Indore and brought home the prestigious J. Jayalalithaa Trophy was also trained by him. He ended his career as Superintendent of Police, Security-Branch CID, a rare achievement for an officer of Armed Reserve. The fact that he was also given a record number of four extensions of service of six months each proved he was an indispensable member of the Tamil Nadu Police force.

Being retained in highly specialised posts for most of one's service is very rare in the police department. IGP Thukkiandi, who started his career in the Naxalite-affected Tirupathur sub-division, fitted the bill. Later, his services were so much in demand that he worked in the Q-Branch, Crime Branch, and Directorate of Vigilance for almost 20 years. He was involved in the investigation of most of the sensational cases, including the wealth case against the Chief Minister, J. Jayalalithaa.

Yes, all these stars have, each one in his own way, contributed to the upliftment of the department.

Veerappan, India's Most Notorious Outlaw

Hide and seek was the game Veerappan played,
As mine-fields around the forest he laid;
The STF stepped in, the brigand to book,
While Veerappan stayed quite safe in his nook.
But Veerappan's luck had to one day, run out.
He succumbed to an ambush in his very last bout

To the present generation, jungle bandit Veerappan's life and exploits may seem extraordinary and unprecedented. But there have been other daring dacoits and outlaws who committed several murders and dacoities, defying the police over several years.

Maan Singh, the most dreaded dacoit of Madhya Pradesh, took advantage of the inaccessible Chambal River valley just as Veerappan made use of the 4000 sq. km forest which marked the boundary between Tamil Nadu and Karnataka. Maan Singh had committed 185 murders and 1122 dacoities before he was killed by the Gurkhas on 24th August 1955. After him, two women dacoits left their mark in the valley. One of them, Putli Bai, was finally shot dead on 23rd January 1958 when she tried to escape from the police by swimming across River Kunvari, a tributary of the Chambal.

Phoolan Devi was subjected to a lot of humiliation, including gang rape by the Kshatriyas, simply because she was of a 'low caste.' She turned the tide by killing 22 Thakurs (Kshatriyas). After this, she became an outlaw on her own. When she was caught, she was convicted and sentenced to life term. But after 11 years in captivity, the Samajwadi Party had her released. She then joined the party and contested three parliamentary elections. She lost one and won two. In the third election, she defeated the BJP candidate by over two hundred thousand votes. On 25.7.2003, Sher Singh Rana, a criminal turned politician, shot her dead near her residence in Delhi. He was sentenced to life term.

Tamil Nadu, too, had been home to a few notorious dacoits. The most dreaded of them were Koolan Kalan (Salem), Kathirvel Padayatchi (Thanjavur), Jambulinga Nadar and Chinnasamy Thevar (Tirunelveli), Malaikallan Thangaiah (Munnar), and Mamattiyan (Mecheri). It will be of interest to the present generation that the STF formed in 1993 to nab Veerappan was preceded by a similar force formed in 1861 to capture Koolan Kalan and his six brothers. After the brothers had been captured or killed, the headquarters of the force was shifted from Salem to Attayampatti.

Thangaiah, a tea-estate worker, did a stint in the army before returning to his family in Munnar. Unwilling to become an estate labourer, he took to a life of violent crime. His most daring attempt was targeting a bike-borne British Assistant Manager carrying the salaries of his workers in the Aathukad Division of Pallivasal Estate as he slowed down to take a hairpin bend. However, Thangaiah's gunshot narrowly missed the manager. Incidentally, my father, also a World War II veteran, was the Field Conductor in the same division. Thangaiah followed this failure with several robberies on either side of the state border and acquired the sobriquet of 'Malaikallan' (hill thief). Later, in 1960, he and an associate robbed 25 picnickers at the Kumbakarai waterfalls near Periakulam on the Kodaikanal slope, thus becoming the most feared criminal in both states. He was arrested by the Madras State Police in Madurai and transferred to Kerala, where he made a dramatic escape from Devikulam sub-jail. While escaping, he helped himself to a .410 musket but had no ammunition. For this, he targeted two beat policemen near Senthamaram in Tirunelveli district, his native place. While PC 2538, who had been attacked by him, was grappling with him despite deep cut injuries, PC 310 shot him dead, thereby bringing the curtain down on the inter-state hunt for the most wanted criminal of the time. PC 2538 was awarded the President's Police Medal for gallantry, and PC 310 received a reward of Rs.500/-, which at that time was a princely sum.

Later on, when I visited Senthamaram police station, I tried to get details of the two beat constables. I found to my dismay that nobody knew their names. Those were the days when even the wives and children of the constables and Head Constables referred to them only by their numbers! It was on my request that the Chief Minister ordered the humanisation of the constabulary. Now, they proudly carry their name badges above their shirt pockets, and everyone refers to them by name instead of by their numbers as in the past.

Jambulinga Nadar's main area of operation was on either side of the then Madras Presidency – Travancore border. He was shot dead by the police on 20.3.1923. Kadirvel Padayachi was another dacoit who terrorised Tanjore District in the thirties. SI of Police Arokiasamy Naidu, who killed him in 1933, was awarded a gallantry medal.

Ayyadurai Padayachi, also known as Mamattiyan or Mammati Vayan (spade-shaped mouth), became an outlaw in 1959 after killing nine members of his uncle's family to avenge his father's murder following a property dispute. He never indulged in dacoity. While five of his associates were hanged and his brother Oomaiyan was shot dead by SI Dowlath Ali near Mecheri, Mamattiyan eluded the police for five years and finally met his end on 27.3.1964 in Sigarallahally village at the hands of Karuppan, a parisal operator. In recognition of this service, Karuppan was presented with a licensed gun and a monetary reward by the government. However, he went on to terrorise the public with his newly acquired toy! He was later acquitted in a murder case in Karnataka, after which he went back to operating his parisal six kms downstream from Hogennekal, where I met him in 1981. He died a few years later of natural causes. I also met Paramasivan, who had earlier survived Mammatiyan's attack and had gone on to become an MLA. I also met Mamattiyan's wife and son in 1982, where they were working as coolies. Here, I must record my appreciation of the efforts of ASP A.K. Viswanathan, IPS, presently DGP, in reconstructing the story of Mamattiyan for the benefit of later generations.

Chinnasamy Thevar, a dacoit belonging to Valliyur in Tirunelveli District, was active between 1965 and 1968. I was, at that time, ASP, Tuticorin. The dacoit's area of operation was outside of my jurisdiction, but I got the SP's permission to go after him. I then led a search party comprising members of the district police shooting team into the jungles between Tirunelveli District and the Neyyar River in Kerala. Although we could not track him down in a six-day venture, we were able to expose many of his hideouts in the forest, as a result of which he was soon after shot dead by the police.

Now coming to Veerappan... Displaced by the construction of Mettur Dam in the years 1929-1934, a large number of farmers in Tamil Nadu, whose villages had been submerged by the waters of the dam, took shelter on the Karnataka side of the water-spread. Deprived of their fields, they started living off forest produce—sandalwood and elephant tusks for money and other jungle animals like spotted deer, sambar, and wild boar for meat. It was a grave mistake on the part of the two governments not to provide them with means of livelihood in the newly formed settlements. Even as a 13-year-old boy, Veerappan started to live off the forest under the leadership of Sevi Gounder. After gaining some expertise in shooting, he formed his own gang. However, as all his activities were confined to the Karnataka side of the forest, the Tamil Nadu police did not pay much attention to his activities. Veerappan started taking shelter in the Tamil Nadu side of the forest after committing serious crimes in Karnataka.

There have been outlaws of notoriety who defied the government and society over several years, but none of them equalled Veerappan in terms of cunning, multiplicity of crimes ranging from theft of forest property, killing of elephants for tusks, extortion from granite owners, brutality in eliminating rivals and men in khaki belonging to both Karnataka and Tamil Nadu, and converting the 4000 sq. km forest into his private domain. Judging by any standards, Veerappan tops the list of outlaws since India's independence 76 years ago.

The first time I heard about Veerappan was during the general elections in 1991. I was then IGP Armed Police and was sent to ensure the peaceful conduct of the election. The information we received was that he and his gang would prevent the voting because the PMK party had announced that it would boycott the elections. I went to the area with C. Sylendra Babu, who was then ASP, Gobichettipalayam, and visited all the polling booths. On Election Day, we also kept watch on the area, but Veerappan neither turned up nor disrupted the election. In one of his search operations, C. Sylendra Babu's party was fired at by Veerappan's gang at Makkampalayam. The ASP and his men returned fire, and the gang members escaped. As a result of the police action, Veerappan left the election area and returned to Karnataka. The election was conducted without any incidents.

Harikrishna of Karnataka was the first Superintendent of Police who took up the challenge of arresting Veerappan. On 19.2.1992, he shot dead Gurunathan, Veerappan's arms supplier. In retaliation, Veerappan raided Rampura Police Station on 20.5.1992, killed five constables, and escaped with the station's firearms. It was then that a special force was created under Harikrishna to nab Veerappan.

On 24th August 1992, Harikrishna was informed by Veerappan through Kamal Nayak, an informant, that he was prepared to surrender but that he should come alone to a specified place. Harikrishna drove the vehicle himself and told the police party not to follow him. That turned out to be a fatal mistake. The treacherous Veerappan killed him and two of his subordinates. With that, the Karnataka police were left without a leader until DIG Shankar Bidari volunteered to lead them.

It was at this point that the Karnataka Police sought the help of the Tamil Nadu Police because Veerappan, a Tamilian, would take shelter in Tamil Nadu after each major crime. After a meeting with the IGP Karnataka, I selected SP Gopalakrishnan, a tough and fearless officer who belonged to Mettur, close to Veerappan's area of operation. Incidentally, he too, like Veerappan and his followers, belonged to the martial race of Padayachis. Gopalakrishnan took his assignment very seriously and, with only a small team to assist him, extended all help to the Karnataka Police. Sensing the threat posed by Gopalakrishnan, also known as 'Rambo,' on account of his powerful physique, Veerappan made him his next target.

In April 1993, posters appeared in Mettur and nearby places challenging Gopalakrishnan to enter the Karnataka side of the river Palar. Gopalakrishnan was not one to be deterred by such threats. At about 9:30 AM on 9.4.1993, he, along with the equally gallant Inspector Ashok Kumar of Naxalite fame, 13 other police personnel, one forest guard, two forest watchers, one private driver, and 16 forest workers, left Kaveripuram in two Karnataka police vehicles. The SP was in the first vehicle, and Inspector Ashok Kumar followed him in the second. At about 11:00 AM, when the convoy reached Soraikaimaduvu, three kilometres from the river Palar on the Karnataka side, a powerful explosion blew up the first vehicle. On seeing the SP's vehicle being blown up, Inspector Ashok Kumar and his party opened fire at Veerappan's group, who were closing in to kill the injured and take their weapons. But for the brilliant rear-guard action of Inspector Ashok Kumar and his team, the gangsters would have killed those remaining, including SP Gopalakrishnan, and would have managed to seize all the arms and ammunition. Because of the heroic action of Ashok Kumar, Veerappan and his gang members left the area, leaving behind an injured member of their gang, Simon. Simon was later tracked down to a private hospital by Ashok Kumar. It was on his information that a large number of minefields, each much larger than the one that killed 22 people, were located and neutralised.

The blast had killed five policemen of the Tamil Nadu police, one forest watcher, one forest guard, and 15 civilian labourers—22 in all. SP Gopalakrishnan, who was standing at the door of the vehicle looking out for signs of Veerappan's gang, was seriously injured and was shifted to a hospital in Salem where he was visited by CM Jayalalithaa. His injuries and prolonged treatment rendered him unfit to rejoin the field force.

The day after her visit to the hospital, CM J. Jayalalithaa called for a meeting with Veerappa Moily, the CM of Karnataka. Both of them agreed on a joint command. Jayalalithaa sent me a note across the table asking whether I would head the Joint Command. I readily agreed, and the Joint Command was set up with DIG Shankar Bidari as Commander of Karnataka Police and Sanjay Arora as Commander of the Tamil Nadu Unit. Thus, the STF was born.

With the efficient Shankar Bidri of the Karnataka police

The fearless Gopalakrishnan (Rambo)

That Fateful Day – 21-2-'94

Six months to walk again, they said,
As they put me onto a hospital bed.
But I, determined to prove them wrong;
I would not be in bed that long.
But it wasn't the power of will alone.
This, I admit, I have always known.
My well-wishers prayed; with God they talked.
God heard their pleas, and soon, I walked.

When I was given the responsibility of leading the STF, I was already holding the post of ADGP (L&O) with jurisdiction over the whole state. However, I managed to juggle my time between the two responsibilities. The time spent on the dual responsibility was split into blocks of 7-10 days in the forest and 3 to 5 days either in Chennai or some other central place to brief the CM on the progress of the search and also to look into office routine. Those were pre-mobile phone days with no means of communication from the forest to the outside world and vice versa.

On 21.2.1994, after a hectic four-day search operation on the Karnataka side of the forest, I left for Theni to check on the bandobust arrangements for the inauguration, by the Chief Minister, a week later of the All Women Police Station in Theni. After briefing the officers, including the newly posted ASP Jayant Murali, I left for Madurai Airport to take the evening flight back to Madras. I was in the front seat of a

Police Maruti Gypsy driven by Naik Duraisamy of the Armed Reserve, Madurai City.

Earlier on my way to Theni, I had stopped by the Periyakulam Police Station and borrowed the station's Part-IV register to read the entries about the exploits of dacoit "Malaikallan" Thangaiah. I was so engrossed in reading that I did not know what had hit me. I was semi-conscious, but unaware of what had happened. Why was I in pain? Why was I being carried? Why was I not able to talk? I became aware that something, not quite on my schedule, had taken place. Our vehicle had crashed into a bus, and worse, in the impact, my driver was killed. I had a providential escape from death, probably because it was my jaw, not my head or chest, that took the impact of the crash when I was thrown forward onto the dashboard.

I was identified by the passengers on a bus that passed by and taken to the nearest hospital in Chekkanoorani for first aid. By then, news of the mishap had been passed on to K.V.S. Murthy, the Commissioner of Police, Madurai. He arranged to keep the road clear of all traffic to enable the ambulance carrying me to reach Jawahar Hospital in Madurai at the earliest. This arrangement brought normal life in Madurai to a standstill. With me in the ambulance were AC Tallakulam Thamaraikannan, ADC Veeranan, and Dr. Jayasarathi, the owner of Jawahar Hospital, where I was given first aid and my jaw, broken into three pieces, was attended to. An anxious DC Sarabjit Singh and his wife Pammi were at the hospital when I arrived. While it was being debated whether I should remain in Madurai or be taken to Madras, Chief Minister Jayalalithaa insisted on having me taken to Chennai. She also arranged to hold up the Madurai-Madras flight for me. It was the same flight I was to have taken to Madras. K.V.S. Murthy, retired SP P.V.R. Reddiar, ADSP Veeranan, and three doctors accompanied me on the flight.

I must mention here that after Prema and Anita were informed of the mishap, DIG Letika Saran rushed over to be with them, giving them the moral support they so badly needed. Pammi, after consulting the doctors in Madurai, thoughtfully called Prema to inform her that although I was badly injured, none of the injuries was life-threatening. At Madras, arrangements were made to keep the route clear to rush me from Chennai Airport to Vijaya Hospital, where orthopaedic surgeon Dr. Mohandas of MIOT, Dr. Soloman Victor, the renowned heart specialist, and his equally renowned wife Dr. Sunithi Solomon were awaiting my arrival. So was SP Subramaniam of Madurai Rural District, where the accident had taken place, but who happened to be away in Madras that day. Dr. Kabir and his wife Priscilla, both close friends of ours, were waiting with Prema and Anita at the airport. Dr. Kabir had come into our lives in Nagapattinam, where I was Superintendent of Police and his adopted father Paulraj was the DSP. He, and later his wife, Priscilla, have been a part of our lives ever since.

At the hospital, CM Jayalalithaa was received by Prema. I was conscious enough to hear her stern voice asking, "Mr. Davaram, how many times have I told you not to travel by that jeep?" But I was in no condition to reply. She then asked Dr. Mohandas about the nature of my injuries and the time it would take for my complete recovery. His reply that it would take a minimum of six months gave me a jolt, but I should have anticipated it considering I had sustained as many as ten fractures: a triple fracture of my jaw, multiple fractures on my right leg, and fractures on my right shoulder blade and collar bone.

Prema can never forget the concern and thoughtfulness of a friend from Vellore. It was late at night after I had been admitted to the hospital. She was waiting outside my ward when a familiar worried face approached her. It was Mohanlal, a friend from our Vellore days. He had rushed to Madras on hearing the news of my accident on TV. After making quick enquiries about how I was, he pressed a cover into her hand saying, "You will need this. It's only what I had at home," turned around, and disappeared into the night. Mohanlal has been the same thoughtful friend down the years, even today.

Prema's parents arrived the next morning and took charge of the house. Anita took on the responsibility of being with me during the day. It helped that she held a diploma in Hospital Administration, was well-versed in hospital protocol and procedures, and could ask all the right questions. This left Prema free to juggle her time between home, her job with Saudi Arabian Airlines, and overnight stays at the hospital.

The most touching display of departmental loyalty was the padayatra undertaken by SP Subramanyam of Madurai North District and his subordinates, numbering more than 200, to Alagar Koil. He also installed a trishul close to the accident spot. It is now called Karuppusamy Temple, where motorists still stop for a moment and pray for a safe journey.

My recovery, I was told, would be a long-drawn-out process. The hospitalisation itself was expected to last six months. But thanks to the efficiency of the doctors and perhaps my own will-power, my stay in the hospital was reduced to just nine weeks. The corrective operation on my broken jaw, a procedure that took four hours, was carried out by Dr. Ramesh, a Maxillofacial Surgeon, and Dr. Rajendran, a Plastic Surgeon.

The surgery to set the bones of my fractured leg was undertaken a week later by Dr. Mohandas and Dr. Barry Rozario.

Tuesday, the 19th of April 1994, the 63rd day after my accident, was a red-letter day for me. Dr. Mohandas, while on his rounds, asked me to hold onto the shoulder of a nurse and try to take a step. I took one, then another, and yet another! I was walking! On seeing the progress, the doctor said that I could be discharged in a fortnight; however, he mentioned that my office would have to be moved to the ground floor as I would not be able to climb the steps up to my office on the first floor. That Tuesday was also of special significance because Priscilla, the wife of Dr. Kabeer, had taken a vow of a Novena, to pray at the shrine of St. Antony on nine consecutive Tuesdays starting the day after my accident. 19th April was the 9th Tuesday. As she had done over the previous eight Tuesdays, she came to my ward after her 9th visit to the shrine and found me walking. St. Anthony had answered her prayers. Prema also remembers with gratitude the holy picture with a Novena prayer given to her by Dr. Cynthia Alexander, the kind-hearted and benevolent wife of IGP Intelligence A.X. Alexander.

From that day on, every evening after the doctors had left for the day, Prema and I would quietly step out of my ward into the deserted corridor, much to the consternation of the nurses Uma and Soundarapandi, and practise climbing up and down the steps leading to the floor above. The result of my efforts was that I could return to my office on the first floor on the very first day of my return to work.

My prolonged hospitalisation must have resulted in speculations regarding my successor and even efforts to occupy the vacant chair. But the CM was very firm that I would continue to hold the post no matter how long my recovery took. From the second month onwards, I had my tapals (files) brought to the hospital, and I would go through them while reclined on my hospital bed. Administration continued as always.

While in the hospital, I was visited by several VIPs, senior government servants, police officers, men and women of the department, sportsmen, and even unknown members of the public. They were regulated and requested to make entries in a visitors' book and were allowed to visit me, depending on my condition. As many as 7,821 well-wishers had entered their names in the visitors' book, and another 3,815 had sent messages wishing me a speedy recovery. Those who were allowed into my ward were distraught to see that I had lost my 'signature' moustache due to the surgery on my broken jaw. Actor Sivakumar, a friend of my surgeon Dr. Ramesh, decided something had to be done about this and brought me a false moustache to wear whenever there were visitors. The discerning eyes of CM Jayalalithaa saw through this when she visited me; she made a joke of my deception. Another important visitor was actor Sivaji Ganesan, whose visit was initiated by the Tamil magazine 'Ananda Vikatan.' The Chief Minister continued to visit me once every ten or 15 days. I took advantage of that to recommend my fellow in-patients for government help to cover their hospital expenses. She helped each one of them.

Back at my desk, I called on the Chief Minister, who again advised me to go slow on my fieldwork and to shelve my STF responsibilities for a while. On the first of July, I was back in the jungle on a 25 km search operation that resulted in the discovery of an oil barrel full of rice, dhal, and condiments, and hidden under them, currency notes amounting to Rs. 1.5 lakh. Veerappan must have buried several more such barrels in various places in the forest. We were able to uncover just a few of them. I am sure currency notes hidden in several other places must have just wasted away. It is also possible that a few of these barrels might have been unearthed by tribals in the area.

Many people said the accident was God's way of protecting me from a worse fate in a jungle operation, but my reappearance in the forest was a boost to the STF. I was absolutely fit and able to lead them in the jungle operations, thanks to the grace of God, the goodwill of the Chief

Minister, and the prayers of friends and well-wishers, police officers, men and women.

While making enquiries about the accident, I was told that the bus driver concerned had been suspended by Rani Mangammal Transport Corporation and the police had registered a case against him for rash and negligent driving. I immediately got in touch with the authorities concerned and got the suspension revoked and the case withdrawn. The driver and his family visited me in the hospital to convey their gratitude.

My driver's oldest daughter, just 19 at that time, was enrolled as a constable, and another daughter was employed as a Junior Assistant in the Police office. It is ironic that the totally mangled jeep found its resting place in the same Armed Reserve ground in Madurai where I had had my training 30 years earlier. Was it to condole the death of the driver or to celebrate my survival?

The STF

The Special Task Force is a team elite,
Formed any dangerous mission to meet;
With strength to conquer any terrain,
And stamina to face sun, wind and rain.
Formed at first, a brigand to nab,
The nation's attention, they soon did grab;
Now Special Task Forces from far and near,
For tough jungle training they all head out here.

As the founder and head of the STF with a very pressing and perilous assignment on hand, I went all-out to select and train a strictly voluntary force consisting of the boldest and fittest officers and men. IGP K. Vijay Kumar, who was in charge of the Chief Minister's security, sent his second-in-command SP Sanjay Arora and 15 Inspectors and SIs, all members of the CM's security force. Apart from them, 250 subordinate staff gave their willingness. After a strict selection process, 180 of them were selected. My greatest disappointment was that no senior officer or even young ASPs, DSPs, Inspectors, and SIs responded to my call. It is not that many of them had not managed difficult law-and-order situations from time to time, but when I asked them why they did not volunteer for a rare and once-in-a-lifetime opportunity, they cited reasons like the unwillingness of their wives, family commitments, children's education, 'aged' parents, etc. Did not those who responded to my call have those problems? But they were eager to prove their loyalty to the department and were willing to sacrifice their personal safety and the comfort of home and family life.

Thinking back, I am reminded of a song by actress Padmini in a Tamil movie from my college days, 'Veerapandiya Kattabomman.' 'Pogathey pogathey enkanava, pollatha swapnam nanum kanden' (Don't go, don't go, dear husband, I had an ominous dream). But her husband, Commander Vellaiya Thevar, brushed aside her pleas, led the army against the East India Company, and died a heroic death. So did the Palla General Katta Karuppan Sundaralingam and Kattabomman's brother Oomaithurai. Eventually, Kattabomman was hanged in Kayathar, bringing the heroic episode to a close.

It is true that every man has a family as well as family responsibilities. But can there be a greater gift to his children than their father's courage and sacrifice? Even now, I hear some of them introducing themselves as children of those who had sacrificed their lives or spent several years in the war against Naxalites, religious fundamentalists, or Veerappan's gang. I said 'or' because the conjunction 'and' applies only to SP Ashok

Kumar, who started his colourful career as an SI by eradicating naxalism from Tamil Nadu, tracking down the Muslim fundamentalist Imam Ali to his hideout in Bangalore, and wiping out the entire gang, and finally taking part in the anti-Veerappan operation from day one. Of course, there are officers like Vijay Kumar, Tamil Selvan, Sanjay Arora, 'Rambo' Gopalakrishnan, Inspectors Karupusamy, Rajarajan, Hussain, Mohan Nawaz, Sampath Kumar, and others who proved that they were of a different calibre from their colleagues who kept themselves out of difficult and dangerous assignments.

With the intrepid Ashok Kumar

Of course, Vijay Kumar, Sanjay Arora, and I had the advantage of our wives being willing to live with the constant threats their husbands faced. During the Anti-Naxalite operation in the 1960s, Prema stayed in the poorly maintained government guest houses in Dharmapuri, Tirupathur, Jamunamaruthur, and Yelagiri, anxiously awaiting my return from raids that lasted anything between five and ten days. Similarly, Vijay Kumar's wife stayed in Satyamangalam throughout her husband's three long spells of jungle operation. Sanjay Arora's wife would stay in remote places like Thattakarai and Thamaraikarai, both accessible to Veerappan. As for SI Mohan Nawaz, he refused to get married until the assignment was over.

It is against this background that the names of those few officers and men who stayed on in the operation from start to finish (1993 to 2004) deserve a permanent place in the annals of valour and sacrifice. They fall into three categories:

a. Those who volunteered when the STF was formed after the Palar bomb blast and who stayed on till the campaign was over.

b. Those who left the STF when operations were suspended after the kidnapping of Kannada actor Rajkumar and who hastened to rejoin the force in 2001 and stayed on till the end of the operation.

c. The third category of heroes was those who were severely injured in encounters with the Veerappan gang, but on their discharge from hospital, rushed back to rejoin the STF. They were IGP Tamil Selvan, SP Gopalakrishnan, and SI Mohan Nawaz. IGP Tamil Selvan had lost half his palm and two middle fingers. Gopalakrishnan had to spend more than a year in the hospital. Mohan Nawaz went straight from the hospital to the field of operation. Could they have had a more valid reason than this God-given chance to stay away from the Veerappan operation? But they cited, as an example, my return to the jungle soon after my discharge from hospital after my serious road accident. The following extract from K. Vijay Kumar's book is relevant here: "Meanwhile, Walter Davaram, chafing in a hospital bed after suffering a life-threatening accident, defied the orders of his doctor to be on bed rest for 12 weeks and returned to the field. After nearly 8 weeks, he rushed 500 km by road and rail with several broken bones held in place by steel rods."

DSP Thirunavukarasu, who is in charge of the CM's security and who is a talented writer, singer, and commentator, was yet another officer who chose life in the jungle over the comfort of a station posting.

After a month of intensive training in jungle warfare, stamina-building exercises, and jungle survival tactics, we planned to enter Veerappan's kingdom on 10th May 1993. The Chief Minister of Tamil Nadu gave the following pep talk to the entire team: "As a woman, I would not like to send any one of you into the forest. But this is a matter of great importance to the two governments and the people living on both sides of the border. Come back with success and without any one of you getting hurt."

And, Operation Veerappan was launched.

When I led the STF with Sanjay Arora, 28 Inspectors and Sub-Inspectors, and 160 Other Rank personnel, it was with the words of the song by Oscar Hammerstein II ringing in my mind:

'O, give me some men, who are stout-hearted men

Who will fight for the right they adore

Start me with ten who are stout-hearted men

And I'll soon give you 10000 more"

With some of my stout-hearted men, my dream of '10000 more' remained a dream. But each one of my original stout-hearted men completed the campaign and received the government's generous awards. Of the two matchless and remarkable leaders, K. Vijay Kumar went on to serve as the Security Adviser to the Ministry of Home Affairs, Government of India, for a period of ten years (2012-2022), and Sanjay Arora is now Commissioner of Delhi. Both of them belong to the Tamil Nadu cadre. All they carried with them was the 'Veerappan Insignia.'

With Sanjay Arora and Ashok Kumar

Operation Veerappan commenced on 8.5.1993. The entire strength was assembled at Salem Airport and divided into ten groups to cover the large extent of the forest. I took a small team comprising HC Krishnaswamy and four policemen and entered the forest at Chinnamalai Kanavai along the river Palar in Karnataka. At dawn, when we stopped to have our breakfast, I decided to study the river and its approaches. I directed my team to follow me at a distance of 50 to 100 metres on either side of the path and to report any human movement. We had trekked for four hours in the forest cover along the river when I saw a country-made gun resting against a tree. It could have been a weapon either of an animal hunter or of Veerappan's lookout. I waited for the rest of the team to join me, but before they could reach me, a man, obviously the gang's lookout, rushed back and reached for his gun. Before he could take aim, I shot him down. The sound of gunfire unfolded an unexpected drama as nearly 100 people, including women who were bathing in the meandering river, jumped out and ran into the jungle on both sides of the river. As I kept firing, a member of my team called out to say that three men had been hit by my bullets. Later on, we learnt that they were very important members of the gang—Sunda Vellaiyan, Chinnaraj, and Rangasamy—who succumbed to their injuries subsequently. I was disappointed that neither Veerappan nor his brother Arjunan was among them. It was the first encounter with the gang after the formation of the STF. We carried the weapons left by them and walked nearly 15 km to the Karnataka border check post on the way to M.M. Hills, the jungle headquarters of DIG Shankar Bidri.

In another major search operation led by Vijay Kumar and Inspector Rajarajan, the entire party escaped being blown up by landmines planted by the gang. They were fortunate that the wire connecting the explosives to the ignition had snapped. On combing the mined area, the STF dug out 300 kg of gelatine, 100 kg of ammonium nitrate, and six country-made bombs. The minefield had as many as 85 pits compared to the 14 pits that had killed 22 in the Palar River blast. About 10 kg of explosives had been packed into each pit, connected by a cortex wire that had been taken to a vantage point where three of Veerappan's observers kept watch day and night. Had the blast materialised, Vijay Kumar and his entire party would have been wiped out.

I must also explain the presence of Vijay Kumar in the forest when he was supposed to be in charge of the CM's security. As his mind was totally fixed on the jungle adventure, he would sneak out of Chennai to join the operation. The CM, who understood his mindset, turned a blind eye to his absence. I first met the super-fit Vijay Kumar, the son of an SI of Police belonging to the Tamil Nadu cadre, at the National Police Academy, Hyderabad, where I had gone to conduct the riding test for the IPS probationers. Vijay Kumar was late for the test as he had gone to write the IAS examination. He passed the exam but shocked everyone by deciding to continue in the IPS.

Few people know that Mohan Nawaz, who almost lost his life in an ambush, returned to the jungle straight from the hospital. Till the end, he remained the brigand's No.1 enemy because of his mastery in jungle craft, skill in shooting, and thorough knowledge of the jungle.

The brave and dedicated Mohan Nawa

The most dangerous aspect of the jungle warfare was the presence of minefields everywhere, one of which had caused the blast killing 22 persons. I narrowly escaped the mines twice. During a routine search operation, my team, consisting of Inspector Mohan Singh and three others, came across four men carrying country-made weapons. They told us they were local tribals hunting animals for food. As we neared the forest clearance, we saw a camp with arrangements for cooking and sleeping, which more or less confirmed my suspicion that the armed men were watchers from a lookout point. We spotted one such watcher who had been left behind at the observation post. Before he could reach for his gun, I shot him dead. Mohan Singh and his team accounted for the others.

Clearing the land mines

While on the lookout for members of Veerappan's gang, we had to be extremely careful not to mistake tribals for gang members, as they also carried weapons for hunting. However, they also violated the Government Order preventing the shooting of wild animals. There had been occasions when the tribals shared their meat with us. We decided that instead of looking for landmines, it would be better to locate the spotters who were covering each landmine, waiting to set off the explosives when police parties entered those areas. We had to go up to the highest point on the hill to locate the watchtowers and shoot the watchers. Never was any innocent villager or hunter killed by the STF, as some organisations and even police officers had alleged. I always led the team because I was confident in distinguishing a gang member from a tribal. On one of our forays into the jungle, we chanced upon a man sleeping with a gun beside him. We took away his gun and, upon questioning him, found he was an important member of the gang involved in several murders. The members of my team wanted to kill him, but I thought it better to arrest him and send him for remand, which itself was a difficult job when one is in the middle of the forest, but not as difficult as having to conduct an inquest at the spot by the RDO and then having to carry a body to a hospital 35 km away. He is still in prison along with Mathaiyan, the older brother of Veerappan; also, Simon, who was injured in the firing by Inspector Ashok Kumar after the bomb blast at Soraikaimadavu on 9/4/1993. It was through Simon that we got to know of several landmines on both sides of the state border.

I am proud to say that the STF I founded has become the most permanent outcome of Operation Veerappan. It has been retained and has gained a reputation as the most experienced jungle operation unit in the country. SP Karuppusamy, Inspector Sorimuthu, and Commandant Murugan have developed it into an excellent training centre where members of the Indian Administrative Academy, the Central Police Academy, the Central Forest Academy, and special Units of several states are sent for jungle rescue and survival courses.

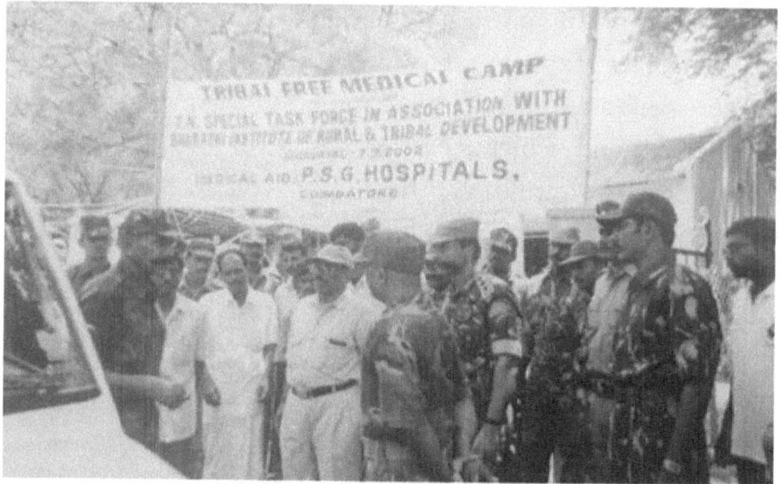

Medical camps conducted by the STF for the villagers and tribals

They Who Dared

The mission was daunting, I could not deny;
Volunteers I called for, "with me do or die"!
The STF formed thus, a force resolute became;
Rid the forest of that brigand! 'Twas their only aim.
Those stout-hearted men who answered my call,
Ready to stand by me, or with me fall.

I was back in action 90 days after my accident and was able to cover a distance of 25 km and a climb of nearly 1000 metres to one of the advanced posts. One could write an entire book on the Veerappan saga, but I will restrict myself to the most important encounters with the gang after they had moved out from their original camp near Chinnamalai Kanavai, the scene of my first shoot-out on 8.5.1993.

After intensive combing of the forest, SI Mohan Nawaz located Veerappan's new shelter in Nachipoli. On 29th Sep '93, a combined team of the STF and the BSF led by DIG Shankar Bidri and SP Sanjay Arora closed in upon a three sq. km area and sprayed bullets into the thick jungle cover. Veerappan was not there, but his brother Arjunan, who was in charge of the camp, and the male members of the gang escaped, leaving behind Veerappan's wife Muthulakshmi and two other women. They were taken to our camp in Bannari and later to a shelter in Coimbatore, where they remained until the whole operation was over. Veerappan never attempted to rescue them as we hoped he would; instead, he went on a killing spree, in which several villagers and tribals whom he suspected had led the police to his hideout were massacred. Within a month, he had killed five villagers in Gethasal, seven in Manjugomapatty in Tamil Nadu, and five in Bedhuhali and six in Pulinjur in Karnataka. Among those killed were a 16-year-old boy and a 12-year-old girl. The villagers in both states, fearing for their safety, began to avoid the police.

In another encounter at Thalaimalai on 17th Sep '94, DIG Shankar Bidri narrowly escaped death, but his gunman HC Ponnaiah lost his life. Sanjay Arora and Inspector Chennamallan narrowly escaped but lost SI Senthil Kumar and constable Ramesh of the Tamil Nadu police and Lance-Naik Bhupinder Singh of the BSF.

Misfortune pursued us relentlessly. On the night of 25.06.1995, constable Ananjay Kumar of the Tamil Nadu STF left the camp without informing the sentry PC to answer the call of nature. When returning to the camp, he brushed against a bush, and the sentry PC, assuming that the disturbance was caused by either a wild animal or a member of Veerappan's gang, aimed his automatic weapon at the bush and fired. When the team reached the spot, they found the bullet-ridden body of Ananjay Kumar. The sentry PC, distraught by what had happened, tried to shoot himself but was restrained by those around.

On 17.2.1996, the jeep carrying SP Tamil Selvan, SI Loyola Ignacius, Mohan Nawaz, HC Selvaraj, Constable Raghupathi, and driver PC Elangovan, going towards Arraypalayam, was ambushed by Veerappan. HC Selvaraj, an All-India Police swimming champion, died on the spot, and all the others except Constable Raghupathi were seriously injured. But thanks to effective counter-fire by those injured, Veerappan was forced to leave the place without killing them or taking away their weapons. Except for SI Loyola, whose head was embedded with pellets, all the others returned to the jungle operation after they recovered.

Veerappan's loss of revenue from sandalwood smuggling and elephant poaching, and his failure to get the STF out of the forest, made him turn to kidnapping. On 3.12.1994, he took the STF by surprise when he kidnapped DSP Vigilance and Anti-Corruption, Chidambaranathan, his brother Rajagopal, an HC, and a relative Sekar Raja from their farmland adjacent to the forest near Sirumugai. They had gone there to check on their crops despite a specific warning by the STF against doing so.

The abduction was followed by unreasonable and outrageous demands like a ransom of Rs.100 crore, the withdrawal of the STF from the forest, and the release of all his gang members who were in prison. While C.V. Shankar, the District Collector of Coimbatore, was negotiating with the bandits, we continued our efforts to locate the three kidnapped men, who we suspected were being held somewhere near the river Bhavani. But Veerappan had given a stern warning that should any effort be made by the police to cross the river Bhavani to rescue the kidnapped, the hostages would be killed. Meanwhile, he had sent his brother Arjunan to Coimbatore for eye treatment. No one, not even the press who had met Arjunan, was aware of the gallant role played by DSP Ashok Kumar and Inspector Karuppasamy. Ashok Kumar played the role of the Collector's 'Dafedar,' complete with the white uniform, waistband, and red cross belt. Karuppasamy played the role of Deputy tahsildar and even shared a room with Arjunan. Had Arjunan even suspected the ruse, he would, as had been his practice, have brutally killed the Inspector. The unarmed Inspector Karuppasamy sharing the room with an armed criminal was an example of matchless courage.

Knowing that coracles (parisals) crossing the river Bhavani could be spotted from Veerappan's lookout points, we decided to reach the riverbank from the hills. I formed three parties, one each under SP Sanjay Arora, Mohan Nawaz, and me. We started from Sholurmattam near Kotagiri, 6000 feet above the Bhavani River, and made our way down the jungle slope. It was an arduous venture that had to be carried out in total silence and darkness. The three parties took up positions around the area we suspected was where the three hostages were being held captive. It was Sanjay Arora's party that was first sighted by Veerappan's gang, which opened fire, injuring one of the constables. Sanjay Arora returned the fire very effectively and rescued all three hostages. He also arrested four important members of the gang, Govindan, Iyyandurai, Rangasami, and Kadambooran, each carrying a bounty of Rs.20 lakh on his head. Two muskets, 21 cartridges, four elephant tusks worth Rs.2.5 lakh, and Rs.18 lakh in cash were seized. All four were remanded to custody along with Arjunan. Again, Veerappan and four of his gang members managed to escape. Even so, this was a significant victory in our fight against his gang. Three of the four accused and Arjunan were taken by the Karnataka police in connection with cases pending in their courts. The following day, we received a message that all four of them had committed suicide by consuming poison! As all four had been searched while in our custody and later in the custody of the Karnataka police, the poison theory was difficult to swallow. "Bullet for bullet" is the rule of law in an armed conflict, not "poison for bullet." Custodial deaths demean the police.

The rescued hostages were brought to the Coimbatore Collectorate for a press meet addressed jointly by the Collector and me. The police had a difficult time controlling the crowd that had assembled to see the rescued trio. According to the Indian Express, "The STF's operation had exposed the hollowness of the criticism by some parties that the State Government was ineffective in fighting Veerappan's gang."

STF frees hostages, Veerappan escapes

From Our Special Correspondent

COIMBATORE, Dec. 30.

The three men held hostage by the sandalwood smuggler Veerappan for 27 days were rescued by the Special Task Force personnel from deep inside the Sirumugai forests between the Nilgiris and Bhavanisagar in Tamil Nadu on Thursday afternoon.

Four armed men of Veerappan's gang — Ayyandurai, third lieutenant of the outlaw carrying Rs. 20 lakhs on his head, Rangaswamy and two Irulas, Kadamburan (instrumental in helping the smuggler take the three men hostage) and Kunjan — who were at the hideout were taken by surprise and they surrendered. But Veerappan and four other men escaped.

A total of 300 STF personnel headed by the Additional Director General of Police, Mr. Walter Davaram, and Mr. Sanjay Arora, carried out the operation. The three they rescued were Mr. Chidambaranathan, Deputy Superintendent of Police, Vigilance and Anti-Corruption, Mr. Rajagopal, head constable, CID, Erode, and Mr. Sekar Raja, a physical training instructor. Kadamburan, one of those arrested, was working in Mr. Chidambaranathan's farm.

Mr. Davaram said at a crowded press conference here on Friday afternoon that there was no bloodshed during the mission though shots were fired. The hunt for Veerappan would continue. Veerappan's movement has been restricted to an area of 150 sq. km and he is left with only four armed men — Sethukuliyur Govindan, Baby Veerappan, Rangaswamy and Madhesh. Mr. Davaram said he would not fix any time limit for the capture of Veerappan and his men in view of the hostile terrain in which the STF had to operate.

The three hostages rescued were shown to the press as also the huge stocks of ammunition, cartridges, tusks and food articles seized from the deserted hideouts of the forest brigand.

Veerappan's brother and second in command in his gang, Arjunan, now undergoing treatment here for a knee injury and the four who surrendered to the STF had been arrested for various offences including murder and would be remanded to custody. The firearms they had in their possession had been confiscated and they would be proceeded against for their offences.

The Additional DGP said Veerappan was free to surrender if he wanted to do so either before court or the District Collector and face prosecution for the offences he had committed. There was no question of the Government granting him and his men general amnesty.

Mr. Davaram said anybody who joined the brigand's gang or attempted to help him in any way would also be treated as a criminal and dealt with accordingly. Since the STF was continuing its combing operations in the forests, Mr. Davaram cautioned against anyone entering the area. The police would open fire at anybody seen there. Mr. Davaram said he had to issue this warning as during the intervening few days when the STF combing operations were temporarily suspended to facilitate negotiations between Veerappan's emissaries and the District Collector, some were reported to be joining his gang and supplying him essentials and arms and ammunition. During this period, Veerappan had stored 8-1/2 bags of rice, several litres of ghee and oil, batteries and devices for automatic refilling of cartridges. The STF had seized these and also two pairs of tusks worth Rs. 2.5 lakhs.

The Additional DGP denied the allegations that women in the forest areas or those relating to Veerappan had been held under the custody of the police or were being molested.

The Tamil Nadu Additional Director-General of Police, Mr. Walter Davaram, and the Coimbatore District Collector, Mr. C. V. Sankar, addressing a press conference in Coimbatore on Friday. The three persons rescued from the sandalwood smuggler, Veerappan's hideout are standing behind them.

The Hindu, dated 31ˢᵗ December 1994, had published the following:

1. The three men held hostage by Veerappan for 27 days were rescued by the STF from deep inside Sirumugai forest. Four armed men of Veerappan's gang, each carrying Rs.20 lakh on his head, were also arrested. But Veerappan and four others escaped.

2. "The STF personnel, headed by the ADGP Mr. W.I. Davaram and SP Sanjay Arora, carried out the operation. Mr. Davaram said that but for the injuries caused to a constable, there were no casualties. The hunt for Veerappan would continue. Veerappan was left with only four armed men—Sethukuli Govindan, Baby Veerappan, Rangasamy, and Madhesh. Mr. Davaram said he would not fix any time for the capture of Veerappan in view of the hostile terrain."

At the Medal Parade held in Coimbatore on October 8, 1995, Chief Minister J. Jayalalithaa presented appreciation certificates to the following officers:

W.I. Davaram, IPS (ADGP L&O), Sanjay Arora, IPS (Commander-STF), M. Ashok Kumar, Deputy Commandant, STF, K. Kuppusamy, DSP, Inspectors K. Chennamalan, K. Gopalsamy, Karuppasamy, and SIs Balasubramaniam, Mohan Nawaz, Gnanasekaran, Krishnasamy, and Kandasamy.

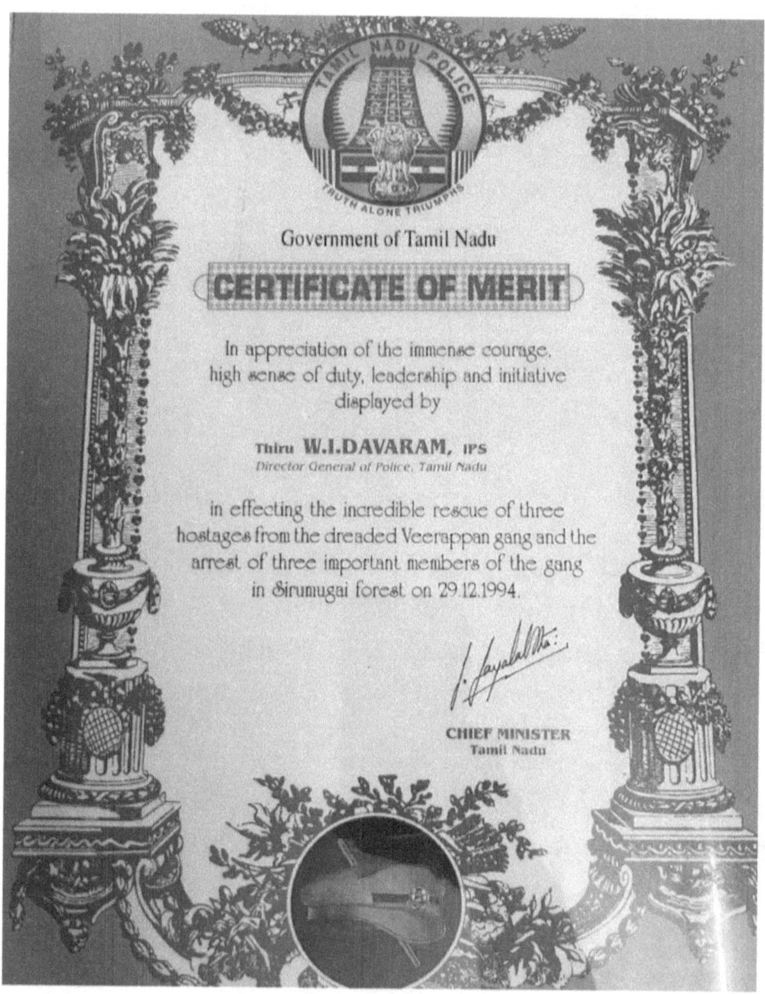

Readers would find it difficult to visualise the hardships we underwent in the forest. We could carry food for only two days. After that, we survived on fish from the jungle streams and fruit from the forest trees. When we came across tribal villages, we shared their food, paying them in cash. Cash was a rare and welcome commodity for those in the forests where the barter system still existed.

Sentry duty was assigned to every member of the team, irrespective of rank. I preferred the early morning shift as it gave me the chance to pluck out leeches from my body. My record was 34 of them clinging to me, with another 20 or 25 having dropped off, leaving streaks of blood. Looking at the men sleeping on the ground without cover, braving the heavy rain, suffering leech and mosquito bites, my heart would be filled with remorse, as it was I, not Veerappan, who had subjected them to such hardship.

I lost count of the STF's several encounters against the gang. I personally led the men in seven of them, accounting for 15 members of the gang. I had spent more than 100 nights in the jungle as ADGP and DGP L&O, and another 125 nights when I was recalled after my retirement to lead the STF once again.

Veerappan sprang a surprise by kidnapping popular Kannada actor Rajkumar from his house on the state border. He warned both governments that the actor would be killed if any attempt was made to rescue him. The government had to take his threats seriously, as any harm to the actor would have resulted in a large-scale killing of Tamilians in Karnataka. Both Chief Ministers met and appointed journalist Nakkeeran R.R. Gopal as the government emissary. A total of 14 demands were sent to the government, the most ridiculous ones being that the River Cauvery dispute should be referred to the International Court of Justice, that all those detained under TADA should be released, and that Tamil should be made a medium of instruction in Tamil Nadu up to Std X. Meanwhile, the Karnataka High Court ordered the release of 56 TADA accused. But a retired Karnataka police officer, Abdul Kareem, whose son Shakeel Ahamed, along with SP Harikrishna, had been killed by Veerappan, approached the Supreme Court to cancel the order of the High Court. The Supreme Court asked for my views. I submitted my opinion to the Supreme Court as follows:

'Allowing the detenus to go free would create a lethal combination of crime and politics.'

The SC accepted my view and overruled the High Court order.

However, the STF was withdrawn from the forest, and most of the volunteers returned to their original Units. Those who did not were asked not to venture into the forest. Meanwhile, Nakkeeran Gopal was also replaced by former Congressman Nedumaran and DK leader Kolathur Mani. Finally, after 108 days of captivity, Rajkumar was released on 15.11.2000. The conditions of the release and the amount that was paid are still not known.

When the AIADMK returned to power in 2001, CM Jayalalithaa invited me to head the STF. Whereupon, three civil rights organisations challenged my appointment, calling it an 'extra-legal' and 'extra-constitutional police authority.' But their objection was overruled by the court. She also brought Vijay Kumar from Delhi to assist me. Though I had spent more than 250 days and nights in the forest, I had failed to complete the mission - a failure that will remain a thorn in my life forever.

After my year-long deputation was over, Vijay Kumar continued to lead the STF. He survived a serious injury caused by a rampaging elephant, which forced him into three weeks of rest, the longest he ever had in his lifetime.

After a year, Vijay Kumar was posted as CoP Chennai City, and ADGP R Nataraj was posted to the STF. Two encounter deaths in Chennai, one of criminal Veeramani and another of don Venkatesa Pannaiyar during Vijay Kumar's Commissionerate, created a controversy. Vijay Kumar's frank statement to the press was as follows: 'If you trust a policeman to carry a gun, then you must trust him to use it wisely and effectively under the law. We do not carry weapons around us as ornaments.' This comment resulted in the media accusing him of being trigger-happy.

Vijay Kumar was once again posted to the STF; he was glad that he had got yet another chance to nab Veerappan. To him, posts like that of Commissioner of Police or even DGP did not mean much when compared to an opportunity to get Veerappan. I leave out much of the details of the final showdown, which have been given in great detail by Vijay Kumar in his book 'Veerappan – Chasing the Brigand.'

Ruthless as he was, Veerappan was naive enough to think that he could leave the forest and join the LTTE; so naive that he believed that ardent, dedicated freedom fighters, who would sacrifice their lives for their cause, would welcome a forest brigand into their fold. Lured by this hope, he agreed to be taken to Prabakaran after an eye treatment in Salem. Police driver Saravanan was groomed to drive a police vehicle camouflaged as an ambulance to take Veerappan and his associates out of their hideout, supposedly to an eye hospital. He was to be accompanied by SI Velladurai, a bold and resourceful officer with past experiences of encounters and who had spent several days in Veerappan's camp posing as an LTTE member. A third person who had established a close relationship with Veerappan was to arrange the consultation with the eye specialist. The "ambulance" was to be driven to a particular point near Pappireddipatty in Dharmapuri district, where Vijay Kumar's ambush party would be lying in wait. Vijay Kumar, Senthamaraikannan, Rajarajan, and Inspector Charles had planned the placement of the parties and the tracking equipment for the ambush.

Finally, at 10 pm on 18th October 2004, the ambulance reached the pre-determined spot. Everything went as planned. Driver Saravanan stopped the vehicle on the pretext of having to check one of the tyres. He alighted and hid behind a tree. Velladurai got down on the other side after rolling a grenade into the vehicle where Veerappan was seated. That was the signal for the ambush party to open fire. The encounter lasted 20 minutes, described by K. Vijay Kumar as a 'rapid climax to a 20-year wait.' The entire team of officers and men lying in wait at their respective points jumped out, shouting "Long live the STF!" and hoisted Vijay Kumar and Senthamarai Kannan onto their shoulders.

The victorious Vijayakumar

On hearing the good news from Vijay Kumar, I called the Chief Minister and requested her to announce a one-rank promotion and a cash prize of Rs. 1 lakh for all those who had taken part in the operation. However, she announced the news the next day: a one-rank promotion, a cash award of Rs. 3 lakhs, and a house site for each member of the STF. Altogether, 177 officers and men received awards.

There have been cases of injustice as well, a classic example of which was the relegation of ADSP Thirunavukarasu. He had to take his place below six DSPs of his batch and 12 of his previous batch whom he had overtaken through the CM's Special Order. He had to take his place below the 18 whom he had superseded. Today, he is still an SP, but he ought to have become a DIG.

But one 'Hero in Khaki' defied conventions and calculations, injustice, and hardship by returning to the jungle outfit after shunning highly coveted posts in Coimbatore and Chennai Cities. He was of great assistance to Commandant Shankar Jiwal in building the jungle in a stretch of poromboke land near Bannari and completing it into a No.1 Jungle Training Centre in the country. Even after his retirement from the STF, after completing 18 years of service, he continues to give lectures and instructions in jungle craft to the visiting trainees from all over India. He is none other than Karuppasamy, who joined the service as an SI and retired as an IPS officer, winning several gallantry medals.

The dauntless Karuppusamy

I would like to end this chapter on a happy note. Mohan Nawaz had spent as many as 11 years of his life in the forest. When his original batch of SIs had become eligible for promotion to the rank of SP, Mohan Nawaz was No. 12 on the promotion list and just days away from retirement. As usual, the bureaucratic red tape kept the file moving back and forth with queries and answers while time was running out. My taking up the issue with the DGP, who personally took the matter up to the Hon'ble CM, and my personal request to the CM's Personal Secretary, Tr. Udayachandran, to speed up the relevant file bore fruit, and Mohan Nawaz's promotion order was issued on the 30th of March 2023. He took charge as one of the DCs (SP) of Chennai City Police at 10:30 AM on the 31st of March and retired as SP at 5 PM that same day! It was the same Tr. Udayachandran, IAS, who ordered the promotion of an Adivasi constable to DSP after all the others had let him down. I would like to express my gratitude to him, DGP Dr. C. Sylendra Babu, and last but not least, the noble-hearted CM, Tr. M.K. Stalin.

Extract from K. Vijay Kumar's book 'Veerappan – Chasing the Brigand'

The first few years of service went by in a blur as I learnt the ropes. It was during this stint that I first served under the legendary Walter Davaram, who later became the first head of the Tamil Nadu STF. Walter was a tough, adventurous officer who believed in leading from the front – the more dangerous the situation, the better. He was an interesting combination of brains and brawn. As a student, he had spent most of his time playing various sports. He also had a photographic memory that had helped him top the M.A. history course at Annamalai University. He was an ace shooter and was responsible for triggering a passion for shooting in me. My scores in shooting at the academy were nothing much to write home about. But Walter inspired me to practise relentlessly. The more I shot, the better I got, and the better I got, the more enthusiastically I practised.

July 2001.

Walter patiently emptied about 20 dead leeches from one boot. He extracted a similar number from his other boot. He had just returned to the Travellers' Bungalow after spending a day trekking through the jungle, chasing elusive leads. As usual, he had ignored the fact that leeches and the blood-thinning medicine the doctors had ordered him to take were not a good combination.

At 60-plus, the legendary super-cop still retained his fire and ability to motivate all those who served under him. With a bristling moustache and imposing physique, he instantly commanded attention even if one had not heard of his awe-inspiring achievements. I was delighted to be reporting to him once again. While I was serving as SP in Dharmapuri and Salem between 1981 and 1985, he was my boss as DIG, Vellore. He was credited with wiping out Naxalism in the area. He had set many records, including being the only officer to have visited each of the over 1,100 police stations in Tamil Nadu, during which he left delightful visiting notes.

Most of my weekends were spent conducting raids or going on treks led by Walter, who liked nothing better than to be out in the field. That suited me just fine, because I too deeply disliked sitting behind the desk pushing papers. Exactly a month after the Good Friday blast, the STF entered Veerappan's den in his first ambush against Veerappan. Walter nearly succeeded in getting him, but not only did the wily bandit escape, the STF ambush in Veerappan's core area produced one of the most interesting episodes in STF history.

Acknowledgement

I would especially like to acknowledge the lion-hearted efforts of Walter Davaram and Shankar Bidri. Between them, they reduced the Veerappan gang's number to single digits.

The Bravest of the Brave

Among our edifices that stand out tall,
There's one that's tallest of them all;
Volunteered for every hazardous mission,
"Never give up", his only vision;
The graver the danger, the greater the thrill,
He gave of his best; his war-cry, 'I will'.
"Who is this Bravest of the Brave"?

'He' started his career as a Sub-Inspector of Police in 1976, and within four years of service, volunteered for the Anti-Naxalite operation. 'He' had accompanied me in many of the inter-state raids and accounted for several wanted Naxalites.

After the Naxalite menace had been controlled, 'he' went back to routine police work, but not for long. When forest brigand Veerappan's activities extended into Tamil Nadu and volunteers were called for, his was the first hand to go up.

When another serious problem arose in the form of Muslim fundamentalist Imam Ali, who had destroyed the RSS office in Madras, killing 13 RSS members, 'he' was my natural choice when Shukla asked for help to tackle the situation. 'He' again lived up to his reputation, laid siege to the hideout, and killed Imam Ali and four others in a well-controlled shoot-out without causing any civilian casualties.

After the Veerappan operation, 'he' was posted to the Q-Branch, dealing with religious and political extremists. 'He' continued with his dangerous field operations until the day he retired. The IPS was conferred on him, but he unfortunately missed his promotion to DIG due to procedural delays, denying him the distinction of becoming the first SI to rise to the rank of DIG.

'He' was not only brave but highly principled and an epitome of honesty and self-respect.

'He,' the Bravest of the Brave, is none other than SP Ashok Kumar.

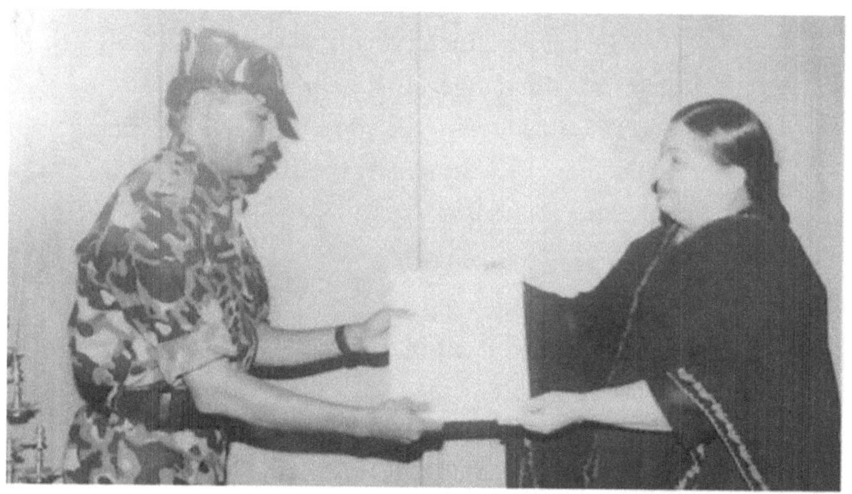

The Family Travelogue

Far, far away, where earth meets the sky,
We wished to be there, spread our wings out and fly
Above starry firmament; and from up there to see,
What's beyond the horizon, the mountains and sea.
We climbed every mountain that stood around our home,
We forded every stream that lay where'er we'd roam;
When our homeland beckoned, with so much more to see,
We did our best to cover it, Himalaya to the sea.
And then, we looked around and saw the world before us lay,
Too big, we thought; a bit for now; the rest, perhaps, some day.

For most of us who were born and brought up in the hills in the 40s, walking was 'a,' or rather, 'the' way of life. We walked everywhere. This was true of life in Munnar, where I was born and brought up, and in Coonoor, where Prema was born and brought up.

In Munnar, the only cars were those owned by a few British managers. The other managers and assistant managers, all of them British, owned motorbikes. Public transport meant the three buses, each one making just one return trip a day between Munnar and Udumalpet in Tamil Nadu and Kottayam and Alwaye in Kerala. Udumalpet and Alwaye were the towns with railway stations from where we could take trains to our intended destination. As such, walking to school and back from various estates, unmindful of the distance of even 10 to 15 km one-way, was the norm and nothing out of the ordinary; and as if that were not enough, my father would make my sisters and me go for runs in the bracing early morning chill. With the Munnar scouts, I have climbed past the Eravikulam Ibex Sanctuary up to Anamudi peak, which at 8,842 feet is the highest peak South of the Himalayas. To me, waiting for a bus was more tiresome than walking to my destination. Some of the walks that defied convention have been walking back 26.5 km to Tambaram after watching a movie in a cinema hall or a football match at the Jawaharlal Nehru Stadium and then attending an NCC parade early the next morning, all spruced up and looking fresh; or walking the 20 km to Bhavani Sagar Dam from the NCC camp at Sathyamangalam.

Coonoor, on the other hand, was even then a well-developed hill-station. The British had built good roads connecting the towns of Coonoor, Ooty, and Kotagiri to Mettupalayam in Tamil Nadu, to Mysore in Karnataka, and to Sultan's Battery in Kerala. The missionaries of yore had established excellent day-cum-boarding schools in Coonoor and Ooty. It may be relevant to mention here that Prema's mother, Prema, and our daughter Anita, all three of them, passed through the hallowed portals of St. Joseph's Convent, established in Coonoor in the year 1900 by the nuns of a French order, the Missionaries of St. Joseph of Tarbes.

Prema grew up with a love of the great outdoors instilled in her by her parents. Her father was a champion tennis player, but could get neither Prema nor her brother to follow in his footsteps. A Sunday outing usually meant a hike up to the top of Teneriffe, the highest peak in Coonoor, berry-picking (the slopes used to be covered with shrubs of hill guava, locally known as 'thavuttu pazham') along the way. Or they would drive up to Ooty and hike up, picnic hamper in hand, along the narrow path through thorny bushes to the top of the highest peak in the state, Doddabetta. The motorable road did not exist then.

Prema's father with the Cowley Brown trophy

So, it was that when I married Prema, I had married a kindred soul who, like me, was a child of the hills and shared with me the love of mountains, long walks, and everything outdoors.

Prema and I needed no excuse to walk. Often, en route to Coonoor, we would get off at Law's Falls, 10 km down the Ghat Road, and walk up the mountain paths to reach the town. We would do the same to reach

Yercaud from Salem. I remember how, on one such walk, we passed women estate workers who muttered in Tamil disdainfully, "Look at that miser. He's making that poor lady walk when he could have taken her up by bus." When on holiday in Coonoor, hikes up to the top of Teneriffe or down the hill to Runnymede Railway Station on The Nilgiri Mountain railroad and back, or walking from Coonoor to Ooty along the railway track, was nothing out of the ordinary. In Tanjore, our quarters stood all by themselves in a large compound with the front gate opening onto the Trichy-Tanjore Road and the back gate onto the Trichy-Pudukkottai Road. Whenever I was in headquarters, we would walk out of the front gate, reach the point where the highway forked, take the Pudukkottai branch, and reach our back gate, covering a distance of about 8 km. When we were posted to Trichy, we would walk from our quarters in Kimber Gardens to the cantonment area and back, a distance of around 14 km. Often, we took in a movie at the Plaza Theatre. The Sangam Hotel was then just a restaurant serving delicious dosas, dripping with ghee. Naturally, we had to walk home faster to rid ourselves of the guilt!

Our daughter Anita, an avid trekker, started hiking at the tender age of two. Part of the hike at that time would, of course, be on my shoulder. She has come a long way since then. She has done most of the hikes in The Nilgiris: Mukurthi, Rangaswamy Peak and Pillar, Western Catchment, Kolaribetta Earthen Dam, Beermukh Hill, Echo Rock, Droog, and also the Nonsuch-Pillur hike. She has done treks in the Himalayas as well. Her first one was with her son Amitesh to Hampta Pass (14,009 ft) and Chandra Tal. They went with a group organised by Renok Adventures, who sent them a long list of essentials to be equipped with before reporting at Manali. The most exciting part of the five-day trek was the river crossings with no bridges. The swift-flowing, waist-deep, ice-cold mountain streams were crossed expertly by a human chain stretched across from bank to bank. This was probably why the group had to wear 'quick-drying' clothes. Their 2021 vacation took them backpacking through the deserts of Rajasthan, they came on camel-back, spending nights under the starry skies, and then backpacking through other parts of the state. Anita has done several other Himalayan treks with her classmates from PCK and her best friend from St. Joseph's, Niranjala. They have done the Valley of Flowers (11,500 ft), Hemkund Sahib (15,000 ft), Mana, the last village in India (12,500 ft), and Yuksom and Dzongri (13,100 ft). In 2022, Anita and Amitesh did the Kashmir Great Lakes (KGL) trek, starting at Sonamarg and ending at Naranag with seven days of steep ascents and descents, crawling over huge boulders, crossing icy glacial swift-flowing streams while covering 73 km, and reaching the highest point of 13,800 ft. After the trek, they decided to be even more adventurous and backpacked to Gurez Valley, which lies along the LOC in the northern part of Kashmir, and then onto Chakwali, the last village on the Indo-Pak border. Amitesh carried on from there and completed the Spiti circuit (Shimla, Kinnaur, Spiti, Manali). He stayed a couple of nights at the Key monastery and visited Tabo, the oldest monastery, Komic, the highest monastery, and also the monasteries of Kibber and Dankar. He also visited the last village on the Indo-China border, Chitkul, in the Sangla Valley. He was thrilled to be able to visit the highest post office at Hikkim. Backpacking his way, he has visited Rasol, Malana Village, Magic Valley with its glacier, Kheerganga, Rudranag, and Triund up to the snow line at 10,900 ft. Interacting with the locals and other backpackers was an experience he found very enlightening and fulfilling. As all the places he visited drew trekkers from all over the world, language was never a problem and every meal was a delectable surprise.

Amitesh and Anita at the Kashmir Great Lakes, the Indo-Pak border on the Thar desert, the Indo-Pak border at Chakwali, and Amitesh at the world's highest post office at Hikkim.

Dev, my older sister's second son, now settled in Canada, leads a life of adventure. He has hitchhiked or cycled all over Canada and New Zealand. His latest adventure was cycling from the West Coast to the East, covering a distance of 9,000 km. The same sister's youngest daughter-in-law, Nalini, takes part in full and half-marathons and has won several medals as a veteran athlete. My youngest sister, Della, was a champion athlete in college. My doctor sister's son was also a good athlete and football player.

*Nalini, Dev, Della and Jaimitt with
the Subroto Cup winning football team*

Prema and I had always been great walkers, but coming across books on the exercise programmes VBX and XBX, formulated for the men and women of the Canadian Air Force, got us interested in planned exercising. However, I did not find this form of exercise appealing. Eventually, I went back to my daily walks, while Prema carried on. In Chennai, she took to gymming and aerobics; and now, COVID-19 has introduced her to the Schellea Fowler exercise programmes and Tai Chi.

443

I was one of those to whom hills were like magnets. The sight of even a little hillock roused in me the urge to climb it just to see what lay on the other side. I was like the bear in the nursery song:

'The bear went over the mountain
To see what he could see;
And all that he could see,
Was the other side of the mountain.
Was all that he could see'

I have climbed all the peaks in The Nilgiris – Kolaribetta, Mukurti, Rangasamy Peak, Glenmorgan, Teneriffe, and Droog; the topography of Coonoor is such that there is no 'flat' at all. So, every walk was either down-and-up or up-and-down. I have also climbed Perumal Peak in Kodaikanal. The downhill walk from Top Station, the upper terminal of the ropeway in Munnar, to Kurangani, the lower terminal of the ropeway, and back was just a way of life for me because the ropeway, perhaps for reasons of safety, was to transport only tea, not people. Little wonder then, that walking was second nature to me and followed me into my life on the plains, preparing me for the physically demanding operations against the Naxalites and later, against the Veerappan gang.

Apart from our outdoor activities, Prema and I shared an interest in languages. Prema had studied Hindi in school and French in college. She could speak Tamil and learnt to read it from her mother. Her father helped her with Malayalam from the newspapers that the local bakers, all of them Malayalee, used to wrap their freshly baked bread. I, from Munnar, knew Malayalam and Tamil; also, Hindi, which was a compulsory subject in Kerala. During the Anti-Naxalite operations, I found that there was a lot of cross-border Naxalite activity between Tamil Nadu and Andhra Pradesh. I realised that I needed to know Telugu. I engaged a Telugu pundit to teach me to speak the language, but he encouraged and taught me to read and write it as well. Our Nagapattinam posting gave us the opportunity to interact with the captains and crew members of the several Japanese ships that docked there. We got interested in the Japanese language, and 'Linguaphone' made its way into our lives. Prema even won the first prize in an elocution competition conducted by the Japanese Embassy. We got interested in Spanish after meeting an Indian nun who had spent several years in Spain, and we learnt the language, again, through 'Linguaphone.' To keep in touch with these languages, Prema and I had our Spanish and Japanese days until I left for the Veerappan operation. Those were the days when communication systems were not what they are today, and communicating with Prema even in English, let alone in Japanese or Spanish, was rarely possible.

I was fortunate to have E.L. Stracey as my IG, as he encouraged officers to take annual vacations and return to duty rejuvenated. All our vacations were in winter to coincide with our daughter Anita's school holidays. In those days, the school year for schools in the hills ran from February to November. This was convenient because we could plan winter holidays in the Himalayas. Come June, we would choose a destination and get the TTK map of the place. These maps included a small list of three or four hotels in the area. Prema would write to them for details. A couple of months (yes, months) later, replies from the hotels would trickle in, asking for a day's payment to reserve a room for us. Based on the facilities offered, mainly running hot water, we would choose a hotel and send off a 'Money Order' or M.O., as it was called, for the amount. M.O.s were handled by the Post Office. You filled in a form with details of the sender and recipient; there was also a blank space for any communication. The filled in form and payment in cash were handed in at the post office. A never-fail system of money transfer. Several weeks later, we would receive the acknowledgement from the hotel, and Prema would carefully put it into the 'holiday file.' Although communication systems were hardly advanced, they were dependable; and we always arrived at our destination to find our room ready and waiting for us. Those were days when nobody took winter holidays, but we booked our accommodation so we would know where to go once we reached our destination. On those holidays, we enjoyed the undivided attention of the hotel staff. How nice to be welcomed back after a day of winter sight-seeing with bowls of hot soup!

Even nicer to climb into bed and have our freezing toes encounter the comfort of a hot-water bottle. Sheer bliss! Would those of the present generation understand this pure 'bliss' now that their lives have been 'air-conditioned' and 'centrally heated?'

When Sikkim beckoned, it took a bit of planning because Gangtok, in those days, was not easy to reach. We decided to couple our holiday in Sikkim with stop-overs at Kalimpong and Darjeeling. Kalimpong was misty and a lot like Coonoor, while the skyline in Darjeeling was dominated by the Kanchenjunga.

One of our most rewarding experiences was going up to Tiger Hill near Darjeeling. We were woken up early in the morning by the caretaker of our guest house and walked uphill in the dark to a viewpoint to watch Mount Everest come alive with the rising sun; just black when we took up positions at the viewpoint, turning to dark purple, then pink, orange, yellow, and finally, white. An unforgettable celestial drama!

Our hotel in Gangtok, a brand-new Sikkim Tourism Department one, was perched atop a hill. Our room had a large picture window framing the majestic Kanchenjunga; the awesome sight we woke up to every morning of our holiday there.

Our holiday in Nepal was no less enthralling. Our long bus ride to Pokhara was made less tedious by the Annapurna Massif, which seemed to be travelling alongside us. At Pokhara, it was the Machapuchare that was framed in our window. It looked to be within touching distance, so much so that Anita worried about an unwelcome visit from the 'Abominable Snowman!' Back in Kathmandu, we were lucky to have a clear day to take the 'Everest Flight,' which gave us a mesmerising view in slow motion, so to speak, of all the Himalayan peaks from west to east. The flight then turned around and did the entire stretch from east to west for the benefit of the passengers on the other side of the plane. Each of us was given a chart of all the peaks in order, named for easy identification. Thanks to the several foreign mountaineers who make Nepal their base, we found many inexpensive, but neat shacks serving delicious soup, pizza, and apple pie.

We owe all that we experienced in Ladakh to my batchmate A.V. Liddle. He was with the ITBP based in Srinagar and helped us join the first convoy that went up when the road opened in summer. Leh, at that time, was not a tourist destination. It was a two-day drive with an overnight halt at Kargil. The first day's drive had us with our hearts in our mouths as we navigated a rough road only as wide as the minibus we were on. On one side, the cliffs rose vertically and high into the sky; on the other was a sheer drop of thousands of feet into a deep valley where we could see a serpentine emerald ribbon of a river. The memorials along the road made us appreciative of the efforts of the members of the Border Roads Organisation who had lost their lives building and keeping this perilous road open. We reached Kargil by sundown after a brief tea stop at Dras, the coldest place in India and one of the coldest in the world. The second day's drive was easier, and we could enjoy the colours of the mountain desert that we drove through. Leh stood at 11,500 ft, which was probably why we found oxygen cylinders in our room in the ITBP guest house; also, a hotline to the hospital with instructions to just lift the receiver should we feel any discomfort. We did not have to use these emergency measures as, having grown up in the hills, acclimatisation was no problem. We were also able to take the trip to Khardung La at 17,500 ft. Our flight back to Delhi was even more mesmerising. We gazed down with awe at the Himalayan peaks and the wondrous spectacle of snow-bound formations below us as we glided over them until we cleared the range. The mighty Himalayas from 30,000 ft above - an unforgettable experience.

One enjoyable holiday was the one that covered Nainital, Raniket, and the foothills of the Himalayas to Dehradun and Mussoorie. We were to take a bus, but all our efforts to check the schedule drew responses that started with 'if the bus comes,' as the route was landslide-prone. We decided to take the situation in our stride. After all, we were on holiday.

The bus did arrive eventually, and we were on our way. We broke our journey in Karnaprayag and found accommodation in a strategically placed Travellers' Bungalow. It was already dark when we arrived, but we could hear the gurgling of a river far below. We woke up the next morning to the beautiful sight of the Pindar River meeting the Alaknanda. Our journey the next day took us past the confluence of the Alaknanda and Mandakini at Rudraprayag and that of the Alaknanda and Bhagirathi at Devaprayag to Rishikesh, where we saw the Ganges and the Lakshman Jhula (bridge). We went to Dehradun and on to Mussoorie, where I showed Prema and Anita the Institute where I started my career. Our holiday in Meghalaya was a dampener because of bad weather. We could not make it to Cherrapunji, but Anita was lucky to visit it with her PCK friends a couple of years back.

Anita with her friends at the
double decker root bridge at Cherrapunjee

Another unforgettable holiday was our trip to Nagaland and Manipur. We took the train from Calcutta to Dimapur, the railhead. The first thrill came when we crossed the Farakka Barrage over the Ganges. We were awed by the vastness of the river. At the midpoint, we could see neither bank. The express train was speeding over the barrage, and even then, the crossing seemed to take an eternity. We were awed by the

Ganges, the River of India. Our train journey took two days, not only because of delays en route but also because we had to skirt Bangladesh and Meghalaya. At Dimapur, we took a bus to Kohima. The highlight of our solemn visit to Kohima was the beautifully tiered war cemetery. The touching epitaph by John Maxwell Edmonds reads:

'When you go home, tell them of us and say,
For your tomorrow, we gave our today.'

We also visited my batchmate Haridas Kachari. I was meeting him for the first time since our Mount Abu days.

We continued to the war cemetery at Imphal, our next stop. There, the memorial read, 'Their name liveth for evermore.' We then took a stroll around the Ima Keithal, the 500-year-old all-woman market. For Prema and Anita, this was their first visit to Nagaland and Manipur. But for me, it was a joyous revisiting of places that had been so much a part of my pre-IPS days. I was filled with nostalgia as I showed Prema and Anita all the old familiar places, especially the DM College where I had worked. We met my colleagues from the college, Menon and Lokendra Singh. This holiday was also something of a lesson in geography. Latitude-wise, we were approximately 24 degrees North. This meant the winter days were shorter, and it would be dark by 5 PM. However, our longitudinal position was approximately 93 degrees East; so, when night fell, it was only 3.30 PM IST! This not only cut short our sight-seeing hours; it also made our evenings long and dreary. But it was a worthwhile experience that made us wonder why India didn't have more than its single time zone set for longitude 82.5 degrees East.

We flew back to Calcutta with a change of flight at Agartala. Our flight from Imphal to Agartala was unforgettable because we had among our travel companions local villagers, a goat, and a basket of cackling chickens! Given the difficult nature of the terrain, flights at subsidised fares were the most feasible mode of transport.

Once again, the lure of the Himalayas drew us to the Western Himachal towns of Dalhousie, McLeod Ganj, Dharamshala, Chamba, and Kangra for magnificent views of the Pir Panjal and the Dhauladhar Ranges of the Lesser Himalayas. At all of these places, we walked to our hearts' content. Thanks to Nazeem, an IAS officer of the Himachal Pradesh cadre whom we got to know when he was on deputation to the Tea Board in Coonoor, we were able to get inexpensive accommodation in PWD and Electricity Board guesthouses.

Our winter holiday in Manali was planned because our grandson Amitesh, 8 years old at the time, wanted to see snow. Prema visited the Himachal Pradesh Tourism office housed in the Tourism Complex in Chennai, where the helpful lady-in-charge recommended we take the overnight 'very comfortable high-tech luxury Volvo' for the 14-hour drive from Delhi. We were diffident. Fourteen miserable hours on a bus? We took it, anyway, buying our tickets from the same office. We found the semi-sleeper bus more than just comfortable. After the dinner stop at Chandigarh, we were lulled to sleep through the night, waking up only when the bus arrived in Manali to our delight, as the town had had its first snowfall of the season.

Our hotel, Snow Valley Resort, was one of the last in a string of hotels up a steep road, and we were the lone guests. We woke up the next morning to heavy snowfall, with no let-up over the next four days. From our third-floor room, we gleefully watched the sunken open-to-sky quadrangle below fill up and the steps leading down to it disappear one by one under the snow. We listened to thuds as snow piled up on the gabled roofs slid off onto the veranda that ran alongside the rooms; we watched the concrete 'tables' on the open terrace begin to look like iced Christmas cakes. We were in fairyland! When it finally stopped snowing, we had just a day of our holiday left. We ploughed our way through the snow to take in what we could of the town, the river Beas, and a trout meal that Manali is known for. Amitesh had had his fill of snow.

Our last Himalaya holiday, this time in Eastern Uttarakhand, was more recent. We were no longer young and were aware that we would not be able to rough it as we had done on our previous holidays. As luck would have it, one of our Tamil Nadu officers, Mehboob Alam, on deputation to the ITBP, was stationed in Delhi. We left it to him to organise our holiday there, telling him that views of the Eastern Himalayas were our top priority. In the ITBP camp at Munsiyari, our room had a picture window framing the Panchchuli peaks, which appeared to be next door to us. In fact, they were constantly in view, wherever we went—Pithoragarh, Bunsar, and Almora. Kausani gave us a breathtaking panoramic view of the range from Trishul and Nanda Devi to the Panchachulis. At the end of our holiday, we were sorry to leave the mighty Himalayas behind us. Would we ever see them again?

Our holiday in Hyderabad was planned mainly to spend time with friends Ravi and Rema Gnanadickam. They took us sight-seeing in Old Hyderabad with its Charminar, the Golconda Fort with its ancient history, and the Salar Jung museum with its mind-blowing collection of artefacts and the statue of Margaretta and Mephistopheles placed strategically in front of a mirror. They also took us to Nagarjuna Sagar, the dam across the river Krishna. We left Hyderabad with memories to cherish.

Our first holiday in Karnataka, more than four decades earlier, was with our daughter Anita. We roughed it, travelling by bus and staying in tourist bungalows. We went to Belgaum with the ruins of the 'Kitoor' Rani Chenamma Fort and were awed by the spectacular Jog Falls, which we realised were actually four falls: Rocket, Roarer, Rani, and Raja. We went on to Badami, known for its rock-cut cave Temples, Pattadakal with its Hindu and Jain Temples, and Aihole with its Durga Temple, so different from other Temples we had seen. Our last stop was Hampi. Apart from the ruins and Temples, what really caught our admiration was the beautifully carved stone chariot drawn by two stone elephants. Our bus ride from Hampi to Bangalore was far from comfortable. It was a travel-weary trio that checked into East West hotel in time to be perked up by the New Year's Eve Party.

Our second holiday in Karnataka was with our grandson Amitesh. It was a comfortable and well-organised holiday, thanks to IGP Shankar Bidari, who had worked with me on the Karnataka side in our joint operation against the brigand Veerappan. At the Bannerghatta National Park, Amitesh was crestfallen when we explained to him that the signboards which read 'Adopt a Tiger' did not mean that we could take home a tiger on a leash! We covered Mysore and the Brindavan Gardens. At the Nagarhole National Park, we sighted tigers frolicking in the river—our only sighting ever of tigers outside of a zoo, never mind that we were safely up on a 'machan.' We visited the Tibetan settlement at Bylakuppa and spent a few days in Coorg, where, at the Dubare Elephant Camp, Amitesh got to help bathe an elephant. This made up for not being able to take home a tiger.

Our delightful Christmas beach holiday in Goa with Anita, then nine years old, made us feel that Goa is the place to be at Christmas time. The Christmas spirit was everywhere. Our hotel, catering mainly to foreigners, displayed a signboard which read, much to our amusement, 'Enjoy your stay with us. Just wear a little more than a smile!'

Another holiday we will always remember is the one in Bhutan. We were thrilled to see Mount Everest from above when our pilot pointed it out to us. Landing at Paro airport was gripping because we flew in through what seemed to be a narrow space between high mountains before touchdown. It was only later that we learnt we had landed at one of the world's most difficult airports. We were able to visit Thimphu and Punakha and the beautiful monasteries and dzongs. We also went to Phobjikha Valley, the breeding ground of the black-necked crane. We couldn't help but admire the residents of the valley for the sacrifices they had made for the safety of the birds. The valley had no electricity at all because electric posts and wires would have endangered the lives of the birds. When darkness fell, the valley lit up with the heart-warming glow of candles, Petromax, and kerosene lanterns. We made the mistake of keeping the best for last—the Tiger's Nest Monastery. It rained, so we had to satisfy ourselves with viewing it from a distance. We marvelled at the highly disciplined Bhutanese people, so proud of their country and going all-out to preserve their heritage. Every building followed the same attractive, colourful pattern, even petrol bunks and public toilets. We did not see any Bhutanese, young or old, in Western clothes.

Prema had always enjoyed planning our holidays and working out itineraries and schedules. So, it was that, when we knew we were nearing the end of our district and range days, she took a course on airline fares and ticketing. Those were pre-computer days when fares were calculated manually and air tickets hand-written. Prema's stint with Northwest Airlines, Japan Airlines, and Saudi Arabian Airlines got us free tickets, which enabled us to travel abroad.

To make the most of our American holiday, we took the Northwest Airlines VUSA (Visit USA) pass. We covered San Francisco, Los Angeles, Universal Studios, Disneyland, Las Vegas, the Grand Canyon, Disney World, Philadelphia, Washington, New York, Denver (the mile-high city), the Grand Canyon, and also Montreal and Toronto, from where we drove to Niagara Falls and went across the falls on the 'Maid of the Mist.'

Our holiday in Mexico was fraught with anxiety because, at immigration, we were handed a booklet with a long list of 'don'ts' for our safety. At one point, we lost our bearings. We asked a passer-by in Spanish, "Por favor, dónde estamos nosotros?" He gave us an incredulous look and said, "¡En México!" Anyway, we managed to take in all the sights in Mexico City, the Diego Rivera murals, make a trip to see the Pyramids of the Sun and Moon, and even watch a football match. The football stadium stood right next to the bullring. We had a choice – to our left, football or to our right, bullfight. I must admit, we didn't think we could stomach a gory bullfight! So, football it was! We even cheered for the team 'Cruz Azul' and bought our grandson a jersey from that club. We left Mexico unscathed and happy that we could use our Spanish.

Our holiday in Britain took in all the sights in and around London, Stratford-upon-Avon, and Oxford. We also went to Bolton to visit Peggy Walsh. Her father, one of the last British police officers in the erstwhile Madras Presidency, had returned to England after Independence. Peggy, after the death of her husband, came to India only to visit Coimbatore, where her father had worked and where she had spent a few years of her childhood. I arranged for DSP Robson to escort her. After that visit, Peggy made annual trips to Chennai with the sole purpose of spending time with the Robsons and us. Later, when Prema and I visited her in England, Peggy, knowing I was a football fan, took us on an 'Old Trafford Tour,' which we thoroughly enjoyed. She also took us on a delightful drive through the Malvern Hills and the picturesque villages of the Cotswolds.

We then left Peggy and Bolton for Scotland, covering the Lake District, taking in the beautiful countryside en route to Glasgow, where we saw the beautiful Glasgow Cathedral. In Edinburgh, we visited Edinburgh Castle and walked the Royal Mile. We returned to London via York. In York, we walked the 'Wall' built by the Romans. We also visited the magnificent York Minster (Cathedral) with a history dating back to 627 AD. Back in London, we toured Wimbledon, where I took a picture of Prema with Centre court behind her, remarking poignantly, 'My father dreamt of seeing me here; and here I am!' We ended our holiday in England by spending a few days with my cousin Stella and her daughters Lita and Hema, who had migrated to England several decades ago.

In Egypt, we realised we ought to have booked our tours before arrival. As a result, we found ourselves at the mercy of unscrupulous taxi drivers who would drop us off near groups of 'helpful boys' who would misguide us for a fee, leading us into the hands of another group of boys who would give us the right directions—for a handsome fee, of course! All the misguidance notwithstanding, we managed to see the Pyramids of Giza and realised they were not located closely one behind the other as pictures often suggest. But that did not matter as we were on camels. We also saw the Sphinx. We could not take the Nile Cruise because that, too, had to be booked in advance before we got to Egypt. Instead, we took a bus to Alexandria, where once stood Cleopatra's Needle.

The situation in Syria might have been the same as in Egypt had we not encountered a retired Professor of English who worked as a tour guide. He organised our most rewarding and enjoyable holiday, taking in the historical towns of Palmyra with the ancient ruins of the Roman Theatre, Temple of Bael, and several other monuments; Aleppo with its Citadel and the dead city of Serjilla; Hama with its water wheels, and Krak des Chevaliers of the Crusades. The beautifully preserved ancient city of Damascus transported us back to Biblical times; we walked down the 'Street Called Straight' to the house of Judas, who sheltered Saul of

Tarsus (who later became Paul the Apostle) and where Ananias restored Saul's eyesight. We also visited the house of Ananias. All of Damascus had been beautifully preserved, exactly as it had been in Biblical times. Our guide even showed us the gap in the wall of the city through which Saul made his escape, lowered in a basket.

Our holiday in Sri Lanka was planned because Anita, then 11 years old, complained, 'When you go too far away countries, you never take me.' The thrill of landing in a foreign country, going through immigration, and having her passport stamped wore off within a few miles of our drive from the airport to Colombo. A disappointed Anita exclaimed, 'But this is only somewhat abroad!' Her disappointment notwithstanding, we had a delightful holiday. Our IPS friend Unnikrishnan, on deputation to RAW, was in the Indian High Commission there. He helped us organise our Sri Lankan holiday. After Colombo, we went to Galle and on to Hikkaduwa with its glass-bottom boats from which we could see the beautiful coral reefs and shoals of colourful fish. We also covered Kurunegala, the Sigiriya fortress on a massive monolith, Kandy with its Temple of the Sacred Tooth, and Nuwara Eliya, which we found was not much different from the tea estates back home. We could not visit Batticaloa as the town had been cut off by recent floods, but we could go to Trincomalee. We returned to India via Talaimannar and a ferry ride to Rameswaram.

We have visited Thailand a few times simply because it was an affordable holiday destination. On our first visit, we were able to see 'Thailand in Miniature,' which was close to Bangkok. We walked the Bridge on the River Kwai—the real one, not the movie one. We also visited the Rose Garden and took a cruise on the River Chao Phraya. Our last visit to Thailand was with our grandson Amitesh when we went to Chiang Mai with its Old City. Our main destination, however, was the Tiger Kingdom, where Amitesh got to play with tiger cubs.

In Malaysia, we have 'done' Johor Bahru, Seremban, Terengganu and Melaka (originally called Malacca, whose history goes back a few centuries), Penang, and the Genting Highlands. Kuala Lumpur was our port of entry and exit; but it was also to visit my college mate Hari and his wife Vasantha, who live there. Hari has retired after a successful career as a surgeon in the Malaysian Government Service. He and Vasantha often visit us in Chennai. Being devout Hindus, visits to Temples are always a part of their holiday plans.

We were fortunate to have planned our only visit to Singapore in late October. We were there to find the island a Christmas Wonderland, an experience we truly enjoyed.

Our first visit to Japan was thanks to my three-month course there. I had a good allowance, so when Prema joined me, we could visit Nikko, which had already had its first snowfall of the season. We also visited Owakudani, taking the ropeway across the valley, viewing the sulphur vents and hot springs from above. We rode the expensive Shinkansen (the Bullet Train). We were able to take in all the sights in Tokyo. Our knowledge of Japanese helped us get around on our own. We broke our journey at Hong Kong on our way back to India. Our second visit to Japan was 16 years later, with Anita. A lot had changed; everything had become expensive, almost unaffordable. It helped that we found an en-suite family room in a youth hostel for our stay there. We could only do Tokyo.

Our holiday in Europe was a delight. To our luck, that year, the Eurail Pass had become available against payment in Indian rupees and allowed 21 days of unlimited First Class travel on trains and buses all over Europe. In Italy, we visited Rome, Naples, Capri, Florence (we looked up in awe at Michelangelo's David), Pisa with its leaning tower, Venice (Gondola ride, of course), Verona (of Romeo & Juliet fame), Padua (the shrine of St. Anthony), and Milan (Leonardo da Vinci's 'The Last Supper'). In Spain, we covered Barcelona and its Olympic stadium, Granada, Seville, Madrid, and the medieval town of Toledo. The best part of our visit to Germany was the bus ride, also covered by the Eurail Pass, on the 'Romantic Road' from Munich to Frankfurt, which avoided the highways and took us through the picturesque countryside and pretty villages and towns like the beautifully well-preserved medieval town of Rothenburg and the lovely University town of Augsburg. As we made that trip on a Sunday, we were able to enjoy a few Sunday markets. The beauty of the towns of Switzerland like Lucerne, Interlaken, Montreux, and Bern is unforgettable; likewise, Innsbruck, Vienna, and Salzburg in Austria. We also covered Antwerp and Amsterdam (Anne Frank's house). All in all, it was a trip we truly enjoyed.

I had to reopen this chapter when a long-overdue trip to a state that had eluded us for years finally materialised. Orissa, or Odisha as it is now known, had been on our bucket list of states to visit for a very long time. We decided to finally do a road trip, much against the protests of friends and well-wishers who felt Prema and I would not be able to handle the drive, especially since Anita would be driving throughout. We set out from Coonoor, with our first stop being Chennai as we needed to pick up Amitesh and our summer clothes! We drove through Andhra Pradesh with an overnight stop in Guntur, crossing the mighty Krishna and the awesome Godavari with its never-ending bridges to our next stop, Visakhapatnam. Walking through the historic submarine Kursura, riding the cable car up to Kailashagiri with beautiful views of the sea, and visiting the tribal coffee area of Araku were some of the highlights of our stopover at Vizag. We drove on to Bhubaneswar, where we did the usual tourist circuit of Cuttack, the Lingaraj Temple with its amazing architecture, the Dhauli Shanti Stupa with its sound and light show, and the beautiful Khandagiri and Udayagiri Jain caves dating back to the 1st century BC.

Odisha is home to two officers belonging to the Tamil Nadu cadre. Now retired, DGP Tripathi and ADGP Mahali have moved back to Bhubaneswar, where they've been given prestigious posts. We met them over lunch and had an enjoyable afternoon recalling memories of our days as serving officers. I was pleasantly surprised to receive a visit from

DIG Dhirendra Kumar of the BSF, who, during one of his postings, worked with the STF during the Veerappan operation.

With the Tripathis and Mahali in Bhubaneshwar

Our next stop was the Sun Temple at Konark. Seeing it in person was a revelation. We were definitely not prepared for its magnificence, intricate carvings, and superior workmanship. No trip to Odisha is complete without a visit to Puri, with its famous Jagannath Temple, never-ending clean beaches, and delicious street food.

On our way back, we stopped at Vijayawada specifically to drive across the Prakasam Barrage. We missed seeing the Borra Caves on our way to Araku because, in Andhra Pradesh, they take their lunch break seriously and close even tourist attractions between 12 and 2. We have realised there is so much more in Odisha that we have to cover—the forests, sanctuaries, and hills. Does this call for another trip?

The wedding of the grandson of a doctor friend took us back to Nagapattinam, 50 years after my posting there in 1971-73. Unfortunately, we couldn't go into the house we lived in but got to see it from the outside. We were distressed to see it in such a dilapidated condition. We also visited Tranquebar with its Danish history and Poompuhar, places which were so much a part of our lives when I was SP of Tanjavur East District.

As Vice President of the Indian Athletic Association, I have led the Indian Team several times to Asian and World meets in Japan, China, Korea, Indonesia, Kazakhstan, Sri Lanka, Vietnam, and Italy.

I have been on family vacations to other parts of the world, but I still consider touring India with its cultural, linguistic, and historical wealth more rewarding and enriching than all those other trips.

Smorgasbord

My readers I invite to come on board,
And have a taste of my smorgasbord;
Of tributes that have to me been paid
In spite of mistakes, I'd sometimes made;
Of my hits and misses I do write here,
Hoping you'd laugh till you shed a tear,
To keep up with the times I'd often failed;
But yet, through life, I smoothly sailed.

xxxxxxxxxxxxx

Sir, Keep It Yourself

When on "camp," I would go on my morning walks, taking with me a few coins to give to beggars. I would usually return to my place of stay for my morning tea. One day, I had taken a long and circuitous route and realised that it would take me another hour or more to return to the guest house. I stopped by a roadside teashop and had a bajji with a cup of tea. I gave the shopkeeper Rs. 2. He looked at it and said, "Sir, keep it yourself." It was then that I realised times had changed since my college days when one could get a cup of tea for ten paise and a bajji for 15 paise. I later sent Rs. 15 to the shopkeeper, by which time my naivety had become the talk of the town.

XXXXXXXXXXXXX

Who Will Win the Tug of War – IGP or the SP?

I had given clear instructions to all my subordinates that I did not want anyone to open the car door for me, although this had been the practice over several years or rather decades. There had even been instances of the receiving officer being reprimanded for not opening the car door for the visiting superior officer. On one of my trips to supervise a major bandobust, several officers had assembled to receive me. When my car stopped, the SP ran up to open the door for me. I held on to the handle from within my car, resulting in a tug of war between the two of us. Of course, it was I who won.

XXXXXXXXXXXXX

'Dorai' and the Sentry PC

E.L. Stracey, the last of the IP officers, used to go on his morning walks in mufti. Few recognised him as the DGP. On one of his walks in Chennai, he stopped by a police station, and the sentry PC, out of respect for the 'foreigner,' invited him in and said, "Dorai, please take your seat." Stracey obliged and engaged the sentry in friendly conversation in his halting anglicised Tamil. When he got up to leave, the PC said to him,

"Dorai, please give me something for my tea." Stracey gave him some money and asked him to bring two cups of tea, one for the sentry PC and one for himself. Stracey left after having had the tea. Only later did the sentry learn that it was no 'Dorai' who happened to be walking past the station but the DGP who had treated him to a cup of tea.

'Dorai' was a term used to address European and Anglo-Indian officers, as well as senior Indian ones. In fact, even I started out my police career in Tuticorin as a 'Dorai.'

xxxxxxxxxxxx

Prime Minister's Visit to Ooty:

India's first non-Congress Prime Minister, Morarji Desai, was to visit Ooty. The inspection of the Aranmore Palace, where he was to stay, was carried out by the Intelligence Chief, Mohandoss. After inspecting the reception centre, drawing room, and dining room, Mohandoss said, "Now, let us check the dining room." I was taken aback because we had just left the dining room behind us. It was only when he led the way to the toilet that I realised he was referring jocularly to the Prime Minister's widely known belief in 'urine therapy.'

xxxxxxxxxxxx

A Mystic Experience

(Taken from my visiting notes – 12.02.1988)

Today, I witnessed a great miracle – the miracle of a man sleeping in an upright position.

I have seen the horizontal levitation of the human body. I have seen a man entering a Samadhi four feet below the earth's surface and coming out of it alive after 24 hours. I have seen fakirs and sadhus in the lower Himalayas in various stages of philosophic abstraction, sublimation, and transcendental meditation. I have even seen one with the palm of his permanently clenched fist pierced through by his overgrown nails, and yet another who had torn off his eyelids to fulfil a vow never to close his eyes in sleep.

All these have been achieved through mesmeric, tantric, or yogic powers, gained through years of practice. Yet none had, till today, acquired the ability to sleep on his feet, a facility which has, hitherto, been enjoyed only by certain four-legged animals like horses and, to a lesser extent, elephants.

When I realised that this miracle was performed by a member of the City Police, my heart swelled with pride. There he was, standing right in the middle of the main entrance to the Basin Bridge Police Station, feet apart, body well-balanced, hands crossed across his chest and face turned towards the road. He gave the appearance of keeping diligent vigil. Only when I walked past him did I realise that he was in a state of supreme bliss, totally unaware of his earthly existence. When I came out of the station five minutes later, he was still in the same state of hypnotic trance. But for my worldly responsibilities, I would have straightaway sat at his feet or followed him to the nearest hill-top, seeking enlightenment. Instead, I helped myself to his cap and returned home.

However, should anyone who reads this want to follow such a course, I shall be only too happy to reveal the identity of the great yogi who has achieved total supremacy of mind over body and, perhaps, a final solution to the ever-growing problem of living space.

Sd/-

(W.I. Davaram)

xxxxxxxxxxxx

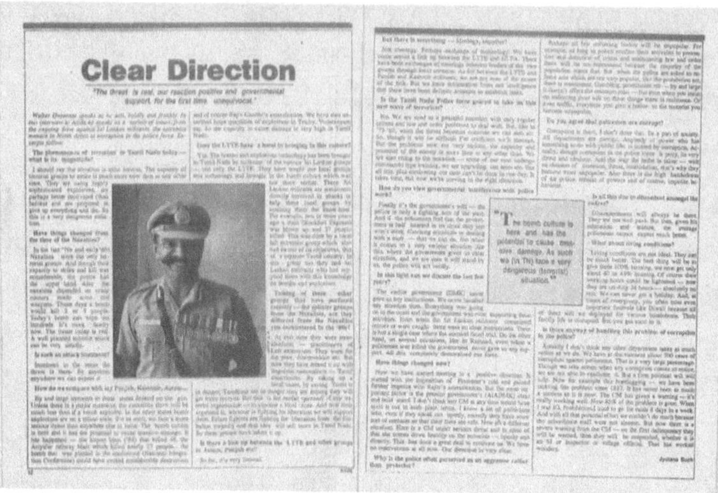

Top Secret

Dated: 25.5.2002

MEMORANDUM

(a) After the release of Dr. Rajkumar from the captivity of Veerappan, the TN Police arrested several TNLA cadres who were with Veerappan, including Maran, Govindarajan, Chezhian, Selvam, Andril, etc., and supporters of Veerappan, viz., Kolathur Mani @ T.S. Mani and Pandian @ Muthukumar (TNRT), were arrested by Karnataka Police. All of them are detained in prisons. It is learnt that Veerappan had nurtured a plan to abduct a VIP/official with the help of some locals to secure the release of T.S. Mani.

(b) A conspiracy has been hatched by Veerappan and his associates to do away with former DGP, Thiru W.I. Davaram.

(c) There were also inputs earlier that Veerappan and his gang members were planning to abduct Thiru W.I. Davaram during his visit to The Nilgiris District and do away with him.

(d) In view of the above information, it is requested that all concerned may be sensitised, all necessary precautionary measures be taken, and security for Thiru W.I. Davaram be further beefed up.

Sd/-

For Addl. Director-Genl. of Police, Intelligence

To:

The Superintendents of Police, Erode, The Nilgiris, Coimbatore, Salem, and Dharmapuri

Copy to the Dy. Inspectors-General of Police, Coimbatore & Salem

Copy to the Inspector-Genl. of Police, L&O, Western Zone

Copy to the Addl. Director-Genl. of Police, Special Task Force

Based on the above memo, an armed guard was sent to my flat on the third floor. A guard was to remain outside the door of my flat, to be replaced every three hours. The first guard had already arrived and taken up his position between the door of my flat and that of the opposite one, leaving no space for the movement of the people staying in the flats. I directed the officer to withdraw the guard as there was no need for the same. We could look after ourselves.

xxxxxxxxxxxxx

A drama of the wild

By W. I. DAVARAM

One clear winter afternoon last year, I was trekking in the Western Catchment, an undulating grassland dotted with small sholas at an altitude of 8200 ft. in the Nilgiri hills when a sudden movement on the opposite slope caught my attention. I was in time to see a long black shadow detaching itself from one of the dark "sholas" and moving gracefully across the grass to the next shola, a distance of about four hundred yards.

Realising that the shadow was none other than a black panther on the prowl, a sight seldom to be seen by man, I took cover behind a rock in eager anticipation of witnessing this jungle drama from a ring-side seat. The panther had neither scented nor seen me as I was downwind of it with the sun behind me.

The panther, obviously on a hunting foray, was searching the sholas for Sambar or Black Langur, the only animals found in those parts apart from the Ibex, otherwise called the "Nilgiri Thar", which occupy the inaccessible rocky crests or the peaks above. As the panther approached each shola, it went around it in a slow, wide circle, carefully watching the intrior of the woods for any signs of its quarry. After three or four circles, each one smaller than the one before, it gingerly entered the woods, came out again and proceeded to the next shola. The first three sholas were void of any animal life and by the time the panther reached the fourth, it was already evening and the whole hill side was bathed in the brilliant yellow light of the setting sun.

As the panther measured its way around the shola, the slopes echoed with a sharp belling sound as a Samber stag, sporting a magnificent pair of antlers, rushed out of the shola and stood in the open, facing the panther. The panther, which would have preferred the cover of the woods to stalk and surprise its prey was left in the open, face to face with it. Now both animals, the hunter and the hunted, began to move in a slow circle, the panther manoeuvring for a vantage position whence to launch its attack; the stag, careful not to expose its defenceless flanks and hind-quarters to its feline adversary.

The panther then sidled up a rock and positioned itself directly above the stag. A more impressive tableau for the final act of the drama could not have been signed—the stag hurling defiance at the panther with an occasional yell; the panther a perfect study in sepia, crouching motionless in the hushed stillness of the jungle evening.

Now the attack looked imminent. But the gallant stag stood its ground, always facing the panther squarely thereby shielding its vulnerable body with its formidable antlers. The panther could neither catch the stag off-guard nor was it prepared to risk a frontal attack.

As the sun dipped beyond the Western hills the panther decided to call it a day, got up and nonchalantly walked up the slope with never a glance at the stag, as if to say that the grapes were sour. The stag, still fearing a surprise attack, stood watching the retreating killer till it went out of sight and then, with a triumphant Whee-onk! Oo-onk! strode down to the stream below.

Copy of my letter to a bully and a coward

It is the responsibility of the Commissioner of Police or the District Collectors to detain rowdies, repeat property offenders, and other bad characters under the Goondas Act. The proposal for this will be initiated by the field officers or, in the case of prohibition offenders, by the DIG, Prohibition.

As Commissioner of Police, I received a proposal from the then DIG, Prohibition to order the detention of a bootlegger under the Goondas Act. As I required some more details before issuing the order, I had kept the paper pending. The next day, at his staff meeting, he asked the Inspector concerned whether I had signed the detention order. When the Inspector answered in the negative, the DIG said, "Oh, the Commissioner of Police is afraid." Most of his subordinate officers could not stomach his comment about me and promptly informed me. Given below is the copy of the letter I sent to him the same day.

Commissioner of Police

Chennai Police

02.05.1994

Dear ------------------------,

This relates to your referring to me as "Oh, the Commissioner of Police is afraid" when the Inspector concerned told you that I had not yet signed the proceedings to book a particular person under the Goondas Act. You said this in the daily meeting with your staff.

I may have a few human weaknesses, but certainly "being afraid" is not one of them. I am afraid only of God and not of His creations: human beings, wild animals, or nature's challenges in the form of mountains, oceans, rivers, and deserts. But to say that I am afraid of a bad character is the biggest insult that can be levelled against me. I need immediate requital. I leave it to you to decide the time, place, and weapon. I give you two days to inform me of your decision.

Sd/-

(W.I. Davaram)

Commissioner of Police,

Chennai Police

Upon receipt of my letter, he went all-out to placate me so as to avoid the intended duel. I refused to meet him until I had received a reply to my letter. I do not want to go into the details of his desperate efforts to convey his apologies through a number of people known to me. Finally, I accepted his unconditional surrender and closed the matter.

xxxxxxxxxxxxx

SAVED BY A TWIG

Coonoor had been witness to days of incessant rain, which had resulted in several landslides. Information about a major landslide on the Coonoor-Mettupalayam ghat road in 1993 brought Inspector Govindaraj to the spot. As he surveyed the magnitude of the disaster, he saw a twig protruding from the mud. All was calm after the storm and all the trees still, but the twig was swaying. This prompted him to dig further to find a hand holding the twig. He desperately dug deeper to find the owner of the hand—he was alive! Govindaraj's presence of mind that day saved the man who would otherwise never have been found.

XXXXXXXXXXXXX

The President and I

One event in my life that I will always cherish is my meeting with the President of India, Dr. A.P.J. Abdul Kalam, in the awe-inspiring Darbar Hall of the Rashtrapati Bhavan.

Dr. Abdul Kalam was a great hero to most of us because of his extraordinary life and achievements. Born under poor circumstances on Rameswaram Island, he had his primary and middle school education in the Panchayat Union Primary School and in the Rameswaram Government School. He sold newspapers to supplement his family's income. He completed his high school studies at the Schwartz Higher Secondary School in Ramanathapuram. On my first official visit to Ramnad district, I went all the way to the island just to see his house. I also visited the Schwartz Higher Secondary School and was shown his name in the school register (1946-1950). His higher education, entry into the world of aerospace engineering, and the launch of the successful SLV-3 are too well-known to be included in this write-up. However, I must mention his return to his village after the successful launch. He was met by district SP Dr. K. Radhakrishnan, IPS, who suggested he have an armed guard at his house. He politely declined the offer. He remained simple and amiable all his life.

Though I have received several service medals—gallantry, life-saving, and duty meet medals—from Governors and Chief Ministers of various States, I have never done anything so great as to receive one from the President of India at the Rashtrapati Bhavan. The opportunity to be part of the austere Arjuna Award ceremony was given to me by India's greatest woman athlete, Anju Bobby George Markose. She had been awarded the Arjuna Award in 2002, but she was away in Europe representing India at an international athletic meet on the day she was to receive the award. She requested me to receive the medal on her behalf, which is why I was there at the award ceremony at the Rashtrapati Bhavan. While handing the medal to me, the President inquired, in Tamil, about my health and my retired life and even mentioned my visit to his house in Rameswaram. I was elated. Looking back, I still wonder why Anju chose me to receive the award on her behalf over her father, who, recognising the talent in his little daughter, had tirelessly taken her for her early morning training sessions; or Bobby George, her national triple-jump champion husband-cum-coach. I felt truly honoured.

xxxxxxxxxxxxx

Theirs – The Roof of the World:

Few people know of the Tibetan refugee influx into India, as it did not lead to any conflict since they were not a militant group. Also, it was restricted to the Indo-Tibetan border, and the refugees were taken care of by the Indian government in well-organised settlements in several states.

The first time I saw them was in Mussoorie in 1963, where they had their settlement close to the IAS Academy. Because we did not know their language and they did not know ours, we could not communicate with them; but their polite and gentle demeanour endeared them to us. Years later, I met some of them in the Bylakuppe settlement in Karnataka and in two other colonies close to the Tamil Nadu-Karnataka border. Interestingly, Bylakuppe boasts a magnificent Buddhist Temple that attracts a large number of tourists, both Indian and foreign.

There had been several attempts by the Tibetans to free themselves from Chinese occupation, of which the outside world was not aware. India was very supportive and even helped the Tibetans raise a well-trained army. It was during one of our long treks out of Mussoorie that my colleague A.V. Liddle and I crossed the river Yamuna and reached Chakrata, where the Tibetans were being trained by the Indian army. Sadly, the Chinese army was far more formidable, and Tibet became part of China. Following the Dalai Lama's escape to India and the setting up of his headquarters in Dharamshala in Himachal Pradesh in 1959, more than a hundred thousand Tibetan refugees were placed in 39 settlements across India. Many others found their way to various other places as small traders. Even today, we have a small group of Tibetans in Ooty selling woollens; they have no hope of ever going back to Tibet. The major refugee villages are in Karnataka, thanks to Chief Minister Nijalingappa's concern for them.

Unlike the rival groups of Sri Lankan militants, the Tibetans are very peaceful in their demonstrations, whether it be a Tibetan awareness programme, a rally, or a hunger strike for the cause of Tibet. Always present with them is one Indian—Asha Reddy. She looks after their welfare, including the admission of their children into schools and colleges and finding jobs for them. I first met her when I was Commissioner of Police and have helped her with some of her welfare efforts. I have also attended some of their peaceful demonstrations for a free Tibet and their Uprising Day function, observed on March 10 every year. They call her 'Asha Aunty.' Her selfless service to the Tibetans has been recognised, and she has been awarded the Martyrs' Award "Pawo Thupten Ngodup" by the Tibetan Government in exile. The doors of the Dalai Lama's palace in Dharamshala are always open to her.

Asha Reddy with the Dalai Lama

Pot-Pourri

The Family mix

My brother Mitra and Prema's brother, Kumar,
both of whom were in the IAF

Amitesh receiving the 1st prize for the OOTY 200 photography
competition from MP Raja & Minister Ramachandran
and Dt Collector Mr. Amrit

Friends who are family

Niranjala, Preena, Vijyalakshmi, K.K Muthusamy & family,
Govindaraj & family, Robsons

Relaxing with pets

A little bit of this and a little bit of that

With Usha Uthup

Boat ride with the K.V. S's

At Mussoorie

Shailendra Babu

Adios Khaki

With this last chapter, I close my book;
T'was an awesome journey that I undertook
To tell of my life as a khaki-clad guy;
Those action-filled years, they just flew by.
Each station in the State has the notes that I wrote;
I've visited most tribal villages remote.
With my subordinate staff, I built a rapport;
If I couldn't do that, what was I there for?
But I've never sat in a mufti-job seat;
So, am I really a policeman complete?

The one person children hold in awe is the policeman; the traffic policeman, to be precise. They marvel at how, with one sweep of his outstretched arm, he can bring the entire traffic to a grinding halt. The children then graduate to playing 'police and robbers,' giving the policeman the role of 'thief-catcher.' It cannot be denied that the policeman is an integral part of society and that every little town has its own 'Mr. Plod' of Enid Blyton fame patrolling its streets.

To the general public, it would seem that the police are there only to maintain law-and-order, prevent and detect crime, and regulate traffic. But there are other behind-the-scenes activities going on that keep the wheels of the department running smoothly; Vigilance and Anti-Corruption, Intelligence, Crime Branch, Fire and Rescue Service,

Prison and Railway Police, to name a few. Deputation to central police organisations like the IB, CBI, BSF, CRPF, and ITBP is also a part of the IPS curriculum vitae.

Considering all this, I certainly cannot call myself a 'full-fledged police officer' because all through my service, I have been in charge only of Law-and-Order, Armed Police, Enforcement, and Training; I have never been out of uniform. But then, I must admit that the posts I held brought me challenges aplenty, which gave me immense satisfaction. Besides, it was me the government always chose when dealing with serious law-and-order problems anywhere in the State.

I visited all the 1076 Police Stations in the State, whether they were under my jurisdiction or not, and left visiting notes in each one of them. My visits to areas outside of my jurisdiction were on the orders of the Government or of the DGP to deal with major law-and-order situations. Inspecting police quarters, getting in touch with the families, and redressing their grievances gave me immense satisfaction. During my tenure, I visited almost all the tribal villages in the remote jungle areas of The Nilgiris, Anaimalais, and the Servarayan, Kalrayan, and Javadhu hills. While on my hunt for Naxalites and, to a lesser extent, for the Veerappan gang, I have trekked to the sources of most of the important rivers in Tamil Nadu, Kerala, Andhra Pradesh, and Karnataka. Organising bandobusts at two Mahamahams in Kumbakonam (1980 and 1992), six Karthikai Deepams in Thiruvannamalai, and important festivals in the 'Arupadai Veedugal,' more than 80 Vaishnav Divya Desams, and more than 600 Kumbabishekams were the challenges I faced. I must say I was received with great respect at all the religious centres, although all of them knew that I would not spare even places of worship if they were being used to foster communal hatred. I am sure the Muslims of Pulianthope would not have forgotten that incident in which Muslim fanatics killed one of their own, thinking him to be a Hindu, simply because he did not know Urdu. To them, it seemed inconceivable that a Muslim would not know Urdu. I reached the spot to find AC Magudabathi trying to keep the determined Muslims and the incensed Hindus apart. I entered the Mosque without a second thought, arrested 60 Muslims hiding there, recovered a cache of weapons, and brought the situation under control.

I did not believe in wasting my time or that of subordinates by conducting needless meetings or sending papers down the line, which often got delayed or, even worse, went astray. I rarely stayed in my office beyond 5.30 p.m., thus enabling the subordinates to leave their offices soon after. Beyond office hours, there was enough to attend to, like the management of sports associations and the conduct of major national and international meets. Prema and I have attended as many as 3218 police weddings of all ranks and functions connected with the police and their families, irrespective of rank. We now have the pleasure of attending the weddings of their children and even grandchildren.

Punishing subordinates never appealed to me; instead, I considered all their appeals and genuine requests favourably. As DGP, I cancelled all the minor punishments of subordinate staff lest their promotions be affected. I have appreciated and acknowledged each one's good work and have taken special effort to get them medals, rewards, cash awards, and accelerated promotions.

During my service, I have handled several law-and-order situations and, in the process, have opened fire on ten occasions. The first was on violent workers of the Cordite Factory in Aravankadu within two months of my first tenure as SP, The Nilgiris; the last was shortly before my retirement when I fired warning shots over the heads of rioting fishermen sheltering themselves in the sea off Tuticorin during a communal flare-up.

As a firm believer and advocate of leading from the front, I have led encounters against Naxalites and Veerappan's jungle bandits and stood in front while dealing with other law-and-order issues. I have faced judicial and magisterial inquiries 17 times and have been summoned by the courts in Tamil Nadu, Karnataka (Veerappan operation), Andhra

Pradesh (Naxalite operation), and twice by the Supreme Court—once for the alleged violation of civil liberties and once for protesting against the decision of the Governments of Karnataka and Tamil Nadu to take a conciliatory stand with Veerappan on the actor Rajkumar issue. The Supreme Court agreed with my view that criminals should not be allowed to take part in the peace talks and also overruled the order of the Madras High Court releasing 56 TADA detenues belonging to Veerappan's gang.

There has been a general feeling that I was trigger-happy and harsh on criminals. But the duty of the police is to protect the life and property of law-abiding citizens, not to safeguard the so-called rights of the law-breakers. I have always been on the side of the victims of crime and injustice, of those who had lost their property and even lives to criminals. Investigating officers should go all-out to recover stolen property and the weapons used by the criminals. In most cases, this is not possible without the use of minimal force. For instance, in today's scenario of inter-religious violence, how can the police unearth weapons and explosives clandestinely hidden away by extremists to be used against other religions? By persuasion? No. By repeated questioning? No. By promises? No. The only way to get the vital information is by using force. We do not deserve to be called police officers if we cannot safeguard the lives and property of innocent citizens. This has always been my personal conviction and instruction to my subordinates.

The lengthy jungle operations gave me the opportunity to meet the tribal population and to study their basic requirements. Apart from helping them get basic facilities like roads, hospitals, and schools, I also recruited more than 180 tribal youngsters, including several borderline Naxalites, into the Police Department.

The most fulfilling facet of my service is the camaraderie I fostered with the entire force, irrespective of rank. I always believed in assuming full responsibility for the situation and sharing in the perils and triumphs of my subordinates.

Recently, 25 years after my retirement, I had the privilege of addressing the 937 Sub-Inspector trainees. I took with me gallantry medallists SP Ashok Kumar, woman Inspector Rajeswari, and the first woman SI A.V. Usha to inspire and motivate them. Bribery has of late been the bane of the Police Department, so it was a memorable moment when I made all the trainees stand up and take an oath that they would not accept bribes. My family are sure the trainees are still laughing behind my back at my naivety!

I would not be true to my conscience if I did not admit my failures. The first major failure was the death of more than 40 pilgrims at the Kumbakonam Mahamaham in 1992. As ADGP, L&O, I was in charge of the bandobust, including ensuring the safety of the Chief Minister. I therefore ought to take the entire blame for the tragedy. My second failure was not preempting the assassination of Rajiv Gandhi. Although I was not in charge of the function where he was assassinated, as ADGP L&O for the whole State, I should take the blame. In fact, Mohandas, DGP, Intelligence, and I had succeeded in disarming all the militant factions in one stroke, but sadly and incomprehensibly, we were asked to return to the LTTE the weapons we had confiscated from them. We ought to have, but failed to keep track of the movements of the Sri Lankan conspirators—one-eyed Sivarasan, Dhanu, Subha, and Murugan—who had stayed back in India to carry out the assassination.

My deepest anguish lies in my failure to bring the brigand Veerappan to book, despite having formed the STF and heading it for over 5 years. It was left to the brave and resourceful DGP K. Vijay Kumar to bring the curtain down on the jungle drama. He magnanimously shared his victory with all of us who had been part of the operation in its various stages.

As the time of my retirement was approaching, there were many offers from private concerns wanting me to join them either in a supervisory or counselling capacity, but I was firm in my decision not to work for anyone or any private concern after 35 years of dignified police service.

The Chief Minister did indicate his wish to give me an extension of service, but I did not think it proper to accept it, as it would have affected the promotion of the officer below me in the hierarchy. DGP L&O Rajasekara Nair, my colleague and friend over several years, arranged an excellent farewell parade for me, which was attended by a large number of officers, policemen, women, and trainees. What more could a police officer want while hanging up his khakis and the brown boots that he had worn for 34 years than the exhilarating memory of those eventful days gone by?

I am but a speck in the 150-year-old history of the Madras (Tamil Nadu) Police, but I am proud to have been a part of it. Officers may come and officers may go, but the Tamil Nadu Police will go on forever.

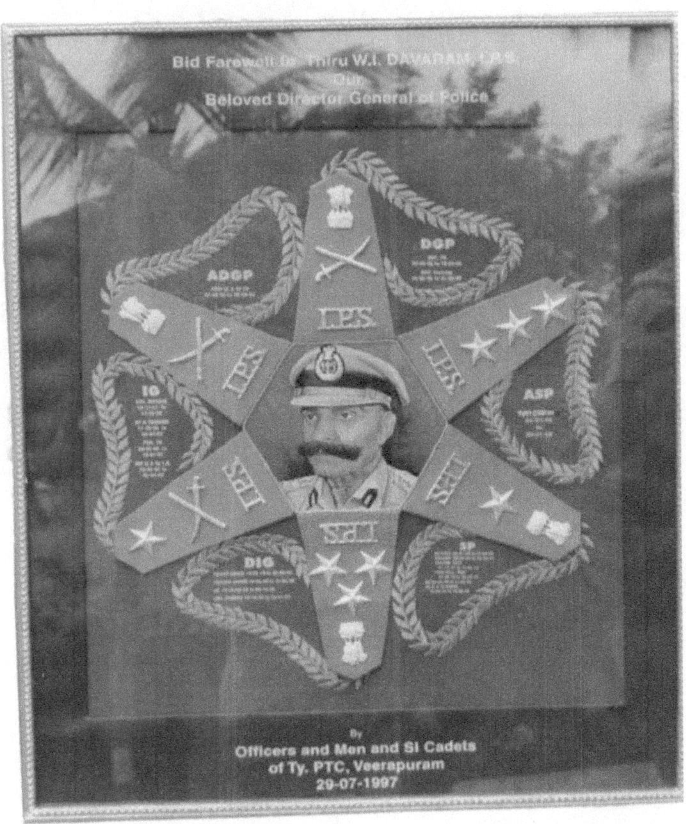

Arriving for my farewell parade

At my farewell parade

Taking the final salute on my last day in office

Epilogue

A little bit of this, and a little bit of that,
A little bit of ease and of course, of combat.
Some snippets here, and some trifles there,
At times a dream and at times nightmare.
These are what made my life worthwhile;
Now I 'm retired; I can sit back and smile.
There were hardships aplenty, I surmounted them all;
Those halcyon days now, are a joy to recall.
I can just be here, I can just be there,
I can travel the world in my rocking chair.

Thank you for reaching out.